The Cambridge Companion to American Modernism

The Cambridge Companion to American Modernism provides a comprehensive and authoritative overview of American literary modernism from 1890 to 1939. These original essays by twelve distinguished scholars of international reputation offer critical accounts of the major genres, literary culture, and social contexts that define the current state of modern American literature and cultural studies. Among the diverse topics covered are nationalism, race, gender, and the impact of music and visual arts on literary modernism, as well as surveys of the achievements of American modernism in fiction, poetry and drama. The book concludes with a chapter on modern American criticism. An essential reference guide to the field, the *Companion* gives readers a chronology of key events and publication dates, covering the first half of the twentieth century in the United States, and an up-to-date bibliography of further reading organized by chapter topics.

D0141415

THE CAMBRIDGE COMPANION TO

AMERICAN MODERNISM

EDITED BY

WALTER KALAIDJIAN

Emory University

CAMBRIDGE
UNIVERSITY PRESS

CAMBRIDGE UNIVERSITY PRESS
Cambridge, New York, Melbourne, Madrid, Cape Town, Singapore, São Paulo

Cambridge University Press
The Edinburgh Building, Cambridge CB2 2RU, UK

Published in the United States of America by Cambridge University Press, New York

www.cambridge.org
Information on this title: www.cambridge.org/9780521829953

© Cambridge University Press 2005

First published 2005

Printed in the United Kingdom at the University Press, Cambridge

A catalogue record for this book is available from the British Library

ISBN-13 978-0-521-82995-3 hardback
ISBN-10 0-521-82995-X hardback
ISBN-13 978-0-521-53680-6 paperback
ISBN-10 0-521-53680-4 paperback

CONTENTS

ILLUSTRATIONS

Citation Acknowledgement

"Flight to the City," "The Red Wheelbarrow" and "The Right of Way" by William Carlos Williams, are taken from *Collected Poems: 1909–1939*, Volume I, 1938, New Directions Publishing Corporation. Reprinted by permission of New Directions Publishing Corporation. ©

LIST OF CONTRIBUTORS

RITA BARNARD is Associate Professor of English and Director of the Comparative Literature Program at the University of Pennsylvania. She is the author of *The Great Depression and the Culture of Abundance* (1995) and *Beyond Apartheid: South African Writers and the Politics of Place* (forthcoming). She is currently completing a collection of essays on American modernism and mass-mediated culture.

JOHN DUVALL is Professor of English and Editor of *MFS Modern Fiction Studies* at Purdue University. He is author of *The Identifying Fictions of Toni Morrison: Modernist Authenticity and Postmodern Blackness* (2000) and *Faulkner's Marginal Couple: Invisible, Outlaw, and Unspeakable Communities* (1990), as well as the editor of *Productive Postmodernism: Consuming Histories and Cultural Studies* (2002) and the co-editor of *Faulkner and Postmodernism* (2002).

WALTER KALAIDJIAN is Professor of English and Director of English Graduate Studies at Emory University. He is the author of *Understanding Literature* (2004), *American Culture Between the Wars: Revisionary Modernism and Postmodern Critique* (1994), *Languages of Liberation: The Social Text in Contemporary American Poetry* (1989), and *Understanding Theodore Roethke* (1988). His forthcoming book is titled *The Edge of Modernism: American Poetry and the Traumatic Past.*

JANET LYON is Associate Professor of English at Penn State University where she teaches literature and gender/sexuality studies. She is the author of *Manifestoes: Provocations of the Modern* (1999); she is completing a book manuscript titled *The Perfect Hostess: Salons and Modernity.*

DOUGLAS MAO is Associate Professor of English at Cornell University. He is the author of *Solid Objects: Modernism and The Test of Production* (1998), a former president of the Modernist Studies Association, and a member of the editorial board at *Textual Practice.*

MARK MORRISON is Associate Professor of English at Penn State University. He is the author of *The Public Face of Modernism: Little Magazines, Audience, and Reception, 1905–1920* (2001) and was a co-founder and executive board member of the Modernist Studies Association. He is completing a book that examines the confluence of early particle physics, occultism, and literature during the modernist period.

CARY NELSON is Jubilee Professor of Liberal Arts and Sciences at the University of Illinois at Urbana-Champaign. His twenty-four books include *Revolutionary Memory: Recovering The Poetry Of The American Left* (2001), *Anthology Of Modern American Poetry* (2000), and *Repression And Recovery: Modern American Poetry And The Politics Of Cultural Memory* (1989).

MICHAEL NORTH is Professor of English at the University of California, Los Angeles. His most recent books include the Norton Critical Edition of T. S. Eliot's *The Waste Land* (2001), *Reading 1922: A Return to the Scene of the Modern* (1999), and *The Dialect of Modernism: Race, Language, and Twentieth-Century Literature* (1994).

MARJORIE PERLOFF is Sadie D. Patek Professor Emerita in the Humanities at Stanford University and is currently Scholar-in-Residence at the University of Southern California. Her most recent books are *The Vienna Paradox* (2004), *Differentials: Poetry, Poetics, Pedagogy* (2004), and *21st Century Modernism* (2002).

PAULA RABINOWITZ is Professor of English at the University of Minnesota and an affiliated member of American Studies, Feminist Studies and Critical Studies in Discourse and Society. Her book publications include *Black and White and Noir: America's Pulp Modernism* (2002), *They Must Be Represented: The Politics of Documentary* (1994), *Labor and Desire: Women's Revolutionary Fiction in Depression America* (1991), and the edited collection *Writing Red: An Anthology of American Women Writers, 1930–1940* (1987).

JED RASULA is Helen S. Lanier Distinguished Professor of English at the University of Georgia. His most recent books are *Syncopations: The Stress of Innovation in Recent American Poetry* (2004), *This Compost: Ecological Imperatives in American Poetry* (2002), and *The American Poetry Wax Museum: Reality Effects, 1940–1990* (1996). He is a contributing author to *Blackening Europe* (2003) and to *The Cambridge Companion to Jazz* (2002); jazz is central to a book in progress titled *Phantom Sensations: The Pathic Receptacles of Modernism*.

MARK A. SANDERS is Associate Professor of African American Studies and English at Emory University. He is the author of *Afro-Modernist Aesthetics and the Poetry of Sterling A. Brown* (1999) and the editor of *A Son's Return: Selected Essays of Sterling A. Brown* (1996).

STEPHEN WATT is Professor of English and Chair of the Department of English at Indiana University-Bloomington. His most recent books include the anthology *The Cultural Politics of Ian Fleming and 007*, edited with Edward Comentale and Skip Willman (2004), and *What We Did Last Winter: Essays on Campus Activism and Disciplinary Change*, co-authored with Cary Nelson (2004). He is working on a book-length study tentatively entitled *Beckett's Ghost*.

CHRONOLOGY

1890 Battle of Wounded Knee
      Jane Addams founds Hull House
      Sarah Orne Jewett, *Tales of New England*

1891 First international copyright law
      Thomas Edison patents the "kinetoscope"
      Ambrose Bierce, *In the Midst of Life*
      Mary E. Wilkins Freeman, *A New England Nun and Other Stories*

1892 Homestead (Pennsylvania) steelworkers' strike
      Death of Whitman (b. 1819)
      Joel Chandler Harris, *Uncle Remus and his Friends*
      William Dean Howells, *The Quality of Mercy*

1893 Financial panic of 1893
      World's Columbian Exhibition opens in Chicago
      Muckraking journal *McClure's Magazine* founded
      Paul Laurence Dunbar, *Oak and Ivy*
      Stephen Crane, *Maggie: A Girl of the Streets*
      Henry James, *The Real Thing and Other Tales*

1894 Coxey's Army of the unemployed marches on Washington
      George Washington Cable, *John March, Southerner*
      Kate Chopin, *Bayou Folk*
      Samuel Langhorne Clemens (Mark Twain), *The Tragedy of Pudd'nhead Wilson and the Comedy of Those Extraordinary Twins*

1895 Invention of the motion picture
      Stephen Crane, *The Red Badge of Courage, The Black Riders and Other Lines*
      Alice Dunbar-Nelson, *Violets and Other Tales*

1896　Klondike Gold Rush begins
　　　Supreme Court defines "separate but equal doctrine" in *Plessy* v.
　　　Ferguson
　　　Abraham Cahan, *Yekl*
　　　Paul Laurence Dunbar, *Lyrics of Lowly Life*
　　　Sarah Orne Jewett, *The Country of the Pointed Firs*

1897　Edwin Arlington Robinson, *Children of the Night*
　　　William James, *The Varieties of Religious Experience*
　　　Kate Chopin, *A Night in Acadie*

1898　Spanish-American War
　　　Stephen Crane, *The Open Boat and Other Stories*
　　　Henry James, *The Turn of the Screw*

1899　US intervenes in China's Boxer Rebellion
　　　Charles W. Chesnutt, *The Conjure Woman*
　　　Kate Chopin, *The Awakening*
　　　Charlotte Perkins Gilman, *The Yellow Wallpaper*
　　　Frank Norris, *McTeague*

1900　Founding of International Ladies' Garment Workers' Union
　　　Pauline Elizabeth Hopkins, *Contending Forces: A Romance
　　　Illustrative of Negro Life North and South*
　　　Theodore Dreiser, *Sister Carrie*

1901　President William McKinley is shot by Leon Czolgoz and
　　　dies on September 14; he is succeeded by Theodore
　　　Roosevelt
　　　Founding of United Textile Workers of America
　　　Charles W. Chesnutt, *The Marrow of Tradition*
　　　Frank Norris, *The Octopus*
　　　Booker T. Washington, *Up from Slavery*

1902　United Mine Workers Strike
　　　Charles Alexander Eastman, *Indian Boyhood*
　　　Ellen Glasgow, *The Battle-Ground*
　　　Henry James, *The Wings of the Dove*

1903　Wilbur and Orville Wright achieve first sustained heavier-than-air
　　　machine flight on December 17
　　　W. E. B. Du Bois, *The Souls of Black Folk*
　　　Henry James, *The Ambassadors*
　　　Jack London, *The Call of the Wild*
　　　Gertrude Stein, *The Making of Americans*

1904   National Child Labor Committee formed
        Charles Alexander Eastman, *Red Hunters and the Animal People*
        Henry James, *The Golden Bowl*
        Jack London, *The Sea-Wolf*

1905   Industrial Workers of the World union organized in Chicago
        W. E. B. Du Bois initiates the "Niagra Movement"
        Willa Cather, *The Troll Garden*
        Edith Wharton, *The House of Mirth*

1906   San Francisco earthquake
        Atlanta race riots
        Congress passes the Meat Inspection Act and the Pure Food and Drug Act
        Upton Sinclair, *The Jungle*

1907   Financial Panic of 1907
        Presidential restriction of Japanese immigration
        Henry Adams, *The Education of Henry Adams*
        Henry James, *The American Scene*
        Edith Wharton, *The Fruit of the Tree*

1908   Henry Ford produces first Model T Ford
        Mary E. Wilkins Freeman, *The Shoulders of Atlas*
        Jack London, *The Iron Heel*

1909   W. E. B. Du Bois founds National Association for the Advancement of Colored People (NAACP)
        W. C. Handy composes "Memphis Blues"
        Gertrude Stein, *Three Lives*
        William Carlos Williams, *Poems*

1910   Mann Act ("White Slave Traffic Act") prohibits the transportation of women across state lines for "immoral purposes"
        Great Migration of Southern African-Americans to urban North begins
        William Dean Howells, *My Mark Twain*
        Ezra Pound, *The Spirit of Romance*

1911   Triangle Shirtwaist Company factory fire
        Supreme Court dissolves Standard Oil Company for restraint of trade
        Theodore Dreiser, *Jennie Gerhardt*
        Charlotte Perkins Gilman, *The Man-Made World*
        Edith Wharton, *Ethan Frome*

1912   Titanic collides with an iceberg and sinks on its maiden voyage
Founding of *Poetry* magazine
Mary Antin, *The Promised Land*
Willa Cather, *Alexander's Bridge*
Sui-Sin Far (Edith Maude Eaton), *Mrs. Spring Fragrance*
James Weldon Johnson, *The Autobiography of an Ex-Colored Man*
Edith Wharton, *The Reef*

1913   The New York Armory Show
Willa Cather, *O Pioneers!*
Robert Frost, *A Boy's Will*
Ellen Glasgow, *Virginia*
Edith Wharton, *The Custom of the Country*

1914   Archduke Francis Ferdinand is assassinated in Sarajevo triggering
World War I
Panama Canal completed
Ludlow Massacre at the Colorado Fuel and Iron Corporation
Carl Sandburg, *Chicago*
Gertrude Stein, *Tender Buttons*

1915   German submarine sinks the ocean liner *Lusitania*
Willa Cather, *The Song of the Lark*
Albert Einstein, *General Theory of Relativity*
T. S. Eliot, "The Love Song of J. Alfred Prufrock"
Robert Frost, *North of Boston*
D. W. Griffith films *The Birth of a Nation*

1916   Congress enacts Workman's Compensation
John Dewey, *Democracy and Education*
Hilda Doolittle, *Sea Garden*
Ring Lardner, *You Know Me Al*
Amy Lowell, *Men, Women, and Ghosts*
Carl Sandburg, *Chicago Poems*
Mark Twain, *The Mysterious Stranger*

1917   Russian Revolution
United States enters into World War I
Pulitzer Prize established
T. S. Eliot, *Prufrock and Other Observations*
Edna St. Vincent Millay, *Renascence and Other Poems*
Ezra Pound, *The Cantos*
Edith Wharton, *Summer*

1918 Influenza epidemic
      Willa Cather, *My Ántonia*
      Theodore Dreiser, *Free and Other Stories*
      Mary E. Wilkins Freeman, *Edgewater People*
      Georgia Douglas Johnson, *The Heart of a Woman and Other Poems*
      Edith Wharton, *The Marne*

1919 Congress passes Prohibition Act
      Founding of American Communist Party
      Versailles Treaty
      Sherwood Anderson, *Winesburg, Ohio*
      Amy Lowell, *Pictures of the Floating World*
      John Reed, *Ten Days that Shook the World*

1920 Nineteenth Amendment gives women the right to vote
      F. Scott Fitzgerald, *This Side of Paradise*
      Robert Frost, *Mountain Interval*
      Sinclair Lewis, *Main Street*
      Eugene O'Neill, *The Emperor Jones*
      Ezra Pound, *Hugh Selwyn Mauberly*
      Edith Wharton, *The Age of Innocence* and *In Morocco*

1921 Alice Paul founds National Woman's Party
      Sherwood Anderson, *The Triumph of the Egg*
      John Dos Passos, *Three Soldiers*
      F. Scott Fitzgerald, *Flappers and Philosophers*
      Edith Wharton receives the Pulitzer Prize for *The Age of Innocence*
      Anzia Yezierska, *Hungry Hearts*

1922 Supreme Court upholds 19th Amendment granting women
      the right to vote
      Willa Cather, *One of Ours*
      T. S. Eliot, *The Waste Land*
      Sinclair Lewis, *Babbitt*
      Eugene O'Neill, *The Hairy Ape*
      Edith Wharton, *The Glimpses of the Moon*
      Anzia Yezierska, *Salome of the Tenements*

1923 Steelworkers negotiate an eight-hour workday
      Willa Cather, *A Lost Lady*
      Robert Frost, *New Hampshire*
      Wallace Stevens, *Harmonium*
      Jean Toomer, *Cane*
      William Carlos Williams, *Spring and All*

1924 The Teapot Dome scandal
Restrictive immigration laws passed by Congress
Marianne Moore, *Observations*
Eugene O'Neill, *Desire under the Elms*
Edith Wharton, *Old New York*

1925 Scopes trial
The *New Yorker* magazine founded by Harold Ross
Willa Cather, *The Professor's House*
John Dos Passos, *Manhattan Transfer*
Theodore Dreiser, *An American Tragedy*
F. Scott Fitzgerald, *The Great Gatsby*
Ernest Hemingway, *In Our Time*
Alain Locke, ed., *The New Negro*
Anzia Yezierska, *Bread Givers*

1926 US Marines invade Nicaragua
Hart Crane, *White Buildings*
William Faulkner, *Soldier's Pay*
Ernest Hemingway, *The Sun Also Rises*
Langston Hughes, *The Weary Blues*

1927 Charles Lindbergh pilots *The Spirit of St. Louis* in a solo flight
from New York to Paris
Execution of Nicola Sacco and Bartolomeo Vanzetti
Willa Cather, *Death Comes for the Archbishop*
Countee Cullen, *Copper Sun*
Langston Hughes, *Fine Clothes to the Jew*

1928 William Mulholland's St. Francis Dam collapses
Djuna Barnes, *Ryder*
Nella Larsen, *Quicksand*
Eugene O'Neill, *Strange Interlude*

1929 St. Valentine's Day massacre
"Black Thursday" 24 October, stock market crash
Countee Cullen, *Black Christ and Other Poems*
William Faulkner, *The Sound and the Fury*
Ernest Hemingway, *A Farewell to Arms*
Nella Larsen, *Passing*

1930 Television broadcasting begins
Hart Crane, *The Bridge*
William Faulkner, *As I Lay Dying*
Mike Gold, *Jews Without Money*
Katherine Anne Porter, *Flowering Judas and Other Stories*

1931   The "Scottsboro Boys" trial begins
        Pearl S. Buck, *The Good Earth*
        e. e. cummings, *Viva*
        William Faulkner, *Sanctuary*

1932   Amelia Earhart becomes first woman to make a solo flight across
        the Atlantic
        Benjamin Nathan Cardozo becomes first Hispanic judge appointed
        to the US Supreme Court
        Sterling A. Brown, *Southern Road*
        John Dos Passos, *U. S. A.*
        Ernest Hemingway, *Death in the Afternoon*
        Langston Hughes, *The Dream Keeper*
        Gertrude Stein, *Three Lives*

1933   Federal Deposit Insurance Corporation, Federal Emergency Relief
        Act, Public Works Administration, and Civilian Conservation
        Corps are created
        Sherwood Anderson, *Death in the Woods*
        Ernest Hemingway, *Winner Take Nothing*
        James Weldon Johnson, *Along This Way*
        Mourning Dove (Okanogan), *Coyote Stories*

1934   Founding of Federal Housing Administration
        Drought and storms result in the Great Plains "Dust Bowl"
        Kenneth Fearing, *1933*
        Lillian Hellman, *The Children's Hour*
        Zora Neale Hurston, *Jonah's Gourd Vine*
        Edna St. Vincent Millay, *Wine from These Grapes*
        Ezra Pound, *Make it New*
        Henry Roth, *Call it Sleep*

1935   Rural Electrification Administration and Works Progress
        Administration created
        Harlem riot
        William Faulkner, *Pylon*
        Ellen Glasgow, *Vein of Iron*
        Ernest Hemingway, *Green Hills of Africa*
        Zora Neale Hurston, *Mules and Men*
        Marianne Moore, *Selected Poems*

1936   Spanish Civil War begins
        Akron rubber workers strike at the Goodyear tire company
        Djuna Barnes, *Nightwood*

John Dos Passos, *The Big Money*
William Faulkner, *Absalom, Absalom!*

1937   William H. Hastie becomes first African-American federal judge
"Memorial Day Massacre" at Republic Steel in Chicago
Ernest Hemingway, *To Have and Have Not*
Zora Neale Hurston, *Their Eyes Were Watching God*
Younghill Kang, *East Goes West*
John Steinbeck, *Of Mice and Men*
Wallace Stevens, *The Man with the Blue Guitar*

1938   House Un-American Activities Committee (HUAC) founded
William Faulkner, *The Unvanquished*
Zora Neale Hurston, *Tell My Horse*
Thornton Wilder, *Our Town*
Richard Wright, *Uncle Tom's Children*

1939   Germany signs non-aggression pact with Russia and invades Poland
World War II begins
William Faulkner, *The Wild Palms*
Lillian Helman, *The Little Foxes*
Zora Neale Hurston, *Moses: Man of the Mountain*
Katherine Anne Porter, *Pale Horse, Pale Rider*
John Steinbeck, *The Grapes of Wrath*

WALTER KALAIDJIAN

Introduction

Slightly ahead of his time, Walt Whitman welcomed the new energies of American modernism with his 1876 poem "To a Locomotive in Winter." In it, he hailed the steam engine as "type of the modern – emblem of motion and power – pulse of the continent."[1] Only seven years earlier at Promontory Summit, Utah, the Union Pacific and Central Pacific Railroads were linked by a golden spike driven into the final tie of the nation's first transcontinental rail network. Dynamic, transformative, and "unpent," modernism's new social, cultural, and technological economies of scale would rapidly remap space, time, and distance in ways that were heretofore unimaginable. Such accelerating velocities of change would increasingly define the quickened "pulse of the continent." Soon, American modernism would exceed the parochial limits of nation formation in the global reach of its imagined community. Such was the pace of modernization that by 1880 the steam locomotive would be eclipsed by Thomas Edison's demonstration of the electric train in Menlo Park, New Jersey. Two decades later, Harvard professor Henry Adams would be so awed by the giant electromagnetic dynamos on display at the Great Exposition of 1900 that he would "see only an absolute *fiat* in electricity" defining the modern age.[2] Reflecting on the major scientific advances of the 1890s such as Wilhelm Conrad Röntgen's discovery of X-rays, Edouard Branly's and Guglielmo Marconi's experiments with radio waves, Marie Curie's detection of radium in pitchblende, Adams "wrapped himself in vibrations and rays which were new, and he would have hugged Marconi and Branly had he met them, as he hugged the dynamo" (381). Extending Whitman's celebration of the "unpent" forces mobilized in modernism's newer technologies, Adams's fascination with the "supersensual world" of *fin de siécle* science described a modern world outlook defined by "Multiplicity, Diversity, Complexity, Anarchy, Chaos" (455).

As harbingers of change, such key terms increasingly characterized the new physics that would quickly leap ahead after 1905 in Einstein's special theory of relativity, Max Born's and Werner Heisenberg's quantum mechanics,

Heisenberg's uncertainty principle, Paul A. M. Dirac's prediction of antimatter, and so on. Not coincidentally, multiplicity, diversity, complexity, anarchy and chaos could just as easily be mapped as defining rubrics across the contemporaneous fields of culture, aesthetics, and politics of the modern American age; they aptly describe the social experience of the new masses coming together in the cosmopolitan urban centers of modern American big city life. Waves of immigration from around the globe through New York City's Ellis Island, coupled with the Great Migration of Southern African-Americans to the industrial North, dramatically transfigured the American scene in the early twentieth century. By the 1910s, New York City had a population of some five million city dwellers, 40 percent of whom were first-generation émigrés. Writing in *Our America* (1919), Waldo Frank exclaimed that "the rebels from the West met Europe in New York and made it theirs . . . What a godsend for the hungering New Yorker! What a leaven! Slowly, the ferments moved the lump of the Eastern seaboard. Slowly, New York became the nervous city."[3] It was the social diversity of the "nervous city" that the young, former Columbia College student and social critic Randolph Bourne praised in his landmark essay "Trans-National America" (1916). Adding to this ethnic mix, the urban centers of the Northern United States further received tens of thousands of transplanted working families during the so-called Great Migration of African-Americans from the South. During the first two decades of the twentieth century, African-American populations doubled in such major industrial centers as Chicago and Detroit. In contrast to the South – marked by crop failures, flooding, job scarcity and Jim Crow discrimination – the urban North offered an alternative vision of prosperity and racial uplift. Indeed, Howard University professor Alain Locke described a "new vision of opportunity" in Harlem, which he considered a cultural "laboratory of a great race-welding."[4] During these years, the campaign for a diverse, cosmopolitan, and progressive socialist culture was sustained by the literary network of little magazines like the *The Masses*, *New Masses*, *Craftsman*, *Crisis*, *Fire*, *Opportunity*, *The Messenger*, *Comrade*, *International Socialist Review*, *Coming Nation*, *Mother Earth*, *New York Call*, and many more.

By far the most popular of these venues, *The Masses* was originally launched as a muckraking publication by Piet Vlag in 1911 and later edited by Max Eastman. The term "muckraker" was coined by President Theodore Roosevelt in a 1906 speech to describe the wave of novelists, writers, and investigative journalists who waged a cultural campaign against abusive labor practices, corporate monopolies, and corrupt politicians at the turn of the century. Reflecting back on this time, Eastman wrote, "Our magazine provided for the first time in America a meeting ground for revolutionary *labor* and the radical intelligentsia."[5] *The Masses* offered a lively forum for the era's political journalism, manifestos, cartoon art, poetry, fiction, and drama. But equally important, it fostered the kind of salon culture hosted in Greenwich Village parties by socialites, patrons, and cultural radicals such as Mabel Dodge, Alyse Gregory, and Gertrude Vanderbilt Whitney. At these social get-togethers, Dodge wrote, one could come upon "Socialists, Trade-Unionists, Anarchists, Suffragists, Poets, Relations, Lawyers, Murderers, 'Old Friends,' Psychoanalysts, IWWs, Single Taxers, Birth Controlists, Newspapermen, Artists, Modern-Artists, Club Women, woman's-place-is-in-the-home Women, Clergymen, and just plain men."[6]

Multiplicity, diversity, complexity, anarchy and chaos not only described such modern American salons, but also characterized the aesthetic dimension of American modernism as witnessed in such historic exhibitions as the New York 1913 International Exhibition of Modern Art. Popularly known as the Armory Show, this famous venue featured some 1,250 works of painting, sculpture, and decorative art mounted at New York's 69th Regiment Armory on Lexington Avenue between 25th and 26th streets. Reflecting a rich and complex range of modernist aesthetics, the Armory Show exhibited European masters such as Paul Gaugin, Henri Matisse, Paul Cézanne, Marcel Duchamp, Pablo Picasso, Constantin Brancusi, Georges Seurat, Toulouse-Lautrec, Wassily Kandinsky, and Ernst Kirchner alongside such American modernists as George Bellows, Marsden Hartley, Walt Kuhn, Joseph Stella, Abraham Walkowitz, John Marin, John Sloan, Anne Goldthwaite, and Patrick Henry Bruce, among others. American modernist writers like William Carlos Williams were delighted by the shocking break with convention that the Armory Show inaugurated. "I laughed out loud," Williams would later write, "when I first saw it, happily, with relief."[7] Journalists, for the most part, were not as amused and like Kenyon Cox writing in the *New York Times*, found modernism's departure from "any representation of nature . . . any known or traditional form of decoration" to border on the "pathological." As far as Cox was concerned, the Armory Show was simply a way of "making insanity pay."[8]

Despite such dismissals, the formal innovations of American modernism would indeed make "insanity pay" and not just in the art world. Soon, the example of American modernism would quickly spread to the other arts, in poetry, fiction, experimental film, Hollywood cinema, the visual techniques of advertising, and in popular culture generally. Indeed, as Thomas Crow has written, the avant-garde in America served as "a kind of research and development arm of the culture industry."[9] As early as 1922, the year T. S. Eliot published *The Waste Land*, Matthew Josephson argued in the avant-garde journal *Broom* that the true innovation of American modernism lay precisely in its fusion of experimentalism and popular culture. In his essay, entitled "The Great American Billposter," Josephson avowed that America, not Europe, was defining modernism not just through its commerce in advertising billposters, but through the lively spectacle of the American scene: "where athletes play upon the frenetic passions of baseball crowds, and skyscrapers rise lyrically to the exotic rhythms of jazz bands which upon waking up we find to be nothing but the drilling of pneumatic hammers on steel girders."[10] Thus the rubric of American modernism – as the contributors to this Cambridge Companion volume demonstrate – refers not just to an arts movement, a literary period term, or a particular cultural nationalism but, more broadly, signals the expansive paradigm shift emerging at the *fin de siécle*. It encompasses the global contexts of social change roughly between 1890 and 1939 in industry, commerce, technology, politics, and aesthetics of what came to be considered as a distinctively American public sphere.

Engaging the question of what constitutes the "American-ness" of modernism in literature, culture, and society, Mark Morrisson's opening chapter on "Nationalism and the modern American canon" explores competing models of what defined American national culture at the turn of the century. Negotiations over how national identity should be defined, as Morrisson demonstrates, did not produce a seamless consensus among America's various societal constituencies divided as they were along ethnic, racial, and class lines. On the one hand, nativist impulses – as in William Carlos Williams's call for a "rediscovery of a primary impetus, the elementary principles of all art" – would ground modernism in "the local conditions" of regional America.[11] Similarly, even expatriates such as Ezra Pound would identify modernist aesthetics with Walt Whitman's inaugural identity as quintessential American. On the other hand, such nativist impulses were inescapably mediated by the global scope of modernism as it was being conceived in such international urban cities as Moscow, Berlin, Paris, and London. Morrisson teases out the competing tensions between nativism and internationalism in the make-up of an American modernist canon by examining the publication history of the period's major little magazines such as *Poetry*, *The Seven Arts*, and *The Dial* as well as the shaping influence of notable anthologies and pedagogical textbooks of the American New Critics. In particular, Morrisson provides a case study of Margaret Anderson and Jane Heap's *The Little Review* from its inception in Chicago in 1914 – as a venue for Midwestern American poets – through 1926 and its increasingly transnational representation of such aesthetic movements as Imagism, Cubism, Vorticism, Dadaism and Surrealism. Quoting Anderson, Morrisson sums up the mutually enabling exchange that made up the nativist and international cast of this important cultural venue: "*The Little Review* was the first magazine to reassure Europe as to America, and the first to give America the tang of Europe."

The first of three chapters on modern American literature, Rita Barnard's essay takes Alfred Kazin's retrospective study *On Native Ground* (1942) as its starting point for a consideration of how modern American fiction addresses "the need to learn what the reality of life was in our modern era."[12] Noting the era's transition from an economy based in industrial production to one increasingly defined by the consumption of abundant things, goods, services, and images, Barnard questions how these social and cultural transformations altered narrative form in terms of such basic categories of experience as space, time, and value. To begin with, Barnard examines the distinctively modern "location of culture" in the American settings of such urban American novels as John Dos Passos's *Manhattan Transfer* (1925), Waldo Frank's *City Block* (1922), and Albert Halper's *Union Square* (1933). Moreover, in reading Ernest Hemingway, Mike Gold, Henry Adams, Richard Wright, and Willa Cather, Barnard demonstrates the changing presentations of modern American place, subject to the period's shifting demographics of race, class, and ethnic migration. In addition, Barnard notes the accelerating rhythms of modern industry as they reshape perception, sensation, and psychic sensibility in the experimental narrative techniques of Gertrude Stein, Sherwood Anderson, Hemingway, and Dos Passos. The stylized presentation of temporality pioneered by these authors, Barnard argues, influences such proletarian works of fiction as Tom Kromer's Depression-Era novel, *Waiting For Nothing* (1936). Finally, Barnard considers how modern American fiction negotiates changing notions of value, money, and economic exchange. Modern American self-fashioning, she argues, is powerfully mediated by the new narratives of fiscal accumulation and expenditure, profit and loss, class status and social mobility.

The interface between literary experiment and the new economic, cultural, and social energies of American modernism likewise shapes the rich rhetorical inventiveness of modern American poetry. As Cary Nelson demonstrates in his overview of the verse genre, modern American poetry's creative breadth, its variety of forms, and diversity of voices exceed any single or monolithic account of the period. Indeed, the dominant story of the modern Image – promoted by Ezra Pound, T. S. Eliot, F. S. Flint, and H. D. (Hilda Doolittle) – is no longer considered as *the* defining template for modern American poetry. Moreover, he argues, literary Imagism, as a "founding movement in modern American poetry . . . is richer and more diverse than we have been inclined to think." To take one example, image-text traditions in the arts, popular culture, and advertising discourse influence the collage techniques of such *291 Gallery* talents as Agnes Ernst Meyer and Marius de

Zayas in experimental works like "Mental Reactions." As a vehicle of poetic innovation, modern collage, as Nelson shows, encompasses a remarkable presentational range of forms and techniques in the poetry of T. S. Eliot, Ezra Pound, and Mina Loy. Similarly, Nelson surveys the verbal experimentalism of Gertrude Stein, Marianne Moore, and Hart Crane. Equally important, as Nelson notes, such otherwise distinctive poets as Robert Frost, Claude McKay, and Edna St. Vincent Millay share a common agenda of masterfully appropriating traditional verse forms like the sonnet, ballad stanza, and dramatic monologue in powerfully original modes of new social expression. Beyond literary formalism and the compositional strictures of the Imagist movement in American verse, Nelson's critical survey also shows how the new social discourses of race, empire, class, and gender – not to mention the period's defining historical events such as the Spanish Civil War – complicate and enrich the literary heritage of modern American poetry.

In "Modern American drama" Stephen Watt begins with American theatre's roots in such nineteenth-century American traditions as the Virginia minstrels and the popular drama of James Pilgrim who featured narratives of Irish immigration in *Ireland and America* (1851) and *Irish Assurance and Yankee Modesty* (1854). Moving on to the rise of the Theatrical Syndicate in the 1890s, Watt argues that a diversified national drama arose far from the commercial venues of New York's Broadway theatre district. Chicago's Hull-House community theatre, the Chicago Little Theatre, and Provincetown Players offer models of an alternative, modernist drama that emerged in America during the first decades of the twentieth century. Such vital scenes of American modernist theater produced works like Susan Glaspell's *Suppressed Desires* (1914), *Trifles* (1916), *Bernice* (1919), and *The Verge* (1921) and Eugene O'Neill's *The Moon of the Caribbees* (1918), *Beyond the Horizon* (1920), *The Emperor Jones* (1920), and *Desire Under the Elms* (1924). In addition to these sites of emergent, modern American drama, Watt considers the influences of melodrama and realism on the productions of James A. Herne, David Belasco, and Clyde Fitch, as well as new dramatic narratives of desire, emancipatory feminism, and socialist politics in works such as Elizabeth Robins's *Votes for Women!* (1908), Rachel Crothers's *The Three of Us* (1906), *A Man's World* (1910), and *He and She* (1911), Elmer Rice's *The Adding Machine* (1923), and Clifford Odets's *Waiting for Lefty* (1935).

The first of three essays on the cultural dimension of American modernism, Mark Sanders's essay on the New Negro Renaissance reads the flowering modern African-American culture against contemporaneous philosophical, political, and anthropological currents of American pragmatism. Surveying the influence that William James, John Dewey, Franz Boaz, and W. E. B. Du Bois had on American pragmatism, Sanders also takes into account such public intellectuals as Van Wyck Brooks, Waldo Frank, Max Eastman, Randolph Bourne, William Carlos Williams, V. F. Calverton, and Alfred Stieglitz. Against earlier formalist models of an aesthetic "high modernism," Sanders lays out the case for a new "constellation of ideas, movements, publishing venues, and artistic communities that comprised a *heterodox modernism* in which New Negroes participated fully." In this vein, Sanders examines the "little magazines" and publishing houses that sponsored New Negro Renaissance writers such as Langston Hughes, Zora Neale Hurston, Jean Toomer, James Weldon Johnson, George Schuyler, Nella Larsen, Rudolph Fisher, Jessie Fauset, and Sterling Brown. Finally, in close readings of the work of Zora Neale Hurston, Sterling Brown, and Jean Toomer, Sanders considers the key contributions that these three authors made to the American modernist tradition. Hurston's "free indirect discourse," that fuses folk vernacular and third-person narrative in *Their Eyes Were Watching God* (1937), Brown's recovery, in *Southern Road* (1932), of the American democratic ideal animating Walt Whitman's poetics, and Toomer's verbal impressionism, narrative fragmentation, and mixed generic modes in *Cane* (1923) are three exemplary African-American interventions in modern letters.

The vital connection between African-American vernacular culture and modernism is further explored in Jed Rasula's survey of the jazz age from its folk origins in the blues to the more cosmopolitan rhythms of ragtime, on through the heyday of Big Band Jazz, and into the bebop era. Tracing the cultural geography of jazz from its inception in New Orleans and subsequent migration to such Northern urban centers as Chicago, Kansas City, and New York, Rasula examines how jazz culture became synonymous with the industrial and commercial energies of American modernism as witnessed in such classic works as F. Scott Fitzgerald's *Flappers and Philosophers* (1920) and *Tales of the Jazz Age* (1922). But not just commercial entertainment, jazz's aesthetic novelty – its formal orchestration, sensuous tonalities, and syncopated rhythms – offered an "acoustic counterpart" to the radically new pictorial and literary forms of experimental modernism. Indeed, as an international phenomenon, jazz did not just set the tone for American modernism across the color line of the pre-Civil Rights era, but was a musical inspiration for such European composers as Claude Debussy, Darius Milhaud, Igor Stravinsky, Paul Hindemith, Maurice Ravel, and George Antheil, among others. A mass-mediated art form, jazz came of age with the emergence of such technologies as the radio and phonograph and, as Rasula shows, gave the modern era its distinctive "sound track."

What the Frankfurt school critic Walter Benjamin described as the "age of mechanical reproduction" also characterizes modernism's highly mediated visual culture beginning with the invention of the daguerreotype in 1837 and evolving so rapidly that by the 1880s George Eastman had invented paper-based photographic film and the Kodak roll-film camera. Between 1880 and 1904 – as Michael North discusses in his essay on the "Visual culture" of American modernism – photography began to circulate routinely in newspaper dailies, while these decades also mark the invention by Louis Lumière of the first motion picture camera in 1895 and Thomas Edison's vitascope projector the following year. For the European avant-gardes, American modernism was synonymous with the new visuality represented in journals such as Alfred Stieglitz's *Camera Work* as well as the kind of popular culture forms that Gilbert Seldes analyzed in *The Seven Lively Arts* (1924): Hollywood cinema, advertising billposters, and the visual antics of Charlie Chaplin, the Keystone Kops, and Krazy Kat comics. Moreover, as North shows in his reading of Georg Simmel's 1903 essay "The Metropolis and Mental Life," the accelerated panoramas of daily life mobilized through rapid train and automobile travel left their imprint on the visual imagination in ways that mirrored the experience of motion picture viewing. In North's analysis, the shifting perceptions of America's emerging society of the spectacle also mark the themes and new literary forms pioneered by American modernist writers, notably William Carlos Williams.

The influence of visual culture on Williams's compositional techniques, as Marjorie Perloff demonstrates, has another linkage to the more rarefied aesthetic traditions of the historical avant-gardes in American modernism. Tracing the term "avant-garde" back to its military origins, Perloff explores the ways in which Williams as well as Marcel Duchamp, Francis Picabia, Man Ray, Mina Loy, Baroness Elsa von Freitag-Loringhoven, Marius de Zayas, and Gertrude Stein, among others, provocatively challenged the traditional notions of artist and authorial identity, the art object and the literary work, and aesthetic form and generic conventions. Noting that New York Dada as an avant-garde aesthetic movement was actually the production of Europeans such as Duchamp, Picabia, von Freitag-Loringhoven, and Loy, Perloff also locates its origins two years prior to the 1916 inception of European Dada at Zurich's *Cabaret Voltaire*. The artistic scene of American modernism that flourished in New York through such sites as the 1913 Armory Show, the Walter Arensberg salon, and the 291 *Gallery* produced some of the most radically fresh expressions in modern art, sculpture, and prose. Duchamp's "readymades," Alfred Stieglitz's photography showcased in his little magazine *Camera Work*, the typography of Marius de Zayas, Picabia's "mechanomorphic" drawings, Man Ray's "objects,"

Mina Loy's erotic surrealist verse are all notable examples of an avant-garde tradition that flowered in New York City during the modern period.

Not just an avant-garde poet, however, Mina Loy also imagined new models of feminist agency, gender and sexuality in the modern public sphere. As Janet Lyon explains, Loy did not limit herself to the political agenda of suffragettes such as Dorothy Day, Margaret Sanger, or Elizabeth Gurney Flynn. Equally important, Loy inaugurated new discourses of women's sexual difference in the cultural arena through the arts of poetry, art, conversation, performance and fashion. As Lyon shows, the cosmopolitan settings of American modernism fostered shifting social arrangements between men and women that radically altered traditional understandings of gender and sexuality. In close readings of Loy, Willa Cather, Ernest Hemingway, Gertrude Stein, Hart Crane, and Wallace Thurman, among others, Lyon further explores the ways in which literary form inscribes the fungible relations among sexuality, gender, and modern identity. In addition, Lyon considers the salon communities hosted by figures like Mabel Dodge, Alfred Stieglitz, Natalie Barney, Gertrude Stein, A'Lelia Walker, and Josephine Baker that fostered the era's cultural experimentation in art and life.

Amplifying the local contexts of American modernism, John Duvall examines the ways in which regionalism signified social difference in asserting emergent varieties of gender, race, class, and ethnic identities. To begin with, Duvall questions the notion that regionalism – insofar as it is traditionally tied to realist and naturalist writers of "local color" – is anathema to the experimental, cosmopolitan, and international connotations of modern culture. In accounting for the regional resources of American modernism, Duvall shows how such major modernists as Kate Chopin, Willa Cather, Ernest Hemingway, Robert Frost, Zora Neale Hurston, Richard Wright, and William Faulkner, among others, employed local, vernacular cultures – rooted in such settings as say, Michigan, Nebraska, Mississippi, Florida, and Vermont – to forge levels of psychological characterization, thematic complexity and formal innovation that we otherwise associate with the difficult intensities defining international modernism. Similarly, as Paula Rabinowitz demonstrates, the novel forms of communal association afforded by the rise of modern big-city life were defining aspects of American modernism for authors such as John Dos Passos, Muriel Rukeyser, Gertrude Stein, Joy Davidman, W. E. B. Du Bois, Hart Crane, Jean Toomer, James Agee, Nella Larsen, Meridel LeSueur, and Anzia Yezierska, among others. Like Janet Lyon, Rabinowitz explores urban space as a social site that provided radically new modes of self fashioning. As Rabinowitz shows, the urban experience of modern city life – increasingly characterized by a multiplicity, mobility, and diversity of social exchange among bodies, machines, commodities, information, and signage – offered fresh opportunities for gender, ethnic, class, and racial cross-identifications that departed radically from traditional understandings of American national identity.

Completing the coverage of the *Cambridge Companion to American Modernism*, Douglas Mao's final chapter examines the major figures, schools, and movements of modern American literary criticism. To begin with, Mao presents the push for a so-called "New Humanism" that would revitalize the study of language and literature undertaken by figures such as Irving Babbitt, Paul Elmer More, Stuart P. Sherman, and Norman Foerster. Mao goes on to examine the lively aesthetic debates gathered in such classic collections of the era as *American Criticism* (1924). Against the conservatism, Puritanism, and old-line moralism of the New Humanists, critics like Joel Spingarn, Ernest Boyd, Van Wyck Brooks, H. L. Mencken, Max Eastman, Waldo Frank, and Randolph Bourne campaigned for more liberal, progressive, and experimental readings of American modernism. In addition, Mao presents the emergence of the period's "New Negro" aesthetic and cultural initiatives promoted by Spingarn, W. E. B. Du Bois, Alain Locke, James Weldon Johnson, Charles Johnson, William Stanley Braithwaite and Jessie Fauset, among others. The agitational criticism of Mike Gold and V. F. Calverton ties the race agenda of the former group to Marxist readings of literary form that are further refined in works such as Granville Hicks's *The Great Tradition: An Interpretation of American Literature Since the Civil War* (1930), V. L. Parrington's *Main Currents in American Thought* (1927–1930), and Edmund Wilson's *Axel's Castle* (1931). Mao further reviews the origins of psychoanalytic criticism in America and considers the shaping influence of such regional initiatives as the evolving Fugitive, Southern Agrarian and New Criticism movements as well as the Chicago school, ending finally with a study of the New York school associated with the *Partisan Review* of the 1930s. Thus, as the twelve distinguished contributors to this volume show, the "Multiplicity, Diversity, Complexity, Anarchy, Chaos" that, for Henry Adams, described the emerging "grammar" of the twentieth century become most fully patent in the literary, cultural, and social energies that define American modernism. At no point in American history has the "pulse of the continent" been more vital, its aesthetic expression more bold, and its imaginative range more "unpent."

NOTES

1. Walt Whitman, "To a Locomotive in Winter," in *The Complete Poems of Walt Whitman*, ed. Francis Murphy (New York: Penguin Books, 1986), 483.
2. Henry Adams, *The Education of Henry Adams*, ed. Ernest Samuels (Boston: Houghton Mifflin, 1974), 381.

3. Waldo Frank, *Our America* (New York: Boni & Liveright, Inc., 1919), 177–178.

4. Alain Locke, "The New Negro," in *The New Negro*, ed. Alain Locke (New York: Albert and Charles Boni, 1925), 6, 7.

5. Max Eastman, *The Enjoyment of Living* (New York: Harpers, 1948), 409.

6. Mabel Dodge Luhan, *Movers and Shakers*. Vol. 3 of *Intimate Memories* (New York: Harcourt Brace, 1936), 83; quoted in Rebecca Zurier, *Art for the Masses* (Philadelphia: Temple University Press, 1988), 105.

7. William Carlos Williams, *The Autobiography of William Carlos Williams* (New York: Random House, 1948), 134.

8. Kenyon Cox, "Cubists and Futurists are Making Insanity Pay," *New York Times*, March 16, 1913, magazine sec., pt. 6, 1; quoted in Allan Antliff, *Anarchist Modernism: Art Politics and the First American Avant-Garde* (University of Chicago Press, 2001), 47.

9. Thomas Crow, "Modernism and Mass Culture in the Visual Arts," in *Modernism and Modernity*, ed. S. Guilbaut and D. Solkin (Halifax: Press of the Nova Scotia College of Art and Design, 1983), 253.

10. Matthew Josephson, "The Great American Billposter," *Broom* 3 (November 1922), 304.

11. Williams, *The Autobiography*, 146.

12. Alfred Kazin, *On Native Grounds: An Interpretation of Modern American Prose Literature* (New York: Harcourt, Brace, 1942), viii, ix.

I

MARK MORRISSON

Nationalism and the modern American canon

London was a Mecca for modernist writers and visual artists, with its Bloomsbury experiments in aesthetics and lifestyles, its avant-garde exhibitions and arts workshops, its audacious poetry readings, and its fiercely independent small presses and little magazines. But as Hugh Kenner has noted, none of the "masterpieces" of modernist literature (*Ulysses*, *The Waste Land*, or the first third of Ezra Pound's *Cantos*, for instance) were written by English writers. Moreover, the English language and English literature itself had become decentered: Kenner went on to argue that "by mid-century . . . English was the language not only of the Three Provinces but also of several masterpieces best located in a supranational movement called International Modernism."[1] The literature that he espoused – primarily the work of T. S. Eliot, Ezra Pound, Wyndham Lewis, James Joyce, William Carlos Williams, William Butler Yeats, Marianne Moore, and Samuel Beckett – all, in Kenner's view, belonged to this "supranational movement." Indeed, modernism has often been conceptualized as a stridently international phenomenon across art and literature.

But if we accept such a vision of modernism as international, what could the phrase "American modernism" possibly mean? Does it refer to a specific subset of international modernism (that is, work produced by American modernists), or to a different kind of writing altogether? In the late nineteenth and early twentieth centuries, many American writers (modernist or not) were grappling with the "American-ness" of their own writing, seeking to understand what could define their literature as a national literature and not simply as a provincial footnote to English literature. American literary nationalism proved a powerful cultural force even as modernists began to engage with international avant-gardism. The national (or international) identity of modernism was by no means as lucid then as later scholarly assessments, including Kenner's, might suggest.

As America increasingly asserted itself on the world stage – becoming an imperial power at the turn of the century, reluctantly but successfully entering

World War I, and grappling with its relationship to the League of Nations after the war – nationalism and understandings of the arts' relationship to national identity metamorphosed a number of times. Nationalist political progressives of the late nineteenth and early twentieth centuries believed that European cultural refinement would gradually come to the American masses and that immigrants would be assimilated into this culture. Young cultural insurgents, among them many modernists, argued vehemently against gradual cultural progress and in favor of a cultural revolution or renaissance (two different rhetorical flourishes in the service of much the same goal) that would sweep away stifling, empty American conventions and replace them with a truly vibrant indigenous culture.[2] During the war, the Espionage Act was used to shut down several periodicals (including ones publishing modernism) that were deemed to be subversive and un-American; much of the American Left, however, saw itself as working for a better, more just, national culture, not subverting American ideals.[3] Progressivist notions of American identity were challenged by pluralism and then by nativism in the 1920s, a decade that also saw a resurgence of populist nationalism.[4] And most forms of American cultural nationalism drew not only from the country's history (a history whose very writing was a nationalist project) but also, at least since the early nineteenth century, from its varied and often spectacularly extreme landscapes.[5]

But just what is a nation? The issue was hotly debated in America during the modernist era. Could immigrants *become* American by enculturation, as progressivists imagined, or were they always somehow non-American culturally, even if they had attained American citizenship? Was "American culture" essentially Anglo-Saxon, as many would have it? Others argued that America's great strength as a nation was its very pluralistic composition. Was there a national identity that superseded regional identities? Were African-Americans and Native Americans truly American? Some claimed that America's major cultural contributions were primarily those of African-Americans, and they pointed to jazz, blues, dances, and folklore. Much of the discourse about modern American literature during the period was in the service of creating an American "imagined community" (Anderson) as a living organism, one that might be expressed and even *grown* by a national literature.

Against the backdrop of nationalist debates about American identity and American culture – about the nature of the imagined community that was "America" – many experimental writers began to forge something that could be called "American modernism." But which writers and artists truly represent American modernism? And who gets to decide? Editors of modernist little magazines or of mass-market periodicals? Mainstream or avant-garde publishers? Anthologists? Literary prize committees? The writers themselves? Patrons? Critics? University professors and their growing numbers of student readers of American literature? The answer is that all of these have contributed, in varying degrees and at different times, to an ever-developing American modernist canon. They still do. But the notion of a *single* canon, even if it is understood as an ever-changing inventory, may be too simple, as we shall see.

Over the last few decades, scholars who study the processes of canonization have often relied upon two seemingly competing understandings of how canons are formed. An "aesthetic" model of canon formation assumes that creative writers *themselves* create the canon by their interaction with each other's work and that of their predecessors. By contrast, an "institutional" model suggests that cultural institutions dictate what is read and valued.[6] Some scholars have argued that both models might be necessary for a complete, historically nuanced picture of how a canon, or even alternative canons, might be formed in various historical periods.[7]

The modernist period saw a shift in the institutions of canonization in America. During the first quarter of the century, the writers who helped establish the reputations of other writers and artists worked in a range of publication venues – from the little magazine, small press anthology, and limited-edition book on the one end of the spectrum to the mass-circulation magazine, popular anthology, and mass-market book on the other. Poet-critics such as T. S. Eliot and Ezra Pound exerted their influence on the reception of new literary work and the processes of canonization by publishing criticism and commentary in little magazines, wider circulation magazines, and books. They also influenced the offerings of publishers from the small-scale Egoist Press to the far larger Faber & Faber. But by the late 1930s, especially with the advent of the New Criticism, the academic institution – professors, the college English classroom, the textbook market – had begun to play a crucial part in canonization. While alternative canons, often directly influenced by poets and novelists themselves, persisted throughout the twentieth century and into the present, the academy remains highly influential in determining what work is valued and what is completely overlooked. As we explore the formation of the American modernist canon in the light of these models, we must consider the role of American literary nationalism in the stridently international aesthetic revolution of modernism.

American literary nationalism: Whitman and modernism

The nationalistic sense that America was a special country, a new country on the verge of a major cultural renaissance, was widespread in the pre-First

World War period. As scholar Charles C. Alexander explains, "the vision of a genuinely native, nationally representative artistic expression was the single most significant feature of American cultural commentary in the years after 1900 and up to the Second World War" (xii). American modernists who primarily stayed in the United States – such as William Carlos Williams, Hart Crane, John Dos Passos, Marianne Moore, and William Faulkner – were preoccupied with American national identity or with regional identities within the United States. Even many of the expatriate writers, often seen as exemplars of internationalist modernism – Ezra Pound, Gertrude Stein, H. D., and Ernest Hemingway, for instance – had, at various times, shown serious commitments to exploring American identity. Pound, from his vantage point as an expatriate in London, expressed grave frustrations with American culture, but he also argued in *Patria Mia* (1912–1913) for the exceptional artistic potential of that American identity. Predicting an American renaissance, Pound declared that "there is more artistic impulse in America than in any country in Europe."[8] He imagined that the "mongrel" nature of America, the migratory status of its evolving population, its constant state of flux, the ingenuity of its pioneers, its "crowd pagan as ever imperial Rome was, eager, careless, with an animal vigour unlike that of any European crowd that I have ever looked at" (104), and even the southern climate of the country all made America like a medieval culture rife for an exemplary intellectual awakening (103–112). Many of these characterizations of American culture were common currency at the time, echoing, among others, Frederick Jackson Turner's "frontier theory," which imagined the great national virtue of the country to derive from the pioneer spirit of rugged democratic individualism as well as egalitarianism (see Alexander, *Here the Country Lies*, 89).

Adopting, for the moment, an aesthetic model of canon formation, we must confront the reputation and influence at the birth of American modernism of Walt Whitman – the poet who, for many, most captured those "national" features of vigor, flux, ingenuity, democracy, and almost careless exuberance. The most popular conception of an American canon at the time was based upon a poetics of presence, which, as Timothy Morris explains, "means the belief that a work of art conveys the living presence of the artist, and the implied value that a work is better as the artist is more present in it."[9] Such a notion stretched back, as Morris notes, to early American literary nationalism and later found its most significant model in Whitman.

Whitman's work and reputation caused an "anxiety of influence" (as Harold Bloom puts it) for the modernists, offering them an example of a distinctively modern American voice that could assault the genteel tradition of the later nineteenth century but also generate imitators who were already stultifying and sloppy, by the early twentieth century, and could potentially rob the modernists of their own originality. Pound felt compelled both to endorse and attack Whitman, even in the same breath. In a 1909 article written in London, he claims an international perspective ("From this side of the Atlantic I am for the first time able to read Whitman . . . from the vantage of my education and . . . my world citizenship"), but immediately falls back into assertions of Whitman's – and by extension, his own – identity *as* American culture: "I see him as America's poet . . . He *is* America. His crudity is an exceeding great stench, but it *is* America . . . Mentally I am a Walt Whitman who has learned to wear a collar and a dress shirt."[10]

In *Patria Mia*, Pound could use his assertion of Whitman's *identity* with America as a tool to dismiss his aesthetic value: "Now Whitman was not an artist, but a reflex, the first honest reflex, in an age of papier-mâché letters. He was the time and the people (of 1860–80)" (110). Yet his primary target here is Whitman's aesthetic progeny, with whom Pound clearly does not wish to be identified: "His 'followers' go no further than to copy the defects of his style" (110). In a poem published the next year, though, Pound famously made his "pact" with Whitman, his "pig-headed father," observing that "It was you that broke the new wood, / Now is a time for carving. / We have one sap and one root – / Let there be commerce between us."[11]

This anxious relationship to the increasingly canonical status of Whitman was a pervasive feature of much modernist American poetry. Though William Carlos Williams sought to avoid what he saw as a lack of structure in the poetry of Whitman and Sandburg, he, like Whitman, emphasized American subjects, and he particularly aimed at a poetic idiom that could grapple with the local.[12] *Paterson*, his effort to write an epic poem grounded in the daily life and speech of a particular locality, owed some debt to Whitman, and it clearly influenced Charles Olson's *Maximus Poems* of the post-World War II era and inspired many American poets across the century. Hart Crane's important volume, *The Bridge*, likewise marked him as a poet in Whitman's line, so much so that the quotation from Malcolm Cowley used to publicize the book noted, "THE BRIDGE is in many respects the most important volume of American poetry since Whitman's *Leaves of Grass*."

Even into the 1930s, Whitman's legacy for American literary nationalism remained both significant and contentious for modernists. In a 1937 review of Edgar Lee Masters's *Whitman*, the expatriate poet H. D. struggled with Masters's attempt to base American identity on the prairie and to map his vision of literary patriotism onto Whitman. Rather than arguing against literary nationalism or undermining the notion of an American identity, H. D. simply claims Whitman for the eastern United States, and she thus ties him firmly into what Celena Kusch describes as an "expatriate literary nationalism" that links America to its European origins.[13]

Poets who were not modernists also laid claim to Whitman – often more stridently than those now called modernists. The subsequent canonization of modernist poets over the extremely popular and even experimental poets who published alongside them in many journals and anthologies – poets such as Vachel Lindsay, Edgar Lee Masters, and Carl Sandburg – is a story that cannot fully be told through an aesthetic model of canonization. We must turn to an institutional model to comprehend the larger picture of modernism's growing dominance in the canon of early-twentieth-century American literature.

The little magazines

In *Patria Mia*, Pound execrated the conservative and stultifying conventions of American literary magazines as the greatest impediment to his much desired American Risorgimento, or renaissance (110). One poet who shared both Pound's sense of an impending American renewal and his assessment of the American literary magazines was Harriet Monroe, who lived in Chicago. She decided to found her own literary magazine in 1912 – and named it simply *Poetry*. Monroe turned to Whitman for inspiration, choosing his words for the motto of *Poetry*: "To have great poets there must be great audiences too." And while Monroe published and lauded some non-American poets, her goal for *Poetry* was very much inflected by the cultural nationalism of the moment. Her ideal developed out of a progressivist vision of American culture that saw a blending of different racial and ethnic strains as the country's strength. "In this American melting-pot," she wrote, "the English language becomes the mother tongue."[14] The American poets she had in mind – the "second-generation Swede" Carl Sandburg, the "Italian" Arturo Giovannitti, the "Yiddish Jew" Morris Rosenfeld, and "the Syrian" Arjan Syrian, as well as only a few poets of "Anglo-Saxon stock," Edgar Lee Masters and C. E. S. Wood – are "bent upon the same business – in the deepest sense a poet's business – of seeing our *national* life in the large – its beauty and glory, its baseness and shame" (Monroe "Chicago Granite," 90–91, my emphasis). Monroe's formulation of an American national poetry deployed the common racialized understanding of ethnicity, but she saw those racial/national identities of immigrants as blending under the banner of the American English language into something distinctly American.

It had become so common for English and American critics to urge American writers and artists to express "American" subjects in their art that Amy Lowell, writing in *Poetry*, complained of the demand for "a narrow and purely surface 'Americanism.'"[15] But even Lowell affirmed an American mission for poetry that was based upon the same logic of identity that Pound had adopted in *Patria Mia*: "A nation is its character, just as a man is" (35). Instead of deliberately choosing a preconceived set of "American" subjects, American poets, in simply expressing themselves, by virtue of their being American, will create American poetry. "Poe and Walt Whitman," she went on, "share the honor of being America's greatest poets. And what a difference! How unlike are the subjects which inspired them, and how utterly unlike their forms of 'attack'" (Lowell, "Nationalism," 36). While rejecting calls for American subject matter, Lowell never seems to have questioned that *Poetry*'s agenda should be to encourage great American poetry. And *Poetry* was only the first of many such little magazines in America that would help create an audience for modernism and shape a modernist canon.

The little magazine was the quintessential genre of modernist publication – and one of modernism's many contributions to twentieth-century literature. This genre is, indeed, a logical starting place for any institutional exploration of American modernist canon formation, and it is the genre that had the most direct input from the authors themselves (the editors, too, were often modernist authors). The late nineteenth century saw the cost of printing and paper drop dramatically, and modernist editors with small budgets could act fairly independently of the constraints of mass-market periodicals; they could publish obscure or wildly experimental work and advocate aesthetic and social revolutions. Many of the most famous works of modernist literature appeared to readers first in the pages of little magazines and only later in book form. Emphasizing the genre's importance to the modernist canon, George Bornstein notes that "Part of the extraordinary success of the modernists in canon formation came from their attention to editorial presentation of new or neglected writers . . . in little magazines (such as *Poetry*, *Little Review*, or the larger *Dial*)."[16] Even though individual little magazines often had short lives and small print runs, the genre has flourished ever since. Already by the middle of the twentieth century, over a thousand different little magazines had been published, and hundreds more have since come into existence.

In spite of the strikingly international content of many of these magazines and their espousal of "International Modernism," many of them (even those edited by expatriate Americans) emerged out of the American cultural nationalism of the early twentieth century and meant to contribute to an American cultural renaissance. In the pre-World War I period, the magazine *The Seven Arts* (1916–1917) forcefully expressed an American cultural nationalism inspired by Walt Whitman. Under the editorial guidance of James Oppenheim, Waldo Frank, and Van Wyck Brooks, the journal epitomized what Charles Alexander terms "romantic nationalism." In a circular sent around to American authors, Oppenheim declared that "It is our faith and the faith of many, that we are living in the first days of a renascent period, a time which means for America the coming of the national self-consciousness which is the beginning of greatness . . . It is the aim of *The Seven Arts* to become a channel for the flow of these new tendencies: an expression of our American arts which shall be fundamentally an expression of our American life."[17] Oppenheim, Frank, and Brooks frequently called for Americans to forge their own traditions, to make their own art, to put their own theatrical productions on the stage – essentially, to overcome the timidity and self-destructive conventions of American culture and create a new nationalistic art. While *The Seven Arts* published work by writers such as John Reed, Theodore Dreiser, Carl Sandburg, Floyd Dell, and H. L. Mencken, who were not at the forefront of literary modernism, it also included work by Amy Lowell, Robert Frost, Sherwood Anderson, Eugene O'Neill, and John Dos Passos, and its editors seemed to have made no aesthetic distinctions among its diverse set of contributors.

The periodical featured the cultural criticism of Brooks, whose famous essay in *The Dial*, "On Creating a Usable Past," argued for creating a past that could have value to the present, for understanding the failures of Emerson, Thoreau, and Whitman to live up to their full potential in a difficult American cultural environment, and for inspiring a sense of communal purpose in revamping American national culture. Brooks made several of these points in a *Seven Arts* essay, "Young America," from December 1916. The magazine also featured the work of the young American nationalist, Randolph Bourne, whose influential writings argued against the "melting pot" of American progressivism and instead for a cultural pluralism. Bourne advocated a vision of America not as an Anglo-Saxon nation but as the first cosmopolitan and transnational country (Alexander, *Here the Country Lies*, 80–83).

From the turn of the century to the 1920s, as Walter Benn Michaels has argued in *Our America*, the idea of America and of national identity in general had changed significantly (2). Michaels tracks the rise of nativist pluralism not just to claim it as a context for understanding key modernist texts of the 1920s (for instance, Faulkner's *The Sound and the Fury*, Hemingway's *The Sun Also Rises*, Cather's *The Professor's House*, Fitzgerald's *The Great Gatsby*, and the poetry of William Carlos Williams) but rather to argue that nativism and modernism were "efforts to work out the meaning of the commitment to identity – linguistic, national, cultural, racial – that . . . is common to both" (3). He suggests the primacy of identity itself in American cultural debates of the 1920s, noting the similar logic of two significant acts passed by Congress in 1924: the Johnson Immigration Act, which restricted immigration, and the Indian Citizenship Act, which honored Native Americans. "Pluralism," Michaels writes, "is, in a sense, built into nativism since the essence of nativism is its preference for the native exclusively on the grounds of its being native . . . [T]he commitment to pluralism requires in fact that the question of who we are continue to be understood as prior to questions about what we do" (14).

In the 1920s, a pluralist nationalist vision could be explicitly wedded to a kind of modernism in the little magazines – a nativist modernism. In the opening manifesto of the journal *Contact*, edited by William Carlos Williams and Robert McAlmon from 1920–1924, the editors proclaimed that "We are here because of our faith in the existence of native artists who are capable of having, comprehending and recording extraordinary experiences . . . We will be American, because we are of America . . . Particularly we will adopt no aggressive or inferior attitude toward 'imported thought' or art."[18] The magazine published the work of American authors such as Marianne Moore, Wallace Gould, Marsden Hartley, Wallace Stevens, John Gould Fletcher, Kenneth Burke, and, of course, Williams and McAlmon, as well as that of Americans abroad, such as H. D., Ezra Pound, and Kay Boyle. Williams called *Contact* "the first truly representative American magazine of art yet published."[19] As Michaels has shown, Williams's own commitments to identity, pluralism, and "pure writing" – his efforts to create a materialist American aesthetic in which writing itself was reality and not merely an imitation of it – were in line with the broader political and cultural climate of 1920s nativism (76–77).

While Williams chastised the expatriate American writers and referred to the quickly canonical masterwork at the center of modernism, Eliot's *The Waste Land*, as "the great catastrophe to our letters" (quoted in Michaels, *Our America*, 75), even the American expatriate magazines often aimed at American audiences and hoped to rejuvenate American literature. Harold Loeb's *Broom* (1921–1924), which was published in Rome and then in Berlin, proclaimed itself "an international magazine of the arts" and published a wide variety of American and Continental work, but it translated all of the non-English-language work into English so that Americans could read it. And Eugene Jolas's *transition* (published in Paris from 1927–1938), the most famous of all American expatriate modernist magazines, published all of its literature in English translation from its founding in 1927 until 1933, when Jolas announced that he would publish all texts in their original languages. As Craig Monk notes, "Proceeding from what the editor, Eugene Jolas, hoped would be a developing enthusiasm in the United States for world literature, *transition* sought to encourage a host of international contributors, initially translating their works into 'a language Americans can read and understand.'"[20] One of the most international of modernist magazines could thus see itself as contributing to American culture, but it had clearly moved a long way from the romantic nationalism of *The Seven Arts*.

The Little Review: A case study

The publishing history of Margaret Anderson and Jane Heap's *Little Review*, one of the most significant American modernist little magazines, illustrates the common tension between American cultural nationalism and internationalist aspirations in the early period of modernist canon formation. *The Little Review*, which began publication as a monthly in Chicago in March 1914, self-consciously positioned itself as a manifestation of America's recently emerging culture of youth, capitalizing on the energies of American advertising culture and on the image of Chicago as a new city characterized by youthful exuberance and idealism.[21] Its nationalism was not based on the country's past and its traditions but on a sense of the limitless possibilities inherent in its very newness.

During its early years, most of the poets publishing in *The Little Review* were American. Even as late as the Autumn 1922 issue, William Carlos Williams could write, "I hope I may be permitted to say that the *Little Review* is American, that it, yes, alone, is worth while because it maintains contact with common sense in America. It is the only important reaction to the American environment, the only reaction that is not a coat of paint on the stanchion."[22] The poets who appeared most frequently during the magazine's Chicago years can be categorized into two groups: first, Midwestern poets, and second, poets adopting the emerging Imagist poetics. In the first group were Iowa poet Arthur Davison Ficke, Chicagoans Eunice Tietjens, Ben Hecht, Carl Sandburg, and Edgar Lee Masters, and Vachel Lindsay, also from Illinois. The Imagist-inspired poets frequently appearing during the Chicago years were Amy Lowell and Maxwell Bodenheim and the British poet Richard Aldington (with a single appearance by H. D. and John Gould Fletcher). Aldington and Ezra Pound also wrote essays for the journal.

These two trends in the contents of the *Little Review* reveal two competing visions of an American modern poetry canon developing during the pre-First World War period. The first was epitomized by Lindsay, Masters, and to some extent Sandburg, and it represents a continuation of the Whitman-inspired canon. As in *Poetry*, Whitman was frequently lauded in the early *Little Review* and was discussed in at least ten essays, reviews, and letters in the first two years of the magazine. Margaret Anderson herself used lines from Whitman as an epigraph to her first poem in the *Little Review*. Whitman was seen as an American master whose poetics of presence, cosmic sensibility, and advocacy of democracy had much to offer the young modern generation; as one *Little Review* contributor put it, Whitman "opened the door for (y)our generation – the dear old pioneer . . . the pillar of cloud by day."[23]

Critics in the *Little Review* quickly drew comparisons between Masters and Whitman. John Cowper Powys placed Masters with Theodore Dreiser, whom the early *Little Review* had crowned as the great American novelist. Powys noted, "The true literary descendants of the author of the *Leaves of Grass* are undoubtedly Theodore Dreiser and Edgar Masters. These two, and these two alone, though in completely different ways, possess that singular 'beyond-good-and-evil' touch which the epic form of art requires."[24] Carl Sandburg's review of *The Spoon River Anthology* (1915) even cited Ezra Pound to justify his admiration – a judgment from which Pound would soon back away.[25] Masters's brief portraits in *Spoon River* of the recently deceased denizens of a rural Illinois town were seen as poetry of the highest order, embodying something important about America ("striking, indigenous, out of the soil of America as a home-land" as Sandburg put it [43]), but also universal in the best sense: "They are Illinois people. Also they are the people of anywhere and everywhere in so-called civilization" (43).

The other Midwestern poet to garner the adulation of the early *Little Review* was Vachel Lindsay, author of the poem "General William Booth Enters Into Heaven," which was published in *Poetry* and widely seen as a breakthrough poem for modern American poetics. One *Little Review* essay argued that "Lindsay has sung out humanly and delightfully a more acceptable ideal of democracy than any American has yet sung. The rest of us would-be artists are creating things that can appeal to a small number. Lindsay is chanting to all America, and all America is listening – we, the artists, as well as the littlest country school-boy."[26] Lindsay was famous for the lively performances of his poetry, his loose (sometimes breathless) verse, and his American themes, and *The Little Review* often associated him with Whitman.

Yet even as many contributors and readers of *The Little Review* sang the praises of Lindsay and Masters and Whitmanian poetics, another American poetry quickly rivaled this aesthetic – Imagism. As will be discussed below, Imagism itself was a canonization strategy, designed to give a coherent focus to the otherwise disparate work of poets ranging from Pound, H. D., and Aldington to D. H. Lawrence and James Joyce. By the time *The Little Review* had begun publishing, Imagism was being discussed on both sides of the Atlantic in little magazines.

During its Chicago years, the *Little Review* not only published several Imagist poets – some of them frequently – but also took on the work of critical advocacy for Imagism, publishing at least six articles on Imagism and reviews of the Imagist anthologies, Pound's *Des Imagistes* and Amy Lowell's *Some Imagist Poets*. Imagism became a dominant poetic, even influencing several minor poets who were not part of the Imagist anthologies. And while there was not much open hostility between the espousers of Whitman, Masters, and Lindsay and the advocates of Imagism, it was clear that a battle was being fought that would have far-reaching consequences for modernism. In short, even before Ezra Pound became the Foreign Editor of *The Little Review* (beginning with the May 1917 issue), Imagism had won that battle, and American modernism carried on more fully in the line of Imagism than in the line of Whitman. In April 1917 the *Little Review* announced the winners of its "Vers Libre Prize contest." While Eunice Tietjens, a more traditional American poet, was one of the three judges, the other two were William Carlos Williams and Helen Hoyt, both poets sympathetic to Imagism. And the winners were American Imagist poets: H. D. and Maxwell Bodenheim. The free verse revolution in American poetry had come, in the pages of *The Little Review*, to be an Imagist revolution. Above all, Imagism forged a tie with the British modernist scene in London and helped pave the way for *The Little Review*'s turn to British modernism and Continental avant-gardism beginning in 1917.

What was to come, of course, made Imagism seem like a reform rather than a revolution. *The Little Review* largely remained in Chicago through the January 1917 issue, and then it moved with its editors to New York. The influx of Continental avant-gardists into New York during World War I made the lively Greenwich Village bohemian scene even more international and aesthetically daring. Anderson and Heap made contact with artists and writers in New York, and, especially after the war, with European artists and American expatriates in Paris. From London Pound helped channel much of the best British and Continental modernist work to the *Little Review*. The magazine continued to publish American modernists who remained in America (William Carlos Williams published twenty-two poems in the magazine between 1917 and 1926, and Marianne Moore, Wallace Stevens, Amy Lowell, Marsden Hartley, and several others appeared in the journal), but *The Little Review* also published much poetry by American expatriates such as Stein, Hemingway, H. D., Pound, Djuna Barnes, Malcolm Cowley, and Eliot. The magazine made lasting contacts with European avant-gardists and eventually published a number of poets associated with Dada and Surrealism, including Tristan Tzara, Paul Eluard, Francis Picabia, and Jean Cocteau.

Fiction had played very little role in the Chicago years of *The Little Review*, but it became prominent during the magazine's tenure in New York. Pound and others helped bring work by Wyndham Lewis, Mary Butts, Hemingway, Dorothy Richardson, Barnes, Jean Toomer, and others to the magazine. *The*

Little Review's biggest coup, though, was the serial publication of James Joyce's *Ulysses*, which began in the April 1918 issue. (A legal action using obscenity laws forced the magazine to suspend publication of Joyce's novel after twenty-two installments.) And, along with fiction, art began to be much more prominent in the magazine. Anderson and Heap published much writing about art, including Dada, Italian Futurist, and De Stijl manifestos, and included many plates of artworks by Americans such as Man Ray, Joseph Stella, Arthur B. Davies, and Stuart Davis. Many European modernist artists, including those involved in the key aesthetic movements of the day – e.g., Surrealism, Parisian and Berlin Dada, Blaue Reiter, Vorticism, Cubism, and Constructivism – were also represented. While the magazine had only published the work of four artists during its Chicago years, it published the art of ninety-three others, including Brancusi, De Chirico, Duchamp, Kandinsky, and Picasso, after it moved to New York.

While readers in 1917 occasionally complained about how British and foreign the magazine was becoming, others praised the change of direction and reveled in the lively transatlantic connections the magazine was forging. Still, *The Little Review* remained committed to constructing an American canon, and it continued to publish special "American Number" issues that featured American writing. Moreover, it devoted special issues to particular American modernists – Pound, Stella, and even the recently deceased Henry James. As Margaret Anderson put it in an advertisement for the magazine in the September-December 1920 issue, "*The Little Review* was the first magazine to reassure Europe as to America, and the first to give America the tang of Europe."

A small-circulation magazine like *The Little Review* can only provide a partial view of the developing American modernist canon, but it is an important example of an institution through which much of the conversation about American modernism occurred among modernists themselves and their earliest readers. This brief sketch of Anderson and Heap's magazine shows how editors, contributors, and readers could imagine an American cultural revival that increasingly saw itself as part of a multinational movement in the arts.

Anthologies, presses, and collective identities

As little magazines offered an institutional outlet in which modernists could shape and discuss the nature of American modernism, the anthology and the small press book publisher also contributed to one part of the dynamic of canonization – the forging of collective identities. Anthologies contributed much to the American modernist canon in short fiction and poetry. One example of how anthologies helped create group identities can be seen in the history of the Imagist anthologies. Ezra Pound developed his sense of Imagist poetics in exchanges with T. E. Hulme, Ford Madox Ford, H. D., and several others on the London scene, and the history of Imagism's emergence shows how opportunistic and strategic the name "Imagist" could be. In an oft-rehearsed episode in early modernism, H. D. recalled how Pound in 1912 appended "H. D. Imagiste" to the manuscript of her poem "Hermes of the Ways" to help publish and publicize her work in *Poetry*.[27] Pound then published programmatic statements of Imagist poetics in the March 1913 *Poetry*, launched a campaign to publicize the "movement" in other little magazines, and finally in 1914 published an anthology entitled *Des Imagistes* (presumably to emphasize the Continental, avant-garde nature of the undertaking). The anthology printed poems by Aldington, H. D., F. S. Flint, Skipwith Cannell, Lowell, Williams, James Joyce, Ford Madox Hueffer (soon to become Ford Madox Ford), Allen Upward, John Cournos, and of course Pound himself. While much of the work featured in the anthology did not resemble the description of Imagist principles that Pound had directed into *Poetry* (Ford even denied being an Imagist at all), the "movement" was launched, the group identity forged, and the press could then talk of Imagism as if it were a well-established aesthetic, often described as a haiku-inspired descriptive poetry. When a rift developed between Lowell and Pound, Lowell went on to publish her own series of Imagist anthologies with Houghton Mifflin between 1915 and 1917. *Some Imagist Poets: An Annual Anthology* featured the work of Aldington, H. D., Fletcher, Flint, D. H. Lawrence, and Lowell. With group publications like these anthologies to garner reviews and discussion in the press and among modernist poets, a sense of a distinctive aesthetic direction began to emerge in modernist poetry, one that took on a life as a largely American alternative to French symbolism, with Williams and H. D. perhaps as its most significant poets.

Other anthologies created a collective focus based not on a small group but on a racial or regional identity. Alain Locke's *The New Negro* (1925) is a key document of the Harlem Renaissance, helping establish the important authors emerging from Harlem during the 1920s. Alice Corbin Henderson likewise began to shape a regional Southwest canon that included several modernist writers in her anthology *The Turquoise Trail* (1928). Other anthologies cast a broader net but still attempted to fashion a unique identity for the work published. For example, Harriet Monroe and Alice Corbin Henderson published *The New Poetry: An Anthology* (1918) with a major publisher, Macmillan, to give shape to the poetry renaissance in America and Britain. The broader an anthology became, though, the less it could contribute to the ongoing process of canon formation. The anthologist William

Stanley Braithwaite, for instance, did much to keep new poetry before the eyes of the American poetry-reading public with his annual *Anthology of Magazine Verse and Year Book of American Poetry*, which began in 1913 and published its final volume in 1958. Yet Braithwaite took the all-inclusive approach, and he published modernist poems culled from little magazines alongside hundreds of traditional poems from major mainstream publications like *The Century Magazine, Scribner's*, and *Good Housekeeping*.

In addition to anthologies, small presses themselves could give a kind of collective identity to authors that helped shape the modernist canon. Key modernist presses included Sylvia Beach's Shakespeare and Company, Harriet Shaw Weaver's Egoist Press, Nancy Cunard's Hours Press, Harry and Caresse Crosby's Black Sun Press, Leonard and Virginia Woolf's Hogarth Press, James Laughlin's New Directions and also larger publishing houses such as Faber & Faber. As Lawrence Rainey has shown of the often hand-printed luxury editions of modernist work from small presses (the most famous example of which is the first edition of Joyce's *Ulysses* brought out by Shakespeare and Company in 1922): "By the early 1920s it had become a routine step in a tripartite publishing program – journal, limited edition, and public or commercial edition – that was now normative for the avant-garde."[28] Such a publishing path was also a path toward canonization, with authors who were associated through publication in an especially noteworthy small press gaining a group identity and a kind of cachet on the book collectors' market as well as in the press.

Prizes and the American modernist canon

The literary prize could be a fast track to canonization. Prizes ranged from small monetary awards given out by modernist little magazines to the Bollingen Prize, awarded by the Fellows in American Letters of the Library of Congress, or even the Nobel Prize. Harriet Monroe began giving out annual poetry prizes through *Poetry* in 1914, with the Levinson Prize as the key award – and through 1936, when Harriet Monroe died, all of the Levinson Prizes were given to American poets. The first four winners – Carl Sandburg (1914), Vachel Lindsay (1915), Edgar Lee Masters (1916), and Cloyd Head (1917) – were Illinois poets in the Whitman tradition. Monroe's choices for prize winners sometimes came under criticism for popularizing poetry rather than seeking quality.[29] But the Levinson Prize was, in fact, given to a number of modernist poets as well, including Stevens, Frost, Lowell, Crane, Moore, H. D., cummings, and Williams. The magazine used the Levinson Prize and several other small prizes to recognize a wide range of poetry, though, and the awards never became essential in forming an American modernist canon.

Two prizes that *did* make major interventions in that canon were the Dial Award of 1922, given to T. S. Eliot for *The Waste Land*, and the Nobel Prize for literature awarded to William Faulkner in 1950. Both illustrate the role that prizes can have in canon formation and the kinds of manipulations that must occur to pave the way for such distinction. Lawrence Rainey has chronicled the negotiations and decisions that led up to Eliot's agreement to publish *The Waste Land* virtually simultaneously in October 1922 in two periodicals – his own journal, *The Criterion*, in Britain and *The Dial* in the United States – and then in book form in December 1922 with the American publisher Horace Liveright. Pound was attempting to find a single publisher to bring out the works of the modernists he considered important, and he sought to make that arrangement with Liveright (Rainey, *Institutions*, 82). Naturally, Pound suggested Liveright as a publisher for *The Waste Land*, the work Pound was espousing as "the justification of the 'movement,' of our modern experiment, since 1900" (quoted in Rainey, *Institutions*, 81). But the choice of American magazine venue was more complicated. Pound and Eliot discussed both the *Little Review* (with a circulation of around 3,100) as an option, as well as the more mass-market popularizer of modernism, *Vanity Fair* (with its vastly larger budget and circulation of around 96,500), but they instead negotiated the poem's appearance in *The Dial*, whose circulation was around 9,500 (Rainey, *Institutions*, 98). Because of Pound's reputation as a discerning critic and an impresario of modernism, the editors of *The Dial*, who wanted the magazine to become *the* major American publisher of modernist writing, were convinced that they had to be the first American publishers of the poem. Eliot shrewdly saw that *The Dial*, not the more commercially successful and mass market-oriented *Vanity Fair*, would bring the cultural status and distinction to his poem that he wished for it (Rainey, *Institutions*, 105). The end result was that without even having seen the poem, the editors of *The Dial* agreed to pay Eliot $150 for it and, above all, to award it the 1922 Dial Award of $2,000 (a sum worth more than $40,000 in the late 1980s, when Rainey first published his research). As Rainey notes, "It was not simply the institutions that were the vehicle of the poem; the poem also became the vehicle of the institutions" (106).

If the publication of *The Waste Land* and the Dial Award given Eliot in 1922 represent the institutional forces of canonization created by modernists during the period before the academy gained preeminence in canon formation, the resurgence of William Faulkner's reputation and his triumphant canonization and Nobel Prize represent institutional dynamics of the post-World War II period. In his exploration of Faulkner's career, Lawrence H. Schwartz "wondered how was it possible for a writer, out of print and generally ignored in the early 1940s, to be proclaimed, in 1950, a literary genius, perhaps the best American novelist of the century."[30] Schwartz argues that for Faulkner to reach the height of canonical status he had achieved by the mid-1950s, his work had to be reinterpreted positively by critics of major stature – a task taken up by two esteemed critics of the postwar era, Malcolm Cowley and Robert Penn Warren. This reinterpretation was especially carried on by Southern writers tied to the New Criticism in American academia – such writers as John Crowe Ransom, Allen Tate, and Cleanth Brooks – as well as by Katherine Anne Porter, Eudora Welty, Kay Boyle, James T. Farrell, and Conrad Aiken. Moreover, Schwartz notes, this reinterpretation came as America rose to new heights of prosperity and world dominance after the war. The postwar American hegemony emerging during the cold war gave an ideological and strategic underpinning – and traction – to the new interpretations of Faulkner. As Schwartz shows, New Critics and other literati in New York, along with the Rockefeller Foundation, "came together in the 1940s to set a cultural agenda, and they used and promoted Faulkner for their own ends" (5). But the critical reception and ideological advocacy of Faulkner also coincided with the expansion of cheap mass-market paperbacks in the American publishing industry after the war. Some of Faulkner's novels became widely available to readers just as his works were being championed by influential critics and university professors.

As with the case of Eliot's Dial Award for *The Waste Land*, Faulkner's Nobel Prize for Literature in 1950 was made possible by a number of different institutional manipulations and needs. Does this mean that these canonizations were not based in any way on literary merit? Not at all, though literary merit is a vexingly subjective concept. Institutional models of canonization help explain how some works become, at least for a time, canonical.

The New Criticism

The story I have been telling has been one of authors, poet-critics, and editors engaging the institutions of the publishing world to advance competing visions of a modern American canon, but by the late 1930s, one institution quickly became (and has remained) the dominant force in canonization: the American university classroom. A group of professors who have come to be known as the New Critics (after John Crowe Ransom's 1941 volume, *The New Criticism*) influenced the rise of university English departments and pedagogical anthologies as key sites of literary evaluation and canon formation, and they were major voices in debates about modernist poetry and American literary nationalism. These men, including Warren, Brooks, Tate, and Ransom, were, as Golding notes, "poets first, professors second: men (for they were all men) who could be termed poet-professors . . . a distinctive kind of literary professional" (*Outlaw to Classic*, 71). The influential critical methods these poet-professors developed emphasized the sharpening of close reading skills. New Criticism privileged the evaluation of poetry as the justification of literary scholarship – not the biographical and bibliographical work that had characterized the profession for many years, or the fetishization of isolated aspects of a poem (such as metrics), or the narrow focus on moral import, or the deep political engagements of, for instance, the Marxist critics of the same era. Brooks and Warren's *Understanding Poetry* (1938) became one of the most influential college poetry textbooks of the 1930s and continued to be revised and reprinted well into the 1970s. In their "Letter to the Teacher" at the beginning of *Understanding Poetry*, Brooks and Warren cautioned: "This book has been conceived on the assumption that if poetry is worth teaching at all it is worth teaching as poetry."[31] In other words, New Criticism would explore the text as an autonomous work of art. Its close reading tools meant to show students how a work of literature employs formal techniques and such devices as irony, tension, and wit to create meaning.

Not surprisingly, New Criticism spawned an interest in challenging poetry that would demonstrate the utility of New Critical tools – poems such as Eliot's *Waste Land* and Yeats's later work, as well as the works of Emily Dickinson and John Donne. Poetry that best fit the aesthetic criteria of the New Critics was emphasized in important classroom teaching anthologies. Poetry less conducive to the New Critical quest for tensions and ironies, like the work of Williams, Stein, Pound, or, for that matter, Whitman, Lindsay, or Sandburg, was not. A critical method thus helped ensure the ongoing classroom use of certain poets and the almost complete eclipse of others.

Moreover, the New Critics were manifestly Anglophilic in their taste. Their understanding of the canon – of the literary "tradition" – was, as Golding puts it, "a transhistorical narrative of the writing of metaphysical poems" (*Outlaw to Classic*, 88). This ahistorical perspective allowed them to view Donne, Dickinson, Blake, and Eliot as each essentially doing the same thing. It also enabled them to see the tradition as an English one. Even though many of the modern poets they privileged in their criticism and teaching anthologies were American, the "American-ness" of any of those poets was irrelevant. Indeed, they held American literary nationalism to be a kind of parochialism, and they could not imagine American poetry to emerge from a tradition other than the English one they had elaborated (Golding, *Outlaw to Classic*, 88–89).

Eliot himself had prepared the way for such a reading of the "tradition" in "Tradition and the Individual Talent" (1919). In this essay, Eliot elaborated his theory of the impersonality of the great artist, arguing that "The progress of an artist is a continual self-sacrifice, a continual extinction of personality . . . the more perfect the artist, the more completely separate in him will be the man who suffers and the mind which creates."[32] And in a move that succinctly states what became a New Critical truism, he wrote: "Honest criticism and sensitive appreciation is directed not upon the poet but upon the poetry" (53). Of course, experiences that are transmogrified by the artistic process are specific to a particular artist in a particular time and place. But from Eliot's perspective, the success and the value of a poem do not derive from a reader's knowledge of the poet's biography. Instead, they derive from Eliot's ability to be aware of and write in a great literary tradition. Eliot argues that the ability to write in this tradition involves acquiring "the historical sense": "[T]he historical sense involves a perception, not only of the pastness of the past, but of its presence . . . a feeling that the whole of the literature of Europe from Homer and within it the whole of the literature of his own country has a simultaneous existence and composes a simultaneous order" (49). Eliot and the New Critics elaborated this tradition as monolithic – and largely English.

As the New Critics developed this canon, they challenged efforts to assert a specifically American literary tradition as an alternative to the one they advocated. Because the poetics of presence had been a foundation of the American poetry canon for almost a century, with Whitman its most prominent example, Whitman drew special fire from the New Critics. As Golding has shown, Whitman became a ground upon which the New Critics assaulted other competing critical schools and sensibilities, and this battle was far from a disinterested pursuit of poetic value. The New Critics competed with schools of nationalist thought during the 1930s that assigned value to literature according to extraliterary criteria (such as anticapitalist or progressive politics) and that attempted to define American literature in terms of essential American traits. There was, of course, a political valence to these arguments by the culturally conservative New Critics over Whitman and literary nationalism. (Whitman had been seen by the Communist Party and the Popular Front as a progressive and essentially American voice in American literature [Golding, *Outlaw to Classic*, 87–94]).

While we have seen that some modernists, including Eliot, Lowell, and, in a more complicated way, Pound, were critical of Whitman and of some American literary nationalist ideals, the New Critical attack on Whitman had consequences for the American modernist canon of the 1930s to the 1950s. Poets who had been published alongside Pound, Eliot, and Yeats in the early years of modernism and often considered key modern American poets by readers of modernist little magazines and anthologies – in particular, Lindsay, Sandburg, Masters, Williams, Crane, and Edna St. Vincent

Millay – were also under attack. These poets were still espoused by read-ers and publishers of classroom textbook anthologies that competed with the modern poetry texts of the New Critics. This somewhat greater diver-sity of modern American poets in anthologies persisted into the 1940s. By the 1950s, though, the New Critical insistence on evaluation, on depth over breadth, had finally won out in the American classroom. The canon, even in the American literature anthologies, had significantly narrowed in a way that approached the "tradition" of the New Critics (Golding, *Outlaw to Classic*, 111).

The canon after the New Criticism

In the New Critical classroom of the late 1940s, as Hugh Kenner remem-bers it, Eliot and the later Yeats were central to the modernist canon whose narrowness, however, extended beyond the bounds of modernist poetry. Summarizing the 1948 National Council of Teachers of English review of American literature in the college classroom, Paul Lauter notes that only three women (Dickinson, Wharton, and Cather) were included in the ninety survey-course syllabi that the study examined, and, as Lauter puts it, "by the end of the 1950s, one could study American literature and read no work by a black writer, few works by women except Dickinson and perhaps Marianne Moore or Katherine Anne Porter, and no work about the lives or experiences of working-class people."[33]

Yet at the beginning of our current century, a course in American mod-ernism might include poetry not only by Eliot, Frost, and Stevens but also by Williams, Crane, the Pound of the *Cantos*, H. D., Gertude Stein, Langston Hughes, Louis Zukofsky, Marianne Moore, and Amy Lowell – or, to add some fiction corollaries, by Zora Neale Hurston, Djuna Barnes, John Dos Passos, and Kay Boyle and not just Hemingway, Fitzgerald, and Faulkner. How has the canon changed so much, given that much of the New Critical pedagogical emphasis on close reading skills has remained in the American classroom?

Part of that shift is explained by changes in the academic institution. The rapid expansion of the postwar American university and, in particular, of English departments and English graduate programs brought about several changes in research methodologies and indeed in the very nature of literary scholarship. A scholarly return to historical work like source hunting, for instance, after many years of New Critical ahistoricism, was only a mod-est first step. The assault on New Criticism *within* academia had already begun even in the 1950s.[34] Frank Lentricchia traces the opposition to New Criticism within the academy back even into the 1940s, but he notes that "by around 1957 the moribund condition of the New Criticism and the literary needs it left unfulfilled placed us in a critical void"[35] – a void that was about to be filled by a blossoming of theoretical approaches. By the 1960s and 1970s new paradigms, including structuralist, poststructuralist, psychoanalytic, feminist, and new Marxist critical theories moved well beyond the return to historical scholarship in modernism to change English departments radically. The rise of feminist scholarship in the 1970s and 1980s effected a sea change in the modernist canon, not only making it impossible to continue ignoring Stein, H. D., Moore, and Barnes in the classroom, for instance, but also bringing them to the center of the canon and ensuring the return to print of most of their works. Likewise, the increasing complexity and strength of African-American studies in American universities brought back into print much work from the modernist period and has helped set the terms for critical assessments of the Harlem Renaissance as a modernist phenomenon.[36] Similarly, the emergence of queer theory has brought renewed interest in the works of Stein, Crane, and other modernists who had been neglected in the classroom, and it fostered new homosocial readings of more "canonical" writers.

But another part of the story of the canon after New Criticism confirms an aesthetic model of canon formation, as poets and poet-critics reread their modernist forebears – and often turned to a different set of modernists than those their New Critical professors had asked them to read. New generations of poets have constructed a different canon of modernism and have stridently revisited the literary nationalism that the New Critics had all but effaced. An exemplary set of texts in this revision of modernism by post-World War II poets is Donald M. Allen's highly successful anthology, *The New American Poetry* (1960), and its companion piece, *The Poetics of the New American Poetry* (1973, edited by Allen and by Warren Tallman). Allen's brief introduction to his collection immediately positions its "New American" poets as the heirs of an actively creative set of American modernists. He explicitly refers to the late work of Williams, Pound, H. D., cummings, Moore, and Stevens as "American poetry" and lines up the poets in the anthology as participating in the "singularly rich period" of postwar American poetry.[37] The anthology covers poets associated with Black Mountain College in North Carolina, poetry of the "San Francisco Renaissance," and the "Beat Generation," and the so-called New York Poets, and work by poets not explicitly associated with any of the above groups.

These were poets who took "American-ness" seriously, not in a narrowly nationalistic way, but from several different perspectives on American identity, the American city, the American landscape, and the American tradition in literature. But this tradition was neither subordinated to an English tradition nor dictated by New Critical conceptions of metaphysical poetry. The preface to *Poetics of the New American Poetry* made sense of an American literary tradition, beginning with an allusion to Walt Whitman's 1856 letter to Emerson calling for a new poetry for the New World.[38] Both "Beat poet" Ginsberg and his predecessor, Pound, are positioned in Whitman's line. The modernist ancestors are clearly not those of the New Critics: Yeats is dismissed as "a magnificent poet but . . . perhaps nearer to some endpoint of a great British line than to the emergence of a new American poetry," and Eliot, the favorite of the New Critics, is seen as "casting back rather than moving forward, more urbane perhaps than urgent" (x). Brooks and Warren's *Understanding Poetry* is deemed too traditional and ineffective for the new reader. And a catalogue of the modernists who now count in the "New American Poetry" quickly follows: Pound, Williams, Stein, H. D., Lawrence, Crane, and Zukofsky (x). This alternative American poetry canon has continued to remain significant for experimental poetry in America as newer generations of poets have turned again to Pound, Stein, and Zukofsky for inspiration rather than Eliot, Stevens, or Yeats.

Canons clearly change over time for numerous reasons. This brief examination into the role of nationalism in the American modernist canon should suggest that as much as modernism *is* an international phenomenon, we do cultural history a disservice by ignoring the nationalism often at play at different moments and in different ways in the history of the modernist movement. Indeed, much of the richness of American modernism emerges from its frequent efforts to imagine the nature of an American identity as America increasingly became a nation that embodied – in perhaps the most pronounced ways – the tensions and strains of modernity.

NOTES

1. Hugh Kenner, "The Making of the Modernist Canon," in *Canons*, ed. Robert von Hallberg, 3 (University of Chicago Press, 1984), 363–375 at 367.
2. Charles C. Alexander, *Here the Country Lies: Nationalism and the Arts in Twentieth-Century America* (Bloomington: Indiana University Press, 1980), 30–33.
3. See Cary Nelson, *Repression and Recovery: Modern American Poetry and the Politics of Cultural Memory, 1910–1945* (Madison: University of Wisconsin Press, 1989).
4. See Walter Benn Michaels, *Our America: Nativism, Modernism, and Pluralism* (Durham: Duke University Press, 1995), and Karen A. J. Miller, *Populist Nationalism: Republican Insurgency and American Foreign Policy Making, 1918–1925* (Westport, Conn: Greenwood Press, 1999).

5. See Angela Miller, *The Empire of the Eye: Landscape Representation and American Cultural Politics, 1825–1875* (Ithaca and London: Cornell University Press, 1993), and Stephen Daniels, *Fields of Vision: Landscape Imagery and National Identity in England and the United States* (Princeton: Princeton University Press, 1993).

6. Alan Golding, *From Outlaw to Classic: Canons in American Poetry* (Madison: University of Wisconsin Press, 1995), 41–47.

7. *Ibid.*, and von Hallberg, ed., *Canons*, 2–3.

8. Ezra Pound, *Patria Mia*, in *Ezra Pound: Selected Prose, 1909–1965*, ed. William Cookson (New York: New Directions, 1975), 99–141 at 112.

9. Timothy Morris, *Becoming Canonical in American Poetry* (Urbana and Chicago: University of Illinois Press, 1995), xi.

10. Ezra Pound, "What I feel about Walt Whitman," in *Ezra Pound: Selected Prose 1909–1965*, ed. William Cookson (New York: New Directions, 1975), 145–146.

11. Ezra Pound, "A Pact," in *Personae: The Collected Shorter Poems of Ezra Pound* (New York: New Directions, 1971), 89.

12. Michael Bernstein, *The Tale of the Tribe: Ezra Pound and the Modern Verse Epic* (Princeton: Princeton University Press, 1980), 198.

13. Celena E. Kusch, "How the West Was One: American Modernism's Song of Itself," *American Literature* 74, no. 3 (2002), 522–523.

14. Harriet Monroe, "Chicago Granite," *Poetry* 8, no. 2 (1916), 90.

15. Amy Lowell, "Nationalism in Art," *Poetry* 5, no. 1 (1914), 33.

16. George Bornstein, "Introduction: Why Editing Matters," in *Representing Modernist Texts: Editing as Interpretation*, ed. George Bornstein (Ann Arbor: University of Michigan Press, 1991), 1–16 at 2.

17. James Oppenheim, "An Expression of Artists for the Community," *The Seven Arts* 1, no. 1 (1916), 52–54.

18. William Carlos Williams and Robert McAlmon, "CONTACT," *Contact* 1 (December 1920), 1.

19. William Carlos Williams, "Comment," *Contact* 2 (January 1921): [11].

20. Craig Monk, "Eugene Jolas and the Translation Policies of *transition*," *Mosaic* 32, no. 4 (1999), 18.

21. Mark Morrisson, *The Public Face of Modernism: Little Magazines, Audiences, and Reception, 1905–1920* (Madison: University of Wisconsin Press, 2001), 133–166.

22. William Carlos Williams, "The Reader Critic," *The Little Review* (Autumn 1922), 60.

23. Will Levington Comfort, "Letter to *The Little Review*," *The Little Review* (March 1915), 56.

24. John Cowper Powys, "Theodore Dreiser," *The Little Review* (November 1915), 9–10.

25. Carl Sandburg, "Notes For a Review of 'The Spoon River Anthology,'" *The Little Review* (May 1915), 43.

26. Daphne and Michael Carr, "The Prophet in His Own Country," *The Little Review* (May 1916), 41.

27. Humphrey Carpenter, *A Serious Character: The Life of Ezra Pound* (Boston: Houghton Mifflin, 1988), 187.

28. Lawrence Rainey, *Institutions of Modernism: Literary Elites and Public Culture* (New Haven and London: Yale University Press, 1998), 101.

29. Ellen Williams, *Harriet Monroe and the Poetry Renaissance: The First Ten Years of Poetry, 1912–1922* (Urbana: University of Illinois Press, 1977), 179.

30. Lawrence H. Schwartz, *Creating Faulkner's Reputation: The Politics of Modern Literary Criticism* (Knoxville: The University of Tennessee Press, 1988), 1.

31. Cleanth Brooks, *Understanding Poetry* (New York: H. Holt and Company, 1938), iv.

32. T. S. Eliot, *The Sacred Wood* (1920) (London and New York: Methuen, 1986), 53–54.

33. Paul Lauter, *Canons and Contexts* (New York and Oxford: Oxford University Press, 1991), 27.

34. Murray Krieger, *The New Apologists for Poetry* (Minneapolis: University of Minnesota Press, 1956).

35. Frank Lentricchia, *After the New Criticism* (University of Chicago Press, 1980), 4.

36. See Houston A. Baker, *Modernism and the Harlem Renaissance* (University of Chicago Press, 1987), and Michael North, *The Dialect of Modernism: Race, Language and Twentieth-Century Literature* (New York and Oxford: Oxford University Press, 1994).

37. Donald M. Allen, *The New American Poetry* (New York: Grove, 1960), xi.

38. Warren Tallman, "Preface," *Poetics of the New American Poetry*, ed. Donald Allen and Warren Tallman (New York: Grove, 1973), ix.

I

GENRE

2

RITA BARNARD

Modern American fiction

Introduction

There is no need for us to quarrel with Alfred Kazin when he writes in the introduction to *On Native Grounds* (1942) that modern American fiction is "at bottom only the expression" of American life in the late nineteenth and early twentieth century. No one cause or project can be singled out as the defining feature of this diverse body of writing. "Everything," says Kazin, "contributed to its formation." Its roots were "nothing less than the transformation of our society in the great seminal years after the War" and its project was ultimately a cognitive one: "the need to learn what the reality of life was in our modern era."[1]

The social transformation in question has been characterized in many different ways, both before and since Kazin's day. The historian Warren Susman saw the period as marking a transition from a producer-capitalist culture (with a focus on work, thrift, and self-denial) to a new culture of abundance (with a focus on leisure, spending, and self-fulfillment). This broad shift, he observed, was partly the consequence of new communications media, which affected not only the distribution and circulation of goods and ideas, but altered perceptions of time and place and thereby changed consciousness itself. The novelist John Dos Passos, whose *U. S. A.* trilogy (1938) is a veritable archive of the technological, political, and linguistic changes that shaped the nation from the turn of the century to the Great Depression, saw these years in terms of the "crystallization" of monopoly capitalism out of an earlier, more individualistic competitive capitalism.[2]

But it is an older writer, Sherwood Anderson, who gives us the most vivid thumbnail sketch of the changes from which modern American fiction emerged. In *Winesburg, Ohio* (1922), Anderson observes that the readers of his day may already find it difficult to understand the sensibilities of people whose lives were shaped by an earlier world of harsh agricultural labor:

The coming of industrialism, attended by all the roar and rattle of affairs, the shrill cries of millions of new voices that have come among us from overseas, the going and coming of trains, the growth of cities, the building of the interurban car lines that weave in and out of towns and past farmhouses and . . . the coming of the automobile has worked a tremendous change in the lives and in the habits of thought of our people of Mid-America. Books, badly imagined and written though they may be in the hurry of our times, are in every household, magazines circulate by the millions of copies, newspapers are everywhere. In our day a farmer standing by the stove in the store in his village has his mind filled to overflowing with the words of other men . . . [He] is brother to the men of the cities, and if you listen you will find him talking as glibly and as senselessly as the best city man of us all.[3]

The "revolution" of modernity, as Anderson calls it, was not the exclusive experience of urban sophisticates: it extended unevenly but inexorably across the nation – even into the country store and into the minds of the folks who still gathered around the woodstove to chat.

Now, it is easy to come up with a long line-up of writers – from Upton Sinclair to John Dos Passos, from Theodore Dreiser to Nathanael West, and from Abraham Cahan to Henry Roth – who have tackled such issues as urbanization, industrialization, immigration, and the rise of the mass media in their work. But to say that modern fiction takes these topics as its subject matter does not fully address the way in which it might "express" its historical moment, especially given the fact that this "moment" may not be experienced everywhere in the same way, nor at the same pace. How exactly did the transformation of modern life change narrative form? And does modern fiction in fact provide that special knowledge about modern "reality" of which Kazin speaks? Or is there something about modernity that disables cognition, if not narrative itself?

In his "Literary Prophecy" of 1894, the novelist Hamlin Garland, taking courage from what he saw as the positive evolution of society, predicted the shape that the fiction of "modern man" was to take. He got several things right, even though his belief in progress now makes his essay seem like the product of a bygone age. Garland believed that the emergent literature would react against the traditions of the past and attend fearlessly to the uglier contemporary aspects of reality. Narrative techniques, he predicted, would be streamlined: "Because the novels of the past were long, involved, and given to discussion and comment upon the action," he observes, "so the novel of the future will be shorter" and less obvious in its method. Its "lessons" will be brought out, not by explanation, but "by placing before the reader the facts of life as they stand related to the artist."[4]

Though few modern writers, living in the wake of World War I and the stock market crash of 1929, would have endorsed Garland's optimistic beliefs, there were certainly some who found in the speed, scale, and technological inventiveness of the age a stimulus for new forms. Nathanael West, for one, also imagined that the short novel would become the quintessential American form, since it is more suited to a "hasty" people than the long "Scandinavian" tomes of yesteryear. Modern works of fiction only had time to "explode" like "cannon balls." In a culture where "violence is idiomatic," where a brutal crime may not even make it to the front page of a newspaper, there is no need to follow a Dostoyevsky in spending whole chapters providing the psychological motivation "for one little murder." A new kind of fiction, adapted to an environment of screaming headlines, would have to be devised, even if the writer had to turn to commercial forms like the comics for inspiration.

If some American writers could, in a spirit of national bravado, dispense with traditional narrative forms (or pretend to do so), the most important European theorists of modern fiction, Georg Lukács and Walter Benjamin, saw the decline of such forms as a cognitive and political crisis. For Lukács the realist novel offered a way of understanding historical causality – the workings of the entire social process – by representing the interaction of human subjects and the objective world. When this dialectic vision is abandoned, he argues, narration loses its dynamic quality: it becomes fixed either on the subject or the object. The result is either an overemphasis on the inner psychological world or an overemphasis on the external world. Antithetical though these two strategies may seem, they are for Lukács identical in their presumption of a static world: they tend to produce series of disjointed scenes and to turn human lives into still lives. Moreover, while the traditional omniscient narrator, deploying the retrospective vantage of the past tense, was able to provide the reader with a sense of the overall direction and significance of the action, the modernist writer, often using the present tense and experimental points of view, is caught up in a flux of emotions, memories, and sense perceptions. In Lukács's view, this loss of an interpretive purchase on the world cannot be offset by attaching a symbolic meaning to objects or incidents. In fact, all of modernism's technical experimentation seemed dangerous to him in that it undermined the significance and transformative potential of human action: hence the harsh prescriptiveness that characterizes his work.[5]

Though more sympathetic to modernism than Lukács, Benjamin also despaired of drawing any "lesson" or useful knowledge from modern fiction. Experience itself, or so he declared in his "Storyteller" essay of 1936, had "fallen in value": its inherent meaningfulness and narratability had been lost. Thus the soldiers who returned from the battlefields of the World War I had "grown silent, not richer – but poorer in communicable experience." But unlike Lukács, for whom the realist novel represented a cognitive ideal, Benjamin regarded the novel itself as an early symptom of a crisis in narration. While the storyteller, whom Benjamin locates in a pre-capitalist world of artisanal production, could readily offer advice – the proverbial "moral of the story" – to his auditors, the novelist, who emerges in a bourgeois world of mechanized production and isolated consumption, can reveal the "meaning of life" only at the conclusion of strenuous artistic labors. In the bustle of the modern world, even this hard-won, synthetic meaning threatens to disappear. For as mechanized production accelerates, the novel is gradually replaced by "information" – by the shards of narrative we find in the newspaper. Feeding on experiences that are in constant danger of obsolescence, the fractured format of the daily news destroys our narrative abilities and depreciates experience even further: "modern man no longer works at what cannot be abbreviated."[6] Thus brevity, the very quality that some American writers celebrated as an exciting innovation, comes to be viewed in Benjamin's mournful meditation as a distressing symptom of a reified world.

With these initial reflections on modernist form in place, we are ready for a thought experiment. In light of the terms set up so far, let us ask ourselves what the most thoroughly "modern" American novel might be, and then consider whether or not that novel can be viewed as a representative product of the period. Or to put the question differently and more perversely: which American novel would Georg Lukács have hated the most?

I vote that the prize should go – why not? (we are experimenting here) – to Nathan Asch for *Pay Day*, published to no acclaim whatsoever in 1930. Let me briefly describe its relevant qualities, before returning to broader considerations. *Pay Day* is a compact novel: the action, such as it is, is confined to a twelve-hour period, from the end of one workday to the dawn of the next. Even so, it is episodic, lacking in any sense of cumulative significance. The desultory character of the narration (which is mimicked in the disappointingly plotless movie the main character goes to see midway through the novel) is presented as an effect of the modern settings from which the various chapters derive their titles: "The Subway," "The Street," "The Speakeasy," "The Taxi," and so forth. In the chapter entitled "The L," for instance, the stream-of-consciousness narration records one trivial urban scene after another in rapid succession; it mimics the passive, spectatorial experience of the commuter, looking out at the passing cityscape from a fast-moving train. *Pay Day*'s modernity can also be seen in its obvious economic concerns. Though Asch's novel is devoid of the Jazz Age glamor of, say, Fitzgerald's fiction, it is similarly concerned with the emerging ethos of consumption. The novel's antihero, a spotty young clerk called Jim Cowan, having received his pitifully small paycheck, feels compelled to hit the town and blow his earnings on a date with a waitress. But since Cowan's means are so petty, his version of "nightlife" is entirely unromantic: it merely exacerbates his sense of resentment. Indeed, the rapid oscillation of his emotions, which switch in a matter of seconds from self-satisfaction to self-pity and then to aggression is a symptom of the powerlessness of the white-collar flunkey, liable to be fired at any minute.

But *Pay Day*, while clearly symptomatic of modernity, at times seems diagnostic of it as well: it draws the reader's attention to the way the distraction of urban life impedes active political involvement. The novel takes place on the night of August 23, 1927, the same night that anarchists Sacco and Vanzetti were executed in Boston. Headlines, newsboys, and taxi-drivers constantly remind Cowan of this significant political event. But the barrage of sense impressions to which he is subjected make it impossible for him to reflect on the implications of the men's deaths: he only remembers the executions at the end of the novel, when a new day dawns without bringing much insight or hope to Manhattan's ordinary Jims and Joes.

Pay Day is deeply responsive to some of the quintessential features of social modernity and to the challenges they present to conventional fictional forms. But the truth is that it is neither as apolitical as Lukács would assume, nor is it a particularly typical novel of its day (if there is such a thing), even though it resembles the novels of Dos Passos and West in various ways, and seems to have influenced Richard Wright's *Lawd Today!*, an equally plotless urban novel which takes place on February 12, 1936: the anniversary of Lincoln's birthday. *Pay Day* does what failed works of fiction often do: it serves as a kind of limit text compared to which other more successful or canonical works might seem more traditional, less tailormade to the theorist's or polemicist's order. If we think of the vast body of fiction produced in the United States between 1895 and 1939, the dates that frame this volume, it is clear that brevity, for one thing, did not turn out to be a universal feature. Alongside the many compact novellas and the short story cycles of the period (including Anderson's *Winesburg, Ohio*, Toomer's *Cane*, Hemingway's *In Our Time*, Faulkner's *The Unvanquished* and *The Wild Palms*, Steinbeck's *Pastures of Heaven* and *Tortilla Flat*, Caldwell's *Georgia Boy*, and McCarthy's *The Company She Keeps*), there are also many voluminous works, like the novels of James T. Farrell and Thomas Wolfe. Alongside the many works that are urban in their setting and inspiration, there are also many that take place in far-flung rural places: in Faulkner's Northern Mississippi, in Hurston's Everglades, in McNickle's Montana, in Hemingway's Upper Peninsula, or in another country, for that matter – in rural Spain, on the quay at Smyrna, or in the mud of the Italian front. And alongside works that are concerned with pathological states and experimental points of view, there are also many works, especially in the 1930s, which return to various versions of realism and documentary. Whole new genres concerned with action rather than inner states arose: one might think, for instance, of the many strike novels produced as part of the experiment in Proletarian Literature, and of popular genres like the Western and the hardboiled detective novel. The storyteller's voice, finally, did not entirely disappear: Faulkner's *The Hamlet* (1940) offers us the folksy narration of the loquacious sewing machine salesman, V. K. Ratliffe, while Hurston's masterpiece, *Their Eyes Were Watching God* (1937), presents itself as a life story shared between two friends as they sit on the porch one evening. And West's *Miss Lonelyhearts* (1933), while it traces the debilitating effects of the mass media on individuals' ability to narrate their lives, also recognizes that "lessons" and "advice," which once circulated so freely in traditional communities, had reappeared in commercial guise in advertisements and newspaper sob columns.

Literary critics are fond of quoting famous authors who announce the exact moment (more or less) when social modernity transformed the character of life, whether it is Virginia Woolf, who declared that "on or about December 1910, human character changed," or Robert Musil, who observed that "there was a sudden rift" in European civilization in 1914, when "all of a sudden, the world was full of violence," or Willa Cather, who lamented that "the world broke in two in 1922 or thereabouts."[7] The reason for our attachment to these dramatic pronouncements is perhaps that they relieve us of the obligation of considering the extent to which the old and the new coexist, with varying degrees of tension, in any given period. It is important to remember that the rapid pace of social change brought with it a hankering for tradition and that the revolution of modernity triggered its counter-revolutions. The "New Era" or "Jazz Age," as the historian Lawrence Levine observes, was in many ways backward-looking: it was certainly an age of new technologies and lifestyles, of the automobile, the movies, the flappers, and the cynical "Lost Generation," but it was also a time when many Americans tried to turn the clock back from the ideas and the progressive spirit of the prewar years. Fundamentalism, nativism, and the Ku Klux Klan flourished, Prohibition was instituted, and Left-wing political movements were suppressed.[8] The culture of the 1930s was similarly complex. Even though radical commitments were widespread and Communist Party membership was at a high during this decade, it was also a time when insecurity imposed a certain conformity and when a homegrown idea of "culture" thrived: "The American Way of Life" was, in fact, a coinage of the so-called Red Decade. And if the World Fair of 1939 celebrated modern technology (including the first prototype of television), it was also the year when Colonial Williamsburg was reconstructed and opened to tourists.

It should therefore not surprise us that novels like *Pay Day* and *Gone With the Wind* (to reach for its polar opposite) should be produced within five years of each other. Nor should it surprise us that a novelist like Willa Cather should deploy some of the techniques of the modern novel – its spareness, its attentiveness to point of view and structure – to voice a criticism of modernity and celebrate what she saw as the anti-materialist values of a pioneer aristocracy. Anyone approaching American culture in the first three decades of the twentieth century has to untangle "a web of ambivalence" (204), a manifestation of what Levine identifies as

> the central paradox of American history: a belief in progress coupled with a dream of change, an urge towards the inevitable future combined with a longing for the irretrievable past; a deeply ingrained belief in America's unfolding destiny and a haunting conviction that the nation was in a state of decline.
>
> (191)

The task of offering an overview of modern American fiction is therefore a difficult one, and I would like to approach it by adopting a modernist strategy: that of reducing things to their basic constitutive elements. In the pages that follow, I will consider a number of key works under three very simple rubrics: place, time, and value (both moral and economic). But there is an additional element of narrative – one so fundamental that it often eludes discussion. That element is, quite simply, the word, which modernist writers often tried to make especially visible to their readers by techniques of defamiliarization, repetition, or poetic figuration. Literary historians often cite the powerful passage from Hemingway's *A Farewell to Arms* (1929) in which his narrator summarily bans an entire vocabulary of idealistic generalization:

> I was always embarrassed by the words sacred, glorious, and sacrifice and the expression in vain . . . [F]or a long time now I had seen nothing sacred, and the things that were glorious had no glory and the sacrifices were like the stockyards at Chicago if nothing was done with the meat except to bury it. There were many words you could not stand to hear and finally only the names of places had dignity.[9]

But which words were newly permissible and resonant in the fiction of the period? We might think, first, of the perfectly ordinary words ("beginning," "interesting," "always," and "certainly") that came to seem like familiar strangers in Stein's rhythmic reiterations. Or, we might think of the spare diction of Hemingway's best novels: the way words like "nice" or "utilize" come to seem overdetermined in the conversations of his terse expatriates.

We might think next of the folksy vocabulary Hurston (writing "with the map of Florida on her tongue") introduced into American fiction: not only such playful, earthy words as "woof" and "boogerboo," but also high-toned malapropisms like "monstropolous," "combuction," "diasticutis," and "freezolity." We might think also of those ponderous adjectives like "myriad," "immemorial," "immutable," and "impervious," which, along with a few "grand, truculent *indomitables*," gave the idiosyncratic flavor to Faulkner's work.[10] We might think furthermore of the many brand names that come into play as markers of consumerist know-how: Chesterfields, Wrigley, Coca-Cola, Listerine, Remington, Kodak, and Chrysler. And we might consider, finally, the grim, monosyllabic vocabulary that brought to life the world of the marginal men of the 1930s: words like "vag," "gat," "flop," "bull," "drag," and "stiff," which reminded readers how far America remained from the place of promise and prosperity projected by the utopian writers of the Progressive Era.

For Lukács, the fact that modern fiction made individual words noticeable was yet another sign of its impotence – of its failure to provide the sense of hierarchy, by which words, sentences, and paragraphs could be subordinated to the narrative's overall revelation of the social totality. But for many American modernists it was precisely by attending to words, by revitalizing them and by placing them in new contexts that the novel could begin to do political work. "[W]e have only words" against "Power Superpower," declared John Dos Passos near the end of *U. S. A.* And at the end of *Pay Day* (to return to our typical-atypical modern novel), Nathan Asch puts a striking message in the mouth of a drunk who denounces his fellow subway passengers for their inattention to Sacco and Vanzetti's unjust execution. In a world of headlines, of the easy amusements of sports page and the comics, the orator proclaims, language becomes "old, stale . . . used too much." What is needed is "a way to wake [people] up, to make them realize words."[11] In his insistence on this need, if in no other respect, Asch is a representative voice of his times.

Place

In recent years, a concern with spatiality (as opposed to temporality) has come to be regarded as the defining trait of postmodernism (as opposed to modernism). But broad distinctions of this sort are not, in fact, so readily made. Modernism, after all, has long been associated with a movement from the country to the city – and thus with questions of place and space. Moreover, many of the technical innovations in the modernist novel (e.g., the creation of the impressionistic, synchronous, anti-individualist form of narration that we see in a work like *Manhattan Transfer* [1925]) are the result of an intensified interest in the writer's immediate milieu – in what we may call the "location of culture." The rise of a theoretically sophisticated cultural geography over the past decade or so suggests that critical interest in the socio-spatial aspects of modernist fiction is likely to remain strong. With its emphasis on the dialectics of subjectivity and space and the textual nature of geographical environments, the new cultural geography may enable new readings of virtually forgotten urban novels, such as Waldo Frank's *City Block* (1922) and Albert Halper's *Union Square* (1933), both of which explore the way in which human interactions are defined by complex, but narrowly circumscribed physical spaces.

But postcolonial studies too, with its profound questioning of the relationship between cultural centers and peripheries, may come to provide new perspectives on the imaginative geographies of modern American fiction. In fact, the story that Malcolm Cowley tells in his memoir *Exile's Return* (1934) of a generation's cultural deracination, its exile, and its eventual reclaiming of native turf now strikes one as very similar to the creative struggles recounted some thirty or forty years later by postcolonial intellectuals (and this similarity reveals much about the dramatic shift in power between America and Europe over the course of the twentieth century). Cowley notes that the writers of his generation, the men and women born around the turn of the century, would have considered the site of their childhood – a farm in Wisconsin, a plantation house among the cane brakes, a bluff overlooking the Cumberland, or a Nebraska prairie – as "home." But their formal education was aimed at "destroying whatever roots they had in the soil" and "making [them] homeless citizens of the world." They absorbed the message that art, learning, and literature existed "at an indefinite distance from [their] daily lives" – that "[w]isdom was an attribute of Greece and art of the Renaissance; glamour belonged only to Paris or Vienna."[12] For the modernists of Cowley's generation, as for contemporary writers like Nadine Gordimer and Ngugi Wa Thiong'O, formal education was a matter of cultural alienation, of reading books that took place elsewhere, and their intellectual self-discovery involved either a "journey back" or a rewriting of established cultural geographies – the difficult enterprise of "moving the center," as Ngugi puts it.[13]

In the case of the modern American writer, however, one must specify that the "return" would not exactly be a journey *home*. (We need only recall Hemingway's depiction of a returned veteran's profound dislocation in "Soldier's Home.") The "return" was more likely to involve the discovery of forms in which a sense of being out of place or off-center could be turned to aesthetic advantage. Modern American fiction, as Kazin observes, is characterized by a sense of "alienation *on* native grounds" (ix).

This structure of feeling is captured perfectly in Sherwood Anderson's "Certain Things Last" (1920), a self-reflexive story on the difficulties of finding a place in and about which to write. The city of Chicago, where the story's narrator lives, presents ceaseless distractions to the would-be writer: even as he confesses his problems to the reader, he hears the driver of a horse-drawn coal wagon cursing at the driver of a Ford. His boyhood home, the only place he can turn to in memory, happens to be "a dreary, lonely little place in the far western section of the state of Nebraska." It is, Anderson tells us, the kind of place that makes a "middle-westerner" dream that he is in Italy, or in a Spanish town where "a dark-looking man is riding a bony horse along a street," or that "he is being driven in a sled over the Russian steppes by a man whose face is covered in whiskers." But the narrator realizes almost instantly that his imagined "Italy," "Spain," and "Russia" derive from "the cartoons in the newspapers" or lectures he might have attended in a church hall and the story ends with his recognition that he should write about things closer at hand: about the woman who is with him, or about a certain "moment" that "changed the whole current of his life."[14]

This particular solution is vintage Anderson; but the story is evocative of the challenge confronting many modern American writers and to which they produced an immense variety of responses. Let us consider the case of Willa Cather. In contrast to Anderson's narrator, she seems effortlessly able to discover the stuff of novels in rural Nebraska. By dint of a nostalgic recollection of her childhood on the plains, she is able to project a sense of cultural authority and normativity with regard to the period of early settlement, when pioneer virtue was leavened by the spirit of cosmopolitanism, contributed by large numbers of immigrants from various parts of Europe: Germany, Norway, France, Denmark, Poland, and Bohemia. Cather's success in imaginatively "moving the center" westward is such that her cowboy-scholar Tom Outland in *The Professor's House* (1926) is able to compare the *Aeneid* to a mesa in New Mexico without the slightest sense that the cultural importance of the former outweighs that of the latter. But we should not therefore underestimate the initial difficulty of writing about a place where, as the narrator Jim Burden puts it in *My Ántonia* (1915), "[t]here was nothing but land: not country at all, but the material out of which country was made." This difficulty is strikingly underscored by Cather herself when she reminds us in 1931 that when she published her first novel *Alexander's Bridge* in 1912, the proper setting for fiction was still thought to be a drawing room – and a drawing room full of "smart people and clever people" to boot.[15]

If Cather's work was enabled and her sense of belonging enriched by the historical fact of mass immigration, the opposite was true for some writers of Anglo-American descent. An extreme and early case may be that of Henry Adams, the son of presidents, "American of Americans, with Heaven knows how many Puritans and Patriots behind him," who recorded in *The Education of Henry Adams* (1906) his mournful sense of having been displaced by the new residents of America's cities – the energetic immigrants, "still reeking of the Ghetto" – and who likened himself to "the Indians or the buffalo who had been ejected from their heritage."[16] The anxieties about new demographic configurations and forms of social mobility registered here were exacerbated after World War I, when they influenced the characterization, narrative shape, and symbolic geographies of some of the most celebrated novels of the Jazz Age. For all its interest in social climbing and self-invention, *The Great Gatsby* (1925) seems quite conservative if we attend to its treatment of place, in both the social and geographical sense of the term. Fitzgerald presents New York, "with its racy adventurous feel," as the site of a new urban poetry. But he also imagines it as the all-too-fluid location of a new kind of threat: in the novel's "metropolitan twilight," the pre-eminent place of a wealthy white man is challenged every time a group of "modish Negroes" in a fine limousine happens to pass him in traffic.[17] The established social hierarchy is also symbolically undermined by the undifferentiated desolation of the Valley of Ashes, the uncanny dumping ground through which commuters from the Long Island suburbs must pass on their way to the city. Critics have often remarked on Jay Gatsby's confused sense of geography (social and otherwise), as reflected in his ludicrous claim that he is the scion of a prominent midwestern family from San Francisco. But the closing meditations of Nick Carraway, the novel's cautious narrator, also attach some rather idiosyncratic meanings to the "East" and the "West" of the United States. In a reactionary version of an exile's return, Nick reclaims the West as the "warm center of the world" rather than the "ragged end of the universe," and idealizes the kind of city "where dwellings are still called through decades by a family's name" (184). This resigned conclusion expresses a nostalgic hankering for a landscape in which "Mr. Nobod[ies] from Nowhere" – the charming Gatbsy no less than the uncharming Jewish gangster, Meyer Wolfsheim – would be excluded almost automatically. The novel's symbolic geography lends considerable credence to Walter Benn Michaels's judgment that *The Great Gatsby*, like many of the major novels of the mid-twenties, is fraught with nativist fears that demand narrative resolution: in this case the hope that the hybrid entanglements and "gonnegtions" spawned by a polyglot metropolis may be confined, somehow, to the dangerous "East."

The quintessentially modern sense of dislocation and alienation is also a crucial theme in immigrant fiction. In these texts the protagonists' development of any coherent sense of identity is impeded by a pervasive sense of being simultaneously in America and "in a world somewhere, somewhere else."[18] This peculiar self-division is beautifully captured in the rendering of the immigrants' accented English in Henry Roth's *Call it Sleep*: "Land where our Fodder's Died" turns the anthem "My Country 'tis of Thee' into a parody and makes nonsense of its nativist geography. The confusion captured here is in no way simplified by the fact that second-generation immigrants retained little if any memory of the Europe of their fathers and mothers. In Mike Gold's semi-autobiographical *Jews Without Money* (1930), the young Mikey is able to get some idea of what his mother's beloved Hungarian forests must have been like only during a rare visit to the Bronx Park, and he can understand his father's longing for the communal sociability of his Romanian *stetl* only in a neighborhood wine cellar, where a traditional musician plays the old shepherd songs on the cymbalon. But, for all its old-world associations, the wine cellar – like New York itself – is a hybrid space, offering confused models of identity: on one wall there is a picture of Theodor Hertzel and, on the other, a picture of Teddy Roosevelt charging up San Juan Hill. It is no wonder that Mikey ends up dreaming a syncretic dream of "a Messiah who would look like Buffalo Bill." The difficulty of imaginary journeys "home" makes for a paradoxically "forward-looking nostalgia" in immigrant fiction: it is characterized by a yearning for places, ideals, and forms of expression that are not yet in existence.[19]

The time-honored pastoral tradition, consequently, tends to play out in problematic ways in these mostly urban texts. The opposition between country and city, as James T. Farrell once observed, is not particularly real to people "affected since childhood by the sights, sounds, odors, and objects of an industrial city." But the residual power of this opposition leaves them entrapped in "a technical dilemma, deriving from . . . a dichotomy between the objects and sensations they have sought to describe and the language and symbolism they have inherited."[20] The point is well illustrated in *Jews Without Money*. Though Gold denounces a teacher who preaches about nature to the children of a "petrified city" (to do so, he says, is to offer "snapshots of food to a starving man" [40]), he nevertheless represents the abandoned lots where the tenement children play as the Western plains and rhapsodizes about the clumps of grass which bravely managed to sprout from cracks in the sidewalk. Gold is ultimately unable to imagine revolution without recourse to the most pastoral of tropes: it is figured at the end of the novel in terms of a rebuilding of the ghetto as "a garden for the human spirit" (309). And even Farrell's own work is not entirely free of the dilemma he identifies. His depictions of Chicago's South Side neighborhoods in the *Studs Lonigan* trilogy are by no means romantic; yet there are moments when he turns to natural images to express the energies of an urban scene in which even his more loutish characters are, at times, able to take some pleasure. Thus, in *Young Lonigan*: "Studs looks about at the patches in the grass that Martin and his gang had torn down playing their cowboy and Indian games. There was something about the things he watched that seemed to enter Studs as sun entered a field of grass; and as he watched, he felt that the things he saw were part of himself, and he felt as good as if he were warm sunlight."[21] This persistence of pastoral ideas, however attenuated, incongruous, and ironic, is a mark of modernism's difference from nineteenth-century naturalism: it is one thread in the intricate "web of ambiguity" of modern American culture.

But as with all generalizations, this observation requires qualification. For in the work of Richard Wright, one of the most important American modernists, the pastoral seems to have lost all relevance, even on the level of figuration – and for good reason. For many African-American migrants to northern cities, the historical memory of slavery and the indignities of Jim Crow foreclosed on nostalgia for rural life. The sole utopian moment in *Native Son* (1940) is thus inspired by an urban scene viewed from a prison window: a vision of tall buildings expanding and unfolding as a result of the collective desires and longings of men.

The radical intervention of Wright's dark urban masterpiece is strikingly underscored if we relate it to a problematic moment in "Certain Things Last" that I have refrained from discussing so far. Though Anderson's sketch ultimately dismisses the narrator's dreams of discovering "simpler" milieus in foreign places, it nevertheless holds on to certain primitivist notions as a way of making the modern city more available for fiction. The narrator imagines that the song of a Negro, humming to himself as he goes along the street, might "[freshen] the air above the hot stuffy city" in the way that "a tiny stream running down a hill might freshen the plains below" (4). Such folksy fantasies of redemption are unthinkable in the relentlessly modern and secular world of *Native Son*. For Bigger Thomas, the novel's protagonist, the city of Chicago remains an airless, oppressive place. Though his mother may still hum spirituals (including "Steal away, steal away to Jesus / Steal away home"), her singing cannot mitigate the novel's profound sense of homelessness: a homelessness that is a material rather than a metaphysical condition for African-Americans, inadequately housed as they are in "a prescribed corner of the city."[22] *Native Son*, in effect, replaces the dualities of the pastoral with the more intractable and volatile duality between the white world of comfort and security and the black world of fear, shame, and deprivation. Indeed, duality is too weak a term: for what Kazin describes as the disquieting "irony" in Americans' "possession" of their native grounds (ix) is strikingly politicized in *Native Son*, to the point that it becomes a full-blown ethical and political contradiction. The brunt of Wright's critique of the structural violence of urban segregation is directed at the self-serving morality of the wealthy realtor Dalton, who gives millions of dollars to educate and uplift "Negroes" but makes a fortune out of renting rat-infested properties to them.

The dynamic of blindness and insight exposed here has crucial implications for the novel's form and style. Ways of seeing are simultaneously ways of not seeing; and black and white characters, shaped by their radically different experiences, do not see the same city.[23] This explains why *Native Son*, for all its grimness and interest in social causality, is resolutely modernist, rather than naturalist: though Wright was concerned to get the Chicago street map exactly right, the city is never objectively described. While the young communists, Jan Erlone and Mary Dalton, are able to admire the city's grand skyline and its cultural landmarks, these things are meaningless to Bigger, who can perceive the city only as a treacherous and airless labyrinth, which permits no possibility of escape. Even at the end of the novel, when Bigger's lawyer provides him with a sense of perspective – he gains for a moment "a pinnacle of feeling upon which he can stand and see vague relations he had never dreamed of" (782) – he cannot shake the sense that this vision, like the mendacious promises of cinema and advertising, may lead him into a blind alley.

The nightmarish urban scenes of the novel's second section (reminiscent of the gangster films of the period) are thus essentially expressionist: they reveal Bigger's vulnerability, entrapment, and alienation. But they also hint, at times, at more allegorical interpretive possibilities. The abandoned shells of houses on the South Side, where "windows gape blackly, like the eye-sockets of empty skulls" (661) are also an objective correlative of the blindness of their owners: of the ruling classes, who, as Bigger's lawyer puts it, "could not have built nations on so vast a scale had they not shut their eyes to the humanity of other men" (810). With this sweeping indictment, the implications of the novel move far beyond their immediate time and place, looking ahead to literary and critical movements still to follow: to the work of African-American writers like Baldwin and Ellison, to Existentialism, and to contemporary theory, where questions of blindness and insight, visibility and marginalization, and so forth, have been of paramount concern. In Wright's work, the great modernist discovery of point of view becomes more than a technical device for exploring individual experience. It becomes a matter of ideology, an effect of one's location in the divisive geographies of American Apartheid. *Native Son*, in short, forces us to consider the relationship between power and knowledge and between subjectivity and space in strikingly contemporary ways.

Time

To take on the concept of time in modern American fiction is a risky venture. Not only is it a difficult and abstract topic, but in our postmodern academy it has come to seem like an outmoded one as well: "Time has become a nonperson," Fredric Jameson remarks in a recent essay, and novelists, poets, philosophers, and critics alike have "stopped writing about it."[24] Yet time is not only a constitutive element of all narration, but a major thematic preoccupation in modern American fiction. Modernity, as we have already seen, is intimately connected to the idea of acceleration: in the modern world, as Benjamin suggests, *Erfahrung* (i.e., experience in the sense of wisdom or skills developed over a long period of time) is gradually displaced by *Erlebnis* (i.e., experience in the sense of immediate sensations).[25] Implicit in Benjamin's assertion is a sense that the dominant mode of production affects our most basic ways of processing the world; thus modern consciousness is shaped by the rapidity and seriality of assembly line production. But forms of leisure, too, as we have seen in Asch's *Pay Day*, can affect those aspects of human experience most suited to conventional novelistic treatment: memory, desire, and hope.

In his intellectual history of the period from 1880–1918, Stephen Kern identifies a discovery of interior or "private time" (the kind of flexible temporality we see in stream-of-consciousness narration) as one of the most important cultural phenomena of early modernist culture.[26] This emphasis on interiority and "private time," much as Lukács might denounce it, is not without a social dimension: it is, at least in part, a reaction against the increasing impact of the standardized time of factories, offices, and train schedules. Modernist time, in other words, can itself be historicized, even if the experiments of some modern writers lay in the excision of any sense of historical context and historical causality from their work. It is useful to speculate, along with Jameson, about the conditions that produced modern literature's obsession with time. Modernism, he insists, is best grasped as the culture of an incomplete and uneven modernity. Until World War II, Europe was only partly industrialized and partly bourgeois. The creators of modernist literature were often men and women who had been born in small villages, but who pursued their careers in large industrial cities: they were people who lived in two distinct worlds simultaneously. Though fascinated by the new and absorbed in it in their daily lives, they were also constantly aware of the old: of residual modes of production that they themselves had witnessed or participated in. Their experiments with narrative time can thus be related to the fact that they had to negotiate in their own lived experience the disjuncture between modern and premodern temporalities.[27] Now, it is certainly true that the United States was by the end of the nineteenth century the most modern nation in the world (and the oldest, as Gertrude Stein perversely liked to put it, since it entered the age of mass production the soonest), but the impact of modernity was registered unevenly across its vast territorial sprawl.[28] Many American modernists, like their European counterparts, had a strong sense of alternate ways of living, whether through memories of rural childhoods, through what we might loosely call anthropological experiences, or simply through an alertness to the residual cultural forms still evident in their daily lives. It is no accident, by this logic, that it was Faulkner, the Mississippian, who, of all the major American modernists, had the keenest sense of a pre-industrial mode of production (namely, plantation slavery) and pushed the experimentation with time the furthest.

The obvious entry point for a discussion of the temporalities of American modernism, however, is not the work of Faulkner, but that of William James, to whom we owe that useful and flexible term "stream of consciousness." The project of James's *Principles of Psychology* (1890) was ultimately to enhance our appreciation of the richness of our experiential lives and cognitive processes. It is fair to say, therefore, that James gave certain philosophical weight to the notion of living for the moment: one of the key ideas of the emergent culture of abundance. Experience (in the sense of *Erlebnis*) is of immense importance in James's thinking. Indeed, in his chapter on "The Stream of Thought," he makes the case that each experience we have of a given fact is essentially unique. This is not to say that for him the truth is made up of raw sensory experiences, severed from the past or future: James's concern is not to atomize time, but to "thicken" our sense of the present moment: to imagine a sustained or "specious present," imbued with a "halo" of past experience and future anticipation. James's interest, moreover, is not so much in our perceptions of fixed objects, but in those experiences of direction and tendency that are not readily labeled by nouns – except perhaps by strange new terms like "nextness, andness, and ifness."[29]

The influence of Jamesian psychology is palpable in the early experimental fiction of his student Gertrude Stein: the short story cycle *Three Lives* (1906) and the sprawling, self-reflexive immigrant saga, *The Making of Americans* (1923). Though *Three Lives* takes its inspiration from Flaubert (Stein had tried her hand at translating his *Trois Contes* before embarking on her own stories), it shows no interest in the dense depiction of social milieu that characterizes Flaubert's work, and very little in conventional plotting and denouement. All three of the stories ("The Good Anna," "Melanctha," and "The Gentle Lena") end with the death of the title character, but the death brings no particular lesson or emotional charge. The compositional principle, as Stein liked to say, is cubist: as in the work of Cézanne, "everything is as important as everything else." The moment of closure is therefore no more significant than any other moment and provides no retrospective insight; such meaning as there is, is revealed in the ongoing "habits of attention" by which "the total of character is revealed" (Stein, *Selected Writings*, 243). But it is Jamesian psychology rather than cubism that explains the texture of Stein's prose. Her project (which she was later to describe as "ridding . . . [herself] of nouns") was to devise a style that in its very syntax and lexicon draws our attention to the transitive rather than to the substantive, noun-like aspects of cognition (460). Thus Stein's keywords, especially in "Melanctha," the most experimental of the three stories, are participles like "feeling," "understanding," "beginning," "happening," and "living": words which might be said to hover between verbs and nouns and which alert us to sustained or habitual states of feeling. "He was now never taking any part in this fighting that was always going on inside him" (95) is the kind of thing that counts as an incident in *Three Lives*. In fact, all of Stein's narrative devices – the reiteration of "always" and "never," the meandering reprises, the simple and tentative vocabulary, which seems to suspend any definitive naming of an experience – are intended to give the effect of what she termed a "prolonged present" (417): this despite the fact that the stories in *Three Lives* are written in the past tense.

If the experimental effect of Stein's early prose derives in good measure from a grammatical oscillation between verb and noun, the experimental interest of Sherwood Anderson's story cycle *Winesburg, Ohio* derives from a generic oscillation between the traditional *Bildungsroman* and a form of serial composition that owes much to Stein. Malcolm Cowley once described the aesthetic that animates *Winesburg, Ohio* – and, indeed, all of Anderson's work – as one of "moments," of brief intensities without sequel. Anderson can, to be sure, provide illuminating comments about the broader historical forces that shape his characters' lives. (Indeed, such broader perspectives are essential in order to emphasize the anachronistic nature of his small-town grotesques, who all yearn for things that are no longer, or not yet, possible.) But *Winesburg, Ohio*'s series of structurally identical stories, in which the townspeople, one after another, reveal themselves to the young reporter, George Willard, does not really allow for any development, beyond the climactic moment when the characters articulate (or fail to articulate) their desires, disappointments, or loneliness. The aim of the cycle thus seems to be something quite different from the creation of a conventional plot with a beginning, middle, and end: the stories, as Cowley puts it, "exist separately and timelessly." And yet, the conventional notion of character development does not disappear altogether. The three closing stories ("Death,"

"Sophistication," and "Departure") impose, in a somewhat contrived way, the narrative of George Willard's acquisition of maturity onto the preceding series of fragments, so that by the end of the volume, the grotesques – the very means of Anderson's protest against the commercialism of the modern world – threaten to become "but a background on which to paint the dreams of [the young reporter's] manhood" (243). At the heart of Anderson's most accomplished work lies a narrative and perhaps ideological contradiction between the fractured, lyrical temporality of *Erlebnis* and the more novelistic temporality of *Erfahrung*.

The same could be said of Hemingway's *In Our Time*, where the pervasive irony and imagery of dead babies and unwanted pregnancies should deter readers from approaching the work as a simple *Bildungsroman*, featuring Hemingway's alter ego Nick Adams. *In Our Time* is in fact a challenging experimental work, and one that can be read, as Peter Messent has shown, as an almost point-by-point illustration of Lukács's account of modernist fiction and its fall from dynamic narration to static description.[30] In Messent's reading, the most crucial aspect of Hemingway's famous aesthetic of "leaving things out" is a temporal one: the excision of any sense of historical causality and continuity. Though the collection is tightly knit in terms of recurrent motifs and striking juxtapositions, it dispenses (at least in the "chapters" or vignettes dealing with war, crime, and bullfighting) with any chronological and developmental order. Moreover, the structural disjuncture between the brief, objective "chapters" and the more intimate, subjective stories expresses a stark opposition between the individual and the historical world: no interaction or mediation between subject and object seems to be possible. The vision, in other words, is fatalistic: story after story, vignette after vignette, image after image evoke a condition of being "out of season" in modern times. It is entirely appropriate, then, that the only instance in which Nick Adams enters the sequence of "chapters" (and by extension, the wider social context to which they allude) is when he is wounded on the Italian front. The rituals of masculinity that abound in Hemingway's work in no way contradict Messent's claim regarding the disappearance of agency from Hemingway's early and most interesting fiction. If, as Lukács suggests, the symbol imposes a kind of synthetic meaning on objects and events that have in fact lost their significance, the same kind of thing can be said of the bullfight: however brave and skillful, it is ultimately a synthetic action, removed from the historical world – the only theatre in which actions can have transformative consequences.

These considerations go some way toward explaining the paradoxical effects of Hemingway's simple paratactic prose. Though he consistently writes in the active voice and with an apparently meticulous interest in the sequence of actions, the effect is curiously passive; and though the prevailing tense is the past tense, it provides none of the cognitive advantages of retrospect. The effect is one of extreme immediacy, of what Pound would call "a rain of factual atoms," reproduced in all their confusing singularity. Thus Nick Adams in "Big Two-Hearted River" knows exactly how to set up camp and make coffee, and sets about performing these tasks in the proper way. But the cumulative effect of his activities is to repress, rather than enhance any understanding of, or even any thought about what Lukács would have called the social totality.

The purpose and effect of focusing on the present, rather than on the past or future, is therefore quite different in Stein and in Hemingway. In the case of the former, one might say, it is a quasi-scientific enterprise, and in the case of the latter, a way of blocking out broader (and traumatic) historical truths. To recognize this difference is to register something of the impact of World War I on Hemingway's generation, and especially on the combatants. In Stephen Kern's view, World War I condemned early twentieth-century attempts to conceptually extend the interval between past and future (including those of James and Stein) to obsolescence. The war isolated present experience from the usual flow of time. Not only did the lived moment become extraordinarily compelling, both in its shocking violence and its vast spatial extension (observers of the war needed to attend to distant events taking place simultaneously along a vast front line), but it also attenuated any sense of continuity and tradition (294). Hemingway's *In Our Time*, with its ironic treatment of conventional pieties, its exclusive attention to the luminous moment, and its wide geographical range – with stories and vignettes taking place all the way from Asia Minor to the Midwest – would seem to give some credence to Kern's broad claims.

But while the effects of World War I on the techniques of modern fiction have been amply considered, not enough has been said about the equally far-reaching effects of the Great Depression, with its pervasive insecurities and sudden reversals of fortune. The poetry and prose of the early 1930s, when millions were unemployed and the old American dream of success – or even just the expectation of a meaningful career – seemed to be in tatters, is often marked by a characteristic sense of time. It can be likened to the atomistic and potentially cataclysmic temporality of gambling, of the long shot: the sense that "one minute you are sitting on top of the world the next you are sitting around a jungle fire telling about it," as a hobo in Tom Kromer's *Waiting For Nothing* (1936) puts it.[31]

This novel, based on the author's personal experiences, is one of a number of novels documenting the grim lives of society's bottom dogs, including Edward Newhouse's *You Can't Sleep Here* (1934), Jack Conroy's

The Disinherited (1933), and Nelson Algren's *Somebody in Boots* (1935). But the interest of *Waiting for Nothing* becomes evident when we relate it not to the proletarian novels with which it tends to be pigeonholed, but to the more canonical modernist works we have discussed so far. Kromer's novel adopts not only the mannerisms of Hemingway's early style, but also its implicit attitude toward history: one of fatalistic incomprehension and passivity. The title already draws our attention to a particular kind of temporality. "Waiting" is not entirely a suspension of time ("You do not stay young in a soup line," observes Tom Kromer, the unfortunate protagonist [66]), but rather a suspension of meaningful, directed action. The novel's many reiterations thus serve not to satisfy an aesthetic of abstract composition, but to emphasize the complete inefficacy of personal effort and initiative. Try as he may to improve his situation, Tom finds himself resorting again and again to some variation of the panhandler's humiliating line: "Buddy, can you spare a dime?" The pressing need to find food or shelter ("three hots and a flop," in the novel's harsh vocabulary) renders sustained reflection impossible, and the novel's one instance of historical interpretation is, in effect, censored. When Tom, appearing in court on charges of vagrancy, tries to explain his transgression as the result of a worldwide crisis of unemployment, the magistrate gavels him down, finds him guilty, and moves on to sentence the next bum.

The final chapter of *Waiting for Nothing* offers an attempt at a retrospective assessment, but the futile seriality of his life seems to have disabled Tom's capacity for memory: "I try to think back over the years that I have lived," he laments, "but I cannot think of years any more. I can think only of the drags I have rode. Of the bulls that have sapped up on me, and the mission slop I have swilled. People I have known, I remember no more . . . My life is spent before it is started . . ." (128). The present tense narration thus comes to seem not an experimental option, but an additional mark of privation. The atomistic temporality of Depression-era modernity has not only eliminated any sense of personal significance, but even the promise of religious transcendence: "[S]ince when did Jesus start keeping office hours?" Tom asks himself at the end of the novel, as he stares at the closed door of a mission, above which a giant electric sign flashes the message: JESUS SAVES (124).

The politicized climate of the 1930s, when Gertrude Stein first achieved the celebrity status she craved, provides an interesting perspective on the experiments in narrative time with which I began this discussion. Mike Gold, the tireless Marxist polemicist, described her work as symptomatic of the decay of capitalist culture and as "an attempt to annihilate all relations between the artist and the society in which he lives."[32] And it is true that Stein had little interest in history (except perhaps in the very general and abstract sense of "how everybody is doing everything"). But she was deeply interested in mimicking what she described as her period's characteristic "time-sense" in the "time-sense" of her own composition.[33] She was concerned to represent the one quality that lived history and fiction have in common: the temporality and pace of human experience, which, in Stein's view, was one of the most important distinctions between one period and another.

In this respect, if in no other, Stein resembles John Dos Passos, whose *U. S. A.* trilogy was concerned to examine and represent the speed of history. It is a novel about the socio-political effects of modern technologies of production, and includes among its major *personnages* the historical figures of Frederick "Speedy" Taylor, Henry Ford, and the Wright brothers, whose inventions radically accelerated the pace of human life. The various modes of writing that make up the trilogy – the biographies of historical figures, the narratives of fifteen fictional characters, and so-called "Newsreels" and "Camera Eyes" – are all designed to be read at different velocities.[34] The collage-like effects of the newsreels, for instance, slow down the pace of reading (thus counteracting the high speed at which the language of the media is usually devoured), while the idiosyncratic run-on words (like "pinkishcolored," "nattilydressed," "slightlybulging," "internalcombustion," and "fifteenhundreddollar") accelerate the otherwise steady clip at which we consume the reasonably suspenseful and realistic fictional narratives. In other words, the novel's various experimental techniques alert us to what Dos Passos sees as the multiple and unsynchronized temporalities of twentieth-century life. Modernity in *U. S. A.* is not represented as a simple progression, in which everyone is swept along, but as a dangerous assemblage of unsynchronized forces, which seldom advances the interest of the individual.

It is no accident, then, that the prose poem with which the trilogy opens should represent a young man who is walking "fast but not fast enough . . . to catch the last subway, the street car, the bus." This figure is emblematic, as it turns out, of many of the novel's characters. Even those who are innovators (like the aviator Charley Anderson and the public relations man J. Ward Moorehouse), or those who seem crafty and dogged enough to surf the trends (like the movie-star Margot Dowling), end up being anachronisms, defeated by relentless processes of acceleration and obsolescence in an economy of scale. In the novel's closing prose poem, entitled "Vag," the idea that America has fragmented into "two nations" (1157) – an idea that is also put forward in the stark material oppositions between the haves and have-nots of Kromer's novel – is expressed in terms of temporality and velocity. The poem contrasts the situation of a hungry hitchhiker, who waits by the side of the road while cars and trucks pass him by, with that of a rich man, who flies overhead in a transcontinental plane, and vomits a meal of steak and mushroom into his airsick bag. "History, the billiondollar speedup" has clearly left the young man behind, while the privileged air-traveler is, at least for the moment, keeping up (1240).

If Stein's experiments with time led her in the end to something rather different from fiction, the same might be said, curiously, of Dos Passos. *U.S.A* is a novel without a denouement: the different modes of writing that constitute it all encompass a somewhat different span of time (the narratives seem to end in 1928, whereas the newsreels include events that took place as late as 1936). The various parts of the novel do not end, as it were, on the same beat, nor do they all permit or demand a similar sense of closure. In order to assess the meaning of *U. S. A.*, or so Barbara Foley has suggested, the reader is forced to attend to the drama of real history – to the fortunes of American capitalism during the Great Depression – rather than to seek for any retrospective synthesis within the novel itself.[35] Dos Passos's extraordinary effort at including history (and the mass-mediated discourses that shaped it) in the body of his fictional work requires a degree of experimentation at least as radical as that of the various modernist efforts at excluding history from the work of art.

Value

I started this essay by suggesting, along with John Dos Passos and Warren Susman, that the transformations of American society in the first half of the twentieth century must be understood in broadly economic terms as a transition from competitive to monopoly capitalism, or from a culture of production to a culture of consumption. It seems fitting, then, to conclude with some comments on the sometimes quite intimate ways in which the aesthetic economies of texts – the systems of values and tropes within them – correlate with actual economic conditions. After all, money, as the "material symbol of value itself" is a sign or trope; and many other financial concepts – appreciation, interest, and accounting, for instance – are readily connected to the realm of literature.[36] This last connection is nicely captured in the "Storyteller" essay, where Benjamin describes the novelist as an executor of memories, of a sum of experiences, the value of which often adds up to zero (98–99). Whether or not we agree with his melancholy assessment of the novelist's task, the conception of narrative closure as the moment when the value of the various transactions initiated in a novel is finally calculated remains an intriguing and productive one. It is therefore not surprising that the meeting ground of literature and economics should have proven a fertile terrain for scholarly work, whether focused on the material aspects of literary production or the economic thematics of texts themselves.

As in our earlier investigation of place, Malcolm Cowley's *Exile's Return* provides a useful entry point. If the memoir is, on one level, the record of a generation's conversion from a spirit of deracinated cosmopolitanism to a re-invented literary nationalism or journey home, it is also, on another level, the record of Cowley's personal conversion from the view that "the productive forces of society" were "alien to poetry and learning" to a pre-occupation with the economic conditions and impact of literary creativity (35–36). He argues, for instance, that the values of the Greenwich Village bohemians of the late teens and twenties, though on the surface antagonistic to the materialism of mainstream American culture, actually "fitted into the business picture" quite readily: the ethos of "self-expression" stimulated a demand for all manner of consumer goods from beach pajamas to cosmetics, while "living for the moment" often came down to buying things from radios to automobiles to houses on the installment plan (62–63). Nor were these material concerns and contradictions avoided when the writers of his cadre escaped to Europe. In search of eternal values, Cowley observes, they discovered instead "valuta" (81). The rapidly fluctuating exchange rates for European currencies not only meant that writers were able to support themselves on the strong dollar, but sensitized them to the disjuncture between price and value, utility and worth – a matter that became a major theme in several important fictional works.

An alertness to economic concerns, moreover, was not exclusive to writers who went abroad. In the U.S. savings declined precipitously and debt increased during the Jazz Age. Wealth and class suddenly seemed to be a fluid matter, marked by expenditures rather than by money in the bank: a situation recorded in imaginative detail in novels like *The Great Gatsby* and *The Big Money*, as well as less canonical works like Anita Loos's *Gentlemen Prefer Blondes* (1925). And though the stock market crash of 1929 forced a re-evaluation of the capitalist system and undermined the general faith in the old rags-to-riches dream (Nathanael West's *A Cool Million* [1934] offers the period's most brutal debunking of this theme), the nation's fascination with consumer goods did not decline during the so-called Red Decade. Outrage at the ironic coexistence of plenty and scarcity during the Great Depression frequently animated the fiction of the period. One need only think of the striking passage in *The Grapes of Wrath* (1939), where Steinbeck denounces the wastefulness of a system which demands that "golden mountains" of oranges must be burned to keep up the market price, even though poor children are dying of malnutrition.[37]

If one reads the fiction of this period with an eye to economics, monetary concerns and metaphors come to seem quite pervasive and arise in quite surprising places. For all its thinness of social representation, Stein's *Three Lives*, for example, is shaped by the contrast between the two thrifty German immigrants, Anna and Lena, and the wasteful, impetuous, Melanctha, drawn as she is to speed, gambling, and the pleasures of the moment. Even Willa Cather, who, in a 1922 essay, questioned whether "the banking system and the Stock Exchange [were] worth being written about at all," actually wrote extensively about money and even banks in her two most important novels from the 1920s, *A Lost Lady* (1923) and *The Professor's House* (1925). In the first, Captain Forrester, one of Cather's pioneer aristocrats, finds his mettle tested when the bank of which he is a director fails, and he – alone among the members of the board – decides to refund his investors' deposits dollar-for-dollar out of his own personal wealth. His magnificent impracticality places him and his wife at the mercy of a new generation of money-grubbing, self-seeking businessmen, "who would cut everything up into profitable bits as the match factory splinters the primeval forest."[38] The older values based on good character and trust yield inexorably, in Cather's elegiac assessment, to a new spirit of sheer utility and gain. The narrative crisis of *The Professor's House* is, similarly, a financial one: the plot takes off at the moment when Professor Godfrey St. Peter has finally made enough money through his intellectual work to buy a luxurious new house and the entire novel is structured in terms of a tension (an irresolvable one for Cather) between money and creativity, gifts and acquisitions, reserve and ostentation. The novel asks, in essence, how personal and historical legacies can be valued without "'realiz[ing]' on them" (220): without translating them into the reifying economy of the marketplace.[39]

While Cather (or at least her character Professor St. Peter) seems nauseated by all forms of commercial expenditure and considers the discourse of money to be "a vulgar tongue" (50), Hemingway's attitude, as presented in *The Sun Also Rises* (1926), is more complex. In the moral economy of the novel, anything of value must be paid for (hence the disdain of bankrupts, like Mike Campbell, and of people who expend money in order to avoid giving of themselves, like Robert Cohen). But payment is also intricately involved in a kind of *savoir vivre* or, more seriously, an ethical code for a secular age. One might therefore argue that the aging Greek count (the owner of a chain of stores in the U.S.), who knows how to get value for his money, whether in the form of good service or vintage brandy or female company, is more of a code hero in the novel than is the handsome young bullfighter. There is, moreover, a residual sense that exchange values need, in some way or another, to be in balance with use values and work: Hemingway makes it clear that the fiesta in Pamplona, during which people behave as though there were no consequences to their actions, makes exorbitant demands on the Spanish peasants who attend it: it is not just that the price of wine at cafés seems entirely incommensurate with the value of "the hours worked and bushels of grain sold," but that the fleeting exhilaration of the running of the bulls ends up costing the life of a man, who is gored: "all for fun," as a sober Spanish waiter notes. In its partly serious, partly ironic validation of a "simple exchange of values," the novel seems to simultaneously endorse and recontain the ethos of expenditure and consumerism.[40] It is worth speculating that the popularity of Hemingway's work might be tied to his attempt to salvage a certain masculine austerity (or moral solvency) in a world where the locus of value was rapidly shifting from the traditionally masculine sphere of production to the traditionally feminized sphere of consumption and leisure.

The economic crisis of the 1930s moved many writers (including Hemingway and Fitzgerald) to take a considerably harsher stance toward the emerging culture of abundance. We might think back to Nathan Asch, whose *Pay Day* derives whatever social implications it has through an implicit comparison of the value of the political commitment of Sacco and Vanzetti (for whom August 23, 1927, was "pay day" in a very serious sense of the term) and the trivial and questionable good time pursued by the antihero on his night out. The work of several proletarian authors, including Grace Lumpkin in *To Make my Bread* (1932), or Fielding Burke in *Call Home the Heart* (1932), has a similarly anti-consumerist message. The target of critique in these strike novels is not only the exploitative mill management, but the installment plan, which entraps the members of an idealized rural community in the snares of capitalism in a brand new guise.

However, some of the most important writers of the 1930s do begin in various ways to reconfigure and reclaim aspects of the ethos of expenditure and abundance (which, after all, has utopian as well as repressive implications). In Zora Neale Hurston's *Their Eyes Were Watching God* (1937), for example, the life of the heroine Janie may be read as an "education in expenditure."[41] This education does not imply subservience to the new strategies of business, or to the Keynesian view of consumption as ultimately functional: a means of jumpstarting the national economy. Janie's first husband, Logan Killicks, is devoted to an ethos of production and simple accumulation and he assesses her value merely in terms of her labor. Her second husband, Jody Stark, has begun to understand the idea of conspicuous consumption: he indulges in carefully calibrated expenditures, designed to enhance his own status in the community, and sees Janie largely as a pretty acquisition to put on display. Her third husband, whose very name – "Tea Cake" – suggests something of the sweetness of living for the moment, spends money and time excessively and uselessly, for the sheer playful delight of it. His irresponsible acts of expenditure are certainly open to criticism (he steals $200 from Janie to throw a party and to savor the feeling of wealth), but they are not readily tied to the needs of the mainstream economy and its racialized class structures. Indeed, in the symbolic economy of the text, Tea Cake's reckless spontaneity, of which Janie also comes to partake, seems linked to the recklessness of God, who in his abundance can afford to unleash the destructive power of a hurricane on the world. Needless to say, this is a remarkable vision to put forward in an era when economic deprivation often fostered a spirit of caution and it helps us make sense of the fact that Hurston's reputation only soared several decades after her major works were produced.

Curiously, the writer who comes closest to Hurston in validating an uncalculating generosity, as opposed to a spirit of cheap acquisitiveness, or self-serving accumulation, may be William Faulkner, whose novels are deeply concerned with economic issues. It is fair to say that his characters' attitudes toward money are as important as their attitudes toward time and that his work always comes down on the side of those who give unstintingly, as opposed to the schemers and accountants, like the repulsive Flem Snopes and Jason Compson. In *The Sound and the Fury*, the latter obsessively hoards money and calculates profits; and though he claims to believe that "money has no value: it's just the way you spend it," his interactions with others constantly reveal his instinctive equation of price and value. His miserliness is exposed, significantly, by the black characters in the novel, such as his colleague Job, who feels himself rich enough to give up his two bits in exchange for the immediate pleasure of hearing a man play the saw at a traveling show.[42]

Such details abound in Faulkner's work and this is not the place to record them in any detail. I will close instead by commenting briefly on the relationship between form and economics in his masterpiece, *Go Down, Moses* (1942), where the issue at stake is the historical legacy of slavery. This cycle of interconnected stories, which runs the gamut of money matters – from wagers, treasure hunts, bribes, inheritances, wages, gifts, sales, pay-offs, and robbery to charitable fundraising – begins, strikingly, with a dedication to the Faulkner family's servant, Caroline Barr, whom he praises for her gift of fidelity "without calculation of recompense."[43] Though one might argue that Faulkner has difficulty in imagining a place for African-Americans in the new market economy and that this difficulty is a sign of his residual paternalism, the generosity of Caroline Barr nevertheless marks an ethical position from which to measure the full horror of the story recorded in the ledger book of the McCaslin plantation: a story about the scandal of treating people – even kinsfolk – as commodities. The excessive eloquence of the central story "The Bear," with its interminable, all-inclusive sentences, must be read as a challenge to the language and ethos of the slave owners' ledger book, with its eccentric abbreviations and its terse arithmetic about human lives.[44]

Richard Wright ends *Native Son* with the clang of the prison door, shutting in the face of a condemned murderer in Chicago; Faulkner concludes *Go Down, Moses* by, as it were, picking up the story of the murderer where *Native Son* leaves off. He concludes his fictional investigation of the intersections of race and economics by imagining the aftermath of an execution in Chicago: that of one Samuel Beauchamp, a descendant of the McCaslin and Beauchamp families whose intertwined fates are at the center of *Go Down, Moses*. Like several other stories in the cycle (most notably "Pantaloon in Black"), the final story is about mourning; but once again money matters are at the center of the action. The lawyer Gavin Stevens, out of sympathy for the criminal's grandmother, goes around to collect the necessary funds for the transportation and proper burial of the body from various prominent whites in the local community. Whatever we make of Faulkner's treatment of Samuel Beauchamp and his crime of "[g]etting rich too fast" (370), or of the attitudes of the whites, with their residual sense of paternalistic obligation and their muted, but clearly insufficient recognition of their complicity in Beauchamp's death, it is clear that the funeral will not lay to rest the historical debts of the South. Nor will the intertwined, but nevertheless disjointed stories that make up *Go Down, Moses* yield the kind of closure Benjamin describes in the "Storyteller." And the eschewal of such accounting is precisely the point: the complex, but elusive construction of the cycle as a whole offers a fittingly open-ended way of narrating an "injustice" that, in Faulkner's severe but accurate judgment, "can never be amortized" (226). In its style, structure, and tragic narrative contents, *Go Down, Moses* protests against the reifying language of money. But it is nevertheless through the work's various economic tropes – no less than through the more conventionally poetic symbols like the bear, the deep woods, and the fire on the hearth – that we may trace out Faulkner's major thematic preoccupations: the persistence of the past, and the meaning and cost of modernity.

NOTES

1. Alfred Kazin, *On Native Grounds: An Interpretation of Modern American Prose Literature* (New York: Harcourt Brace, 1942), viii, ix.

2. Warren I. Susman, *Culture as History: The Transformation of American Society in the Twentieth Century* (Washington: Smithsonian Institution Press, 2003), xx; John Dos Passos cited in Townsend Ludington, *John Dos Passos: A Twentieth-Century Odyssey* (New York: Dutton, 1980), 286.

3. Sherwood Anderson, *Winesburg, Ohio* (New York: Penguin, 1992), 70–71.

4. Hamlin Garland, "Literary Prophecy," in *Modern American Fiction: Essays in Criticism*, ed. A. Walton Litz (New York: Oxford University Press, 1963), 30, 32.

5. Georg Lukács, "Narrate or Describe," in *Writer and Critic and Other Essays*, ed. Arthur Kahn (London: Merlin, 1978), 110–148; "The Ideology of Modernism," in *Realism in Our Time: Literature and Class Struggle* (New York: Harper & Row, 1971), 17–46.

6. Walter Benjamin, "The Storyteller: Reflections on the Work of Nikolai Leskov," in *Illuminations: Essays and Reflections* (New York: Schocken, 1969), 83–84, 93.

7. Virginia Woolf, *Mr. Bennett and Mrs. Brown* (London: Hogarth, 1924), 4; Robert Musil quoted in Lukács, "The Ideology of Modernism," 35; Willa Cather quoted in Susman, *Culture as History*, 105.

8. Lawrence Levine, *The Unpredictable Past* (New York: Oxford University Press, 1993), 193–195.

9. Ernest Hemingway, *A Farewell to Arms* (New York: Scribner's, 1969), 184–185.

10. On Faulkner's vocabulary, see Kazin, "Faulkner in his Fury," in *Modern American Fiction* ed. Litz, 170, and Nick Tosches, *Country: The Twisted Roots of Rock 'n' Roll* (New York: Da Capo Press, 1995), 74.

11. Nathan Asch, *Pay Day* (Detroit: Omnigraphics, 1990), 255; John Dos Passos, *U. S. A.* (New York: Library of America, 1996), 1,210.

12. Malcolm Cowley, *Exile's Return: A Literary Odyssey of the 1920s* (New York: Penguin, 1994), 14, 27, 28.

13. Ngugi Wa Thiong'O, *Decolonizing the Mind: The Politics of Language in African Literature* (London: James Currey, 1986), 10–12; and *Moving the Center: The Struggle for Cultural Freedoms* (London, James Currey, 1993), 2–12; Nadine Gordimer, "What Being a South African Means to Me," *South African Outlook* 107 (June 1977), 88.

14. Sherwood Anderson, *The Egg and Other Stories* (New York: Penguin, 1998), 6, 7.

15. See Kazin, *On Native Grounds*, 249–250; Willa Cather, *My Ántonia* (Boston: Hougton, Mifflin, 1954), 7, and "My First Novels," in *Stories, Poems, and Other Writings* (New York: Library of America, 1992), 963–964.

16. Henry Adams, *The Education of Henry Adams* (New York: Random House, 1931), 238.

17. F. Scott Fitzgerald, *The Great Gatsby* (New York: Collier, 1992), 73.

18. Henry Roth, *Call It Sleep* (New York: Farrar, Straus and Giroux, 1991), 23.

19. Mike Gold, *Jews Without Money* (New York: Carol & Graf, 1984), 190; Werner Sollers, "Ethnic Modernism," in *The Cambridge History of American Literature. Volume 6: Prose Writing 1910–1950*, ed. Sacvan Bercovitch (Cambridge University Press, 2002), 482.

20. James T. Farrell, "In Search of an Image," in *The League of Frightened Philistines* (New York: Vanguard Press, 1945), 156.

21. James T. Farrell, *Young Lonigan* (New York: Avon, 1972), 83.

22. Richard Wright, *Early Works: Lawd Today!, Uncle Tom's Children, Native Son* (New York: Library of America, 1991), 682, 550.
23. My reading of Wright is indebted to Charles Scruggs's *Sweet Home: Invisible Cities in the Afro-American Novel* (Baltimore: Johns Hopkins University Press, 1993), 75–79.
24. Frederic Jameson, "The End of Temporality," *Critical Inquiry* 29 (Summer 2003), 695.
25. Benjamin, *Illuminations*, 163.
26. Stephen Kern, *The Culture of Time and Space: 1880–1918* (Cambridge, MA: Harvard University Press, 1983), 8.
27. Fredric Jameson, "The End of Temporality," 699.
28. Gertrude Stein, *Selected Writings* (New York: Vintage, 1990), 73.
29. William James, *Principles of Psychology* (New York: Dover, 1950), vol. II, 608–609; see also Elizabeth Flower and Murray G. Murphey, *A History of Philosophy in America* (New York: Putnam's, 1977), vol. II, 646–647.
30. Peter Messent, "Style: Personal Impressions" in *Ernest Hemingway* (New York: St. Martin's Press, 1992), 5–22.
31. Tom Kromer, *Waiting For Nothing* (Athens: University of Georgia Press, 1986), 116.
32. Cited in Sollers, *Ethnic Modernism*, 377.
33. Stein, *Selected Writings*, 513, 516.
34. See Carin Irr, *The Suburb of Dissent* (Durham: Duke University Press, 1998), 45–46, 56–57.
35. Barbara Foley, "The Treatment of Time in The Big Money," *Modern Fiction Studies* 26 (Autumn 1980), 460–461.
36. Karl Marx, *Capital: A Critique of Political Economy*, I, trans. Ben Fowkes (New York: Vintage Books, 1977), 221–222.
37. John Steinbeck, *The Grapes of Wrath* (New York: Penguin, 1992), 477.
38. Willa Cather, *A Lost Lady* (New York: Knopf, 1923), 106.
39. Willa Cather, *The Professor's House* (New York: Vintage, 1990), 220.
40. Ernest Hemingway, *The Sun Also Rises* (New York: Macmillan, 1986), 152, 197, 72.
41. See Thomas F. Haddox, "The Logic of Expenditure in *Their Eyes Were Watching God*," *Mosaic* 34 (March 2001): 19–34.
42. Faulkner, *The Sound and the Fury* (New York: Vintage, 1990), 194, 231.
43. William Faulkner, *Go Down, Moses* (New York: Vintage, 1973), np.
44. For this insight I am indebted to Eric Dussere, "Accounting for Slavery: Economic Narratives in Morrison and Faulkner," *Modern Fiction Studies* 47 (Summer 2001), 336.

3

CARY NELSON

Modern American poetry

When did modern poetry begin? Who are among its key figures? What does their work have in common? What are the most compelling accounts of the development of modern poetry that we can offer? Is there good reason to distinguish American poetry from developments in other countries taking place at the same time? At what if any point can we say modernity came to an end to be replaced by different practices in a more recent period? These are among the questions that have both vexed and inspired modern poetry scholars since the 1980s. For our answers to all these questions have changed dramatically over that time.

What is increasingly clear as scholars recover the work of forgotten poets and read more widely in original sources, among them not just books but also newspapers and magazines that regularly published poetry, is that American poetry of roughly the first half of the twentieth century is unexcelled in its richness, inventiveness, and diversity. The variety of poetry written and published in the United States in the last century represents a unique explosion of literary creativity. Its range of forms, styles, and preoccupations are in a fundamental sense uncontainable. They exceed any single story we might try to tell about them. And it is a field that continues to change, not only because poetry long out of print is being made available again and given thoughtful analysis but also because scholars continue to discover important early and mid-twentieth-century poetry that missed being published for various reasons. Our literary past is very much a work still in progress.

In the most familiar account of when modern American poetry arrived on the scene, the Imagist revolution of the century's second decade played a key role. One of the Imagist movement's emphases was on extreme concision and on a certain neutrality of description. Ezra Pound's "In a Station of the Metro" (1913) with its title serving as the poem's first line, and William Carlos Williams's "The Red Wheelbarrow" (1923) remain two of its defining texts. Pound's poem is only two lines long:

> The apparition of these faces in the crowd;
> Petals on a wet, black bough.

Williams's poem gets much of its effect from its line breaks and its careful placement of the poem on the page:

> so much depends
> upon
>
> a red wheel
> barrow
>
> glazed with rain
> water
>
> beside the white
> chickens

Yet Imagism from the outset never quite held to this model of concision and descriptive neutrality. John Gould Fletcher (1886–1950) is a clear example of Imagism's less widely recognized, loosely descriptive, and impressionistic mode. His subjects include "the swirling of the seamews above the sullen river," "the iridescent vibrations of midsummer light," the "trees, like great jade elephants" that "chained, stamp and shake 'neath the gadflies of the breeze" and

> Flickering of incessant rain
> On flashing pavements:
> Sudden scurry of umbrellas:
> Bending, recurved blossoms of the storm.

He was also capable of indulging himself in "lacquered mandarin moments" and "crimson placques of cinnabar." With his tendency to echo the writerly excesses of the 1890s, Fletcher is already outside the tradition of Imagist precision and restraint. But the group title of Imagist is even more problematic for Amy Lowell, and H. D. Lowell's work, in fact, soon became too diverse to be classified in any single movement.

With H. D. (Hilda Doolittle, 1886–1961), even in the early poems there is too much throttled self-expression displaced onto nature, too much rhythmic invention, for her work to fit easily within Imagism's more regularly anthologized mode of pictorial detachment. "Hurl your green over us," she calls to the sea in "Oread" (1914), "cover us with your pools of fir." The presence of the speaker here, calling up a force out of nature and intensifying it, enlisting descriptive imagery in a vatic psychological demand, removes "Oread" from any of the conventional paradigms of Imagism. Passages like this in H. D.'s work provoke a whole series of displacements and reversible oppositions. If nature is sexualized, psychologized, and placed in a dynamic, transformative relation with the speaking subject here, the same images invoke demands made of a lover and of the subject's own unconscious. Yet the dynamic psychological torque in this work does not justify assimilating H. D. to the expressive subjectivity we have long associated with lyric poetry. We are not simply in the presence here of a discourse of resplendent or imperiled identity. It hearkens toward an anonymous, sacralized voice, a ritual incantation, in which a transgressive otherness breaks through the discourse of identity. That is partly how we can understand the sense in "Oread" that the body is an animate landscape of vital forces. We cannot choose between such readings in H. D.; these semantic possibilities are simultaneously concentrated in and disseminated by her language. What is clear, however, is that we cannot cast her poetry in the mold of disinterested description. That becomes even more clear in some of her mythological poems. Her 1924 poem "Helen" is a succinct and telling indictment of the relationship between frustrated idealization and misogyny. Though it appears to be exclusively about an earlier age, "Helen" in fact also addresses its own historical moment, not just the period of the Trojan War. It describes the anger some in the culture feel now that women are not simply beautiful objects. "Remembering past enchantments," Greece now "hates / the still eyes in the white face." Only death, it seems, can relieve this tension and recompense the culture for the changes women have wrought:

> Greece sees unmoved,
> God's daughter, born of love,
> the beauty of cool feet
> and slenderest knees,
> could love indeed the maid,
> only if she were laid,
> white ash amid funereal cypresses.

The most famous promoter of Imagism was Amy Lowell (1874–1925), but disinterested description was not her chosen mode either. Lowell's series of poems from 1919 – including "Decade," "Opal," "Madonna of the Evening Flowers," and "Venus Transiens" – are among the most elegantly passionate love poems in modern American poetry. As we can tell from its first stanza, "The Weather-Cock Points South" is remarkable for the way it fuses an eroticized spirituality with explicit physical references:

> I put your leaves aside,
> One by one:
> The stiff, broad outer leaves;
> The smaller ones,

Pleasant to touch, veined with purple;
The glazed inner leaves.
One by one
I parted you from your leaves,
Until you stood up like a white flower
Swaying slightly in the evening wind.

The leaves are put aside at once by a disrobing and by a probing embrace. The poem involves a pursuit of psychic intimacy – a drive to know and celebrate another's inwardness – and an explicit vaginal caress. The flower with its petals and bud is thus both body and spirit, but there is no severing the two. And the woman she describes seems both the object of her gaze and the flower of her own unfolding affection. The flower is both the center of the lover's body and the center of the self, for it becomes the site from which the subject seems to speak. It is also the center of the gardens coalescing in the poem and, implicitly, of nature as a whole. Her unwavering concentration on it gives it the transience of wax and the permanence of stone – "of jade, of unstreaked agate; / Flower with surfaces of ice."

Also appropriately linked with Imagism, if once again idiosyncratically, is the early work of Wallace Stevens (1879–1955). Had Stevens not existed – a lifelong insurance executive writing some of his country's most insistently metaphysical poetry – it would hardly have been plausible to invent him. Yet Stevens had actually committed himself to writing poetry before taking a position with the Hartford Accident and Indemnity Company; the job was a way to earn a living. He was born and grew up in Reading, Pennsylvania, and was educated at Harvard and at the New York University Law School. He began publishing poems in magazines in 1914, but his first book, *Harmonium*, did not appear until 1923.

The book was organized to open with a number of his short, exquisite lyrics, rather than with the longer and more abstract poems that have become the focus of extended critical analysis. Although Stevens lived and worked in Connecticut, a number of his poems drew on the Florida landscape he saw on regular business trips. Indeed the sheer riotous excess and profusion of Florida's flora and fauna often gave him a perfect analogue for the mental life he used nature to evoke. The poems are thus at once referential and devoted to elaborate rhetorical invention that creates a world of its own. In comments in letters that are less than fully trustworthy or definitive, Stevens sometimes denied the poems this double life, but readers should judge for themselves.

The poems are so captivating in their rhetorical inventiveness – the play of words deployed for their sound, the almost palimpsestic thickness of imagery, the wit – that one can easily miss Stevens's regular (if abstract) engagement with the issues of his day, but it is nonetheless a continual feature of his work. Debates both with the world of public events and between contrasting philosophical or cultural positions occur throughout the poems. In "Sunday Morning" (1915) a woman wonders whether her sensual pleasures amount to a belief system comparable to Christianity's obsession with mortality:

> Complacencies of the peignoir, and late
> Coffee and oranges in a sunny chair,
> And the green freedom of a cockatoo
> Upon a rug mingle to dissipate
> The holy hush of ancient sacrifice.

To some degree, such philosophical issues crowd out the sensuous surfaces and the rich music in his later poems. Some critics also find many of the late lyrics too similar to one another. Yet their obsessive circling around related themes of emptiness is a large part of their interest. They form a single, driven project that anticipates postmodern work like W. S. Merwin's poetry of Vietnam War despair.

In the case of Imagism, therefore, we have a founding movement in modern American poetry that is richer and more diverse than we have been inclined to think. But what if there are alternative beginnings literary historians have largely ignored? One major preoccupation for American poets has been race, the country's longest running social trauma. In the standard account of modern American poetry, the issue animates the poetry produced during the mid-nineteenth-century abolitionist debates but then largely disappears until the Harlem (or New Negro) Renaissance of the 1920s. Yet the twentieth century began for many Americans with a debate precisely over race, and poets were a vocal part of the conflict.

In 1900 Morrison I. Swift (1856–1946), a well-known pamphleteer on Left issues, published *Advent of Empire*, a book of poems devoted substantially to America's genocidal war in the Philippines. The New England Anti-Imperialist League met in Boston in November of 1898, but such sentiments were swept aside in widespread national enthusiasm for this first overseas adventure. Literally hundreds of pro-war poems were published in newspapers across the country that year. Echoing the notorious cry "Remember the Maine!" they certified the principle of Manifest Destiny and sanctified the use of military force. Meanwhile, Rudyard Kipling urged action in his notorious poem "The White Man's Burden," and in February of 1899 America embarked on a major war of conquest against the Filipino independence movement. Some 4,000 Americans and over 200,000 Filipinos would eventually die in a war that became increasingly brutal as it shifted from large-scale battles to guerilla tactics.

Late in 1901 public sentiment in the US would shift against the war. By then antiwar poetry would open out into a mass movement. But there were also poets, like Swift, who were in the vanguard of anti-imperialist politics, issuing effective poems highlighting the war's racist politics and economics. In satiric and polemical poems like "Imperial Sam," "Go Die For the President King," "American Love," "Butcher McKinley," "Might and Right," and "The Primitive Races Shall Be Cultured," Swift attacks capitalism and exposes imperialism's hidden logic. Here is Swift, in the midst of the Philippine War, borrowing some of his diction and rhythms from Shakespeare and speaking in the persona of President McKinley. The poem, "Butcher McKinley," 130 lines long, is composed at the turning point of the centuries and driven deep into the rhetoric of its own time. But Swift also reaches back and forward to indict the whole history of imperialism as a form of sanctified racism:

> Sweet friends, sweet fellowmen, sweet voters,
> Call not murder murder if God wills.
> 'Tis blasphemy, abortion, miscontent, abomination,
> Hell's own self, to charge dear God with crime.
> I must as many Filipinos kill as shall appease
> God's wrath at them for spurning my decree . . .
> I am a pious man, a holy man, and member of a church.
> Did I not tell the damned blacks
> To ground their arms? . . .
> Fiends, monsters, toads, green lizards, scorpions,
> snakes . . .
> They must submit. For mean and weak and black
> There is no virtue but submission.
> After submission, – well, we'll see . . .
> It is a law of mine
> That niggers must submit to my sublimity . . .
> And how I love them! God! Everyone that dies
> In disobedience penetrates my soul! . . .
> Send him across the brine to cleave the skulls
> Of those foul imps of mud the Filipinos.

In its condemnation of pious racism, "Butcher McKinley" draws on the history of the abolitionist movement and also looks forward to poems like Langston Hughes's (1902–1967) "Christ in Alabama" (1931). But the poem readily challenges more recent imperialist ventures as well. Part of what is so startling about the poem is the contemporaneity of its insights. The knowledge that racism underlies and underwrites international relations is knowledge we often suppress. Apparently it must be relearned by each generation. American poets had earlier protested slavery. Now some began to

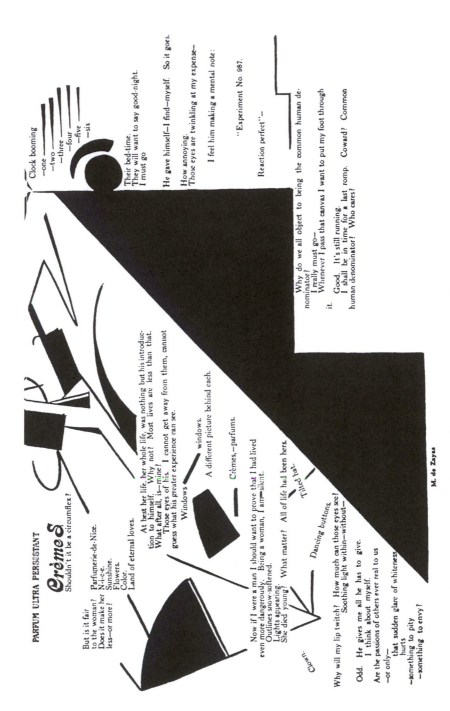

Figure 3.1 Agnes Ernst Meyer and Marius De Zayas, "Mental Reactions," 291 no. 2 (April 1915).

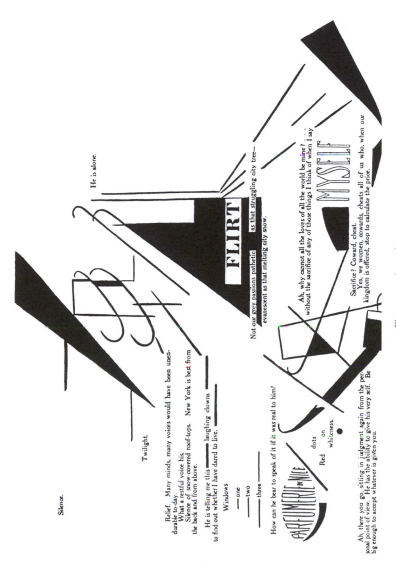

Figure 3.1 (cont.)

realize racism was also a component of our international adventures. There were several interesting volumes by other poets as well, but the most notable anti-imperialist anthology is, no doubt, *Liberty Poems*, issued by the New England Anti-Imperialist League in June 1900.

There are a number of reasons to remember the moment of 1900 and give it a place in a history of modern American poetry. It holds a key position in a 150-year history of American poets writing about race. It helps us recognize that the history of American anti-racist poetry is itself multiracial. Finally, as I shall argue later, it is with poems protesting racism and political repression that American modernity comes to an end. So the moment of 1900 helps frame the first half of the twentieth century in a particularly instructive way.

That makes for a different and quite unconventional starting point for a history of modern poetry. Yet the longstanding consensus about what poetry most mattered – the best that American poets had thought and said – still stands as a reference point for every effort to rethink and deepen our heritage. For decades the single most defining moment of American modernism was taken to be the publication in 1922, by an American then living in London, of T. S. Eliot's (1888–1965) *The Waste Land*. Part of what *The Waste Land* did was to establish collage as a central technique of modern poetry; it also placed radical formal experimentation at the forefront of modernist technique. It was not the first work to adapt visual collage to a literary text. Indeed, Agnes Ernst Meyer's and Marius de Zayas's "Mental Reactions," published in the journal *291* in 1915, made much more radical and disruptive use of the space of the page than Eliot's poem did, and it even used graphic forms to make explicit the connection with artistic movements like cubism. But "Mental Reactions" was a one-shot experiment in a very small circulation journal. Moreover, though aimed at once for a pop-cultural celebration and parody of female stereotypes, it could hardly claim the cultural ambitions *The Waste Land* appeared to embody. Eliot's poem was published in the aftermath of World War I, and it evoked for many readers the ruined landscape left to them after the historically unique devastation of trench warfare and mass slaughter: "A crowd flowed over London bridge, so many, / I had not thought death had undone so many." The poem's fragments mirrored a shattered world, and its allusions, however erudite, recalled a civilized culture many felt they had lost:

> What are the roots that clutch, what branches grow
> Out of this stony rubbish? Son of man,
> You cannot say, or guess, for you know only
> A heap of broken images . . .

Even its tendency to taunt readers with failed possibilities of spiritual rebirth – reinforced by Eliot's own notes to the poem, along with its glimpses of a religious route to joining the pieces of a dismembered god and a broken socius – struck a chord. Eliot was one of many major modernist writers to yearn for a mythic synthesis remaining out of reach.

Years later, with hindsight, the benediction at the poem's end – "Shantih shantih shantih" (The peace which passeth understanding) – could seem to foreshadow the more explicit religiosity of the *Four Quartets* (1936–1942). But that was not apparent in 1922, nor were Eliot's monarchist political conservatism and his reactionary social and racial prejudices yet in evidence. So readers and writers from all points of the political spectrum found inspiration in Eliot's technical innovations. In a surprisingly short period of time, *The Waste Land* became the pre-eminent poem of modernism, the unquestioned symbol of what was actually a much more diverse movement. Eventually, as its shadow came to hide other kinds of modernism – from more decisively vernacular language to poems strongly identified with race or revolution – *The Waste Land* gathered a set of compensatory ambitions and resentments. Of course it was hardly Eliot's aim to make adulation of *The Waste Land* into a justification for ignoring the Harlem Renaissance, a movement barely under way when the poem was written, but conservative literary scholars turned the poem into a weapon with that sort of cultural power.

Meanwhile, the poem itself remains available to be reread. Its mix of multiple voices, its fusion of personal anguish with historical experience, its fragments of narrativity, its riveting imagery and layered allusiveness, all these remain hallmarks of the literary response to modernity. *The Waste Land* is among a tiny handful of poems that define Eliot's career, something that cannot be said of Robert Frost, Langston Hughes, Wallace Stevens, or William Carlos Williams, all of whom wrote large numbers of short poems from which people will choose different favorites. Eliot, on the other hand, has a career that runs more definitively from "The Love Song of J. Alfred Prufrock" (1915) through *The Waste Land* to *Four Quartets*.

At the same time as experimental modernism was under way, however, other American poets were dramatically transforming traditional forms. Robert Frost (1874–1963) regularly worked with traditional forms, using rhyme, meter, and regular stanzas, but he undermined every consolation we might have been led to expect from regularity. Frost cultivated the public image of a New England sage, and the poems, read carelessly in search of platitudes, often seem to support that view. In American high schools Frost's poems continue to be misread to teach little moral lessons that the poems themselves actually decisively undercut. "Take the road less traveled by," students are urged, in a sentimentalized promotion of individual initiative;

or, even more crudely, "don't turn like most toward sin or self-gratification; take the road less traveled by." About the only certainty "The Road Not Taken" (1915) may be said to offer is that of self-deception, for the poem makes it clear there is really no difference to be discerned:

> Two roads diverged in a yellow wood,
> And sorry I could not travel both
> And be one traveler, long I stood
> And looked down one as far as I could
> To where it bent in the undergrowth;
>
> Then took the other, as just as fair,
> And having perhaps the better claim,
> Because it was grassy and wanted wear;
> Though as for that the passing there
> Had worn them really about the same,
>
> And both that morning equally lay
> In leaves no step had trodden black.
> Oh, I kept the first for another day!
> Yet knowing how way leads on to way,
> I doubted if I should ever come back.
>
> I shall be telling this with a sigh
> Somewhere ages and ages hence:
> Two roads diverged in a wood, and I –
> I took the one less traveled by,
> And that has made all the difference.

Frost's poems can be corrosively sardonic, offering a menacing nature or human cruelty as the only alternatives to emptiness. That the voice is so crisp, folksy, and pithy only adds to the underlying sense of terror. Over and over again the poems drain human choices of any meaning, yet they do so in straightforward images, colloquial diction, and rhythms that mimic natural speech. His dark view of human nature would also, remarkably, help him in poems like "The Hill Wife" (1916) to write some of American modernism's most sensitive portraits of women.

The centrality of revolutionary changes in traditional forms, however, is especially clear in the transformation two poets – Claude McKay (1889–1948) and Edna St. Vincent Millay (1892–1950) – worked in the sonnet. Raised in Jamaica and familiar with the history of English poetry, McKay chose the sonnet as the vehicle for his shock and rage at the racism he encountered when he came to the United States. "The Outcast" (1922) is one culmination of several years of his effort to produce capsule indictments of all aspects of race in America:

For the dim regions whence my fathers came
My spirit, bondaged by the body, longs.
Words felt, but never heard, my lips would frame;
My soul would sing forgotten jungle songs.
I would go back to darkness and to peace,
But the great western world holds me in fee,
And I may never hope for full release
While to its alien gods I bend my knee.
Something in me is lost, forever lost,
Some vital thing has gone out of my heart,
And I must walk the way of life a ghost
Among the sons of earth, a thing apart.

For I was born, far from my native clime,
Under the white man's menace, out of time.

Haunted by a past they never knew, exiled to an impossible present, blacks in America may be doubly imperiled. They exist apart from the ordinary social space of lived time and yet are urgently endangered. McKay took the romance and the consolations of the historical sonnet and replaced them with a hand grenade of protest. Compressed and rhetorically proficient anger would now be among the sonnet's resources and its cultural aims; the form would never be quite the same again. Together with Millay, whose anti-romantic sonnets turned the form about face, McKay reconceived the meaning of a centuries-long tradition. Millay's achievements in the sonnet are perhaps most fully realized in her 1923 sequence of seventeen "Sonnets from an Ungrafted Tree." The final number in the sequence opens as the speaker sits at her dead husband's bedside:

> Gazing upon him now, severe and dead,
> It seemed a curious thing that she had lain
> Beside him many a night in that cold bed

and closes in an anti-romantic flourish as she

> . . . sees a man she never saw before –
> The man who eats his victuals at her side,
> Small, and absurd, and hers: for once, not hers, unclassified.

This sort of dramatic rethinking of gender relations in fact takes place across both rethought traditional forms and innovative experimental ones. If there is one signal example of a recently recovered work of experimental modernism predating *The Waste Land* it is probably Mina Loy's 1915–1917 elliptical and minimalist poem sequence "Love Songs." In her "Feminist Manifesto," unpublished but probably written shortly before "Love Songs,"

Loy (1882–1966) argues that "woman must destroy in herself the desire to be loved" and urges that "honor, grief, sentimentality, pride and consequently jealousy must be detached from sex." Employing a form of collage that is primarily conceptual, rather than both conceptual and visual, the "Love Songs" accomplish that and more. Loy concludes that all the values embedded in masculinity and femininity are perilous and destructive. Idealization of female purity and virtue, for example, is "the principle instrument of her subjugation."

As the sequence begins, the speaker has already failed at conventional romance – steeped in all the drama of stereotyped emotions – and opts instead not for unreflective animal sexuality but for something like a verbally inventive biological union. The sequence repeatedly offers up the illusory dramas of gender ("I am the jealous storehouse of the candle-ends / That lit your adolescent learning") only to reject them; repeatedly, in their place, Loy offers us versions of intercourse that invent figures for bodily fluids and anatomy:

> . . . laughing honey
>
> And spermatozoa
> At the core of Nothing
> In the milk of the Moon
>
> Shuttle-cock and battle-door
> A little pink-love
> And feathers are strewn

Some critics have concluded that these are images of degraded lust; they seem instead to be anti-romantic but also celebratory. Moreover, their variety and surprising capacity to recode the rhetoric of romance ("honey," "the milk of the Moon," "pink-love," and "feathers" above all reposition romance tropes) demonstrate that a degendered human sexuality – one freed of cultural cliches about men and women – need not be impoverished. Loy's experimental form is wedded to a cultural project of rethinking the nature of human sexuality.

Yet the other clear masterpiece of experimental modernism grounded in a collage aesthetic is no doubt Ezra Pound's (1885–1972) major lifetime project. Perhaps no other major modern American poet's work is so deeply and irreducibly conflicted. Pound was at once the impresario of high modernism – promoting the work of those contemporaries he admired, among them H. D., Marianne Moore, and James Joyce; editing T. S. Eliot's *The Waste Land* so drastically he is almost its co-author; defining the Imagist movement and making metrical innovation and metaphoric concision central to modernist poetics – and its most tragic figure, undermined by his own arrogance and eventually allied with the worst political impulses of the century. One may compare two early poems, "Portrait d'une Femme" (1912) and "The River-Merchant's Wife: A Letter" (1915), to get a glimpse of how divided his impulses can be; the first is arguably misogynist, the second almost a sympathetic interior portrait. Decades later he would leave officially unfinished, but for all practical purposes complete, a major poem sequence torn between utopianism and bestiality.

Born in Idaho and raised in Pennsylvania, he would earn an MA in Romance Languages at the University of Pennsylvania, teach briefly, and then depart for Europe. But he remained interested in America for years and put himself in direct conflict with his country during World War II. Pound's major poetic achievement, and the focus of decades of his life, is *The Cantos* (1915–1969), a book-length sequence of 116 poems that is unquestionably at once one of the most influential and most controversial documents of twentieth-century literature. The poem's learning and system of unexplained references are immense; like all passionate learning it is also periodically idiosyncratic. No one save Pound himself was likely have ready to hand both the range of classical references and the unconventional economic and cultural theories he cites. Pound himself was effectively the only reader fully prepared to read his poem. Unlike Eliot or Melvin Tolson, moreover, he published no notes with *The Cantos*, though when he read Canto 46 over shortwave radio from Mussolini's Italy in World War II, he did preface it with some glosses, so he was clearly aware that the ordinary reader would either need a course of study or a handbook. Pound pioneered the distribution of what one critic liked to call "radiant gist" throughout *The Cantos*, brief allusions that are designed to invoke a whole historical and emotional context for the reader.

Pound called *The Cantos* "a poem containing history," and in that deceptively neutral, if potentially grandiose, formulation inheres the poem's great challenge. For *The Cantos* is history as Pound saw it; to some degree the poem sequence is also history as he participated in it, albeit in a modest but unforgettable way. Some critics have tried to separate Pound's political views from his art – among them those who supported his receipt of the first Bollingen prize for his "Pisan Cantos" in 1949, an award that sparked a firestorm of debate at the time – but only a casual or self-deceptive reader of *The Cantos* can manage that trick. The poems are replete with Pound's enthusiasm for and defense of the nightmare of European fascism; over fifty million people died in World War II, and Pound believed the wrong side won. Moreover, as Pound looked over history he decided that all the arts were at their best when allied with absolute political power. He made such an alliance himself in Italy, and *The Cantos* repeatedly urges it on us as one route to a new Golden Age. None of this makes the poems easier to deal with, but none of it makes them less interesting either. The relationship between poetry and power receives in *The Cantos* its most compromising realization, as one of our most accomplished poets decides the century's most evil means served glorious ends.

Pound was initially contemptuous of Germany's dictator Adolf Hitler; Mussolini was his contemporary hero. Yet Pound gradually became an admirer of the Nazis, and in a wartime radio broadcast from Rome announced that in *Mein Kampf* (1925), Hitler's anti-Semitic and megalomaniac manifesto, history is "keenly analyzed." Certainly Pound's racial theories found more reinforcement in Hitler than in Mussolini. Yet Pound's anti-Semitism was firmly in place early on; as early as his 1914 *Blast* poem "Salutation the Third," Pound had written, "Let us be done with Jews and Jobbery, / Let us SPIT upon those who fawn on the JEWS for their money." Pound's decades-long jeremiad against usury, or money lending (see Canto 45) was for him also a denunciation of world Jewry. In his 1941–1943 wartime radio broadcasts, published as *"Ezra Pound Speaking": Radio Speeches of World War II* (1978) he rails against the Jews unceasingly, against them and their fantasized allies, "Jews, Jews-playfellows, and the bedfellows of Jews and of Jewesses" (113). "The danger to the United States as a system of government is NOT from Japan, but from Jewry" (86). President Franklin D. Roosevelt he sometimes called "Rosenfeld" to suggest his fantasy dominance by Jewish interests. In Canto 73, published in an Italian military journal in 1945, Pound calls Roosevelt and Churchill "bastards and small Jews." He warned us in the radio broadcasts that "any man who submits to Roosevelt's treason to the Republic commits breech of citizen's duty" (104). Meanwhile, from time to time he tried to persuade American troops they would lose the war. For an American citizen to give aid and comfort to the enemy in the midst of a declared war is a capital offense. When Pound was captured by American troops in 1945 he was headed toward a US trial for treason; government agencies had recorded his broadcasts. The likely verdict was not in doubt, but a group of friends intervened and had him declared insane. It was a ruse, since he was no more insane than some millions of Germans who shared his beliefs, but it kept him alive. The price he paid was to be confined to St. Elizabeth's Hospital in Washington DC from 1946 to 1958.

Despite this anguished history *The Cantos* remains the primary model for an ambitious American poem based on collage and historical and literary citation. Poets at the opposite end of the political spectrum from Pound, including Charles Olson and Robert Duncan, were deeply influenced by Pound's technique. And *The Cantos* themselves are richly conflicted texts – at once lyrical and polemical, visionary and demonic – that well reward the investment required to read them carefully. It is possible also to identify what amounts to the spine of the sequence, a selection that highlights the entanglement of aesthetics and politics, that emphasizes the compromised ambitions that make the poem compelling reading. Canto 1 gives us Pound's epic ambitions at their most pure.

Canto 9 presents the fatal allure of aestheticized power that would haunt Pound for the rest of his life. It is the second of the four 1923 Malatesta Cantos (8–11), which are at the core of Pound's whole project. They concern Sigismundo Pandolfo Malatesta (1417–1468), a famous *condottiere* (Italian leader of mercenary soldiers), military engineer, and patron of the arts. Malatesta grew up in the age when Italian city states, formally subservient to the Pope, warred with one another and competed for power and papal recognition. Malatesta became Lord of Rimini, Fano, and Cesena at the age of fifteen, but he would have to defend his domain for the rest of his days, and his means were sometimes ruthless. Yet he also patronized poets and painters (who often took Malatesta himself as their subject) and employed the greatest artists of his day to design and build a temple at Rimini. The Tempio, honoring Malatesta and his mistress Isotta, was never quite finished and thus remained in part a "monumental failure." For Pound, these aesthetic ends justify Malatesta's sometimes murderous means. He is the prototype for Pound of a leader who kills with warrant in the service of a purported ideal of achievement; Mussolini for Pound would be a contemporary Malatesta. As Pound will note in Canto 80, Malatesta's Tempio was damaged by World War II Allied bombers in the effort to "cwuth Mutholini" (crush Mussolini). Toward the end of World War II Pound thought the Tempio had been entirely destroyed. In effect, *The Cantos* became Pound's own unfinished, ruined Tempio.

Canto 45 (1936) is Pound's towering brief against usury:

> With usura hath no man a house of good stone
> each block cut smooth and well fitting . . .
> WITH USURA
> wool comes not to market . . .
> Usura slayeth the child in the womb . . .

Canto 81 (1948) juxtaposes apologies for fascism with lyrical invocations of nature; for a moment he verges on humility – "Pull down thy vanity" – then rejects it and denies that vanity defined either his ambitions or Mussolini's: "But to have done instead of not doing / this is not vanity." Finally, in a mixture of multi-linguistic collage and counterpointed arguments, Canto 116 and the unfinished fragments give us the competing tensions in Pound's life and work in their most condensed form:

Tho' my errors and wrecks lie about me,
And I am not a demigod,
I cannot make it cohere.

Consistently both conceptual and visual, Pound's lifelong project in *The Cantos* traverses much of the modern period and provides one continuing model for a modernist aesthetic. Yet it is not the only major strain in experimental American poetry. Loy's work, notably, is both conceptually and linguistically experimental and its relentlessly innovative verbal character places it simultaneously in that linked experimental tradition. The major figure in linguistically experimental modernism, inspiration to a whole generation of poets in the second half of the century, is without question Gertrude Stein (1874–1946).

Born in Allegheny, Pennsylvania, Stein studied art and medicine before moving to France in 1902 and establishing what would become a famous Paris salon. By the end of the decade Stein had met her lifelong companion and collaborator, fellow American expatriate Alice B. Toklas. Increasingly influenced by the visual arts and by experimental modernism, Stein wrote both recognizable narratives like *Three Lives* (1909) and playful experimental texts like *Tender Buttons* (1914). In her experimental mode she was arguably the most radical and forward looking of all modernists. "Patriarchal Poetry" is a 1927 prose poem that did not make its way into print until decades later. Yet it may be the only fully realized and rigorous deconstructive poem in American modernism. Can the poem, the title implicitly asks, be *about* patriarchal poetry, or is it to be an instance *of* patriarchal poetry? The parameters of that question are immediately ruptured. For the "poetry" referred to here is not just a literary genre but rather the poetics of everyday thought. "Patriarchal poetry" is the metaphoric logic ruling the meanings that make our culture what it is. The ambiguity of the title thus reflects Stein's judgment that everything one writes will be in some ways patriarchal. A critique of patriarchal poetry cannot be mounted from a position outside it. The only strategy for demolition is a defamiliarizing burlesque from within: "Patriarchal Poetry in pieces."

Using witty and strategically staged repetition, variation, and rhyme, Stein exposes hierarchical and gendered biases built into the most unassuming usages. Repetition short-circuits the expectation that words and phrases can function as neutral syntactic units and frees us to recognize patterns of semantic association that all language carries with it in use: "They said they said they said when they said men. / Men many men many how many many many men men men said many here" (p. 280). "Men," we hear here is always a statement, always an assertion, always a cultural imprimatur. In patriarchal poetics "they said" always means "men said." Patriarchy's differences are really the repetition of the same: the honorific imposition of the law of male priority, "patriarchal poetry as signed."

Repetition and variation let Stein place a variety of words, phrases, and concepts under philosophical and cultural pressure, so that all the components of a statement are shown to be permeated with the assumptions of patriarchal poetry. This technique also isolates and decontextualizes words and phrases, seeming at first to turn them into unstable echolalic nonsense, but thereby severing them from their syntactical functionalism and making it possible to see them as counters in a very different semantic game. On the other side of nonsense is the world view that patriarchal poetics continually reinforces: "Patriarchal poetry makes no mistake"; "Patriarchal poetry is the same as Patriotic Poetry."

Patriarchal poetry is the poetics of unreflective reason and order, of officious segmentation and classification – often to comic effect: "Patriarchal poetry and not meat on Monday patriarchal poetry and meat on Tuesday. Patriarchal poetry and venison on Wednesday Patriarchal poetry and fish on Friday Patriarchal poetry and birds on Sunday." Patriarchal poetry is therefore a poetics of marching: "One Patriarchal Poetry. / Two Patriarchal Poetry. / Three Patriarchal Poetry." It is the signature of the authority of the nation-state and of the corollary authority of the individual male person: "signed by them. / Signed by him." Stein's poem does not proceed in a linear way; that would be to adopt the armature she wants to disavow. So she works by indirection. But the poem does have signal moments of disruption and revelation. The first of these occurs as a serial eruption of the phrases "Let her be," "Let her try," and "Let her be shy." These are pleas for space for women's freedom and commands disseminating women's differences through the language. "Let her be" is also the letter "b," whose additive and secondary character Stein offers in place of patriarchal claims for priority, origin, and power.

Equally – and relentlessly – experimental, though in her own terms, is Marianne Moore (1887–1972). Born in Kirkwood, Missouri, and raised in Carlisle, Pennsylvania, Moore shared a house with her mother all her life, much of it working on a series of jobs in the New York area, but always focusing on writing. Notably, her use of quotation in her poems is as elaborate as that of T. S. Eliot, but to quite different purposes. If Eliot aimed for magisterial allusiveness, Moore aimed for something more complex and subversive, to model the cultural constitution of knowledge and understanding. Her poems braided of multiple sources are, at their most ambitious, social and philosophical investigations of great subtlety. "Marriage" (1924) and "An Octopus" (1924) are the most important poems of this impulse. She also had continuing political and historical interests, as two poems about Ireland – "Sojourn in the Whale" (1921) and "Spenser's Ireland" (1941) make clear.

On one level Moore's "Marriage" is a strikingly even-handed demolition of the illusion that either party to a marriage can so divest himself or herself of self-absorption and self-interest to make a union possible. "He loves himself so much," she writes, "he can permit himself / no rival in that love." But the poem is much more than an analysis of the pitfalls in gender relations. It actually moves centripetally and centrifugally at the same time, treating marriage not only as a site on which individuals and the culture as a whole act out their contradictory investments in independence and community but also as a figural resource that informs all compromised institutions in the culture. Thus the poem is at once about the marriage two people make and about the marriage the states made to form one country – "Liberty and union / now and forever." Both require "public promises / of one's intention / to fulfil a private obligation" and both "can never be more / than an interesting impossibility." Marriage is an institution constructed by contractualized idealization and a model for comparably problematic institutions of other sorts. Marriage in the poem is effectively thus both victim and purveyor of illusions within the culture.

At just under 300 lines, "Marriage" is a relatively long poem. *The Waste Land* was just over 400. They are dwarfed by *The Cantos*, but they all exemplify the modern American interest in the long poem that is formally and verbally experimental. Though equally linked to the lyric tradition, Hart Crane's *The Bridge* (1930) is also an experimental long poem. Born in a small Ohio town, Crane (1899–1932) grew up in Cleveland. He went to New York after leaving high school, but ended up returning to Cleveland until 1923, along the way accumulating work experience in advertising agencies, a newspaper, and in his father's businesses. He faced continual difficulty and much stress supporting himself and had to rely on relatives and a benefactor. The first phase of his career includes such Imagist poems as "October-November" (1916) and the remarkable "Episode of Hands" (1920), one of the most beautiful of explicitly homosexual poems from the modernist period, but his major legacy is *The Bridge*.

The sheer ambition of this book-length project frustrated Crane's attempts to begin it from 1923 to 1926. A change of location from New York City to a summer cottage on the Isles of Pines off the Cuban coast resulted in an outburst of new writing, and all but four of the poem's fifteen sections were substantially complete when an October 1926 hurricane devastated the island. The poem sequence takes its title and the focus of its opening and closing poems, "Proem" and "Atlantis" from a much-celebrated piece of

New York architecture and engineering, the Brooklyn Bridge. Widely considered both an aesthetic triumph and a highly successful technical project, the bridge, for Crane stands as a symbol of American ambition and spirit combined. By reaching back into American history to Columbus's return voyage from the New World ("Ave Maria"), traveling through the Mississippi River region by train in the present day ("The River"), and then imaginatively flying by plane over the east coast of the United States ("Cape Hatteras"), Crane attempts to articulate a unifying vision of America.

Yet if the bridge is a transcendent and ecstatic symbol, the airplane in "Cape Hatteras" is sometimes a demonic one, given over to war rather than cultural poetry. The conflict is resolved, if at all, in the controversial bravado performance of "Atlantis," the final poem, which is one of the most rhetorically flamboyant texts among American long poems. Like Muriel Rukeyser's "The Book of the Dead" eight years later, *The Bridge* chooses commercial enterprises and construction projects as images of both greed and transcendence. Like her poem, too, it creates a unifying myth out of the most resistant materials. Reacting to Eliot's *The Waste Land*, both poets wrote long poem sequences that were American rather than international. Crane also wished to substitute cultural optimism for Eliot's bleak pessimism and to imagine that collaborative human work could offer some hope for the future. At the end, Crane saw little hope for his own; only thirty-three years old, he jumped overboard from a boat returning from Mexico and drowned.

Unlike Crane, from the outset, Rukeyser (1913–1980) was at once a political activist and a visionary. At times, as in "The Book of the Dead" (1938), those qualities were intensified and in those moments she was simultaneously a revolutionary and a mystic. But to grasp the forces that drive her work – through a career that spanned five decades of American history – we have to come to terms with a visionary impulse rooted in time, embedded in a struggle with lived history. Consider as a case in point the rhapsodic images she crafts to voice the mother's anguish at the death of her sons in "Absalom" from "The Book of the Dead." To understand her work we must also embrace the larger, wiser notion of politics that underlies all her poetry. For she understood early on what so many Americans could not: that politics encompasses all the ways that social life is hierarchically structured and made meaningful. Politics is not only the large scale public life of nations. It is also the advantages and inequities and illusions that make daily life very different for different groups among us. Thus Rukeyser understood that race and gender are integral parts of our social and political life. Never officially a feminist, she nonetheless devoted herself, as she does in "Rite," to voicing women's distinctive experience throughout her career.

Although Rukeyser wrote numerous short, tightly controlled poems like "The Minotaur" (1944), it may well be that her most rich and suggestive accomplishments are her poem sequences. "The Book of the Dead" is one of the major poem sequences of American modernism. Based on Rukeyser's own research in West Virginia, it combines historical background, congressional testimony, and the voices of a number of victims in telling the story of a 1930s industrial scandal: a company building a tunnel for a dam decided to double its profit by rapidly mining silica at the same time (without any of the necessary precautions). A great many workers died of lung disease as a result. "The Book of the Dead" is thus also one of Rukeyser's many poems that reflect and contribute to her political activism.

Rukeyser was born and raised in New York City. During the 1930s she regularly wrote for Communist Party publications like *New Masses*. She was in Spain in 1936 to cover the antifascist Olympics in Barcelona when the Spanish Civil War broke out. She described that experience in the long poem "Mediterranean" and returned to the subject throughout her life. Years later, in 1975, she went to South Korea to protest the poet Kim Chi-Ha's imprisonment and anticipated execution; the poem sequence "The Gates" grew out of that trip.

Although "The Book of the Dead" is self-evidently an ambitious experimental long poem, it is usually omitted from accounts of American modernism. There is little question why. For "The Book of the Dead" is one of the highlights of our most pervasively radical political decade, the 1930s, and many scholars, steeped in the anxieties of the cold war, have preferred to ignore this most overtly political poetry. As the Depression deepened in the early 1930s, large numbers of Americans, including both young and established writers, Rukeyser among them, were increasingly drawn to the Left or to the Communist Party. There was a widespread conviction that capitalism had failed, that the old order could not be restored, and that only the most thoroughgoing social and political change could bring about social and economic justice. A number of active poets had already been writing from that perspective in the 1920s. For one thing, the much heralded "roaring twenties" had not brought economic health to everyone. Not only agriculture but also the entire rural economy had remained depressed throughout the decade; moreover, several major industries were already in recession before the stock market crash of 1929. Especially in the South and in depressed areas in the north, working-class and labor poets, along with poets affiliated with socialism, had been writing about economic inequities for years. Subcultural traditions of protest poetry stretched back into the nineteenth century, and some of the poets in those traditions felt themselves to be not only individual voices but also participants in movements for social change.

The Depression's impact on poverty, combined with the continuing influence of the Harlem Renaissance of the 1920s and the resurgence of violent racism in the same decade, would lead to intensified protests against racism from numerous poets. Langston Hughes would open the decade with one of his most compressed and searing indictment's of America's founding betrayal of its ideals, his poem "Christ in Alabama" (figure 3.2).

Two hundred years of racial trauma are driven full force into this thirteen-line, forty-seven word poem. Cast out, vilified, and crucified, the historical Christ returns to earth in serial fashion – in the person of every black man "beaten and black," every slave, every lynching victim, every post-Civil War black denied the full rights of citizenship. It asks a contemporary American reader to understand the black man as the Christ of our time. Of course the archetypal black victim is the product of rape, especially the white rape of a black woman, for then the white father can repress his paternity by murdering his own son. The South's omnipresent and universally denied trinity – white father, black mother, and ostracized black son – form the background for the South's repeated crucifixion scene: *"Nigger Christ / On the cross of the South."*

It is a poem that calls out to waken the world and change it. For a brief moment in American literary history, writing poetry became a credible form of revolutionary action. Reading poetry, in turn, became a way of positioning one's self in relation to the possibility of basic social change. Earlier, the IWW's poems set to music had been among the IWW's most successful recruitment devices. Now, to read a poem like Langston Hughes's "Let America be America Again" (1936) was to find more than an echo of one's own sense of cultural crisis and necessity. It was to find a place to stand ideologically, a concise discursive perspective on America's history and engagement with its contemporary culture. It was also to find a voice one could temporarily take up as one's own. Poetry at once gave people radical critique and visionary aspiration, and it did so in language fit for the speaking voice. It strengthened the beliefs of those already radicalized and helped to persuade some who were not yet decided. It was thus a notable force in articulating and cementing what was a significant cultural and political shift toward the Left. To write poetry under these conditions of readership was therefore to ask not only what one wanted to say but also what other people wanted to read; the sense of audience was pressing, immediate. A revolutionary poem in a magazine or newspaper could be taken up and used by an audience only days or weeks after it was written. Thus when Angelo Herndon, a black Communist unconstitutionally charged with "attempting to incite insurrection" for helping to organize a Georgia hunger march, was released on bail in 1934, poems celebrating his August 7 arrival in New York were written

Christ in Alabama

Christ is a Nigger,
Beaten and black—
O, bare your back.

Mary is His Mother—
Mammy of the South,
Silence your mouth.

God's His Father—
White Master above,
Grant us your love.

Most holy bastard
Of the bleeding mouth:
Nigger Christ
On the cross of the South.

Figure 3.2 Illustration for Langston Hughes's "Christ in Alabama," *Contempo* (December 1931).

and published within days. Alfred Hayes's "Welcome to Angelo Herndon" appeared in *The Daily Worker* on August 9; Michael Blankfort's "Angelo Herndon's Bail" was published in the same newspaper on August 15; and Edwin Rolfe's "Homecoming" was in the August 21 issue of *New Masses*. When such poems offered readers politically committed speaking voices with which they could identify, the poems were in a sense a gift to prospective readers, a text whose authorship was inherently transferrable. To publish a poem that might prove politically persuasive was, in effect, to ask readers to live by way of these words as if they were their own.

The mass audience for poetry in the Depression was, paradoxically, one of the triumphs of a time of widespread suffering. To begin to understand what it meant to be a poet on the Left in the Depression, it is necessary to extend that recognition to the whole cultural field and accept it as a general paradox that typifies life in that period. Hand in hand with hunger and unemployment and the many difficulties of everyday life went a sense of impending revolutionary change. For those poets who participated in the mass movement of the 1930s the period combined sometimes desperate hardship with something like utopian exhilaration. Writing poetry often meant helping to articulate and dramatize both the period's suffering and its characteristic yearnings for change. To write poetry was not only to comment on these cultural processes but also to help shape them. And you were not alone. Down the street, across town, and in towns and cities across the country other poets were contributing to the cultural climate in much the same way.

One of the more interesting changes brought about by the culture's redefinition of poetry's mission was in the concept of authorship, a corollary to a shift away from an emphasis on self-expressive subjectivity. It is perhaps the worker's correspondence poem of the 1930s, the found poem of that era, that most clearly displaced notions of authorship and originality. Tillie Olsen (1912–), who was then writing under her maiden name Lerner, wrote the poem "I Want You Women up North to Know" (1934), based on a letter that had been published in the January 9, 1934, issue of *New Masses*, under the heading "Where the Sun Spends the Winter," a version of the slogan adopted by a Texas Chamber of Commerce as the motto for a tourist campaign. The letter describes the impossible lives of four women who survive by hand-embroidering children's dresses for a few pennies each. The author of the letter, Felipe Ibarro, may well have been a journalist or a social worker or perhaps simply an activist, so the letter is not the direct testimony of the workers described but reported testimony that is already self-consciously rhetorical. Nonetheless, it offers one interesting version of this distinctive 1930s genre. It is worth comparing the opening two paragraphs of the letter with the first three stanzas of the poem. Here is the opening of the letter:

> I want the women of New York, Chicago and Boston who buy at Macy's, Wannamaker's, Gimbel's and Marshall Field to know that when they buy embroidered children's dresses labeled 'hand made' they are getting dresses

made in San Antonio, Texas, by women and girls with trembling fingers and broken backs.

These are bloody facts and I know, because I've spoken to the women who make them. Catalina Rodriguez is a 24-year-old Mexican girl but she looks like 12. She's in the last stages of consumption and works from six in the morning till midnight. She says she never makes more than three dollars a week. I don't wonder any more why in our city with a population of 250,000 the Board of Health has registered 800 professional 'daughters of joy' and in addition, about 2,000 *Mujeres Alegres* (happy women), who are not registered and sell themselves for as little as five cents.

Here are the opening stanzas of the poem:

> i want you women up north to know
> how those dainty children's dresses you buy
>   at macy's, wannamaker's, gimbels, marshall fields,
> are dyed in blood, are stitched in wasting flesh,
> down in San Antonio, "where sunshine spends the winter."
>
> I want you women up north to see
> the obsequious smile, the salesladies trill
>   "exquisite work, madame, exquisite pleats"
> vanish into a bloated face, ordering more dresses,
>   gouging the wages down,
> dissolve into maria, ambrosa, catalina,
>   stitching these dresses from dawn to night,
>   in blood, in wasting flesh.
>
> Catalina Rodriguez, 24,
>   body shrivelled to a child's at twelve,
> catalina rodriguez, last stages of consumption,
>   works for three dollars a week from dawn to midnight.
> A fog of pain thickens over her skull, the parching heat
>   breaks over her body.
> and the bright red blood embroiders the floor of her room.
>   White rain stitching the night, the bourgeois poet would
> say,
>   white gulls of hands, darting, veering,
>   white lightning, threading the clouds,
> this is the exquisite dance of her hands over the cloth,
> and her cough, gay, quick, staccato,
>   like skeleton's bones clattering,
> is appropriate accompaniment for the esthetic dance
>   of her fingers
> and the tremulo, tremulo when the hands tremble with pain.
> Three dollars a week,

two fifty-five,
seventy cents a week,
no wonder two thousand eight hundred ladies of joy
are spending the winter with the sun after he goes down . . .

Olsen works with Ibarro's letter to draw out its drama and intensify the metaphoric power of the suffering it recounts. The poem's title, drawn from the letter, serves as a refrain line that becomes a paradigm for North/South relations and for those who benefit, often indifferently and sometimes in ignorance, from economic exploitation. Olsen uses her own metaphors as well as Ibarro's, but her poem remains nonetheless an inventive extension of the original letter. Keeping true to Ibarro's wish to have women up north understand the economic and social relations that are hidden within the clothing they buy, Olsen adds a passage describing a department store where the children's dresses are sold. Notably, however, the poem's most explicit challenge – a challenge built into the original letter – is not to the businessmen who hire the dressmakers or to the department store owners who sell them but to the consumers who buy them and thus fuel the entire set of transactions. Olsen is not alone in focusing on how ordinary people's actions help sustain economic exploitation – Kenneth Fearing, for example, often satirizes the way people's illusions reinforce the ideology of the marketplace – but attacks on industrialists were certainly more common during the period.

The primary change from Ibarro's text to Olsen's, as with most poems based on worker correspondence, is the generic shift itself, the move from prose to poetry. This is a shift Olsen embraces, but with uneasiness, as her effort to emulate (and thereby critique) a bourgeois poet's lyrical evocation of Catalina Rodriquez's dying efforts at embroidery suggests: "White rain stitching the night, the bourgeois poet would say, / white gulls of hands, darting." Yet Olsen cannot actually cast out the imagined bourgeois poet's literariness without casting out her own as well. She would reject an obfuscating metaphoricity that substitutes fantasies of birds on the wing for hand movements that are actually painful. Yet one could also take the line as celebrating a deft beauty in the midst of suffering. The poem, in short, puts forward an argumentative dichotomy which the poem itself simultaneously destabilizes and undermines, making the reader examine his or her own relationship to the moral and political implications of figurative language.

Such motives animate much of the political poetry of the 1930s, which often focuses on economic hardship and revolutionary change, on general social conditions rather than private experience. Even when individual experience is recounted, it is often recounted because of its representative character, its simultaneous enabling and determination by current history. With individual poets each offering alternative versions of life in the Depression and with poets hearing one another's work at group poetry readings and reading each other's work in books and magazines, it is not difficult to see how one is led not merely to read comparatively but to read chorally, to see these poems not as entries in a competition but as mutually responsive contributions to an emerging revolutionary consensus. That increases the impact of the poems, at least for those reading them as part of a movement. To read or write a 1930s political poem properly, then, is to be continually hailed by other voices. Here, for example, is a collage of quotations from poetry of the period that suggests both a collaborative critique of Depression era capitalism and a collective call for revolutionary change:

> The mills are down
> The hundred stacks
> are shorn of their drifting fume.
> The idle tracks
> rust . . .
> Smeared red with the dust
> of millions of tons of smelted ore
> the furnaces loom –
> towering, desolate tubes –
> smokeless and stark in the sun . . .
> (John Beecher)

> Flanking the freightyards: alleys, wooden shacks,
> And hovels: a grim battalion
> Of crouching rats covered down by the waters
> Of fog that trickles down their slimy backs.
> Near these: the blackened sheds
> Of foundries, smelting furnaces,
> And forges flanking the grey backs of the river
> (Stanley Burnshaw)

> the earth smoked and baked;
> stones in the field
> marked the dead land:
> coins taxing the earth.
> (Sol Funaroff)

> In these days of marking time,
> While the whole tense land marks time
> (Burnshaw)

Where there is no life, no breath, no sound, no touch, no warmth,
no light but the lamp that shines on a trooper's drawn and ready bayonet
                                        (*Kenneth Fearing*)

Our age has Caesars though they wear silk hats
                        (*Joseph Freeman*)

men, pig-snouted, puff
and puke at the stars
    (*Herman Spector*)

They burn the grain in the furnace while men go hungry.
They pile the cloth of the looms while men go ragged.
                            (*Stephen Vincent Benét*)

Under the sign of the coin and the contract,
under the mask of the two-faced double-dealing dollar,
under the fetish of the document, stocks and bonds,
the parchment faces trade in securities.   (*Funaroff*)

Men of paper, robbing by paper, with paper faces.
                                (*Benét*)

The friend of caesar's friend murders the friend
who murders caesar. The juggler of knives
slits his own throat. Tight-rope walkers
find democracy in public urinals.
Black-robed ministers stand with hatchet crosses;
the headsman hacks a worker's life to bone.
                                (*Funaroff*)

Then an end, an end to this. Say enough . . .
                (*Genevieve Taggard*)

The west is dying like a brood of aged birds
In the nests of their decay.
                (*Norman Macleod*)

America today; its fields plowed under . . .
its wide avenues blistered by sun and poison gas
                                (*Rolfe*)

And no lilacs bloom, Walt Whitman.
                (*Mike Gold*)

There is a rust on the land
                (*Benét*)

an unseen hand
Weaving a filmy rust of spiderwebs
Over . . . turbines and grinding gears.
                              (*Joseph Kalar*)

Oh Capital! even in your palaces of learning,
as in your streets and factories,
there is one constant study.

                                        Escape!
                              (*Isidor Schneider*)

We've eaten tin-can stew, tin-can java, tin-can soup
Inside the jungles of America!
We've slept in rain soaked gondolas, across ice-caked bars,
On top of wind-beaten boxes.   (*Robert Gessner*)

I'm not too starved to want food
not too homeless to want a home not too dumb
to answer questions come to think of it
it'll take a hell
of a lot more than you've got to stop what's
going on deep inside us when it starts out
when it starts wheels going worlds growing
and any man can live on earth when we're through with it.
                              (*Kenneth Patchen*)

The million men and a million boys,
Come out of hell
                    (*Horace Gregory*)

From harvest fields rise up
Bone-aching and flesh-sore
Bondsmen
          (*Ruth Lechlitner*)

and crawling back,
maybe they don't know what they're saying,
maybe they don't dare,
but they know what they mean:
Knock down the big boss . . .
hit him again, he cut my pay, Dempsey.
                              (*Horace Gregory*)

Awake and sing, you that dwell in the dust.
                              (*Funaroff*)

Brothers, Comrades, pool the last strength of men
in party, in mass, boil into form, and strike.
                              (*Taggard*)

let the workers storm from the factories,
the peasants from the farms;
sweep the earth clean of this nightmare.
                              (*Freeman*)

you shall rise in the dust of their cities
as a people of grass,
as roots out of dry ground.
                              (*Funaroff*)

If the dispossessed should rise,
Burning anger in their eyes . . .
Oh my brothers in the mire,
Clothe with lightning, shoe with fire . . .
                    (*Henry George Weiss*)

I am black and I have seen black hands
Raised in fists of revolt, side by side with the white
fists of white workers   (*Richard Wright*)

Fists tight-clenched around a crimson banner
                              (*Rolfe*)

Banners of rebellion, surging to the storm,
Rousing men to vision, turning cold blood warm
                              (*Lucia Trent*)

And we think
Of barricades in some red dawn
On the East Side of New York City
                    (*Norman Macleod*)

Split by a tendril of revolt
stone cedes to blossom everywhere
                    (*Muriel Rukeyser*)

The blood's unvoiced rebellion brooding under
This sorrow, this despair.   (*Burnshaw*)

We shall rise up, create our own new lands,
For the last frontiers are taken
                              (*Lechlitner*)

Poets, pickets
Prepare for dawn
          (*Rukeyser*)

Red in the sky our torches write
Resurgence over death
                    (*Lechlitner*)

The red train starts and nothing shall stop it
          (*Louis Aragon/ e. e. cummings*)

Scarlet seas surge
exultant upon new shores
                    (*Funaroff*)

into the red fields of sunrise
                    (*Funaroff*)

to grind the streets into the single lens
of revolution, and converge their massing thunder
to the one pure bolt of proletarian red.
                              (*Ben Maddow*)

Listen, Mary, Mother of God, wrap your new born babe in
the red flag of Revolution.   (*Langston Hughes*)

Now, the red revolution comes.
          (*Isidor Schneider*)

In the early 1930s it was partly the sense that capitalism had run its course and failed that led many of these poets to embrace the possibility of revolutionary change and to join a collective mode of writing. But with Hitler's rise to power in 1933, Japan's invasion of Manchuria, and Italy's invasion of Ethiopia, a new force entered the picture, a threat more terrible than unprincipled exploitation and severe inequity – the threat of fascism. The Communist International, or Comintern, called for a worldwide alliance between revolutionaries and progressives, a Popular Front to defeat fascism, in 1935, but many writers were not entirely ready to heed the call. Even the Communist Party's *Daily Worker* published revolutionary poems up through the early months of 1936. That winter the American Left celebrated a Popular Front victory in Spain, one that seemed destined to grant real relief to Spain's impoverished workforce. Then in July 1936 a group of right-wing army officers allied with conservative clergy, and reactionary politicians staged a revolt against the democratically elected government. The people themselves rose up in Madrid and Barcelona to crush the revolt, and the whole insurgency might well have ended within weeks. But Hitler and Mussolini intervened on the side of the rebel generals. What might have been a brief internal conflict turned into a two-and-a-half-year war with wide international implications. Thousands of volunteers joined the Comintern-organized International Brigades to help defend the Spanish Republic against its own army and German and Italian forces. And the choral poetry of revolution was transformed almost immediately into the still more coherent and more powerfully collective poetry of antifascism.

For a number of modern American poets, the period of the Spanish Civil War was a period when they were no longer primarily *American* writers; they were part of an international political struggle and an international community of writers. Part of what is important about American poets' contributions to the dialogue about Spain, therefore, is that a number of them figuratively gave up nationhood as the ground of their being. It is thus the very reverse of projects like Hart Crane's poem sequence *The Bridge* and William Carlos Williams's critical book *In the American Grain* (1925). If a number of American poets had earlier wondered how to give modernist experimentalism an American inflection, how to interweave collage with American sights and sounds, how to construct a myth that would enable uniquely American identities, now in the shadow of fascism the challenge was to enter the international arena seamlessly. My answer to one of my opening questions – what distinguishes American poetry and justifies giving it partial autonomy – is precisely its continuing obsession with American identity and its ongoing engagement with American history. But Spain is the exception that proves the rule.

Perhaps the quintessential American poem about the Spanish Civil War – because it captures both the idealism of the cause and the sense of loss and exile that followed the Spanish Republic's loss – is Edwin Rolfe's (1909–1954) "First Love" (1943):

Again I am summoned to the eternal field
green with the blood still fresh at the roots of flowers,
green through the dust-rimmed memory of faces
that moved among the trees there for the last time
before the final shock, the glazed eye, the hasty mound.

But why are my thoughts in another country?
Why do I always return to the sunken road through corroded hills,
with the Moorish castle's shadow casting ruins over my shoulder,
and the black-smocked girl approaching, her hands laden with grapes?

I am eager to enter it, eager to end it.
Perhaps this will be the last one.
And men afterward will study our arms in museums
and nod their heads, and frown, and name the inadequate dates
and stumble with infant tongues over the strange place-names.

But my heart is forever captive of that other war
that taught me first the meaning of peace and of comradeship
and always I think of my friend who amid the apparition of bombs
saw on the lyric lake the single perfect swan.

A decade later, the Popular Front consensus would be under sustained assault in the midst of the McCarthy period. For many of the revolutionary poets of the 1930s, 1954 would be a key year. Aaron Kramer (1921–1997) and Edwin Rolfe would each write a series of bleak but sometimes sardonic poems attacking the culture of the witch hunts. In Rolfe's "Little Ballad for Americans – 1954" the wit is inseparable from rage and anguish:

> Brother, brother, best avoid your workmate –
> Words planted in affection can spout a field of hate.
>
> Housewife, housewife, never trust your neighbor –
> A chance remark may boomerang to five years at hard labor.
>
> Student, student, keep mouth shut and brain spry –
> Your best friend Dick Merriwell's employed by the F. B. I.
>
> Lady, lady, make your phone calls frugal –
> The chief of all Inquisitors has ruled the wire-tap legal.
>
> Daughter, daughter, learn soon your heart to harden –
> They've planted stoolies everywhere; why not in kindergarten?
>
> Lovers, lovers, be careful when you're wed –
> The wire-tap grows in living-room, in auto, and in bed.
>
> Give full allegiance only to circuses and bread;
> No person's really trustworthy until he's dead.

For progressive poets writing in the early 1950s, the repressive culture of McCarthyism also renewed their anger at American racism. In 1952 Aaron Kramer published "Denmark Vesey," a long poem sequence about an 1821 South Carolina slave revolt that is a masterpiece of American modernism and the single most ambitious poem about race and African-American history ever written by a white American. His portrait of slave owner culture culminates in a nightmare vision:

> The lovely brocade their ladies wore
> had once been Negro grandmothers' hair.
> The gems that blinked on their arms like stars
> were bright Negro eyes that had lately shed tears.

Nature meanwhile is indifferent:

> Perhaps the free winds and the unbound waves
> rendered the lamentation of the slaves
> in language that the sky might understand . . .
> But from the sky's red mouth no answer came.

The only solution is resistance. A year later Melvin Tolson (1900–1966) published his dense, allusive masterpiece *The Libretto for the Republic of Liberia*. As rich with literary and historical allusions as *The Waste Land* – and with its own set of footnotes – Tolson's *Libretto* instead reflected on the history of slavery and the potential for liberation while the memory of European fascism was still fresh and the ravages of McCarthyism ongoing.

In 1956 Allen Ginsberg (1926–1997) published "Howl" and looked back on recent history, fusing autobiography with political and cultural analysis: "I saw the best minds of my generation destroyed by madness." Three years later Robert Lowell (1917–1977) would issue *Life Studies*. Uncannily, it too came out of a telling conjunction between personal anguish and historical experience, not unlike *The Waste Land*. But Eliot's mask of impersonality was altogether abandoned. Autobiography was now in the forefront of the poem. American modernism had come to an end.

4

STEPHEN WATT

Modern American drama

"Any account of American drama must begin by noting the casual disregard
with which it has been treated by the critical establishment. There is no single
history of its development, no truly comprehensive analysis of its achievement.
In the standard histories of American literature it is accorded at best a marginal
position."

> – C. W. E. Bigsby, *Modern American Drama, 1945–1990* (1992)

As disconcerting as it may be, C. W. E. Bigsby's observation about the "casual
disregard" American drama has suffered is true, perhaps even understated.
Indeed, writing just a few years earlier than Bigsby, Susan Harris Smith
more pointedly characterized American drama as an "unwanted bastard
stepchild," the most "maligned" and "unjustly neglected" area of American
literary studies.[1] She's right. Consider, for example, the paradoxical situation
in which well-known critic Harold Bloom found himself in introducing two
books on Arthur Miller, whose plays *Death of a Salesman* (1949) and *The
Crucible* (1953), among others, remain central to the American theatrical
repertory. In his "Introduction" to a 1987 collection of critical essays on
Miller, Bloom identifies what he regards as *the* "half-dozen crucial American plays": *Death of a Salesman*, which he disparages as reading "poorly";
Eugene O'Neill's *The Iceman Cometh* (1939, first produced, 1947) and
Long Day's Journey Into Night (1939–1941, first produced, 1956); Tennessee
Williams's *A Streetcar Named Desire* (1947), Thornton Wilder's *The Skin
of Our Teeth* (1942), and Edward Albee's *The Zoo Story* (1958). This list is
striking not only because of its brevity, but because of the implication that
no drama prior to the 1940s – the decade in which four of these six plays
had their premieres – is "crucial" to the American stage. Bloom wonders
aloud how a country that can claim such novelists as Nathaniel Hawthorne,
Herman Melville, Mark Twain, and William Faulkner, and poets like Walt
Whitman, Emily Dickinson, Elizabeth Bishop, and Wallace Stevens can
"offer us only O'Neill, Miller, and Williams as its strongest playwrights."[2]
The paradox surfaced again when, some years later, he included Miller in
a series entitled "Bloom's Major Dramatists" yet in a prefatory essay posed
what should be taken not as a rhetorical question, but a serious one: "Does
Miller, like Eugene O'Neill, write the plays of our moral climate, or have we

deceived ourselves into overestimating both of these dramatists?"[3] A "major dramatist," it seems, may not be so major after all, even if the series in which this query appears trumpets the writer in precisely this way. And Bloom is hardly alone in this ungenerous appraisal. In *The Theatre of Revolt* (1962), an influential primer of modernist dramatic ideology from Henrik Ibsen and Anton Chekhov through the absurdist innovations of Jean Genet, Robert Brustein featured only one American playwright, Eugene O'Neill, qualifying his praise in limited ways: "It becomes increasingly clear that O'Neill will be primarily remembered for his last plays . . . No major dramatist, with the possible exception of [Bernard] Shaw, has written so many second-rate plays."[4] A Nobel Prize winner in 1936, the only American dramatist ever so honored with this award, O'Neill developed into a "major talent"; and, as Thomas Postlewait observes, whatever quibbling about individual plays might exist, there is little disagreement in the "established history" that O'Neill brought American drama "to its 'maturity.'"[5]

The advent of a significant American drama in this established historical narrative thus does not coincide with the opening of the first professional theatre in America at Williamsburg, Virginia, in 1752; or with the appearance of Thomas Godfrey's *The Prince of Parthia* (1767), the first play written by an American to be performed by professional actors.[6] Rather, such an account describes an American theatre that struggled greatly even to be born. A warehouse was converted into a rough theatre in Philadelphia in 1749, only to be closed the next year by the city government; other venues were opened in New York and Philadelphia in the 1750s, and in Boston by 1794. In 1798, the Park Theatre, regarded by many as the first "substantial playhouse" in New York, was built to confirm the notion that playgoing was a "necessary concomitant of urban living."[7] Yet, managed by William Dunlap, often regarded as the "Father of American Theatre" and certainly one of its most vocal champions,[8] the Park floundered in the early 1800s, forcing Dunlap to declare bankruptcy in 1805. And, although early republican playwrights like Dunlap and Royall Tyler wrote successfully for the burgeoning American stage, the repertory was nonetheless dominated by British imports. Occasionally an American dramatist like John Augustus Stone would emerge to the forefront, as he did in 1829 with his play *Metamora; or, the Last of the Wampanoags*, a successful representation of a noble Native American chief and staple attraction as portrayed by actor Edwin Forrest. And, in the middle and later 1800s, American actors made their marks both in New York and London, the celebrated Booth family, for example: patriarch Junius Brutus Booth (1796–1852), born in London, and a star in both America and Europe; John Wilkes Booth (1839–1865), infamous as the assassin of President Lincoln; and, the most luminous of them all, Edwin Booth (1833–1893), acclaimed for his productions of Shakespeare, especially *Hamlet*, and well regarded in London as well (in 1881 and 1882, for example, he performed in *Othello* with Henry Irving, alternating the roles of Iago and Othello with his esteemed British counterpart).

Yet, as vital as the nineteenth-century theatre was in such major cities as New York, Philadelphia, Boston, and Chicago, it is difficult to refute Bloom's thesis that American drama prior to the twentieth century was not nearly so accomplished as its poetry and prose. But neither was drama on the nineteenth-century London stage. That is to say, like Bloom's compilation of canonical American poets and novelists of the nineteenth century, a roster of similarly accomplished British writers requires little effort to assemble. All the Romantic poets would make the list, as would Jane Austen, Charles Dickens, William Makepeace Thackeray, Robert Browning, Lord Tennyson, and others. By contrast, the names of successful dramatists like Douglas Jerrold, Tom Taylor, W. G. Wills, Tom Robertson, and, the most prolific of them all, Dion Boucicault (1820–1890), a Dublin-born playwright and actor whose plays achieved enormous popularity in England, Ireland, and America from the 1840s through to the end of the century, are little known or remembered. Just as the American stage required the maturation of Eugene O'Neill, so too the Victorian theatre awaited productions of Henrik Ibsen's plays in the 1880s and 1890s, the talents of such writers as Arthur Wing Pinero and Henry Arthur Jones, and in particular the work of those two transplanted Irishmen, Oscar Wilde and Bernard Shaw. For the most part, then, *modern* drama – a term that will be defined more carefully here but, for the moment, plays that aspired to more than commercial entertainments – was something of a late arrival on the London stage. Shaw's controversial *Mrs. Warren's Profession* was written in the early 1890s, yet not produced for a decade because of opposition by the Lord Chamberlain's Reviewer, a state censor; and *The Importance of Being Earnest*, hardly experimental in form or theme, appeared in 1895. Thus, if American drama before the rise of O'Neill amounted to a bastard cultural form of questionable merit, its British cousins failed also to live up to their more distinguished pedigree.

Why? Happily, the scope of this chapter does not require a consideration of the London and Dublin stages, but it *does* demand answers to more basic questions: What, for example, counts as a modern or modernist drama? What forces in America led both to its cultivation and, conversely, to the arrested development critics allege? To address both questions, a brief return to the nineteenth-century stage is warranted, a kind of revisitation of a troubled history, or histories. Then, the drafting of a kind of revisionist narrative is required, one *less* concerned with evaluation or the assessment of aesthetic value and *more* concerned with the cultural work that modernism and modern drama sought to accomplish. To be sure, this work enacts a revolt from both orthodox aesthetics and a dominant ideology, the very issues Brustein identifies, but also embodies a striving toward a new understanding of both a more complex human subjectivity and a more complicated multi-cultural nation. That is, I want to argue that numerous American playwrights working between 1880 and 1935 – playwrights whose names and work may, in some cases, scarcely be remembered today – were writing modern, if not *modernist*, plays of various formal characteristics that advanced the political and cultural commitments of contemporaneous literary work held in far greater esteem.

The struggle: two familiar stories

The difficult birth of a modern American drama is typically explained – or rationalized – in one of two familiar historical narratives, each based on a different premise. The first of these, perhaps the more commonly offered of the pair, is premised on a particular geography and economy. In it, modern drama's arrested development is attributed to the primacy of New York City, Broadway in particular, and then redressed by a series of movements against Broadway's hegemony. For, while Philadelphia occupied a position of centrality in the early American theatre, by 1825 or so New York rose to prominence, as theatrical expansion on and around Broadway, a central roadway in the city, occurred rapidly in the middle decades of the century. The opening of the 4,500-seat Broadway Theatre, modeled after London's Haymarket Theatre, in 1847 served as an emblem of New York's – and Broadway's – ascendance as the center of the American drama.[9] The centrality of New York theatre continues on to this day, although nothing in contemporary Manhattan can equal the estimated eighty playhouses built in the Broadway area between 1825 and 1900.[10] A similar surge in theatrical activity transformed entertainment in Victorian London. After the repeal of the Patent Act in 1843, a seventeenth-century law that restricted the number of houses allowed to produce so-called "legitimate" drama, some two theatres in London grew to twenty by mid-century and to sixty-one by 1900.[11] All of this industry confirms that drama was on the rise throughout the nineteenth century, attracting large audiences in New York, Philadelphia, and other rapidly expanding cities. But, if this is so, how could it also have suffered the kind of stunted growth its critics allege?

Answers to this question usually originate in nineteenth-century drama's audiences and the economics of theatrical practices designed to appeal to them. The populations of New York, Boston, and Philadelphia were exploding in the middle of the century with newly arrived African-Americans from the South and immigrants from Europe. During the early 1840s, for example, Boston greeted some 4,000 to 5,000 immigrants a year, but absorbed 37,000 new arrivals in 1847 alone, many of them poor Irish escaping the Great Famine that ravaged the country between 1845 and 1851.[12] Equally dramatic, Philadelphia's population of over 72,000 Irish-born residents in 1850 grew to more than 95,000 just a decade later, the majority of whom traveled through New York (where many elected to stay).[13] Poor and often uneducated, these new arrivals sought work in America's nascent industrial economy, and in what little leisure time was afforded them, few attended revivals of Shakespeare or productions of plays featured in a classical repertoire. Consequently, other entertainments emerged to attract popular audiences. Blackface minstrel shows, the origins of which are traced to the later 1820s, evolved in the 1840s and 1850s with such troupes as the Virginia Minstrels and a group headed by E. P. Christy. Not surprisingly, some of the most popular minstrel stars were actually Irish immigrants like Barney Williams (born Bernard O'Flaherty), who throughout the 1850s and 1860s went on to play in a series of successful Irish comedies and eventually managed Wallack's Theatre in New York. I say "not surprisingly," because as numerous cultural historians emphasize, Irish immigrants and African-Americans often found themselves in competition for employment and housing in the cities to which they had moved. In 1850s Philadelphia, for example, the Irish were "thrown together with black people on jobs and in neighborhoods," leading to the Census of 1850 including a class called "mulattoes" for the first time. One popular quip of the day has an African-American laborer complaining that "My master is a great tyrant . . . He treats me as badly as if I was a *common Irishman.*"[14] Williams also starred in *Uncle Pat's Cabin*, an Irish version of *Uncle Tom's Cabin*, which was successfully adapted for the stage within months of the publication of Harriet Beecher Stowe's novel in March 1852;[15] and in a series of comedies that, although succumbing to stereotypes of an inebriate Irishness rivaling those of Africans in minstrel shows, represented the Irish as self-reliant, disciplined, and sufficiently ambitious to survive in a modernizing America. In such vehicles for Williams as *Ireland and America* (1851) and *Irish Assurance and Yankee Modesty* (1854), playwright James Pilgrim "investigated strategies which allowed his comic protagonist to endorse modern values even as he pursued old-fashioned pleasures."[16] The assimilation of such new arrivals into a burgeoning multi-cultural America in the 1850s, therefore, was greatly facilitated by the theatre and such genres as the Irish comedy: important cultural work, in other words, can be achieved by means that might otherwise be dismissed as mere "entertainment."

The same positive valence cannot be found in the minstrel show, as the assimilation of Southern blacks was scarcely one of its *raisons d'être*. On the contrary, the culture of early 1840s New York, as Eric Lott describes in *Love and Theft*, was riven by class warfare: "Working people hit hard by economic disaster in the 1840s were to turn even more urgently to the new minstrel shows" in an attempt "to shore up 'white' class identities by targeting new enemies."[17] The Virginia Minstrels, founded in New York by Dan Emmett in the winter of 1842–1843, and the Christy Minstrels, started in the 1850s, presented such stock figures as Jim Crow, Mr. Tambo and Mr. Bones, and the later urban dandy Zip Coon. Music, lavish costuming and scenery, and conventional comic oratory entertained urban audiences at the same time as they advanced sharply delimited caricatures of blacks and blackness. Minstrel shows evolved after the Civil War, some even moving across the Atlantic (an adolescent James Joyce most likely saw so-called "coon impersonators" like Eugene Stratton in turn-of-the-century Dublin), and of course blackface performers like Al Jolson appeared in the emerging cinema. The influence of the minstrel show, particularly its racist stereotyping, extends into the present, as Ntozake Shange inveighed in her prefatory remarks to *Spell #7* (1979): "the minstrel may be 'banned' as racist/but the minstrel is more powerful in his deformities than our alleged rejection of him."[18] Her work and that of such contemporary dramatists as Amiri Baraka and August Wilson often confront representations of African-Americans that were given fuller expression in mid-nineteenth-century minstrel shows and persist into the present, however transformed or more subtly performed.

In addition to offering representations of immigrants and people of color – some positive, too many derogatory – in a vehicle designed for popular audiences, mid-nineteenth-century drama also entertained by providing elaborate treats for both the eyes and ears. The lavish costumes, music, and dancing of minstrel shows were paralleled by extravagant spectacle in such popular plays as Dion Boucicault's *The Poor of New York* (1857) and *The Octoroon* (1859), and Augustin Daly's *Under the Gaslight* (1867). Like historical drama of the period with its "archaeologically correct" sets and properties, plays like these were masterfully crafted to lead to so-called "sensation scenes": that is, scenes of high emotion and visual spectacle. *The Poor of New York* includes a roaring tenement fire; *The Octoroon*, an exploding steamboat; *Under the Gaslight*, the rescue of a character pilloried to a railroad track. The public's appetite for visual stimulation seemed almost insatiable, as numerous plays and musicals like *The Black Crook* (1866) required nearly six hours to be performed as scenery had to be struck and re-built. More significant than the exorbitant length of time such plays demanded, as one critic of the time complained about *The Black Crook*, were its myriad of aesthetic defects: "the scenery is magnificent; the ballet is beautiful; the drama is – rubbish."[19]

In England, Ireland, and America, this precise criticism of plays demanding elaborate scenic effects, yet based upon deplorable plots and flat characters, was revised into a mantra by proponents of a new and modern drama. Reviewing an extravagant 1895 production starring Henry Irving for the *Saturday Review* Bernard Shaw lamented, "[H]ow am I to praise this [play] when my own art, the art of literature, is left shabby and ashamed amid the triumphs of the arts of the painter and the actor?"[20] Envisioning an Irish Literary Theatre in 1897, William Butler Yeats responded similarly to a rehearsal with the remark that "the modern coats and the litter on the stage draw one's attention away from the dramatic world evoked . . . I want to be able to forget everything in the real world, in watching an imaginative glory."[21] To stage such "imaginative glories," Yeats turned to British designer Gordon Craig, whose stage innovations and writing exerted worldwide influence, not the least of which was felt in America. In his 1919 manifesto *The Theatre – Advancing* Craig, a son of Irving's long-time leading lady Ellen Terry and thus a habitué of Irving's fashionable Lyceum Theatre from the time of his youth, compared the "perishable" theatre with a more durable one. The former, characterized by sumptuous and expensive productions, leaves nothing behind but a trail of messy ledger books and forgettable plays:

> It is a negative affair at best, this present theatre. It has not durable qualities, neither will it perish sufficiently quickly. It costs as much as would a durable theatre, yet endures only a few years. The public of the present theatre is in love with the latest thing, and spends millions of money in order to have one glance at it . . . In fact the present theatre is the triumph of an effete public.[22]

Writing some sixty years after Craig, director Peter Brook leveled a similar charge, comparing a desired "Holy Theatre" with the present "Deadly Theatre" of Broadway and London's West End:

> On Broadway ticket prices are continually rising . . . As fewer and fewer people go through the doors, larger and larger sums cross the ticket office counter, until eventually one last millionaire will be paying a fortune for one private performance for himself alone . . .
> The artistic consequences are severe.[23]

Proponents of the "new drama" – a modern drama – like Craig, Yeats, Shaw, and American writers William Dean Howells, Clyde Fitch, and, in the 1910s, critic Sheldon Cheney expressed their dissatisfaction with the status quo long before Brook made his ominous prediction, advocating, in Howells' case, the advent of an Ibsenite stage realism and, in Cheney's, a Craig-like non-representational, poetic theatre.[24]

From the end of the nineteenth century, New York, especially Broadway, became associated with the promotion of visually sumptuous, yet intellectually mendacious, "eye candy." Moreover, as numerous historians emphasize, a Theatrical Syndicate which monopolized theatre ownership for several decades beginning in the mid-1890s made the production of new, untested dramas even more difficult.[25] One result, evident over the past century, has been a series of movements away from Broadway and commercial dramatic productions, beginning with the community theatre and "Little Theatre" movements of the *fin-de-siècle* and early decades of the twentieth century. Chicago's Hull-House Theatre, to take one example, combined social work with community theatre. Conceived by Jane Addams and Ellen Gates in 1889, the Hull-House Players (1897–1941) and Hull-House Theatre founded in 1901 anticipated what has become known as the Little Theatre Movement across the United States. Two of the most famous of these, Chicago's Little Theatre and Provincetown, Massachusetts's (later New York's) Provincetown Players, prompted British critic and translator of Ibsen, William Archer, to proclaim that modern drama in America was born outside of New York City and Broadway:

> The great hope of the future lies in the fertilization of the large by the little theater, of Broadway by Provincetown . . . in the region of Washington Square and Greenwich Village – or ultimately among the sand dunes of Cape Cod – we must look for the birthplace of the New American Drama.[26]

While the term "birthplace" concretizes a historical origin with more specificity than the facts might support – or, rather, hypostatizes the beginning of a New American drama as 1915, the year in which the Provincetown Players was founded – Archer's observation that a new kind of drama was emerging outside of New York is a trenchant one.

In 1910, British teacher and publisher Maurice Browne traveled to Chicago, motivated, according to biographers, by his love for actress Nellie Van Volkenburg who lived there. Encouraged by her and other friends, and inspired by the 1911 American tour of actors from Dublin's Abbey Theatre, Browne established an intimate playing space on Michigan Avenue across from the world famous Chicago Art Institute and mounted its first production in 1912. Economics, at least in part, determined that Browne's "little" theatre would be even smaller than he had planned. For when he realized he could not afford the rent of $25,000/year on the Fine Arts Theatre across from the Art Institute, he rented a space used for storage in the same building and renovated it into a playhouse that seated only ninety-one spectators.[27] In this way, Browne followed the sentiment William Butler Yeats expressed in a letter to a friend in 1897: "We have a literature for the people but nothing yet for the few."[28] Lady Augusta Gregory, co-founder with Yeats and Edward Martyn of the Abbey Theatre, urged Browne to start a theatre in his own "image," to train amateur actors and avoid "spoiled" professionals, and to overcome the lack of money with originality. Most important, she advised him not to confuse "theatric with literary values" and to remember "that poetry must serve the theatre before it can again rule there" (quoted in Lock, "Maurice Browne," 108). The results of Browne's experiment were enormously influential:

> The Chicago Little Theatre was to name a movement; and transferred – when in 1914 Margaret Anderson named her Chicago periodical *The Little Review* – the word "little" would characterize a style and a politics of modernism.
> (Lock, "Maurice Browne," 109)

That style, that politics, attracted a coterie audience that included Eugene Debs, activist Emma Goldmann, Clarence Darrow, and Theodore Dreiser. During its five years of existence and production of some 130 plays, small audiences at the Michigan Street playhouse witnessed then avant-garde European drama by Yeats, Shaw, their countryman John Millington Synge, Ibsen, Arthur Schnitzler, and symbolist writer Maurice Maeterlinck. They also experienced unconventional stagings and, in increasing amounts not to everyone's liking, puppet and dance theatre as well. At the Little Theatre, in other words, plays never before seen in America were afforded production – and often in ways seldom seen before on the American stage.

Among the attractions the Little Theatre audience did *not* see enough of, however, were new plays by *American* writers, a fact not lost upon two playgoers who called this to Browne's attention and would eventually move east to found the Provincetown Players in 1915:

> "Jig" [George Cram] Cook and Floyd Dell used to scold me, claiming that we presented too few plays by American dramatists. I used to retort that singularly few such plays were submitted, most of them unequivocally bad . . .
> (quoted in Lock, "Maurice Browne," 111–112)

And the few American plays produced at the Little Theatre – including Alice Brown's *Joint Owners in Spain*, a one-act comedy, and Cloyd Head's *The Grotesques* – seldom make even the footnotes or appendices of histories of modern American drama.

Not so with the work of the Provincetown Players, which fostered the talents of two enduring figures in the history of American drama: Susan Glaspell (1876–1948) and Eugene O'Neill. Irritated by the Washington Square Players' rejection of Glaspell's *Suppressed Desires* (1914), a one-act drama that comically skewers the contemporary rage for psychoanalytic theory, Glaspell's husband Jig Cook, with whom she had moved from the Midwest and collaborated, enlisted stage designer Robert Edmond Jones and local actors to produce it himself. In July of 1915, O'Neill appeared at the Cooks' door with a manuscript of his one-act play *Bound East for Cardiff*, one of several he would write from his experiences as a sailor. As produced by the Provincetown Players that summer, O'Neill and Glaspell's plays would eventually find a wider audience, one still growing today. Glaspell's *Trifles* (1916), *Bernice* (1919), and *The Verge* (1921) would all find an important niche in the history of modern American drama, as would an even greater number of O'Neill's plays. Like Browne in Chicago, Cook and his associates converted an unlikely space – in this instance at Provincetown, a ramshackle building on a wharf – into a crucible for the production of serious drama to a small, eager audience. In 1916, the Provincetown Players relocated to New York's Greenwich Village, where its productions would eventually garner the city's attention, especially in 1920 with the productions of O'Neill's *Beyond the Horizon* in February and *The Emperor Jones* in November. The *New York Times* hailed the former production and play as "memorable" and "significant"; *The Nation* asserted that *Beyond the Horizon* established "America's kinship with the stage of the modern world"; and Barnard Hewitt regarded the play as evidence that American drama had "come of age": "No longer need Americans look abroad for the best in contemporary drama; the native product could stand comparison with the finest Europe could offer" (*Theatre U. S. A.*, 333).

At least two points seem pertinent to and inferential from this history. First, for a modern drama to be conceived in America, it needed to escape Broadway and an expensive, commercial – or "Deadly" or "Perishable" – theatre, finding more receptive audiences elsewhere. Of course, at the start of the century some like Clyde Fitch echoed Lady Gregory's admonition to Maurice Browne, demurring in his 1904 article "The Play and the Public" that those who "demand literature in the theatre, at all cost," often ignore the fact that "the first requisite of a *play* is that it be some form of *drama*."[29] As Fitch recognized, drama is inseparable both from the theatrical practices which give it performative life, and from the audiences that grow accustomed to, even demand, certain qualities in the productions it supports. This is precisely why the Little Theatre Movement of the early twentieth century was followed in the 1950s by the so-called Off-Broadway Movement; and it is was off-Broadway where a 1952 revival of Tennessee Williams's *Summer and Smoke* paved the way for famous productions of O'Neill, Samuel Beckett, Edward Albee and others.[30] Similarly, the 1960s witnessed the birth of an "Off-Off" Broadway in warehouses, lofts, and coffeehouses, intimate spaces where non-commercial, alternative theatrical entertainments could be staged inexpensively for an audience very different from the one that supported musicals and comedies on Broadway. The early plays of some of America's most significant contemporary talents, including Sam Shepard, Adrienne Kennedy, Terrence McNally, and Marie Irene Fornés, received their first theatrical production off-off Broadway.

Second, a *modern* drama, either through form or content, attempts to express something new or "just now," as the Latin root of modern *modo* denotes. In the case of Glaspell's *Suppressed Desires*, that "new" reality includes the European psychoanalysis of Sigmund Freud and Carl Jung, an issue given its fullest expression on the American stage in a series of plays O'Neill wrote in the 1920s: *The Emperor Jones, Desire Under the Elms* (1924), *Strange Interlude* (1927), and *Mourning Becomes Electra* (1929). As these titles intimate, new understandings of such issues as "desire" and "mourning," especially those understandings linked to a revised, more complicated conception of human subjectivity, were sweeping America and Europe in the first three decades of the twentieth century. And such matters, however rife for satirical lancing in *Suppressed Desires*, found a receptive audience in America. By the 1910s and certainly by the 1920s, psychoanalysis was a topic of considerable discussion in American intellectual life. So important was it to the art of the Provincetown Players and especially to O'Neill, that Joel Pfister labels O'Neill and the theatre he helped bring into existence as "The Therapeutic Playwright" and "The Therapeutic Theatre." He quotes O'Neill himself in a 1932 essay as providing the most compelling evidence for his thesis:

> [I hope] to express those profound hidden conflicts of the mind which the probings of psychology continue to disclose . . . For what, at bottom, is the new psychological insight into human cause and effect but a study in masks, an exercise in unmasking.[31]

For this reason, O'Neill borrowed one technique from the Classical Greek theatre by experimenting with masks in such plays as *Mourning Becomes Electra* and *The Great God Brown* (1925), the masks connected to the troubled psyches of his protagonists. His deployment of masks provides only one small example of the numerous innovations in lighting, set design, and aural effects a modern drama would demand to realize its ends. Yet a certain subtlety also marks their use, as the burning buildings and exploding volcanoes of the nineteenth-century stage were replaced by nuance and restraint. Or, more accurately, the pyrotechnics required were simply smaller – and very different.

All of which suggests the second "familiar story" referenced above, one that relies upon a formal explanation of modern drama's uneasy development by citing the emergence at the end of the nineteenth century of a realistic drama to counteract melodrama's excesses – and defects. While this second history is theoretically separable from a narrative about Broadway's perishable theatre of spectacular effects, professional stars, and mediocre plays, the two are at another level irreducible. For melodrama, a portmanteau word combining "melody" and "drama," grew to dominate the repertories of mid- and later nineteenth-century companies because of its predictable attractions and excitements. To be sure, the varieties of melodramas that drew crowds to theatres in working-class immigrant neighborhoods were not identical to those produced in more fashionable venues; nevertheless, melodrama can be defined more generally by several formal characteristics. In a foreword to Elmer Rice's *The Adding Machine* (1923), one of America's most influential expressionist plays, Philip Moeller, co-founder of New York's Theatre Guild and director of several of O'Neill's plays in the 1920s, defined melodrama as "the type of play in which the situation . . . 'creates' the people as over against that mightier form called tragedy in which the inevitable character of the dramatis personae creates the situation."[32] In fact, melodramas typically create three predictable characters: a heroine, pure and virtuous, whose selflessness is both tested and re-affirmed by the dramatic action;[33] a villain, heartless and corrupt, who usually harbors both lust and avarice in his (or, occasionally, her) heart; and a hero who, although challenged severely, either saves the heroine or, at times, mourns her loss. Boucicault's antebellum play *The Octoroon* (1859) provides an example. Zoe, a beautiful and Juliet-like octoroon, is desired by both the villainous overseer M'Closky and the likeable, handsome George Peyton, a ladies' man transformed by Zoe's virtue. When George discovers Zoe's racial heritage, he bravely vows to love her whatever the consequences, which because of M'Closky's machinations include the loss of his widowed aunt's plantation and the sale of slaves loyal to her. The only way to save the home, at least as Zoe perceives it, is to allow George to marry a wealthy white woman who has always loved him, and this can only be accomplished by her swallowing poison at the play's conclusion. Punctuated by a fiery "sensation scene" and volatile slave auction where rivals battle over Zoe's purchase, *The Octoroon* both attracted audiences and corroborates Moeller's thesis.

In this explanation, melodrama amounts to "a means of affirming a belief in a reductive perception of reality,"[34] a perception as one-dimensional as the characters who occupy its world. Any filmgoer today understands the potency of such a formula: reduce the complexity of international terrorism (or intergalactic evil) to the motivation of a single "bad guy" or group and oppose this evil with heroes as played by Arnold Schwarzenegger or Harrison Ford; create spectacular effects in battles or calamities; add a beautiful woman to be rescued – or, better, one to help wage a battle against evil. Plays of this kind, in what Thomas Postlewait acutely labels the "suspect history" of American drama, are eventually replaced by a more serious drama represented by an Ibsen-like realism and later refined by the greater artistry of O'Neill. Such "teleological narratives," as Postlewait observes, "are hard to suppress" and even more difficult to support convincingly ("From Melodrama to Realism," 47). After all, *emergent* cultural forms don't simply *replace* prior ones; aesthetic "forms" are hardly ever so pure. "Most of the time," he observes, "we can find melodramatic elements in realistic drama and realistic elements in melodramatic plays." A process involving the "interpenetration of dramatic traits, attitudes, practices, and so on" goes on as the two forms travel parallel courses (55). Indeed, melodrama still thrives today, as I have suggested; it has never been washed away by the wake of a form called *realism*.

In this "suspect history" of American drama, realistic plays by such writers as James A. Herne, Clyde Fitch, and William Vaughn Moody followed in the footsteps of the dramatic revolution instigated by Ibsen, the publication of *A Doll's House* in 1879, and its first production later in London. There, the work of Pinero, Jones, and Shaw followed; in 1880s and 1890s America, a similar phenomenon occurred as vocally supported by such prolific playwright-commentators as Howells. But, we might ask, what was so "realistic" about *fin-de-siècle* realism? For its opponents, it seemed obsessed with the basest of human instincts, with desires that had never quite been represented so vividly on stage before and should never be seen again; for its champions, it marked the resurgence of a serious medium able to confront complex social, political, and psychological issues. Somewhat like melodrama, however, stage realism also relied upon a certain verisimilitude of visual representation, the most apt metaphor of which is the photograph. That is to say, realist drama on stage aspired to the scenic, even scientific, objectivity of the photograph. Such drama, as W. B. Worthen observes, "not only asserts a reality that is natural or unconstructed, it argues that such a reality can only be shown on stage by effacing the medium – literary style, acting, mis-en-scène – that discloses it." The "photographic" objectivity of the stage picture, moreover, also possesses the ability "to govern a behavioristic style of acting."[35] Unlike melodrama, in which actors routinely address the audience in asides and through a self-evident acting style replete with stock gestures, realistic drama demands acting that "erases itself from view"; the actor thus becomes a "vehicle of a fully coherent character" that relates objectively to the audience, seldom speaking to it or drawing it into a kind of pact or confidence (Worthen, *Modern Drama*, 19).

A few examples might suffice not only to illustrate differences between the two forms, but also to underscore Postlewait's wariness of this familiar teleology, based as it is upon a schema in which melodrama is superseded by realism in the later nineteenth century. The playwright often credited with helping refine an Ibsenite realism for the American stage is James A. Herne (1839–1901), an actor and stage manager, collaborator with producer and theatre owner David Belasco (1853–1931), and author of several successful plays. Of these, *Margaret Fleming* proved the most controversial when first produced in Boston in the spring of 1891 and later that winter in New York. The play concerns the infidelity of businessman Philip Fleming, the birth of his bastard child to an unfortunate woman of whom he has taken advantage and who eventually dies soon after childbirth, and the forgiveness of his saintly wife Margaret, who has a one-year-old daughter upon whom she dotes and a lovely home, and is apparently immune to the somber realities of the world. But in the play's opening scene, we learn that Philip has taken a mistress and, despite his efforts to rush her out of town for an abortion, she has stayed and given birth to an infant boy. Family friend Dr. Larkin has visited the woman in her convalescence and reports that she will certainly die, disparaging Philip as an "animal" and sympathizing with the unfortunate young woman in terms critics often associate with the literary *naturalism* of Emile Zola or, in America, of novelists Theodore Dreiser or Frank Norris:

> The *girl's* not to blame. She'd a product of her environment. Under present social conditions, she's probably have gone wrong anyhow. But you![36]

Responding to Philip's fear of scandal should this news be made public, a fear famously shared by such Ibsen characters as Hedda Gabler, Larkin retorts that it isn't scandal but rather "such damn scoundrels as you that make and destroy homes" (*American Drama*, 243). And, as the opening act curtain falls, Philip gazes "sadly" into the fireplace contemplating this very outcome, his wife's professions of love and contentment notwithstanding.

In the next act, Margaret's own medical condition becomes clear: her glaucoma could precipitate her blindness unless "the serenity of her life is not disturbed." Unfortunately, that serenity is impossible to maintain as in Act Three Margaret attempts to help her maid's ailing sister by traveling to the boarding house in which Lena Schmidt, who too conveniently turns out to be Philip's mistress, is eventually found dead. There, Dr. Larkin reads Lena's letter professing her love for Philip, and thus Margaret discovers the truth about her husband's indiscretion. After a few moments of tense dialogue – and others of quiet resignation – a low wail from an infant pierces the scene. The cry jolts Margaret out of self-pity and into the stark reality of her situation, and in a meticulously choreographed curtain scene she rushes to comfort the child, places him in her lap, slowly unbuttons her dress, and offers him nourishment. Her astonished husband enters the scene, standing in "dumb amazement" as the lights slowly fade. In the final act, one Herne rewrote several times, a contrite Philip returns after a long absence and is encouraged by his wife to raise both his legitimate daughter and his illegitimate son, providing him with a name and a father's love. Philip also longs to win his wife back and, although Margaret is not confident that can ever happen, a "serene joy illuminates her face" as her prodigal husband moves to greet both of his young children, now together in the family's garden.

Orthodox New York critics responded to *Margaret Fleming* much in the way conservative critics reacted to Ibsen. *New York Times* critic Edward A. Dithmar railed that the life Herne portrays is "sordid and mean, and its effect upon a sensitive mind is depressing." The *Dramatic Mirror* complained that "If it be the purpose of a play to reproduce, with photographic accuracy, the details of unpleasant and unhealthy forms of everyday life, *Margaret Fleming* can be called a play" (quoted in Hewitt, *Theatre U. S. A.*, 261). Those who endorsed the play, like William Dean Howells, conceded that the play was "pitilessly plain; it was ugly; but it was true, and it was irresistible."[37] Yet it was far from perfect, as even supportive critics like Hamlin Garland detected. For Garland, even though it "forced a comparison with life" and was "worthy to stand for the new drama," *Margaret Fleming* was "overplotted," and the coincidence of Philip's lover being his maid's sister did not stand up to a credible "standard of truth." Recalling Postlewait's argument about the overlapping of dramatic forms, we might also regard the infamous "letter" Dr. Larkin reads to Margaret as replicating the predictable expository methods of melodramatic plots, and Margaret's selfless inner "serenity" as drawing her too close to the sanctity of a melodramatic heroine. In addition, the stage tableau at the end of Act Three parallels the visual sensation to which melodramatic conflict typically led, although the baring of a maternal breast scarcely rivals the explosion of a steamboat or the eruption of a volcano. Still, as supporters of the play frequently emphasized, *Margaret Fleming* represented a "new drama." Historian Arthur Hobson Quinn, although conceding that Margaret's sudden blindness is "bothersome," even goes so far as to say that Herne's "is a powerful problem play unequalled in realism by any other known American drama of its century" (*The Literature of the American People*, 805).

Turn-of-the-century realism, therefore, as Postlewait argues, often contained melodramatic elements, and melodrama often concerned matters more deftly represented by recognizably "modern" forms. For example, of the many plays based on the myriad corruptions of America capitalism before the searing indictments of Clifford Odets in the 1930s, Arthur Miller in the 1940s, and – to take a more contemporary instance – David Mamet in *Glengarry Glen Ross* (1983), two widely seen in their time are Boucicault's melodrama *The Poor of New York* (1857) and Clyde Fitch's *The City* (1909), produced shortly after his death. Both plays concern illegal and unethical banking practices, the ultimate ruination of a prominent banker's family, and the exposure of dubious ethics that more broadly underlie the ascent of America's nouveaux riches. In Boucicault's play, a naive ship captain entrusts $100,000 to the unscrupulous Gideon Bloodgood, who absconds with the money, parlays it into a fortune in the midst of a depression, and heartlessly witnesses the resultant destitution of the captain's family. Predictably enough, a recovered document – specifically, a receipt for the money – eventually exposes the crime, a spectacular tenement fire is set (by Bloodgood in an attempt to destroy the receipt and the former accomplice who possesses it), and a selfless heroine is eventually saved. By contrast, in Fitch's play the dire consequences of a banker's fraudulent practices are visited upon his family, who have moved from the small town of Middleburg to New York. In the opening act, young Cicely Rand exhorts her father to move the family to the city – to "the theatres! The crowds!" – and the excitement. Rand's wife complains of her "empty, humdrum existence" in a place enlivened only by "yesterday's news"; his son George Jr. adds, "We're all choking here . . . *dry-rotting* for *not enough to do*."[38] Their move to the city, however, brings more pain than excitement. There, Mrs. Rand is reduced to an "overdressed, nervous-looking woman"; there, young George's certain nomination as a gubernatorial candidate is undone by the scandal of his father's past, which includes an affair and a now grown illegitimate son; there, more tragically, that illegitimate son secretly marries Cicely and, when his lineage is discovered, kills her before allowing her family's objections to separate them.

While the influence of melodrama is obvious in the city, so too are its more naturalistic elements. Fred Hannock, cast literally as a villainous bastard, loves the young wife he shoots; his action is thus not based upon lust or avarice. He has been wronged by George Rand, Sr., leading to, among other things, his drug abuse (signaled by his use of a needle in full view of the audience). Further, the play's language often transcends the clichés of melodrama: so, when George Jr. reveals to Hannock that Rand *is* his real father, Hannock calls George a "God damn liar." The "sensation" scene, Hannock's shooting of Cicely, unlike those lavishly attenuated on the melodramatic stage, occurs quickly and in the domestic space of the family home. Perhaps most important, the play does not move toward the titillation of visual and emotive excess, but rather to a debate in the closing scene about the effect of urban life on the Rand family. While his sister and mother attribute the family's tragedy to their move to New York, George Jr. offers a long defense of the city, any city large enough to challenge a person to "Make good if you can, or to Hell with you!" (629). A man, he argues, can't lie in the city, because it tests stringently all a man is and wants to be. At the curtain, he vows to start again – to make good as an entirely new person shorn of the past and eager to confront whatever lies ahead.

However problematic, therefore, this second familiar narrative in which an Ibsenite realism supersedes melodrama helps clarify one attraction of a new drama heralded by many of the voices referenced above. But neither this familiar story, nor the one in which the Little Theatre movement is so central, constitutes a satisfactory account of the myriad forms of modern drama in early twentieth-century America and the various cultural work it accomplished. For realism gave way to other forms – expressionism, for example, in the 1910s and 1920s, and the more politically inflected agitprop drama of the 1930s – and American playwrights found ever more complex and socially iconoclastic topics to confront.

The different stories and different forms of modern drama: desire, gender, and class on stage

> The play, indeed, is dull and stupid . . . [It is also] a reeking compost of filth and folly that the crude and frivolous playwright, the late Clyde Fitch, dug out of it, with which to mire the Stage.[39]

Such was New York critic William Winter's opinion of Fitch's play *Sapho*, which was eventually closed by the police in October 1900 on the charge of immorality. But, as I have already suggested, Winter and similarly orthodox reviewers were finally powerless to staunch the flood of plays at the *fin de siècle* and opening decades of the twentieth century that both recognized sexual desire and represented it in unprecedented ways on stage. In the case of Fitch's *Sapho*, the excessive length of onstage kissing and the sight of a young man carrying a more experienced woman to her boudoir at the end of the opening act were more than enough to instantiate a charge of immorality against the play and Olga Nethersole, the actress who starred in it.[40] Yet, although such portrayals of "fallen women" sparked controversy throughout America, it might also be seen as a logical consequence of an increasing interest both in human sexuality and psychology more generally. In his study *Freud on Broadway: A History of Psychoanalysis and the American Drama* (1955), W. David Sievers concedes that the more overt instances of psychoanalytic theory informing modern drama occurred after 1912 in such plays as Glaspell's *Suppressed Desires*, numerous plays of O'Neill, and Alice Gerstenberg's *Overtones*, produced by the Washington Square Players in 1915. For Sievers, Gerstenberg's play marked the "first departure from realism for the purpose of dramatizing the unconscious."[41] Others followed, of course, some in imitation of August Strindberg's earlier *A Dream Play* – dream interpretation being a preoccupation of psychoanalysis – and still other dramas delved into such matters as incest and the so-called "Family Romance," a problematic central not only to Fitch's *The City*, but also in the 1920s to O'Neill's *Desire Under the Elms, Strange Interlude* and *Mourning Becomes Electra*. Sievers's point about *Overtones*, however, concerns more than psychoanalysis. In fact, it reiterates two claims often made about modern drama: one, discussed above, that modern or modernist drama was cultivated in places like Provincetown and the Chicago Little Theatre, not on Broadway; and two, that just as melodrama's dominance was challenged by realism, so too realism would be challenged by other dramatic forms. Indeed, as Charles Lyons suggests about the later contexts of Samuel Beckett's absurdism, "avant-garde playwriting" of the twentieth century seems almost always to assume a "self-conscious antinaturalism."[42] As we shall see, this is the case with American drama of the 1920s and 1930s.

Sievers's interest in the dramatic representation of psychoanalytic themes – the unconscious, for instance, or dream states – might be briefly expanded here to include the representation of desire so central to modernist literature more generally. In this regard, the notorious legal battles in America over the publication and distribution of such novels as James Joyce's *Ulysses*, D. H. Lawrence's *Lady Chatterley's Lover*, and several works by Henry Miller serve to remind us that, in addition to the formal challenges of avant-garde drama, "problem plays" like *Sapho* also exposed to an audience its own hypocritical, often sexist morality – and its aversion to direct conversations about or representations of sexual desire. Sievers regards David Belasco's 1898 production of *Zaza* and 1909 production of Eugene Walter's *The Easiest Way* as heralding a drama that dealt frankly with such topics as prostitution and sexual frustration. Similarly, Walter's 1910 play *Just a Wife* centered around a husband's intimate reasons for taking a mistress.

While lacking the novelist's freedom to represent sexual intimacy in the explicit ways Joyce and Lawrence do, several playwrights developed characters who struggled to express their desire in more indirect, metaphoric ways. In *The Great Divide* (1906) by William Vaughn Moody (1869–1910), for example, Ruth Jordan, an Easterner relocated to southern Arizona, discovers that every day in the emancipating West is "more radiantly exciting than the other" (Richardson, *American Drama*, 269). Left alone one night, Ruth is assailed by three men, all of whom hope to possess her. Through a series of devices including gambling, she is won by – and goes to live with – Stephen Ghent, whom she eventually marries. As she describes these events later, in some ways rationalizing why she did not shoot Ghent when given the opportunity, Ruth exclaims, "My lover came, impatient, importunate, and I – went with him" (283). But it takes her a long time – and a trip back to the repressive East – to reach this conclusion and assert her right to choose her own spouse, however unconventional their meeting. More important, Ruth converts Ghent into a loyal husband, who travels to Ruth's family home in an "old-fashioned" New England town to try and win her back, and in the process of doing so expresses his desire for her in almost Lawrentian terms:

> [T]he first time our eyes met, they burned away all that was bad in our meeting, and left only the fact that we *had* met – pure good – pure joy – a fortune of it – for both of us.

He proclaims, "Our law is joy, and selfishness: the curve of your shoulder and the light on your hair as you sit there says that as plain as preaching" (296). Some twenty years later in Lawrence's *Lady Chatterley's Lover* (1928), Connie Chatterley would be overwhelmed by the "purity" of Oliver Mellors's body; she would bask in the "soft flames" of desire that rippled through her; she would experience the inherent "selfishness" of sexual fulfillment. In the end, Ruth Jordan elects to return to the West, to cross the great divide known as repression, and rejoin her husband, begging him at the closing curtain to teach her to live as he does, to kindle the flame of her desire.

This expression of sexual longing, however indirect, merged on the modern stage with an awareness of gender biases and the ways in which American culture constructs the parameters of gendered identity. On both the British and American stages, this awareness often took on a kind of activist valence. Elizabeth Robins's 1908 play *Votes for Women!* and plays by Dr. Marie Stopes, a sexologist whose plays were produced at London's Royal Court Theatre in the 1920s, championed, in the former case, women's suffrage and, in the latter, women's sexual fulfillment in marriage. In America during the same period, the works of such playwrights as Susan Glaspell, Rachel Crothers, and Sophie Treadwell achieved similar ends. Glaspell's *Trifles*, based on an actual case of an Iowa farmer's murder by his wife, is the best-known and most anthologized work of this period, as the overt sexism of the men investigating the crime renders them incapable of reading the evidence. The women in the play, however, have little difficulty understanding the wife's desperation in attempting to escape the emotional sterility of her life. Further, as a number of critics have argued, Glaspell's structuring of *Trifles* (and other plays) around an unseen woman – the audience never sees Minnie Wright, only learns about her from the dialogue of the investigators and their wives – constitutes an effective feminist practice in "reconfiguring the female subject" and her position of invisibility in American society.[43] Less adventuresome formally, Crothers (1878–1958) in such plays as *The Three of Us* (1906), *A Man's World* (1910), and *He and She* (1911) refined "New Women" willing and able to compete with men in a professional world. Writing mostly social comedies in a realist vein, Crothers took over thirty plays to Broadway, in the process imagining both the professional possibilities awaiting talented women and the difficult choices they would face between their careers and families.

By the teens and 1920s playwrights sought other dramatic forms to represent not only psychical states, but the lived realities of a gendered society riven also by class differences. One of the most significant examples is Treadwell's *Machinal* (1928), which combines the dilemma of Glaspell's housewife with a sharp class consciousness in portraying the complexities of yet another famous murder case, in this instance the 1927 murder trial of Ruth Snyder, the first woman to be sentenced to death in the electric chair by the state of New York. In Treadwell's play, realism gives way to expressionist technique: to an episodic plot structure, a thoughtful lighting design, and a meticulously outlined set of audio effects, all intended to convey the cruelties of life in the city, the protagonist's desperation, and the mechanization of human labor. Treadwell (1885–1970) depicts a vulnerable office worker, a single young woman caring for a difficult mother, who is induced to marry her employer, a vulgar and unattractive man who lusts after her. The staccato dialogue and office noise of the opening scene eventually lead to the young girl's desperate monologue, which delineates her despondence over the prospect of the man's "flabby hands" touching her, yet her awareness that his money will end her acute financial problems and the pressures that accompany alienating office work. Confused, seeking someone's – anyone's – help, she marries the man and suffers his touch, his clumsily executed seduction. Fleeing the marriage to a lover who uses her as ruthlessly as her husband has, she finally murders the latter, endures a trial turned into a media circus, and languishes in a cell before being led to the electric chair. In the final scene, one entitled "A Machine," the shadows of jail bars line the woman's face as a "Negro" spiritual and the whir of an airplane outside are heard. A priest prays in Latin as reporters debate the possibility that the "machine" – the electric chair – might malfunction during the execution. But as one exclaims, "It'll work – It always works!" the audience becomes aware of the final truth of this observation, for Treadwell's young woman has been ensnared in a machine from the beginning. And indeed it has methodically destroyed her.

Treadwell's play was revived by such major theatre companies as England's National Theatre in the 1980s and 1990s, as has another distinguished expressionist play of the period, Elmer Rice's *The Adding Machine*. In Rice's 1923 play, Mr. Zero, an accountant in a department store, finds himself ensnared in a loveless marriage and a dehumanizing job, from which he is eventually fired unceremoniously after twenty-five years of employment. Efficiency experts have convinced Zero's boss that machines can do the calculations better than humans, as the boss endeavors to explain over the increasing roar of machines and the faster revolutions of the stage set: "efficiency – economy – business – *business* – **Business**."[44] This dizzying scene is enhanced by other audio effects, described as "deafening, maddening, unendurable," culminating in a peal of thunder and instant blackness. The Zeros' dinner party in the next scene ends with the police arresting Zero for murder, which leads to his trial and execution. But Rice (1892–1967) and his critique of American capitalism are far from concluded with Zero's death. In the afterlife, he meets a woman with whom he once worked and might have found happiness in the Elysian fields. But he cannot rest, he must remain busy – he must keep working. In the play's concluding scene, he learns that souls are continually refashioned – machine-produced and stamped – in a kind of "cosmic" repair shop, then returned to service. The "culmination of human effort – the final triumph of the evolutionary process," Zero learns, will be the production of perfect machines. In this system, humans are little more than a "waste product," a recycled material that provides the "raw material of slums and wars" (138).

As America headed ineluctably toward the Great Depression, Rice and fellow playwrights Clifford Odets (1906–1963) and John Howard Lawson (1895–1977) refined their criticism of capitalism and class bias even more sharply. For Rice in *Street Scene* (1929), life in urban tenements combined working-class problems with another issue perhaps not so prominent in American cities since the antebellum years of the previous century: the realities of a multicultural society. In Rice's apartment building, blue collar Anglo-Irish Americans reside with newly arrived Italian immigrants and Eastern European Jews. One of the latter, family patriarch qua political theorist Abraham Kaplan, tries in vain to argue with his, at times, bellicose neighbors that "Ve must put de tuls of industry in de hands of de vorking klasses" if a social revolution is ever to be achieved.[45] His irritated disputants descend at times into anti-Semitism, even when rebutting his socialist points in presumably comic ways: "Like I heard a feller sayin': the Eye-talians built New York, the Irish run it an' the Jews own it" (57). Rice's play was preceded by Lawson's *Processional* (1925), an episodic drama set in West Virginia during a coal miners' strike, and was followed by perhaps the most famous agitprop play ever written, Clifford Odets's *Waiting for Lefty* (1935). Somewhat like expressionist plot structure, scenes in agitprop drama typically follow one another not out of some Aristotelian notion of organic development, but rather for more overtly political purposes and not necessarily to develop the conflict of a central character. On the contrary, the scenes in Odets's play can almost be interchanged, as they initially concern a strike of taxi drivers and the plight of their families while the later scenes depict accompanying ethnic and class biases in institutional and industrial contexts. In the work of African-American poet and playwright Langston Hughes (1902–1967), whose angry melodrama *Mulatto* garnered significant success on Broadway in 1935, class issues and economic stability are informed by issues of racial equality in the agitprop piece *Don't You Want to Be Free?* (1938).

Hughes, Lawson, and Odets not only expanded the formal dimensions of a "modern" drama, but also participated in a veritable theatrical revolution of enduring value to the progress of American dramatic art. In Hughes's case, this included the founding of theatres to cultivate the plays of African-American writers, a practice repeated in the 1960s by the Black Arts Movement, while in Odets's and Lawson's it was crucial participation in a theatrical collective known as the Group Theatre. Started in 1931 by director Lee Strasberg, director Harold Clurman, and financial manager Cheryl Crawford, the Group attempted an experiment in theatrical production the results of which are still felt today: namely, a theatrical collective based on equality, not star billing, and on so-called method acting theories adapted from the writing of Konstanin Stanislavsky. Clurman and Strasberg, dissatisfied with commercial plays and predictable acting, were overwhelmed by performances of the Moscow Art Theatre in New York in the 1920s. Along with Crawford, they recruited a cast of young actors and theatrical artisans, exploding onto the New York scene with plays like Lawson's *Success Story* (1932) and Odets's *Awake and Sing* (1935). Their legacy of realistic acting technique, however controversial the theories underlying the technique were then and still are, and socially committed drama is unparalleled in the history of modern American drama.

Thus, the formal experiments of the 1910s and 1920s were continued into the 1930s and beyond by such playwrights as Odets, Hughes, and – later – Thornton Wilder in *Our Town* (1938) and *The Skin of Our Teeth* (1942). The "gauzy realism" of Tennessee Williams, a combination of realism and expressionism realized in such plays as *The Glass Menagerie* (1944), and the hybrid form of much of Arthur Miller's work were soon to follow. Modern drama continued to confront social and cultural issues that had not been given expression on the nineteenth-century stage. Lillian Hellman's *The Children's Hour* (1934), for example, concerns the unjust condemnation of two lesbian teachers, while Hughes's *Mulatto* exposes the racism that underlies lynching, among other less violent discriminations, in the American South.

In sum, a modern drama constantly looks to the present, to the worlds its audience inhabits, and to the values these worlds represent. Modern drama, if it is to be modern, seems always in search of a new form, a fresh way of revealing truths and entertaining its audience. And while its history in America may suggest a kind of stunted growth or second-class literary status, its present and future have never looked brighter.

NOTES

1. Susan Harris Smith, "Generic Hegemony: American Drama and the Canon," *American Quarterly* 41 (1989), 112–122.
2. Harold Bloom, ed., *Arthur Miller* (New York: Chelsea House, 1987), 2.
3. Harold Bloom, ed., *Arthur Miller* (Broomall, PA: Chelsea House, 2000), 9.
4. Robert Brustein, *The Theatre of Revolt: An Approach to the Modern Drama* (Boston: Little, Brown, and Company, 1962), 321.
5. Thomas Postlewait, "From Melodrama to Realism: The Suspect History of American Drama," in *Melodrama: The Cultural Emergence of a Genre*, ed. Michael Hays and Anastasia Nikolopoulou (New York: St. Martin's Press, 1996), 41. I want to acknowledge here the influence this seminal essay has had on my argument.
6. Barnard Hewitt, *Theatre U. S. A., 1665–1957* (New York: McGraw-Hill Book Company, 1959), 29.
7. Don B. Wilmeth and Tice Miller, eds., *Cambridge Guide to American Theatre* (Cambridge and New York: Cambridge University Press, 1993), 341.
8. At the end of the eighteenth century, Dunlap addressed state legislatures on the significance of theatre to a civilized republic, arguing that it was both a "powerful engine for the improvement of man" and a unifying cultural force. See Dunlap's *History of the American Theatre* (1832; rpt. New York: Burt Franklin, 1963).
9. See the entries on New York City Theatres (341–342) and the Broadway Theatre (86) in the *Cambridge Guide to American Theatre*.
10. In another measure of theatrical expansion, Arthur Hobson Quinn notes the appearance of 1,500 professional actors in an 1860 report; by 1900, the total was nearly 15,000. See *The Literature of the American People* (New York: Appleton-Century-Crofts, 1951), 790.
11. See Michael R. Booth, *Prefaces to English Nineteenth-Century Theatre* (Manchester: Manchester University Press, 1980), 1–3.
12. Thomas H. O'Connor, *The Boston Irish: A Political History* (Boston: Northeastern University Press, 1996), 60.
13. Dennis Clark, *The Irish in Philadelphia: Ten Generations of Urban Experience* (Philadelphia: Temple University Press, 1973), 29.
14. Noel Ignatiev, *How the Irish Became White* (New York: Routledge, 1995), 41, 42.
15. Several adaptations of Stowe's novel appeared in 1852 and 1853, with George L. Aiken's version finding so much success that the National Theatre ran morning, afternoon, and evening performances of the play to meet the public's demand. One scholar estimates that the play received over 250,000 performances during Stowe's lifetime.

16. Bruce A. McConachie, "The Cultural Politics of 'Paddy' on the Midcentury American Stage," *Studies in Popular Culture* 10.1 (1987), 2. See also Stephen Watt, "Irish American Drama of the 1850s: National Identity, 'Otherness,' and Assimilation," in *Fleeing the Famine: North America and Irish Refugees, 1845–1851*, ed. Margaret M. Mulrooney (Westport, CT: Praeger, 2003), 97–109.

17. Eric Lott, *Love & Theft: Blackface Minstrelsy and the American Working Class* (New York: Oxford University Press, 1995), 137.

18. Ntozake Shange, "foreword/unrecovered losses/black theatre traditions," in *Three Pieces* (New York: St. Martin's Press, 1981), xiii.

19. John Ranken Towse, *The New York Tribune*, September 17, 1866, as quoted in Hewitt, *Theatre U. S. A.*, 195–196.

20. Bernard Shaw, *Our Theatres in the Nineties*, 3 vols. (London: Constable, 1932), I: 14.

21. *The Letters of W. B. Yeats*, ed. Allan Wade (London: Rupert Hart-Davis, 1954), 308–309.

22. Gordon Craig, *The Theatre – Advancing* (Boston: Little, Brown, and Company, 1919), 25–26.

23. Peter Brooks, *The Empty Space* (New York: Atheneum, 1978), 18–19.

24. See Cheney's *The New Movement in Theater* (New York: M. Kennerley, 1914) and *The Art Theater* (New York: Knopf, 1917), both of which parallel Craig's and Yeats's advocacy of a poetic and symbolist stagecraft of imaginary, not naturalistic, effect.

25. In *American Drama from the Colonial Period Through World War I: A Critical History* (New York: Twayne, 1993), Gary A. Richardson explains that the Syndicate was "a notoriously conservative cartel rarely given to underwriting the dramatic experimentations of even the most successful dramatists" (207). The partnership brokered in 1896 by producer Charles Frohman and several booking agents exerted enormous power, until a rival syndicate, headed by the Shubert brothers Sam, Lee, and Jacob, grew even more powerful.

26. William Archer, as quoted in Louis Sheaffer, *O'Neill: Son and Playwright* (Boston: Little, Brown, 1968), 342.

27. Charles Lock, "Maurice Browne and the Chicago Little Theatre," *Modern Drama* 31 (March 1988), 106–112.

28. *The Letters of W. B. Yeats*, 286.

29. Clyde Fitch, "The Play and the Public," in *Plays by Clyde Fitch*, ed. Montrose J. Moses and Virginia Gerson, 4 vols. (Boston: Little, Brown, and Company, 1915), IV: xxiii.

30. Reviewing the off-Broadway production of *Summer and Smoke*, John Gassner began, "As if to upbraid Broadway for the ignoble season of 1951–52, an intrepid Greenwich Village group calling itself Circle in the Square revived *Summer and Smoke* shortly after the season was officially closed." See "Broadway in Review," *Educational Theatre Journal* 4 (1952), 323–324.

31. Eugene O'Neill, "Memoranda on Masks" (1932), as quoted in Joel Pfister, *Staging Depth: Eugene O'Neill & the Politics of Psychological Discourse* (Chapel Hill: University of North Carolina Press, 1995), 58.

32. Philip Moeller, "A Foreword," in Elmer L. Rice, *The Adding Machine* (New York: Samuel French, 1956), vii.

33. In *The Melodramatic Imagination* (1976; rpt. New York: Columbia University Press, 1984), Peter Brooks argues that "Melodrama typically not only employs virtue persecuted as a source of its dramaturgy, but also tends to become the dramaturgy of virtue misprized and eventually recognized" (27).

34. Jeffrey Mason, *Melodrama and the Myth of America* (Bloomington: Indiana University Press, 1993), 153.

35. W. B. Worthen, *Modern Drama and the Rhetoric of Theater* (Berkeley: University of California Press, 1992), 14, 15.

36. James A. Herne, *Margaret Fleming*, in *American Drama: Colonial to Contemporary*, ed. Stephen Watt and Gary A. Richardson (Fort Worth, TX: Harcourt Brace, 1995), 243.

37. William Dean Howells, "Editor's Study," *Harper's Monthly* (August 1891), 478.

38. Montrose J. Moses and Virginia Gerson, eds., *Plays by Clyde Fitch*, 4 vols. (Boston: Little, Brown, 1915), IV: 459, 469.

39. William Winter, *The Wallet of Time*, 2 vols. (New York: Moffat, Yard and Company, 1913), II: 312–313.

40. For an account of this production, see Joy Harriman Reilly, "A Forgotten 'Fallen Woman'," in *When They Weren't Doing Shakespeare: Essays on Nineteenth-Century British and American Theatre*, ed. Judith L. Fisher and Stephen Watt (Athens: University of Georgia Press, 1989), 106–120.

41. W. David Sievers, *Freud on Broadway: A History of Psychoanalysis and the American Drama* (New York: Hermitage House, 1955), 51.

42. Charles R. Lyons, "Beckett, Shakespeare, and the Making of Theory," in *Around the Absurd*, ed. Enoch Brater and Ruby Cohn (Ann Arbor: University of Michigan Press, 1990), 98.

43. See, for example, Marcia Noe, "Reconfiguring the Subject/Recuperating Realism: Susan Glaspell's Unseen Woman," in *New Readings in American Drama: Something's Happening Here*, ed. Norma Jenkes (New York: Peter Lang, 2002), 9–21.

44. Elmer L. Rice, *The Adding Machine* (New York: Samuel French, 1956), 29.

45. Elmer L. Rice, *Street Scene* (New York: Samuel French, 1929), 52.

2

CULTURE

5

MARK A. SANDERS

American modernism and the New Negro Renaissance

What it means to be a Negro in the modern world is a revelation much needed in poetry.

Sterling A. Brown, *Negro Poetry and Drama*

Rethinking American modernism

By the middle of the twentieth century, the New Critics had installed in the academy a brand of modernism that must have looked quite strange, even alien to the New Negro Renaissance artists of the teens, twenties, and thirties. It wasn't simply that the New Critics' version of modernism excluded New Negroes entirely, though this was certainly the case. More to the point, what would come to be known as "high modernism" robbed the era of the animating ideas and agendas that largely defined New Negro participation. The American modernism focused on Eliot, Pound, Frost, Stevens, Crane, and "lost generation" fiction (and perhaps a few "minor" figures, often women); or a modernism devoted to epistemological crisis, fragmentation, alienation, and cultural exhaustion was for New Negro artists (and, indeed, a much larger group of American writers) but one dimension of a vibrantly multifaceted, tumultuous, often contradictory cultural moment. Much more than the practice of elites, but rather a "full-fledged historical culture,"[1] the modernism to which New Negroes contributed was a multivalent, often discursive era, capable of expressing unbridled optimism and chronic despair in the same breath. It was a moment that saw World War I and the collapse of the Ottoman Empire as both the end and the beginning of modern Western civilization, an era that celebrated democratic renewal, cultural plurality, and potential in mechanization, urbanization, and migration. And yet it was a moment that lamented the death of Christianity, the indeterminacy of language, and the demise of the cohesive self. Put more succinctly, a discussion of the New Negro Renaissance and its relation to American modernism begins not with our received New Critical sense of the era, but with a look at the constellation of ideas, movements, publishing venues, and artistic communities that comprised a *heterodox modernism* in which New Negroes participated fully.

Not to imply that different forms or strands of modernism were mutually exclusive; to the contrary, heterodox modernism, in all its iterations, takes as its points of departure reactions against the limitations of Victorian epistemology and responses to late nineteenth-century modernization. The centrality of God, fixed natural laws, humanity's ability to discern immutable truths, and dichotomous reasoning (human/animal, civilized/uncivilized, free/slave, male/female) largely defined an epistemology ill-equipped for the twentieth century. Indeed, the driving theories of evolution and relativity and the expanding complexities of the subconscious strongly suggested that reality and truth – scientific, social, and moral – were relational and contextual, not natural and transcendent. Furthermore, unprecedented levels of mechanization, and industrialization, the hegemony of industrial capitalism, an expanding middle class, the emergence of suburbs, and migration – both international and domestic – all created an economic, political, and physical world nearly unrecognizable to previous generations.

In response to such rapid philosophical and cultural change, modernism, in Daniel Singal's words, "represents an attempt to restore a sense of order to human experience under the often chaotic conditions of twentieth-century existence" (Singal, "Towards a Definition," 8). Looking more to the American scene, several strands of heterodox modernism – "native" modernism and Afro-modernism in particular – addressed what looked to be the stalled projects of democratic development and nation building. Pragmatism, Boasian anthropology, cultural pluralism, and the nativist project of cultural identification began to define a distinctly American form of modernism. Furthermore, the general emphasis on "aesthetic experience" and art, and on synthesis and new combinations (otherwise known as "super integration") constituted general interests or loose schools of thought that further informed New Negro artistic development, and in turn relied heavily on black participation.

First, addressing pragmatism, this philosophy of utility helped to lay the philosophical foundation for much of American modernism. Ultimately committed to communally beneficial outcomes, pragmatism served "as a form of cultural criticism in which the meaning of America is put forward by intellectuals in response to distinct social and cultural crises. In this sense, American pragmatism is . . . a set of interpretations that attempt to explain America to itself at a particular historical moment."[2] Rejecting both the idealist and realist philosophical traditions, both William James and John Dewey embraced "epistemological uncertainty" and subjected knowledge to the messy subjectivity of experience. James articulated a pluralist universe where absolutes dissolved into contingency, interpretation, and perpetual discovery: "Briefly [pluralism] is this, that nothing real is absolutely simple, that every smallest bit of experience is a *multum in parvo* plurally related, that each relation is one aspect, character, or function, way of its being taken, or way of its taking something else . . ."[3] He extended the evolutionary notion that humans exist in developmental relation to other animals and so attacked head-on the Victorian dichotomy between mind and body, reason and passion. He suggested also that our interpretations of experience (or reality) were always subject to myriad distortions and permutations.[4] Relative to society and the arts, James's sense of pragmatism stressed that individual consciousness and experience, particularly expressed through the arts, would affirm a plural and egalitarian society where communal values would emerge through individual expression.

And Dewey, perhaps even more focused on progressive social change, attacked social barriers and hierarchy while championing cultural pluralism and the deliberative process by which communities exchange values and promote egalitarian principles. For Dewey, the very purpose of social progress "is to set free and to develop the capacities of human individuals without respect to race, sex, class or economic status . . . Democracy has many meanings, but if it has a moral meaning, it is found in resolving that the supreme test of all political institutions and industrial arrangements shall be the contribution they make to the all-round growth of every member of society."[5]

The focus for pragmatism on practice and experience (and on the aesthetics of experience expressed through art) proved enormously important for nativists and Afro-modernists alike. Both would gravitate toward the notion that the arts, as a means of assigning aesthetic quality to experience, could prove "the most effective instruments for training people to cultural pluralism, creative democracy, achieving the widest possible range of human sympathy and understanding . . ."[6] Ultimately, through the arts, "the pragmatist would view the democratic ethos as something to be carried by people in the very structure of their imaginations and feelings, taking on a religious value in harmony with scientific beliefs and day-to-day activities" (Hutchinson, *Harlem Renaissance*, 29). Furthermore, pragmatism leveled the cultural playing field, rejecting any privileged site from which society could be explained. Quite the opposite, that each person and self-designated group contribute to the ongoing process of community building and larger cultural formation, further affirms democratic access and process at the very heart of the philosophical vision (Hutchinson, *Harlem Renaissance*, 80).

For his part, the German-born anthropologist Franz Boas further stressed the relative and contextual nature of reality through withering attacks on Eurocentrism and biological determinism as applied to race. In *The Mind of Primitive Man* (1911) Boas placed European culture in a relative position to supposedly primitive cultures, and further asserted that cultures develop according to their own histories and inner workings and thus should be evaluated accordingly. Across much of his work, Boas posited that "primitive man" was equally capable of complex thought and reason. Finally – and perhaps more to the point for New Negroes – Boas presented voluminous empirical evidence proving that intelligence was largely shaped by environmental factors and not by genetics. Indeed, he found no appreciable differences in intelligence according to race.[7] In refutation of the fundamental argument of white supremacy, he understood racial differences in behavior, custom, and outlook to be products of different social environments and histories. As he put it:

> I believe the present state of our knowledge justifies us in saying that, while individuals differ, biological differences between races are small. There is no reason to believe that one race is by nature so much more intelligent, endowed with great will power, or emotionally more stable than another, that the difference would materially influence its culture.[8]

In short, Boas laid the theoretical and evidential foundation for the constructionist model of race almost universally accepted in the social and natural sciences, and lent greater scientific and ethical weight to fundamental New Negro claims.

While Boas destroyed the Victorian dichotomy between civilized and savage, while James undermined the human/animal binary, and while Dewey challenged the old opposition of intellect and experience, together they helped to usher in a new "integrative mode." Experimenting with new combinations, the three scholars launched an effort "to integrate once more the human and the animal, the civilized and savage, and to heal the sharp divisions that the nineteenth century had established in areas such as class, race, and gender" (Singal, "Towards a Definition," 12). Rather than heightened fragmentation, this strand of American modernism stressed synthesis; a "fusing together of disparate elements" (Singal, "Towards a Definition," 12) or a "super integration."[9] For a burgeoning number of American artists and thinkers looking to indigenous sources for inspiration, super integration would prove the coordinating idea for the reconception of American cultural identity. What George Hutchinson has termed "native modernism" sought to define American cultural identity, largely in American terms, rather then European. Theorists and writers such as Van Wyck Brooks, Waldo Frank, Max Eastman, Randolph Bourne, William Carlos Williams, V. F. Calverton, and Alfred Stieglitz adopted whole cloth "pragmatism's emphasis upon process, its embrace of pluralism, its insistence that truths and morals are produced through historically specific practices, [and] its liberating acceptance of epistemological uncertainty . . ." (Hutchinson, *Harlem Renaissance*, 33). They looked to American's cultural patchwork and championed cultural pluralism – the celebration of ethnic distinction *and* intercultural exchange – in service to egalitarian and democratic ideals. For them the Victorian distinctions between high and low culture, upper and lower classes, free and slave, white and black had to be dismantled and replaced with a synthetic model dedicated to democratic renewal and a "national integration of cultures" (Hutchinson, *Harlem Renaissance*, 90).

Fundamental to this process was the pragmatist notion of the "aesthetic quality of experience" (Hutchinson, *Harlem Renaissance*, 43). All knowledge and understanding flow from the interpretation of experience, and thus from its aesthetic dimensions. Both the individual and the group must enhance its "aesthetic powers" in order to realize fully "one's receptivity to the full range of sensuous experience in the common world" (Hutchinson, *Harlem Renaissance*, 43). It is through the exchange of experience – heightened and made communal through the aesthetic – that inter-ethnic understanding and cultural integration can take place.

And of course, the chief instrument of exchange is art, and literature more specifically. For nativists, art "should give the final touch of meaning, of consummation to all the activities of life" (Hutchinson, *Harlem Renaissance*, 44). Waldo Frank in particular provided a salient model of native modernism, one that directly influenced New Negro artistic self-definition. His most famous volume, *Our America* (1919), served as the virtual manifesto for postwar nativists. Elaborating on Whitman's *Democratic Vistas* (1871) – and thus invoking a nativist progenitor – *Our America* envisioned "a *religious* awakening to the meaning of America" (Hutchinson, *Harlem Renaissance*, 107), again finding meaning in cultural plurality and democratic renewal. Emphasizing an historicized sense of pluralism, Frank conceived the history of American culture as "The flowing of a Stream."[10] Indigenous ethnicities – Native American, Italian-American, Irish-American and so on – serve as tributaries flowing into the greater American cultural stream. For Frank, the metaphor suggests ongoing interchange and amalgamation as American culture and democracy grow in strength due to their multiple sources. And although New Negroes (Jean Toomer in particular) were quick to point out that Frank had omitted African-American culture altogether in his formulation, they still claimed *Our America* as a viable model that at least in theory could envision African-American participation in these processes.

Our America notwithstanding, as one of the founders of *The Seven Arts*, a major nativist journal, Frank strove to promote other modernists and to disseminate nativist ideas. More specific to New Negro artistry, Frank's friendship with Jean Toomer and his aid in developing and publishing *Cane* were crucial not simply for the volume itself, but also for the broader influence the collection had on younger Renaissance writers.

And yet, prior to James, Dewey, Boas, and Frank, it was Walt Whitman and his prophetic call for a national literature of indigenous and varied voices that provided both the vision and artistic model that would fuel both nativist and New Negro agendas. In both ideological and artistic terms, Whitman offered a foundation that would "stamp . . . the interior and real democratic contribution of this American continent, today, and days to come."[11] *Leaves of Grass* (1855), *Democratic Vistas*, and *An American Primer* (1904) served as veritable Ur texts for pluralist/nativist modernism. Whitman's poetry, which discovered the universal in the local and celebrated the regional speech of ordinary people – the voice and idiom of the bearers of the democratic experiment – combined artistic and political concerns for the coming generation. Furthermore, Whitman's formal innovations in verse proved equally as important (clearly seen in Langston Hughes, Sterling Brown, and Jean Toomer), creating prosody that embodied values inherent in the celebration of the common and overlooked voice.

Further amplifying the influence of its architects and defining ideas, native modernism executed its agenda through a broad network of publishing venues, "little magazines" and publishing houses alike. Through European immigration and the accelerated growth of the middle class, the American reading population had grown exponentially from the end of the nineteenth century through the Depression. Appealing to new European immigrants, new publishing houses featuring ethnically specific literature – Russian and Polish for example – began to explore the hybrid identities and experiences of these new immigrants. New magazines, too, explored changes in American culture due to immigration and internal migration, and linked these changes to the ongoing project of democratization. As Hutchinson points out, well before the academy began shaping the American canon, magazines such as *The Nation, The Seven Arts, The New Republic, The Liberator, The Masses, American Mercury*, (and even *The Dial* prior to 1919), set out to define American literature and culture largely in service to pluralist/pragmatist principles. Indeed, "these magazines . . . wanted to distinguish American from English aesthetics, often on grounds of cultural pluralism, vernacular experimentation, and social egalitarianism" (Hutchinson, *Harlem Renaissance*, 126). Magazines and publishing houses alike promoted the "new" American literatures, namely realism, the new regionalism, naturalism, and investigative reporting (or muckraking), in the (re)defining of American culture through attention to ethnic specificity and incisive cultural/political critique.

The overtly marxist *Masses*, for example, addressed American culture in terms of class critique, thus framing working-class white, ethnic, and

African-American experiences in terms of a national (and global) struggle for equal rights. Resurrecting the journal after the war as *The Liberator*, editor Max Eastman – a life-long Dewey devotee – made the magazine one of the most influential magazines for left-leaning artists/intellectuals, black and white alike. (Claude McKay and Michael Gold also served as editors.) Langston Hughes, Sterling Brown, the *Fire!!* group, Jean Toomer, and many more Renaissance writers would comment on the journal's aggressive promotion of plurality and egalitarianism through the arts and cultural critique. Indeed, Toomer published in *The Liberator* some of his first sketches and poems that would later be included in *Cane*. In a similar vein, *The New Masses, The Liberator*'s successor, further promoted a nativist/pluralist agenda with a similar Marxist inflection. It would call for "an art of social engagement" that further advanced the critical realists and cultural pluralist strands of American modernism. The editorial staff at *The Liberator* assembled a veritable "who's who" of native modernists that included Waldo Frank, Sherwood Anderson, Michael Gold, Lewis Mumford, Max Eastman, Van Wych Brooks, Eugene O'Neill, Carl Sandburg, and Louis Untermeyer. Jean Toomer and Langston Hughes also served as contributing editors (Hutchinson, *Harlem Renaissance*, 296).

Perhaps even more nativist in outlook, emphasizing an American democratic tradition over a Marxist one, *The New Republic* and *The Nation* were also crucial venues in the larger nativist web. Both magazines cultivated deep pragmatist roots, directly addressed lynching and other forms of racial injustice, promoted Boasian anthropological and racial theory, and stressed cultural nationalism, all in pursuit of "native cultural resurgence" (Hutchinson, *Harlem Renaissance*, 210). Between them they published works by Carl Sandburg, Sinclair Lewis, Sherwood Anderson, Julia Peterkin, Du Bose Heyward, Paul Green, Claude McKay, Langston Hughes, and more. In a broader sense, the larger network of nativist/pluralist magazines had the dual function of providing significant publishing opportunities for New Negroes and advancing many of the ideas important to the New Negro movement.

So too, new publishing houses such as Knopf, Boni and Liveright, (later A. & C. Boni), Harcourt Brace, Harper Brothers and Viking Press pursued a cultural pluralist vision. Many of these publishing firms were owned and operated by second-generation European immigrants who were very much concerned with ethnic diversity and its relation to national identity. From the beginning, Knopf and Boni and Liveright in particular addressed a new immigrant readership by publishing European literature – Irish drama, French and Russian literature in translation, along with the emerging American literatures. Thus, these houses published the works of "nativists" such as Theodore Dreiser, William Faulkner, Waldo Frank, Sherwood Anderson,

Sinclair Lewis, Max Eastman, Michael Gold, Carl Sandburg, Louis Unter-meyer, and Horace Kallen. And, therefore, it goes without saying that these five or six firms published the writings of virtually all of the New Negro Renaissance writers: Langston Hughes, Zora Neale Hurston, Jean Toomer, James Weldon Johnson, George Schuyler, Nella Larsen, Rudolph Fisher, Jessie Fauset, Sterling Brown, etc.

Again, returning to the notion of multiple strands of modernism, it should be kept in mind how sharply this nativist vein of modernism distinguished itself from "high modernism," particularly relative to race, national iden-tity, and democratic ideals. From a nativist point of view, the formalists (later dubbed high modernists) were the peripheral group, having missed the opportunities that epistemological uncertainty afforded. In reaction to this epistemological "crisis" – and in particular to World War I, the crisis writ large – the formalists deliberately separated aesthetic or technical concerns in art from more overtly material ones. The American high modernists – Eliot, Pound, Stevens, Crane and Frost, for example – focused on poetic form as the location at which much of the crisis would be ameliorated. As we look back through the lens of New Criticism, it was this group's for-mal experimentation that was the most aesthetically rewarding, laying the prosodic foundation for most of twentieth-century poetry privileged by the academy. And yet when placed in a larger historical context, relative to other forms of modernism, it was this group of high modernists that actively tried to avoid the more pressing and immediate implications of modern art for native modernists in general, and for New Negro artists in particular.

For Max Eastman, the formalists' "pure poetry," with its emphasis on self-referentiality and artifice, sought to prop up the Victorian system of class hierarchy and privilege against the erosion threatened by science and "experimental knowledge." Status quo oriented, the formalists eschewed realism because it suggested social action. Even worse, from Eastman's point of view, the formalists shored against the ruins of modern plurality and flux through the reiteration of authority, stability, and control. They resisted change through the invocation of myth, the mastery of technical and linguis-tic intricacy, and through an idealized sense of "tradition." For Eliot and Pound in particular, authority achieved its most brutal form of expression through their fascistic leanings and affiliations.[12]

Given these dramatic differences between formalists and nativists, it is also important to note that Frank and other nativists were not beyond using the racist formulas of the day (in his introduction to *Harlem Shadows* [1922] Eastman refers to McKay as a "pure blooded Negro"[13]). Yet, the nativist philosophical outlook, its commitment to American democracy, and the will-ingness to support and to publish black writers, helped to create ideas and resources that New Negroes could use toward their own ends. Indeed, the celebration of the radically contingent nature of reality, aesthetic experience as the link between art and social progress, the promotion of inter-ethnic exchange and cultural plurality, and the dismantling of binaries in the service of democratic ideals all complemented and supported New Negro political agendas and artistic pursuits. Ultimately, the cross-pollination of ideas and the mutual exchange of personnel and resources fueled both strands of modernism.

Modernism and the New Negro era

Elemental to any discussion of African-American participation in modernism are the immediate and material conditions that shaped black lives at the turn of the century. Despite the great expression and experimentation occurring in the arts, the modernist era witnessed the nadir of race relations in America. From 1882, when the Tuskegee Institute started keeping records, until 1944, at least 3,417 African-Americans were lynched;[14] between 1890 and 1917, "some two to three black Southerners were hanged, burned at the stake, or quietly murdered every week."[15] Disfranchisement, beatings, peonage, and political exclusion of African-Americans were the rule in the South, and across the country, plantation tradition literature, the minstrel stage, advertising, and the new media of film all traded on racial stereotypes. Prevailing thought held that blacks, by definition, were inferior and therefore deserving of second-class citizenship. Indeed, for African-Americans most of the "chaotic conditions" of modernism stemmed not from epistemological concerns, but from the harrowing dissonance between constitutional guarantees and systematic political oppression. To be sure, New Negro Renaissance writers participated in the nativist/pluralist traditions as well as other forms of modernism. But much closer to home, the immediacy of racial politics shaped what has come to be called the Harlem Renaissance, better understood within the context of the New Negro movement.

In an overtly political sense, the New Negro movement, spanning the teens, twenties, and thirties, fought to make palpable Reconstruction civil rights legislation, while the New Negro Renaissance witnessed the first African-American cultural expression of modernity. The term "New Negro," which began to appear in black publications of the 1890s, referred to a new sense of political self-awareness, aggressiveness, and dedication to the cause of black citizenship and empowerment.[16] This post-Reconstruction generation was the first to experience from birth legal and extra-legal exclusion from democratic rights promised to them through the Thirteenth, Fourteenth, and Fifteenth Amendments. In response to America's theoretical promises of equality and the practical reality of subjugation came black America's most unified and organized struggle for citizenship to that point.

Availing themselves of black higher education, the chief enduring legacy of Reconstruction, New Negroes acquired degrees and professional training in unprecedented numbers, and subsequently devoted their training to building organizations and institutions that addressed the failures of American democracy. For example, the Niagra movement, a group of young black radicals frustrated with Booker T. Washington and Tuskegee-styled accommodations, crafted a manifesto that clearly articulated New Negro ideology:

> We want the Constitution of the country enforced. We want Congress to take charge of Congressional elections. We want the Fourteenth amendment carried out to the letter and every State disfranchised in Congress which attempts to disfranchise its rightful voters. We want the Fifteenth amendment enforced and no State allowed to base its franchise simply on color.[17]

New Negroes, then, wanted full access and full inclusion, politically, culturally, and socially. Indeed, some writers went so far as to measure the success (or failure) of American democracy by the degree of inclusion (or exclusion) of the African-American. Most famously, in the title essay of *New Negro* (1925), Alain Locke presents the African-American as the true patriot, embodying American democratic ideals:

> Democracy itself is obstructed and stagnated to the extent that any of its channels are closed. Indeed they cannot be selectively closed. So the choice is not between American institutions frustrated on the one hand and American ideals progressively fulfilled and realized on the other . . . We realize that we cannot be undone without America's undoing.[18]

Thus, New Negroes created institutions such as the Urban League, and the Universal Negro Improvement Association (UNIA), founded independent newspapers, opened schools, and rioted in the streets in the red hot summer of 1919, resisting white racist mob rule. They also pursued legal remedies, perhaps the most noted being cases attacking segregated education and creating the precedents for *Brown* v. *Board of Education*. Furthermore, the list of overtly political New Negroes is legion, including Ida B. Wells-Barnett, Mary Church Terrell, W. E. B. Du Bois, Walter White, William Pickens, Monroe Trotter, Madame C. J. Walker, Carter G. Woodson, Charles Hamilton Houston, and many more.

So too, the New Negro era marked the African-American moment of modernity, one of rapid cultural transformation on the broader modern

American scene. Indeed, in his defining essay, Locke makes clear the inextricable link between New Negro politics and the pressing issue of American and Afro-modernism:

> With each successive wave . . . the movement of the Negro becomes more and more a mass movement toward the larger and more democratic chance – in the Negro's case a deliberate flight not from countryside to city but from medieval America to modern.   (Locke 6)

In one sense, their flight from the countryside was quite literal, as blacks migrated in unprecedented numbers from the rural south to urban centers in the north and midwest. Escaping grinding poverty, lynchings, and Jim Crow, blacks flocked to New York City, Philadelphia, Chicago, and Detroit in pursuit of higher standards of living. And for the first time in African-American history a growing number of folks were no longer farmers, but wage earners, compelled to adjust to a radically different city life and industrialization. Crowded living conditions, regimented time, limited access to land, and more fluid family relationships resulted in new forms of cultural expressions. Thus, as literal migration necessarily led to cultural transformation, older rural folk forms such as country blues, work songs, hollers and spirituals, underwent radical changes that produced gospel music, urban blues, and, of course, jazz.

According to Lawrence Levine, African-American culture experienced an accelerated process of secularization and acculturation, replacing an antebellum version of a unified spiritual world with a bifurcated vision separating the spiritual and the profane. Dramatic changes in collective and individual identity – a new sense of isolation and alienation, as well as access to "mainstream" American culture and thus assimilation – also informed New Negro consciousness and ideology. On the one hand, the impersonal urban environment reinforced feelings of alienation, similar to those created by the post-Reconstruction conundrum of denuded black citizenship. The blues, with its isolated, staunchly secular hero, and stylized lament of "personal catastrophe,"[19] perhaps best expressed the existential crisis marking much of modern black life. Also, in response to the encroaching secularization of modernity, gospel, the new music born in the Pentecostal storefront churches in this new urban environment, reflected the pressing need to make God intensely personal and palpable.

On the other hand, Reconstruction made entry into the American mainstream possible. Thus education, social, and economic upward mobility, and the adoption of middle-class mores all profoundly affected African-American racial identity. Indeed, competing models of Victorian gentility and working-class iconoclasm would define much of the New Negro Renaissance debate over black representation and its effectiveness for New Negro strategy.[20]

In addition to the overarching political milieu, the specifics of the arts scene also played a major role in New Negro Renaissance development. Largely because of the post-World War I economic boom, funding for the arts was at an unprecedented high. Both wealthy individuals and institutions funded writers and artists, mounted museum shows, and financed Broadway productions. Indeed, it was the performing arts, particularly music, which dominated the urban artistic scene in New York City, Washington DC, and Chicago, and which ultimately lent visibility to literary and graphic artists. And at the heart of the music scene was jazz, an upbeat, syncopated style of dance music that synthesized older folk forms, particularly blues and spirituals, as well as "mainstream" forms such as marches, anthems, dance hall standards, and even classical tone poems.

In 1919 James Reese Europe had just returned from World War I, where his 19th regiment had been entertaining the troops with this new style of music. His Clef Club had already become enormously popular in New York, playing concerts and dances across the city, even at Carnegie Hall. At the same time, younger band leaders such as Duke Ellington, Fletcher Henderson, and James P. Johnson led bands in night clubs including the Cotton Club, perhaps the most famous club of the so-called Jazz Age. And all musicians stood in the long shadow of Louis Armstrong, the best-known performer, largely responsible for the creation and popularization of modern jazz. Indeed, through the new technology of phonographs, recorded music, and radio, black music – jazz and blues in particular – swept the entire country, becoming one of the dominant forms of popular music.

Where Armstrong and others popularized jazz, W. C. Handy, "the father of the blues," wrote, produced, and distributed a form of vaudeville blues that would become the standard form of post-World War I performers. His first hit, "St. Louis Blues," was wildly popular, helping to spread the music nationally and to promote the careers of Ma Rainey, Bessie Smith, Clara Ward, and numerous other blues artists.

Responding to the appeal of black music, Broadway featured an unprecedented number of black shows. From the turn of the century through the twenties, black reviews and proto-musicals such as *Clorindy*, *Jes Lak White Folks*, In *Bandana Land*, *The Shoo-Fly Regiment*, and *Shuffle Along* featured spirituals, ragtime, jazz, the blues, skits and comedy acts (with clear roots in minstrelsy) to rave reviews and box-office success. James Weldon Johnson and his brother Rosamond wrote for the Broadway stage, as did Bob Cole and Paul Laurence Dunbar. Simultaneously, a new generation of composers came to the fore. William Grant Still, R. Nathaniel

Dett, and Harry T. Burleigh arranged spirituals as concert art, and more generally composed orchestral works based on black themes. Perhaps most famously, Burleigh helped Antonín Dvořák gather folk themes for his "New World Symphony." And concert singers like Ethel Waters, Paul Robeson, and later Marian Anderson delivered their virtuous solos to packed houses. In Langston Hughes's words, "the Negro was in vogue" largely due to the wide popularity of the music and the performing arts more generally. As a result, much of this attention (and financial support) began to turn to writers, largely through the work of Alain Locke, Jessie Fauset, W. E. B. Du Bois and Charles S. Johnson, and black publishing venues such as *The Crisis* (the journal of the NAACP [National Association for the Advancement of Colored People]), *Opportunity* (the magazine of the Urban League), and *The Messenger* (a black socialist magazine).

Although the period was far too broad and complex to be reduced to a few figures and publications, special attention paid to W. E. B. Du Bois, Charles S. Johnson, and their respective institutions helps to define more sharply the connections between native modernism, New Negro politics, and Afro-modernist literature. First, Du Bois, the foremost activist/intellectual of the era, researched, wrote, organized, and campaigned at such a prodigious rate – between the ages of thirty and ninety-five he published material on average every twelve days[21] – that his work had perhaps the largest influence over the shape and direction of New Negro consciousness. *The Souls of Black Folk* (1903), perhaps his most enduring work, provided three major templates for the era: a definition of twentieth-century politics according to race, an enduring metaphor for black psychic being, and an early articulation of a pragmatist approach to art and African-American culture. And equally as significant, his editorship of *The Crisis*, from 1910–1934, provided an essential venue for New Negro Renaissance literature in the larger context of New Negro ideology.

It is important to keep in mind that as the first black Ph.D. from Harvard, and as a student of philosophy, Du Bois studied under James and became an intimate friend. Indeed, pragmatism profoundly affected his approach to race relations as early as 1903, when, as many critics point out, he framed black citizenship in classic New Negro terms: that the measure of success of our founding democratic ideals is black political inclusion (Hutchinson, *Harlem Renaissance*, 36). This point would be echoed by William Pickens, Alain Locke, James Weldon Johnson, and many more New Negroes, and would ultimately reverberate across the twentieth century through Richard Wright, Ralph Ellison, and James Baldwin, to name the most obvious.

That political rights must be extended to all or remain perpetually in doubt, puts a pragmatist inflection on racial politics, testing the American political system by outcomes, in essence by the benefits it produces. Equally as important, Du Bois advanced a pragmatist approach to education, culture, and art. Reacting against the increasing "Mammonism" of Atlanta and the "New South," Du Bois called for cultural refinement through education, a refinement that would develop greater interracial understanding. Albeit class-conscious and tinged with Victorian gentility, Du Bois asserted that the university was "the organ of that fine adjustment between real life and the growing knowledge of life, an adjustment which forms the secret of civilization." Universities, he argued, serve as "centres of learning and living, colleges that yearly would send into the life of the South a few white men and a few black men of broad culture, catholic tolerance, and trained ability, joining their hands to other hands, and giv[e] to this squabble of the Races a decent and dignified peace . . ."[22] For Du Bois, the realm of "fine" literature is where racism is transcended: "I sit with Shakespeare and he winces not."[23]

Through *Souls*, Du Bois also places race at the center of his understanding of the modern moment. The often quoted line, "the problem of the Twentieth Century is the problem of the color line,"[24] couches the new century in binary terms, dividing white and black, citizen and non-citizen, have and have-not; and thus raising the question of the extension of the Enlightenment experiment. Clearly, Du Bois's vision was global as he anticipated later critiques of European and American imperialism in racial and material terms. For Du Bois, the central question for the modern moment was whether it would extend or restrict the Enlightenment vision of universal human development.

To this end, *Souls* offers perhaps the most pervasive metaphor for the modern black psyche:

> After the Egyptian and Indian, the Greek and Roman, the Teuton and Mongolian, the Negro is a sort of seventh son, born with a veil, and gifted with second-sight in this American world, – a world which yields him no true self-consciousness, but only lets him see himself through the revelation of the other world. It is a peculiar sensation, this double-consciousness, this sense of always looking at one's self through the eyes of others, of measuring one's soul by the tape of a world that looks on in amused contempt and pity. One ever feels his two-ness, – an American, a Negro; two souls, two thoughts, two unreconciled strivings; two warring ideals in one dark body, whose dogged strength alone keeps it from being torn asunder.[25]

The notion of the divided black psyche ever striving for resolution and thus full self-possession would manifest itself through the writings of James Weldon Johnson, Langston Hughes, Zora Neale Hurston, and Sterling Brown. The metaphor well reflects the conundrum of being a part of, yet apart from, American society; of being enfranchised, yet voteless; of being native son, yet alien. Or, to make racially specific Singal's definition of modernism, the "chaotic condition of twentieth-century existence" was black life in the fissure between American ideals and American practices.

Finally, Du Bois's editorial tenure with the *Crisis* further illustrates the pragmatist underpinnings binding Afro- and nativist modernism. Conceiving African-Americans and their culture as integral parts of the American whole, *The Crisis*, similar to the aforementioned nativist journals, concerned itself with national identity, and of course with the black role in forging that identity. Furthermore, literary art would play a crucial role in racial and national identity formation, relaying the experience of African-Americans and thus reiterating black participation (and ownership) in American development. And while Du Bois's sense of literature – that it should represent the best of African-American culture – was clearly too conservative for most of the younger Renaissance writers, the general support and exposure *The Crisis* offered black writers is undeniable, as is the larger nationalist ideology to which most writers, if not all, conformed.

Like Du Bois, Charles Johnson, editor of *Opportunity*, studied directly under a leading pragmatist: Robert Park, a James and Dewey devotee. Johnson fully embraced the theory of cultural pluralism and the necessity of full and equal African-American participation in the American mainstream. A sociologist by training, Johnson worked to document the specifics of black experiences, applying a relatively new methodology to the heretofore academically invisible African-American. So too, Johnson's stewardship of *Opportunity* reflected his sociological training and investments, as the magazine fought prejudice by publishing creative writing and sociological findings that revealed the daily lives of African-Americans. In terms of literature, Johnson "embraced the pragmatist aesthetic theory that the arts are the most effective instruments for training people to cultural pluralism, creative democracy, achieving the widest possible range of human sympathy and understanding" (Hutchinson, *Harlem Renaissance*, 59). And thus the magazine took the lead in publishing black writers, publicizing young talent, creating awards and awards dinners, all in pursuit of greater funding for budding artists. Together, Johnson and Alain Locke – "pre-eminent entrepreneur of black modernism"[26] – and fellow pragmatist, the two engineered much of the Harlem-based writing explosion. For example, at the March 21, 1924 Civic Club Dinner which Locke had helped to arrange, Paul Kellog, editor of *Survey Graphic*, approached Johnson concerning a special issue devoted to New Negro writers. Locke was chosen to collect and edit the materials, ultimately shaping the edition that would give rise to *The New Negro*. Locke's introductory essay and the volume itself afforded an unprecedented level of visibility for Renaissance artists; indeed for some critics, it launched the era.

Again, promoting a pluralist/nativist vision, Johnson framed New Negro literature in terms of "'native values' typical of American writers of the time . . ." Like Carl Sandburg and Edwin Arlington Robinson, New Negro Renaissance writers would look to common and indigenous sources, and thus would affirm egalitarian and democratic principles. Integral to this vision was Johnson's support of "folk realism," the accurate and unsentimental depiction of folk life and experience. Further executing pragmatist ideas, Johnson held that the experience of rural and working-class African-Americans must contribute to the collective project of ongoing community and nation-building (Hutchinson, *Harlem Renaissance*, 58–59). It is no surprise, then, that Hughes, Hurston, and Brown would win *Opportunity* literary prizes very early in their careers.

Three Afro-modernists: Hurston, Brown, Toomer

Hurston

Self-styled "literary anthropologist" – having trained under Franz Boas – Zora Neale Hurston (1891–1960) articulated her own sense of Afro-modernism in at least four ways: her theory of race, her representation of folk culture, her claims to first wave feminism, and her dramatization of double consciousness. Across her writing, Hurston concerned herself with African-American folk culture and folk ways, with the "Negro furthest down," as she put it. She argued that African-American folk culture, if studied closely, expresses its own artistry, indeed a "racial health – a sense of black people as complete, complex *undiminished* human beings . . ."[27]

Raised in the all-black town of Eatonville, Florida, daughter of the three-term mayor and popular preacher, and heir to her mother's inspirational will, Hurston experienced first-hand the color and artistry of storytelling and preaching in her close-knit community. Tall tales, games, songs, the vivid metaphor of the Bible, and the larger-than-life voicings of storytellers on the porch, all shaped her artistic world. In this sense, Hurston's representation of African-American folk life stressed the performative, and ritualistic aspects of black identity. In keeping with Boasian theory, race is rooted in culture and history, in practices that have accrued meaning over time. So too, her approach to African-American folk culture capitalized on the leveling effect of pragmatism and Boasian theory. If modernity is traditionally associated with whiteness, urbanization, technology, and industrialization; and if narrower definitions of modernism employ blackness, the rural, and the pastoral as its enabling antitheses, then Hurston undermines this distorting hierarchy by asserting the folk and the vernacular in a relative (thus equally important) position to allegedly more important cultural formations. And finally, Hurston's address of the folk executes a pragmatist/pluralist approach (as we have seen in Charles Johnson), presenting "folk realism" as a means of communicating experience to a culturally diverse polity.

In addition to her approach to folk culture, Hurston is most often framed in reference to contemporary black feminism, a progenitor for Alice Walker, Ntozake Shange, and others. Yet much of Hurston's feminist politics respond to first wave feminism, roughly 1880–1920, and its influence on modernist thought and art. As Marianne Dekoven points out, issues of gender and changing roles for women were of central concern for modernism. The "new woman" – "independent, educated, (relatively) sexually liberated, oriented more toward productive life in the public sphere than toward reproductive life in the home"[28] – served as a source of inspiration and anxiety for male and female modernists alike. Virginia Woolf, Henrik Ibsen, Kate Chopin, Gertrude Stein, and Ernest Hemingway – to name only a few – all explored the implications of this new feminine type.

Similarly, many of Hurston's female protagonists struggle for independence in male-dominated communities. For example, early short stories such as "Isis" or "Sweat" depict black women resisting their severely circumscribed social spaces. And of course Hurston's most celebrated novel, *Their Eyes Were Watching God*, pits Janie Crawford's vision of herself against her community's definition of black femininity. As a black new woman, Janie exercises choice in her relationships, takes possession of traditionally male-dominated social space, achieves financial independence, and ultimately tells her own tale.

Physical mobility stresses the choices Janie makes in relationships and her ability to end them once they thwart her progress. Indeed Janie exercises her choice by killing, in one way or another, each of her partners, stressing the importance of her growth. She does not simply leave Logan Killicks, but as teller of the tale she renders him a narrative execution, banishing him from the bulk of her story. In response to his abuse, Janie rhetorically executes Jody Starks, exposing his impotence to the community and thus sending him to his death bed. And finally, as the rabid Tea Cake exhibits exaggerated (and lethal) signs of patriarchal possession, she turns the phallic sign of male authority on him and shoots him with his own gun.

Hurston also illustrates Janie's sense of independence and growth through an unqualified celebration of love, sexuality, and the black female body. With language and imagery free of Judeo-Christian implications of sin, and free of the dominant culture's fantasy of excessive black female sexuality, Hurston affords Janie genuine playfulness and curiosity about sexuality. For example, Hurston delivers Janie's first vision of love and emotional fulfillment through a lush, organic depiction of masturbation:

> She saw a dust-bearing bee sink into the sanctum of a bloom; the thousand sister-calyxes arch to meet the love embrace and the ecstatic shiver of the tree from root to tiniest branch creaming in every blossom and frothing with delight. So this was marriage! She had been summoned to behold a revelation. Then Janie felt a pain remorseless sweet that left her limp and languid.[29]

It is the occasion of her first orgasm – not Nanny's preaching or cultural sanction – that enables Janie to envision an ideal marriage and a sense of her fulfillment.

Yet another dimension of Hurston's modernism involves her use of structure and form. In *Their Eyes Were Watching God*, Hurston charts Janie's growth toward subjectivity in the mode of narration itself. What Gates describes as "free indirect discourse" serves as the rhetorical device that creates the illusion of Janie's status of speaking subject, the illusion of the text as a story told to Pheoby. Free indirect discourse seeks to combine the folk oral tradition (direct speech) with the literary (standard English, third person narration), creating folk-inflected narration with the impression of dialogue. Or as Gates puts it, "free indirect discourse is a profound attempt to remove the distinction between repeated speech and represented events."[30] The following paragraph, announcing the end of the hurricane, well illustrates the point:

> And then again Him-with-the-square-toes had gone back to his hours. He stood once more and again in his high flat house without sides to it and without a roof with his soulless sword standing upright in his hand. His pale white horse had galloped over waters, and thundered over land. The time of dying was over. It was time to bury the dead.
>
> (Hurston, *Their Eyes Were Watching God*, 160)

This lyrical narration is "adorned" with metaphor or "word pictures" that Hurston identifies with black idiomatic speech. It is both standard English and colloquial, the report of events informed by the vernacular.

Hurston's use of this "bivocal utterance" reflects a division of consciousness – a double consciousness at the heart of Hurston's Afro-modernism. Though Janie strives to become a speaking subject, her subjectivity remains circumscribed by free indirect discourse; her speech is ever mediated by a narrative strategy creating only the illusion of her full subjectivity. Thus, "double voice unreconciled" serves as "a verbal analogue of her double experiences as a woman in a male-dominated world and as a black person in a nonblack world, a woman writer's revision of W. E. B. Du Bois's metaphor of 'double consciousness' for the hyphenated African-American." Gates goes on to reflect that "Hurston's un-resolved tension between her double voices signifies her full understanding of modernism. Hurston uses the two voices in her text[s] to celebrate the psychological fragmentation both of modernity and of the black American."[31] Ultimately Hurston's narrative strategy comments on the tenuous relationship between black vernacular and a mainstream reading audience, between black women writers and the publishing establishment, and between Hurston's artistic self and American modernity.

Brown

A fellow traveler of the rural black South, Sterling A. Brown (1901–1989) celebrated the folk and modernism largely through poetry. Insisting upon the complexities of New Negro politics and arts, he once said "when you say that I belong to the 'Harlem Renaissance' you are insulting me, but if you say I belong to the 'New Negro Renaissance,' then I will feel as proud as Jelly Roll Morton . . ."[32] Dismissing the Harlem Renaissance as "the show window, the cashier's till, but no more Negro America than New York is America,"[33] Brown claimed New Negro politics while positioning himself as outsider to the Manhattan scene; he roundly condemned the patronage system and Carl Van Vechten, and suggested that Harlem writers prostituted their talents, pandering to whites in search of the primitive and the exotic. While clearly over-simplifying the situation, Brown underscored the uniqueness of his vision for African-American letters and culture. Poet, essayist, cultural critic, anthologist, and ethnographer, Brown devoted his career to the creation of a new artistic and critical vocabulary commensurate with the range and teeming complexity he found in modern black life. He was quick to point out that while Harlem-based writers were courting patrons, he had embarked upon a six-year tour of the rural south. While teaching at successive black colleges and universities, Brown canvassed the countryside, interviewing sharecroppers and field hands, listening to blues singers and tall-tale tellers, and visiting the obligatory juke joint. Real life figures whom he met, such as Mrs. Bibby, Slim Greer, and Calvin "Big Boy" Davis, would become folk heroes in a poetry largely based on folk idioms, voices, and forms.

Brown firmly believed that African-American folk and folk culture were by definition modern, and that folk idiom and vernacular were fully capable of rationalizing and representing the myriad challenges of modern life. Black subjectivity, interiority, and historicity were abundantly evident in folk forms. For Brown, the blues in particular – its strident secularism and direct confrontation of chaos – embodied much of the modernist sensibility inherent in folk culture. Like Hurston, Brown confronted the prevailing assumption of blackness and the folk as the antitheses of modernity and progress. For Brown, perhaps most conspicuously the use of dialect in the plantation tradition articulated the permanent backwardness imposed and reinforced by America's post-Reconstruction white supremacist culture. His entire career, but particularly his poetry, sought to reconstruct black representation in the service of black humanity and democratic access.

A close reading of the opening poem "Odyssey of Big Boy," in his first collection, *Southern Road* (1932), aptly illustrates both the modernity he found in folk culture, as well as the modernism of his own artistry. "Odyssey of Big Boy" introduces the collection with a chronicle of travel and experience, gesturing toward the freedom, self-discovery, and ultimate immortality they might yield. Based on the blues singer Calvin "Big Boy" Davis, Brown creates a blues ballad that delivers the voice of the itinerant performer, yet in an altered form, charged with Homeric implication. As Davis reviews his extended travel and catholic experiences, with the hope of mythic transcendences, the poem builds tension between past and present, thus stressing the temporal moment of vocalization.

Significantly, "Odyssey" is not a standard third-person narrative in the way that other ballads present John Henry, Casey Jones, or Stagolee. It is not simply a chronicle of past deeds and assertions, either. As Davis confronts imminent death, he embarks upon a personal odyssey into the uncertain future, an odyssey that dramatizes contingency and subjectivity, Davis in the ongoing act of interpretation:

> Lemme be wid Casey Jones,
>   Lemme be wid Stagolee,
> Lemme be wid such like men
>   When Death takes hol' on me,
>   When Death takes hol' on me . . .

Fittingly he ends the poem with a similar projection, yet adding and stressing John Henry as the supreme sign of apotheosis:

> An' all dat Big Boy axes
>   When time comes fo' to go,
> Lemme be wid John Henry, steel drivin' man,
>   Lemme be wid old Jazzbo,
>   Lemme be wid ole Jazzbo . . .[34]

Thus framing the history of his life within a vision of the future, Davis's "future link with the past" depends entirely on the oral reshaping of his history; the vocal act of proclamation becomes the odyssey itself, the voice as passage and "mode of knowing." [35]

Urgently Davis delivers a history of robust work and love, travel and conquest, a life exemplifying core heroic virtues in the masculinist tradition: freedom, mobility, autonomy, and physical prowess. Having "seed what dey is to see," the statement of his life should win him passage into the pantheon of cultural gods. But, just as his odyssey depends on the statement of his life, it also relies on the form the statement takes, here the well-known ballad of John Henry. Strictly in terms of stanza form – number of lines, rhyme scheme, and repetition – Davis appropriates the folk ballad "John Henry," specifically the one Brown later anthologized in the *Negro Caravan* (1941). Even the popular melody used to sing "John Henry" would fit "Odyssey of Big Boy." In short, Davis rhetorically recreates himself in the form of John Henry, and therefore constructs himself as both subject and object, the creative agent of the poem as well as its referent. With this symbolic gesture to history, Davis reaches back to the past to claim a form and voice that allows him to envision his future. He grafts his biography onto a cultural continuum; his blues-infected lyrical odyssey from past to future represents not just his progression but that of the surrounding culture.

Equally as important, as we see Davis gesturing toward larger cultural dynamics in his appeal for immortality, he emerges as artist, both musician and poet, able to cull from his experiences "a near tragic, near comic lyricism." [36] His vocalization serves as sign of the artist's ability to shape and recreate one's psychic and culture space, to reshape anguish and chaos into song. And implicit in this reading is Brown himself; here the author in the poem and author of the poem conflate. Ultimately it is Brown who presents Davis and folk culture in this manner; it is he who interprets the urgent black modernity on either side of his mythic southern road; and finally it may well be Brown himself petitioning for immortality on the basis of the force and skill of his lyrical voice.

In a larger sense, the central trope of the road in *Southern Road* alludes to the palpable realities of black life in the South and to the metaphysical contradictions of Afro-modernism. In an immediate sense, the road is literal, a place and locale; it serves as an avenue cutting across the southern land-scape, splitting it in two, providing access for the poet/witness traveling and recording the multiple voices and personae met along the way.

Yet the road is a means of mobility for the southern African-American as well, a way of changing one's material condition through movement from restrictive to liberating space, from object to subject. Symbolically the road refers to separation and mediation as well; divided, it accommodates traffic in opposite directions. [37] Thus such constant coming and going suggests a doubling or unresolved duality that reflects conflicted consciousness, both individual and collective.

In a larger sense, the road is *both/and*, accommodating antagonistic impulses. As Vera Kutzinski puts it, "the characteristic referential ambiguity of "Southern Road" derives from the fact that it leads both away from the South (to a symbolic North), and thus becomes an emblem of adversity, as well as back toward the South, in which case it is transformed into an 'image of kin.'"[38] Ultimately the perpetual ambiguity at the heart of the metaphor (and the collection) references the divided black psyche itself, the both/and of black modernity in response to America's larger contradictions, particularly those relative to race and politics.

Finally Brown stakes his claim to American modernism by taking ownership of one of its progenitors: Walt Whitman. Whitman's commitment to communal and democratic ideals; his attention to the "common man," to the local, and to the "idiom of each existence"[39] help to create the ideological and artistic space for Brown's work. So too, the act of singing – singing the self, chanting saints, singing work songs and the blues, singing the body electric and more – fosters a poetics of celebration, agency, and consciousness. Perhaps stylized vocalization itself serves as the site at which Whitman-influenced modernism and Brown's Afro-modernism intersect.

Toomer

Of all the New Negro writers, the highly enigmatic Jean Toomer (1894–1967) looms as the most obvious modernist, in the conventional sense. Concerned to the point of chronic depression with the fragmented and physically debilitating nature of modern life, Toomer's writings focused on what Rudolph P. Byrd terms "human development," or the perpetual pursuit of spiritual wholeness. Beginning with the critical success of *Cane* (1923), through his Whitmanesque paean to a new America in "The Blue Meridian," and even through his Gurdjieffian-influenced novels and plays, for Toomer "the challenge of modern life was to transcend the fragmentation of modernity itself."[40] Against the ongoing assaults of mechanization and industrialization, either in urban or rural life, Toomer posited the individual in pursuit of a higher state of consciousness, a plane on which the atomized emotion, body, and intellect are reunited. He made full use of many of the modernist experimental techniques and approaches. Fragmented narrative, impressionistic condensation, multi-genre eclecticism, montage, and the imagist "insistence on fresh vision and on the perfect clean economic line,"[41] convey in form and statement the psychic peril of modern life as well as the perpetual possibility of renewal.

Beginning with *Cane*, his greatest achievement, Toomer moves from the racially specific milieu to potentially transcendent truths concerning the human psyche. The compilation of sketches, short stories, drama, and poems are drawn from his experience of black small town and rural life in Sparta, Georgia. Later reflecting on *Cane* and its experiment, he commented on the clash of folk ways and modernization: "The folk-spirit was walking in to die on the modern desert. That spirit was so beautiful. Its death was so tragic . . . And this is the feeling I put into 'Cane.'"[42]

In this sense, *Cane* attempts to capture a late phase of folk life as it gives way to the machine; so too, the volume renders the psychic and emotional toll of transition, while signaling the ongoing potential for revelation and renewal. Embodying this very tension between destruction and renewal, the three-part structure and its analogue unify form and theme in an overtly modernist manner. The three sections – moving from South to North and back to the South, from rural to urban and back again – suggest a circularity and potential completion, gesturing toward wholeness. Making the pattern visual, the first two sections open with a half crescent, while the third opens with two half crescents facing one another yet disconnected. These arcs presuppose thematic curvature as the animating tension between sleeping and consciousness, fragmentation and wholeness, the spiritual and the material move toward their fullest articulation in "Kabnis."

The first section of *Cane*, primarily focused on the plight of black women, addresses the corrosive effects of sexual exploitation, racism, and the lack of self-awareness. Karintha, Becky, Carma, Fern, and Esther all suffer psychic and emotional trauma at the hands of their male-dominated culture, while failing to achieve the self-possession that would allow them to resist their circumstances. And finally, "Blood Burning Moon" dramatizes the inevitability of destruction as a result of racism. While the heavy naturalism of "Blood Burning Moon" threatens to stamp the entire section with a damning sense of fatalism, Fern succeeds in preserving a piece of herself untouched, and Carma's fortitude may well preserve her through her separation from Bane (Byrd, *Jean Toomer's Years*, 47).

The second section, set in Chicago and Washington DC, decries materialism, classism, racism, and the breakdown of community, all exacerbated by the deracinating effects of urban life. Yet this section signals alternative possibilities as well, primarily through "Bona and Paul." Here, with a relationship threatened by racism, Bona capitulates to the prevailing understanding of race, while Paul, who "sprouts new life," is transformed by his embrace of his mixed-blood heritage, and so "takes the first steps toward wholeness" (Byrd, *Jean Toomer's Years*, 22).

Also important for both sections are the poems that "elucidate or set the stage or provide a transition between sketches" (Byrd, *Jean Toomer's Years*, 13). Through foreshadowing or thematic punctuation, they help to create the mode and texture of the milieu. Anticipating *In Our Time* (1925), they function similarly to Hemingway's interchapters, as they condense the metaphoric and thematic effects of the surrounding stories.

Finally "Kabnis" ends the collage, adding history as a crucial element for self-awareness and thus wholeness. In his struggle for epiphany, "Kabnis" echoes Paul's examination of his past as a means of better understanding the present and future. As the drama begins, the protagonist Kabnis is "detached from history." It is the "twisted awful thing" of slavery and ongoing racial exploitation that Kabnis actively denies. Thus, he abuses Father John, the "symbol, flesh, and spirit of the past" (Byrd, *Jean Toomer's Years*, 24), but collapses at Carrie K.'s feet as she attempts to abate his mental anguish, his "fever." He removes his robe and "casts off the lies, illusion, and subterfuges he has employed all of his life as a shield against the truth and the meaning of the past. Kabnis has come through his ordeal with history whole and sane" (Byrd, *Jean Toomer's Years*, 25–26).

Yet in keeping with *Cane*'s sense of unresolved tension, Kabnis can also represent quite the opposite. He is excluded from the circle of light that engulfs Carrie K. and Father John. Indeed, after his collapse he walks "doggedly toward the steps," "savagely jerks [the bucket of coal] from the floor," and silently retreats to the workshop "with eyes downcast and swollen."[43] He has not uttered a word to either Carrie K. or Father John, nor does he display signs of acceptance or transformation. So just as the ending may gesture toward wholeness, it also signals Kabnis's chronic state of psychic paralysis; and just as the arc (both thematic and visual) gestures toward completion, it continues to articulate separation. Indeed, *Cane* effects an "interdependence of theme and structure" (Helbling, 139), where form creates "an aesthetic context that symbolizes as well as fuses with the emotional content . . ." (Helbling, *The Harlem Renaissance*, 140). Here, the fragmentary and eclectic nature of the volume embodies both the atomized individual in the modernist context, as well as the possibility of reunification and wholeness.

The artistic success of *Cane* was not lost on Toomer's New Negro compatriots, nor did it fail to echo and anticipate the formal and thematic experiments of his high modernist contemporaries. Sterling Brown wrote lovingly to Toomer that "I look upon *Cane* as one of the most influential forces in the artistic awakening of the Negro and as one of the most beautiful and moving books of contemporary American literature" (Byrd, *Jean Toomer's Years*, 183). Arna Bontemps said that his generation of writers "went quietly mad," over *Cane*, as the volume legitimized the notion that folk culture could be the basis of New Negro art. In terms of both formal fragmentation and thematic concern for psychic distortion, *Cane* references Anderson's *Winesburg, Ohio* (1919); Toomer's use of the present tense and verbal impressionism (again along with fragmented narration) echoes Stein's *Three Lives* (1909) and anticipates the lyric compression and multi-perspective representation in *In Our Time*. Finally, the loose federation of pieces creating a larger milieu anticipates the narrative mode and effect of Faulkner's *Go Down Moses* (1942).

After *Cane*, Toomer quickly incorporated the influence of Gurdjieff while continuing to focus on mankind's quest for wholeness. This combination found fullest expression in "The Blue Meridian" (1936), his "national epic" (Byrd, *Jean Toomer's Years*, 157) proclaiming America's symbolic potential for universal man. Structured in three parts – Black, White, and Blue meridian – each section represents Gurdjieff's first three levels of consciousness: sleeping, waking, and self-consciousness. So too, the first two sections represent the three American groups, Native Americans, blacks, and whites that will create this new America. The dialectal interaction between blacks and whites creates synthesis in blue, "the harmoniously developed, universal man, free of definition and classification that restrict or confine the vitality of his being."[44] Furthermore, "the imaginary circles which connect both geographical poles and the circle passing through the celestial poles" (Bell, "Toomer's Blue Meridian," 345), the meridian itself represents the very site of synthesis, as the "blue man" signals the perpetual amalgamation of ethnicities into the "race called the Americans." Finally, then, the poem registers America's racial history in Hegelian terms in order "to redeem the past and envision an America that would evolve into the prototype of a society that had achieved universal humanity" (Byrd, *Jean Toomer's Years*, 154).

Toomer's forceful optimism in proclaiming and envisioning America overtly involves Whitman. Indeed, Toomer "thought of himself as Whitman's successor in the American prophet/healer's role,"[45] and so took up a similar vision as well as a similar approach to poetry's craft and purpose. With Whitman in mind, he substitutes linearity for circularity and repetition; uses the "verse paragraph," prose rhythms, and extensive parallelism, as well as the techniques of cataloging emotions.[46] And perhaps most importantly, he saw in poetry the potential to redeem and renew, indeed the vision at the core of *Leaves of Grass*.

In his 1953 essay, "Twentieth-Century Fiction and the Black Mask of Humanity," Ralph Ellison challenged the prevailing New Critical wisdom when he chastised the lost generation for gross "intellectual evasion." Where, for Ellison, nineteenth-century American writers had addressed the defining tension in American culture – "the clash between property rights and human rights" – lost generation writers (Hemingway in particular) had replaced "social responsibility" with technical prowess: "what for Twain was a means [formal mastery] to a moral end became for Hemingway an end in itself. And just as the trend toward technique for the sake of technique and production for the sake of the market lead to the neglect of the human need out of which they spring, so do they lead in literature to a marvelous technical virtuosity won at the expense of a gross insensitivity to fraternal values" (Ellison, *Shadow and Act*, 35). New Negroes cultivated and celebrated a very different sense of modernism; from a New Negro/Harlem Renaissance perspective, American modernism ultimately served as an opportunity to make real the promises of Reconstruction. Taking advantage of the host of theories, methodologies, intellectual communities, and institutions defining nativist/pluralist modernity, New Negro artists depicted African-American life, in all its complexities, with an eye toward the larger American democratic experiment. Their Afro-modernism, then, was one of possibility, an occasion to redefine themselves as full participants, and to redefine their republic as fully democratic.

NOTES

1. Daniel Joseph Singal, "Towards a Definition of American Modernism," *American Quarterly* 39 (Spring 1987), 8.
2. Cornel West, *The American Evasion of Philosophy: A Genealogy of Pragmatism* (Madison: University of Wisconsin Press, 1989), 5.
3. William James, *A Pluralist Universe* (Cambridge, MA: Harvard University Press, 1977), 145.
4. Singal, "Towards a Definition," 16.
5. John Dewey, *Reconstruction in Philosophy* [1920], in *The Middle Works, 1899–1924*, vol. XII, ed. Jo Ann Boydston (Carbondale: Southern Illinois University Press, 1976), 186.
6. George Hutchinson, *The Harlem Renaissance in Black and White* (Cambridge, MA: Harvard University Press, 1995), 59.
7. Franz Boas, *Anthropology and Modern Life* (New York: Norton, 1928), 18–61.
8. Franz Boas, *Race, Language, and Culture* (The University of Chicago Press, 1982), 13–14.
9. James McFarlane, "The Mind of Modernism," in *Modernism, 1890–1930*, ed. James McFarlane and Malcolm Bradbury (New York: Penguin Books, 1976), p. 92.
10. Waldo Frank, *Our America* (New York: Boni and Liveright, 1919), 97.
11. Walt Whitman, *Democratic Vistas* (New York: Liberal Arts Press, 1949), 6.
12. Max Eastman, *The Literary Mind: Its Place in an Age of Science* (New York: Charles Scribner's Sons, 1935), 79–92, and Hutchinson, *The Harlem Renaissance*, 261.

13. Max Eastman, "Introduction," *Harlem Shadows: The Poems of Claude McKay* (New York: Harcourt Brace, 1922), i.
14. Philip Dray, *At the Hands of Persons Unknown: The Lynching of Black America* (New York: Random House, 2002), viii.
15. Leon F. Litwack, *Trouble in Mind: Black Southerners in the Age of Jim Crow* (New York: Vintage Books, 1998), 284.
16. Wilson Moses, "The Lost World of the Negro, 1895–1919: Black Literary and Intellectual Life before the 'Renaissance,'" *Black American Literature Forum* 21 (Spring-Summer 1987), 61.
17. "An Address of the Country," quoted from James Weldon Johnson, *Black Manhattan* (New York: Da Capo Press, 1991), 136–137.
18. Alain Locke, "The New Negro," in *The New Negro: An Interpretation*, ed. Alain Locke (New York: Albert and Charles Boni, 1925), 12.
19. Ralph Ellison, "Richard Right's Blues," in *Shadow and Act* (New York: Vintage Books, 1964), 78.
20. Lawrence W. Levine, *Black Culture and Black Consciousness: Afro-American Folk Thought from Slavery to Freedom* (New York: Oxford University Press, 1977), 5–80, 136–297.
21. Henry Louis Gates, Jr., "Introduction," in *The Souls of Black Folk* (New York: Penguin Books, 1989), ix.
22. W. E. B. Du Bois, "Of the Wings of Atalanta," in *The Souls of Black Folk* (New York: Penguin Books, 1989), 71–72.
23. Du Bois, "Of the Training of Black Men," in *The Souls of Black Folk*, 90.
24. Du Bois, "The Forethought," in *The Souls of Black Folk*, 1.
25. Du Bois, "Of Our Spiritual Strivings," in *The Souls of Black Folk*, 5.
26. William J. Maxwell, *New Negro, Old Left: African-American Writing and Communism Between the Wars* (New York: Columbia University Press, 1999), 2.
27. Alice Walker, quoted in Henry Louis Gates, Jr., "Afterword: Zora Neale Hurston: 'A Negro Way of Saying,'" in Zora Neale Hurston, *Their Eyes Were Watching God* (New York: Harper & Row Publishers, 1937), 190.
28. Marianne Dekoven, "Modernism and Gender," in *The Cambridge Companion to Modernism*, ed. Michael Levenson (Cambridge University Press, 1999), 174.
29. Hurston, *Their Eyes Were Watching God*, 10–11.
30. Henry Louis Gates, Jr., "*Their Eyes Were Watching God*: Hurston and the Speakerly Text," in *Zora Neale Hurston: Critical Perspectives Past and Present*, ed. Henry Louis Gates, Jr. and K. A. Appiah (New York: Amistad), 193.
31. Gates, "Afterword: Zora Neale Hurston," 193–194.
32. Sterling A. Brown, "Ragtime and the Blues," in *Sterling A. Brown: A UMUM Tribute*, ed. Black History Museum Committee (Philadelphia: Black History Museum UMUM Publishers, 1982), 81.
33. Sterling A. Brown, "The New Negro in Literature (1925–1955)," in *The New Negro Thirty Years Afterwards*, ed. Rayford W. Logan (Washington, DC: Howard University Press, 1955), 57.
34. Sterling A. Brown, "The Odyssey of Big Boy," in *The Collected Poems of Sterling A. Brown*, ed. Michael S. Harper (New York: Harper & Row Publishers, 1980), 20–21.

35. Kimberly W. Benston, "Sterling Brown's After-Song: 'When de Saints Go Ma'ching Home' and the Performance of Afro-American Voice," *Callaloo* 5, nos. 14 and 15 (February–May 1982), 39.

36. Ralph Ellison, "Richard Wright's Blues," 78.

37. Rudolph P. Byrd, conversation, December 10, 1996.

38. Vera M. Kutzinski, "The Distant Closeness of Dancing Doubles: Sterling Brown and William Carlos Williams," *Black American Literature Forum* 22 (Spring 1982), 21.

39. George Hutchinson, "Langston Hughes and the 'Other' Whitman," in *The Continuing Presence of Walt Whitman: The Life after the Life*, ed. Robert K. Martin (University of Iowa Press, 1992), 18.

40. Mark Helbling, *The Harlem Renaissance: The One and the Many* (Westport, CT: Greenwood Press, 1999), 149.

41. Walter Kalaidjian, *American Culture between the Wars: Revisionary Modernism and Postmodern Critique* (New York: Columbia University Press, 1993), 83.

42. Quoted from Rudolph P. Byrd, *Jean Toomer's Years with Gurdjieff: Portrait of an Artist, 1923–1936* (Athens: The University of Georgia Press, 1990), 12.

43. Jean Toomer, *Cane: An Authoritative Text, Backgrounds, Criticism*, ed. Darwin T. Turner (New York: W. W. Norton & Company, 1988), 117.

44. Bernard Bell, "Jean Toomer's 'Blue Meridian': The Poet as Prophet of a New Order of Man," in *Jean Toomer: A Critical Evaluation*, ed. Therman B. O'Daniel (Washington, DC: Howard University Press, 1988), 343.

45. George Hutchinson, "The Whitman Legacy and the Harlem Renaissance," in *Walt Whitman: The Centennial Essays*, ed. Ed Folsom (Iowa City: University of Iowa Press, 1994), 211.

46. Robert K. Martin, "Introduction", *Continuing Presence of Walt Whitman*, xiii; and Byrd, *Jean Toomer's Years with Gurdjieff*, 154.

6

JED RASULA

Jazz and American modernism

Approaching the topic of jazz and modernism, one might begin with the emergence of bebop, which was routinely called "modernist" in the 1940s. While the debate about bop replicated aspects of earlier disputes about literary and artistic modernism, the parochial nature of the debate (largely confined to fans, journalists, and record collectors) insulates it from the more compelling issues associated with modernism. An alternative approach to the topic might enumerate encounters with, and opinions about, jazz by recognized modernists. Ezra Pound, for instance, backed George Antheil's concert hall amalgamation of jazz with futurism, even as he disparaged the piano as an agent of jazz (confusing it with ragtime). But most of the modernists had little interest in jazz, and to detect fugitive traces of their encounter with it one would have to scrape deep recesses of the biographical barrel (and, in most cases, the evidence would illustrate a larger pattern of Negrophilia or Negrophobia, adding little to the study of jazz). A third approach, adopted here, is to regard jazz as a conspicuous feature of modernity as it was manifested during and after the Great War. In *that* capacity, jazz unquestionably informed modernism as intellectual challenge, sensory provocation, and social texture.

Around World War I, because of widespread uncertainty about what it was – a kind of music, an attitude to life, a mannerism, cheap vulgarity, or a spirited emotional impulse – the social career of jazz was launched with opportunities for interested parties on all sides of the issue to hold forth. "The word 'jazz,' in its progress toward respectability, has meant first sex, then dancing, then music. It is associated with a state of nervous stimulation, not unlike that of big cities behind the lines of war."[1] F. Scott Fitzgerald's famous pronouncement has served as the decisive link between jazz and modernism for seventy years. Although it is no longer tenable to associate jazz with anything he meant by the term, nonetheless, he pinpoints the controversy that made jazz appear responsible for upending genteel America with its Gilded Age proprieties. The transit of American womanhood from rosy cheeked

Gibson Girl to bobcut flapper was brought about (so it appeared) by the ceaseless incitement to sensual dancing by "jazz" (whatever that was); and moral watchdogs assumed sex was the allegorical gist and practical outcome. In the milieu of 1920 – haunted by the Red Menace, the increasing visibility of blacks in cultural life, and the emancipation of women that combined suffrage with the specter of sexual liberation – jazz was thought to incite licentious abandon. But if jazz was merely distasteful to some – "a low streak in man's tastes that has not yet come out in civilization's wash"[2] – for others its transgressions were a political menace, an "expression of protest against law and order, the bolshevik element of license striving for expression in music."[3] Even fans might speak of a hot solo as "going Bolshevik." The abandon associated with performative mannerisms (particularly in hokum and novelty acts) could not help but signify lack of dignity. It was also widely assumed that black musicians had no formal training, and improvisation was regarded as the last resort of those who could not read music. Musicians were suspected of improprieties in playing their instruments, just as the very presence of novelty instruments in the "spasm bands" was suggestive of illicit activities, and after Prohibition became law in 1919 jazz and speakeasies were virtually synonymous.

Insofar as jazz was thought to be characteristically American in some approved sense, it could be tolerated and even pinched on its upstart cheek with a twinkle in the parental eye condoning youthful escapades. Incarnating unbuttoned postwar swagger, jazz could appear "very American in its snap, speed, smartness and cosmopolitan character."[4] Jazz was the right music for an energetic nation, and in the most positive spirit, it signaled a coming-of-age on the world stage – "a genuine contribution to the gaiety of nations,"[5] as an English admirer put it, possibly even "the National Anthem of Civilization."[6] For Europeans, the Hollywood movies, cars, razor blades, women's fashions, chewing gum, skyscrapers, and jazz-bands (hyphenated in Europe) were ingredients in the vogue for an Americanism synonymous with modernity. Le Corbusier, the leading exponent of modernism in architecture, declared the New York skyline "hot jazz in stone and steel."[7] But others were wary about a music that could be equated with industry. H. L. Mencken pungently called jazz the "sound of riveting"[8] and Waldo Frank hammered the point home:

> Jazz syncopates the lathe-lunge, jazz shatters the piston-thrust, jazz shreds the hum of wheels, jazz is the spark and sudden lilt centrifugal to their incessant pulse. Jazz is a moment's gaiety, after which the spirit droops, cheated and unnurtured. The song is not an escape from the Machine to limpid depths of the soul. It is the Machine itself! It is the music of a revolt that fails. Its voice is the mimicry of our industrial havoc.[9]

Even proponents of jazz recognized that commercialism was a liability, subjecting positive aspects of the music to ceaseless repetition as well as propagating saccharine varieties more amenable to public consumption. Although the stock market crash reduced record sales in the US from 128 million in 1926 to six million in 1932, by 1934 the complaint of "overproduction" was still being made.

Soon after Dvořák's observation in 1893 that American music, to be organically original, must be based on Negro folk tunes, cultural nationalists faced a racial quandary, as ragtime became all the rage. Genteel gatekeepers might accord black spirituals some respect, but for white composers to ground themselves in an inherently alien idiom seemed artificial (if not grotesque, given the pervasiveness of minstrelsy on the popular stage). Besides, to what extent could "the folk" consist of a denigrated minority? When ragtime was succeeded by jazz, the problem of folk music persisted, adding the exacerbating element of a commercialism so conspicuous and invasive that one might question whether any "folk" had ever been involved with jazz at all. Could folk music become commercialized without compromising its integrity? Was jazz authentic folk music, or merely accented with folk elements? In many quarters such questions were beside the point, given that Dvořák and many others had singled out the "sorrow songs" as indubitably authentic, and the prestige of spirituals invariably relegated secular music like jazz to inferior status, even for some of its advocates. Furthermore, surveys and collections of black folk music were often at pains to demonstrate the authenticity of rural folkways, implying that jazz was really a commercialized urban music with only a superficial resemblance to its country cousins (including the blues – which had negative class connotations). Although not noted at the time, jazz was the first thoroughly cosmopolitan music of African-Americans. Its diffusion pattern has traditionally been charted from New Orleans to Chicago to New York, with Kansas City later becoming a magnet for the "territory" bands (with Los Angeles grudgingly conceded as another important site). But in terms of initial impact, Paris was also of singular importance – not only as a reminder of the fact that jazz was an international phenomenon, but because so much of the debate about jazz was complicated by traditional Eurocentricism of the American intelligentsia.

While jazz was unquestionably American, serious attention to it was European. Dvořák's earlier validation of black music in general was narrowed to jazz by visiting composers like Milhaud and Ravel, while European conductors and virtuosi residing in America gave further sanction to its musical viability. For cultural nationalists, jazz was tainted not because it was black but because it was embraced by European modernists, many of whom had earlier been enthused about ragtime. Debussy, for instance, had appropriated rag rhythms, though Americans found his unusual harmonies more disturbing. Before the Great War, modernism was typically associated with forward-looking cultural nationalists like those associated with *Seven Arts* more amenable to a pluralist future. Editor James Oppenheim, observing the prevalence of popular music in American life, bemoaned creeping commercialism while resisting an elitist response, emphasizing instead the need for "prophecy and philosophy and vulgarity in art."[10] Writing in a *Seven Arts* symposium on ragtime in 1917, Hiram Moderwell detected in the music "something Nietzschean in its implicit philosophy that all the world's a dance."[11] Ragtime did indeed set the world dancing. Despite condemnation by the American Federation of Musicians in 1901, ragtime had become the primary agent for the domestic boom in piano sales. After 1910, when the Turkey Trot and similar dances swept the country and then the world, ragtime extended its reign from the parlor to the dance hall. From the eighteenth-century minuet to the nineteenth-century waltz, the introduction of new dance forms incited suspicions of libertine opportunism. Ragtime, however, carried the extra weight of race relations. Nonetheless, ragtime established more dignified career opportunities for African-Americans than had previously been available in public life, facilitating professional opportunities on stage and in the touring "syncopated orchestras" for which the transition to jazz was merely a change of label to meet public expectations.

Terminological uncertainty was rampant in the transition from rags to jazz because, in social terms, the distinction was unclear. Between them, ragtime and jazz pioneered the infusion of dominant white culture by African-Americans, particularly leisure activities like social dancing, cabaret and show music. It is important to stress the role of ragtime during the period when Americans were introduced to modernism. The famous Armory Show occurred as the nation was in thrall to Irving Berlin's hit tunes like "Alexander's Ragtime Band" and "Everybody's Doin' It Now" (Tin Pan Alley homages to ragtime, not rags themselves). That is to say, the thematic aura of popular culture was unavoidably ragtime as the crowds surged through Armory Hall, gazing in bewilderment at the optical assault engineered by French painters (often several decades earlier). Among the numerous American artists transformed under its impact from realists to modernists, Stuart Davis recalled that the Armory Show challenged him with "an objective order in these works which I felt was lacking in my own. It gave me the same kind of excitement I got from the numerical precisions of the Negro piano players in the Negro saloons, and I resolved that I would quite definitely have to become a 'modern' artist."[12]

The perceptual bewilderment occasioned by Armory Show pieces like Marcel Duchamp's "Nude Descending a Staircase" presaged the response to jazz at the end of the war, when the public was confronted by what seemed an aural onslaught commensurate with the cognitive dissonance of modern art. What initially seemed the acoustic counterpart to Duchamp's "explosion in a shingle factory"[13] proved easier to assimilate once the initial novelty wore off and the apparent barrage of noise turned out to adhere to danceable measures. Assimilation of noise being relative, many refused to acknowledge that jazz was anything more than calculated rudeness. In Europe, where the Futurists advocated an "art of noise" and the Dadaists had recently pioneered a repertoire of activities for delivering noise with enviable precision, jazz was understood to be part of an avant-garde continuum. In its homeland, by contrast, jazz was greeted as an unprecedented torrent of commercial licentiousness ravaging the population with the same viral insistence as the influenza epidemic of 1919.

Ishmael Reed shrewdly depicts jazz in *Mumbo Jumbo*, his novel of 1920s Harlem, as the Jes Grew virus, "For if the Jazz Age is year for year the Essences and Symptoms of the times, then Jes Grew is the germ making it rise yeast-like across the American plain."[14] If jazz was a symptom, what was the disease? If it was an essence, what was there to be proud of or inspired by? The choice between symptom and disease mirrored a generational divide rendered conspicuous by war as a historical threshold. Born in 1896, F. Scott Fitzgerald was not so much prescient as in step with his generation by naming his books *Flappers and Philosophers* (1920) and *Tales of the Jazz Age* (1922). His literary generation included John Dos Passos (born 1896), Hart Crane and Ernest Hemingway (both 1899), Thomas Wolfe (1900), Langston Hughes and John Steinbeck (1902); while in the music world there were Sidney Bechet and Fletcher Henderson (1897), George Gershwin and Paul Robeson (1898), Duke Ellington and Hoagy Carmichael, (1899), Louis Armstrong, Aaron Copland, George Antheil, and Kurt Weill (1900), Earl Hines and Bix Beiderbecke (1903), Fats Waller and Coleman Hawkins (1904). Except for Jelly Roll Morton and King Oliver, born like Ezra Pound in 1885, this was the generation that made the 1920s musically roar.

For those of songwriter Hoagy Carmichael's generation, jazz and modernism were variants of the same experience; somehow, the music of African-Americans and the European avant-garde were both intuitively accessible. Living in a small Indiana town, Carmichael heard about Dada from a fellow student, and met soldiers "who had been to Europe, and they talked of jazz now, right out in the open, not ashamed of it. They told me about the tremendous popularity of jazz in Europe during the war and what it was doing over there."[15] He and buddy Bix Beiderbecke, the first white jazz icon, excitedly listened to Rimsky-Korsakov and Stravinsky records together. Whether his memories are accurate or not, it is significant that Hoagy Carmichael portrays a basic reciprocity between jazz and modernism, since both represented for a white Midwesterner the allure of the renegade, the dissident, the upstart.

For blacks as well as the legion of immigrant Jews, on the other hand, being an outsider was a given, and in the cultural pluralism of the postwar years it could be an opportunity. Jewish prominence in the consolidation of the Hollywood film studios is well known, as is the revitalization of the Broadway musical by former Tin Pan Alley songwriters like Irving Berlin and George Gershwin. A significant if less noted role was played by Jews finally breaking into the closed world of Yankee publishing like Alfred Knopf, Horace Liveright, and the Boni brothers, whose firms produced the lion's share of literary modernism as well as the Harlem Renaissance. Wanting a journal as an extension of his publishing house, Knopf engaged H. L. Mencken to create *American Mercury*, in which some of the Chicago jazzmen found their musical tastes mirrored in prose. "That *Mercury* really got to be the Austin High Gang's Bible," recalled Mezzrow. "It looked to us like Mencken was yelling the same message in his magazine that we were trying to get across in our music; his words were practically lyrics to our hot jazz."[16]

In the sweet/hot dichotomy that was to dominate the early years of jazz, the distinction extended to other terms with more conspicuous values attached: restraint versus abandon, civilized versus primitive, sophisticated versus untutored. White and black dance band leaders alike were concerned with the tawdry image conjured by the term jazz, working hard to counter it with all the accoutrements of professionalism, from band tuxedos to a polished ensemble sound, along with a repertoire of waltzes and "sweet" numbers. For band leaders aspiring to loftier venues, the issue of class was more to the point than race. The public demeanor of the predominantly "cool" dance band capable of a few judiciously timed "hot" breaks reflected the mores of middle-class permissiveness which had an appointed (and strictly delimited) place for sowing wild oats. This middle American dominance of the musical marketplace became even more apparent when "jazz" could be dropped altogether in favor of "swing," a term untainted by association with bordellos and gin mills.

Another issue of lasting importance to jazz was the question of musicianship. American symphony orchestras were dominated by Europeans (particularly Germans) well into the twentieth century, and the need for musical approval from abroad hampered efforts to legitimize serious American composition. Wartime nationalism had the unpremeditated consequence of momentarily tarnishing European cultural authority, and lending a certain credibility to indigenous music. What emerged in the form of jazz was not what the musical establishment expected, but its source in the

African-American minority went unnoticed except by the more righteous moral crusaders. Of greater concern was its lowbrow aspect, and after several years of an uninhibited jazz binge provoked escalating public outcry, its reputation was in need of the ultimate sweetener. Debate about jazz took a serious turn in the wake of Paul Whiteman's famous New York recital, "An Experiment in Modern Music," on February 12, 1924, in which he sought not only to establish jazz in the concert hall but to vindicate his belief that the rough edges of the music represented a passing phase. It helped immeasurably that Whiteman had commissioned a work from Tin Pan Alley veteran George Gershwin. Thus Whiteman's "Experiment" succeeded with the public and the critics, mainly on the strength of *Rhapsody in Blue*, vaulting its composer into national prominence and lending credibility to Whiteman's legislative claim to be the King of Jazz. Jazz historians have invariably chosen the Duke and the Count over the King as authentic jazz royalty, but Whiteman's role, like that of white men in general, is central to the intersection of jazz with modernism. While debate about jazz was rampant in the press from the moment the Original Dixieland Jazz Band recorded its million-seller in 1917, Whiteman's "Experiment" changed the nature of the discourse, first by soliciting highbrow response, and second by placing jazz in a more general debate about *modern* music. These terms readily, but not invariably, abstracted jazz from its black roots. For the next two years the pages of *Vanity Fair* vigorously chronicled not only jazz but the black presence in all the arts, and debate spilled over into *American Mercury*, *The Nation*, *Harper's*, and *The New Republic*, among other highbrow weeklies.

Before going on to assess this debate, it is useful to note certain synchronies with modernism. As jazz became a serious subject, a veritable cascade of significant publications made modernism recognizably American. In 1925 alone the following novels appeared: *The Great Gatsby* by F. Scott Fitzgerald, *Manhattan Transfer* by John Dos Passos, *Dark Laughter* by Sherwood Anderson, *An American Tragedy* by Theodore Dreiser, *The Making of Americans* by Gertrude Stein, and *The Professor's House* by Willa Cather, not to mention Ernest Hemingway's story collection *In Our Time*, followed the next year by *The Sun Also Rises*. It was not all fiction, either. *In the American Grain* by William Carlos Williams also appeared in 1925, along with H. D.'s *Collected Poems*, T. S. Eliot's *Poems 1909–1925* and Ezra Pound's *Draft of XVI Cantos* (both titles, however, were published abroad), e. e. cummings's *&* and *XLI Poems*, and Robinson Jeffers's *Roan Stallion*. Marianne Moore's *Observations* appeared in 1924. Pound's collected shorter poems, *Personae*, came out in 1926, along with Hart Crane's *White Buildings* and cummings's *Is 5*. Having featured a black lead in *The Emperor Jones* in 1920, Eugene O'Neill boldly paired Paul Robeson with a white actress in *All God's Chillun*

Got Wings in 1924 – both signal events in James Weldon Johnson's celebration, *Black Manhattan*. In December 1925 Alain Locke's anthology *The New Negro* was published, preceded by Countee Cullen's *Color* and James Weldon Johnson's *Book of American Negro Spirituals*, and a few months before Langston Hughes's *The Weary Blues* appeared, by which point the Harlem Renaissance was in full throttle.

Paul Whiteman is usually consigned to a negligible place in jazz history, even though his historical significance is unquestionable. Hindsight presumes that only a white man could dominate what passed for jazz in the Jazz Age, which may or may not be true. But for his untimely death, a black band leader may easily have been Whiteman's rival. In any case, James Reese Europe merits attention as the single most influential agent in the dissemination of jazz before it was jazz. After a sound musical training under the tutelage of Dvořák's black protégé Harry Burleigh, Europe organized the Clef Club Orchestra, the first black ensemble to play Carnegie Hall (1912). His subsequent association with Vernon and Irene Castle (1913–1915) made Europe famous as the musical impresario behind the prewar international dance craze. Serving in the military, Europe led the Harlem Hell Fighters, whose concerts had a tremendous impact in France. Their return to New York was greeted by a million people, and he promptly signed a record contract as "Jazz King" before his murder at the hands of a band member in 1919. Considering that musicians like Armstrong and Bechet were not recorded until 1923, and in light of his fame, if Europe had lived the entire course of jazz might have been different, not least because its "King" might have been black. By the time Whiteman laid claim to the title, Europe had been dead five years and everything that was known by white people as jazz derived from other whites. Even Whiteman's name has been ridiculed, so some lexical justice is served by recalling the impact on both sides of the Atlantic of a black pioneer named *Europe*.

In 1921 the first musical performed, produced, written, and directed by blacks was a Broadway hit. *Shuffle Along* – written by ragtime composer and pianist Eubie Blake with Noble Sissle, a veteran of Europe's band – launched the careers of Florence Mills, Paul Robeson, and Josephine Baker. Baker was one of many cast and pit band members who ended up staying in Europe when the show toured there to great acclaim in 1923, becoming resident purveyors of a "jazz" that grew increasingly out of touch with the rapid changes the music was undergoing back in the States. Meanwhile, the American musical establishment, being Eurocentric in outlook, began to take note of the fact that serious composers like Milhaud, Stravinsky, Hindemith, and Ravel were keen on jazz. It was while studying in Paris that Aaron Copland was exposed to jazz as a potential ingredient of American art music.

Europeans approved, while the response of a fellow American is indicative: "but that's *whorehouse* music!"[17] In an American context saturated with Puritan instincts and the Protestant work ethic, the Storyville origin of jazz – not to mention its gangster patronage in the bootleg era – was inconveniently near at hand. It was one thing to set aside the cork traditions of minstrelsy and acknowledge the thespian skills of a Paul Robeson or the musical integrity of the spirituals, but for a white man to drag "whorehouse music" into the concert hall was another thing altogether. In the circumstance – and as a prelude to Whiteman's own concert – the most that could be expected was to slip a few "jazz" tunes into a classical song recital, as Eva Gauthier did in 1923, mixing modernist work by Schoenberg, Bartok, and Hindemith with some tunes by Irving Berlin, Jerome Kern, and George Gershwin, who accompanied her on piano for these numbers.

Against this background, then, Whiteman's "Experiment in Modern Music" was a real experiment, and, as with most experiments, the results were not immediately apparent. By early 1925, however, *Vanity Fair* was routinely covering black America as cultural chic. Carl Van Vechten, self-appointed impresario of Harlem for downtown sophisticates, published numerous articles on black music, and introduced Gershwin in "An American Composer Who is Writing Notable Music in the Jazz Idiom." He also presented Langston Hughes to the public along with four of his poems. Virgil Thomson, presumably on the strength of his musical analysis of jazz for *American Mercury*, also became a frequent contributor to *Vanity Fair*, beginning with "How Modern Music Gets That Way." Mocking musical establishment pompousness in the May 1925 issue, Thomson recommended jazzing the classics in the spirit of Dada. But by June he was lamenting "The Cult of Jazz" as "just another form of highbrowism, like the worship of discord or the worship of Brahms."[18] Jazz was indeed becoming fashionable: in *The New Yorker's* "Talk of the Town" it was noted that, with classical virtuosi Heifetz, Paderewski, and Godowsky among its fans, jazz was no longer a parvenu. Although Thomson was skeptical of jazz as fashion, he respected its roots, wisely predicting that "Probably the best negro music will always come from the negroes themselves" (54). As for the immediate concert season, he not only observed the lapse of the "high-brow jazz" fad, but attributed Whiteman's ascendancy to a "cult of Victorianism."[19] In less than six months, then, Thomson had gone from being an advocate of jazzing the classics to lamenting how much "jazzing" the classics were doing, culminating in his dismissal of Whiteman for not doing either the classics or jazz any good.

In his autobiography, Virgil Thomson appreciatively recalled *Vanity Fair* as having "proved that an organ for advertising luxury products is a good place to show far-out culture."[20] A case in point is the May 1925 issue in which Thomson advocated musical Dada. Also in this issue were "Women in the Arts" by Dorothy Richardson, "What, Exactly, is Modern?" by Aldous Huxley, poems by e. e. cummings, and "Is the Realistic Theater Obsolete?" by John Dos Passos – the occasion being the success of John Howard Lawson's *Processional: A Jazz Symphony of American Life*, unflatteringly characterized by George Jean Nathan as "an indifferent work in what may be called hoochie-coochie form."[21] Premiering in January at the Theatre Guild, Lawson's play had not only been a success but also a public event, drawing a crowd of over 700 to a public debate on its merits – and, by extension, on the merits of jazz. It received coverage in several issues of *Vanity Fair*, including a full-page photo of its star with a white saxophonist and a black guitarist. "In the picture above," the caption proposed, "you see Miss Walker with a part of the jazz band which functions in the theatre of Mr. Lawson in the same way as did the chorus in the theatre of Sophocles."[22] In Dos Passos's portentous conclusion, "*Processional* is the Uncle Tom's Cabin of the new American Theatre."[23] *Vanity Fair* implicitly rendered fashionable everything it touched, and it was not only Van Vechten who led the fashion parade of Negrophilia. Mexican stylist Covarrubia sprinkled its pages with the caricatures that have since become enduring images of the Harlem Renaissance.

In its support of the Harlem vogue, *Vanity Fair* mixed fashion with serious reflection. Coverage of the Jazz Age in Mencken's *American Mercury* was less partisan, more sober, but also more divided inasmuch as it consisted largely of shadow combat between Daniel Gregory Mason and Henry O. Osgood (a Whiteman booster and author of the first American book devoted to jazz). Mason was the starched collar of Yankee establishment insularity, waging a lifelong battle against declining musical tastes, for which both jazz and modernism were to blame. "Stravinsky as Symptom," published in the April 1925 issue of *American Mercury*, epitomizes Mason's resentment. Jazz, "the doggerel of music," is merely "a monotonous repetition of short stereotyped figures. For this reason it is popular with listless, easily distracted people."[24] Mason recognized these short, stereotyped figures from elsewhere: namely, "the so-called ultra-modernist composers, headed by Stravinsky" (466). Many in the American music establishment shared Mason's concern that classical composers might abandon traditional craft in an opportunistic bid for immediate popularity. In Europe, by contrast, the jazz influence was welcomed as a necessary phase in the revitalization of serious music, and the younger American composers who lived abroad adopted this perspective.

In November, 1925, Aaron Copland's *Music for Theatre* premiered, and his highly successful career was inaugurated with a patently jazz-based composition. Cultural credentials were abundant in Copland's case, having studied in France during the heyday of Parisian enthusiasm for jazz. For Daniel Gregory Mason and Henry Ford, people like Copland and Gershwin were evidence of a Jewish conspiracy to "Negrotize" American culture. But for others, Copland was just what the world of serious music had been waiting for: the truly modernized native son for whom jazz was an available idiom to be sampled without exaggerated claims. The jazz elements persisted in Copland's *Piano Concerto*, premiering in January 1927. Then, after a brief dalliance with modernist dissonance, Copland went on to forge the idiomatic populism of *Appalachian Spring*, and his jazz modernism receded. The most explosive intersection of modernist dissonance with jazz in 1925 was being undertaken in Paris by expatriate George Antheil – the last of Ezra Pound's many "discoveries" – with his *Ballet mécanique* and *Jazz Symphony*. Antheil was lionized in Paris for being the "bad boy of music" (as he later titled his autobiography). Originally called "Message to Mars," the composer settled for *Ballet mécanique* because it sounded "brutal, contemporary, hard-boiled, symbolic of the spiritual exhaustion, the superathletic, non-sentimental period commencing 'The Long Armistice'."[25] When the work was performed (along with his *Jazz Symphony*) at Carnegie Hall in 1927, the *enfant terrible* was maligned as merely terrible. Antheil blamed the indignity on a huge and "rather tasteless" curtain, "representing a 1927 jazz-mad America," which the producers hung on stage (193). The fiasco also served notice that symphonic jazz was now defunct – proof, if any was needed, of Paul Rosenfeld's gratified obituary: "round us, the Jazz Age writhes in pain and dies away among belated worshippers; and with it fly perverse idealism and counterfeit energy."[26]

The Jazz Age meant many things in the end, but for the period of *Vanity Fair*'s spotlight it had meant the obligation of American composers to sit up and take notice of the native grain. It was only a phenomenon – that is, a flash in the pan – in the popular press, but among certain literati jazz provided one more facet in an increasingly mesmerized encounter with African-American culture. While the upper crust patronage of blacks persisted (Charlotte Mason's stipends to Langston Hughes and Zora Neale Hurston would not begin until the end of 1927), the phenomenon of the New Negro was increasingly evident, and much of the evidence suggested a vibrant autonomy in black cultural affairs. Journals like *The Crisis*, *Opportunity*, and *The Messenger* were filled with profiles of race progress, and even in the white press the publication of Hughes's "The Negro Artist and the Racial

Mountain" in *The Nation* in June 1926 reiterated the Emersonian virtue of self-reliance, newly configured as an appeal to race pride. The burden of patronage apparently being lifted from their shoulders, white enthusiasts could let jazz subside into diversionary entertainment. By the end of 1927, in the whites-only Cotton Club up in Harlem, they could take in the blatantly primitivist floor shows accompanied by a dapper young leader who had given his band, The Washingtonians, a new name, The Jungle Orchestra, to match their new surroundings.

The timing is so precise as to seem contrived, yet that is how it happened. The entire public furor over jazz, along with any sense that jazz and modernism were overlapping phenomena, evaporated just as Duke Ellington's career was getting started. Within a few years – and ever since – Ellington and jazz would be indelibly associated, so that to look back at the Jazz Age is to confront a bewildering anomaly: the Jazz Age was almost entirely lacking in most of what would make jazz a vital part of American life long after its Age had passed. The irony is delicious, and maybe only someone situated at the heart of it could appreciate the irony at the time. The black journals of the period resisted joining in the jazz debate and rarely mentioned the music at all. But in the May 1925 issue of *Opportunity* Charles S. Johnson wrote an editorial on this "new international word" that, in its homeland, "describes not merely music and dancing but a national mood, or, better still, a jumble of moods."[27] Reflecting the white domination of published commentary, Johnson cites Lawson's *Processional* and adds, for technical support, Van Vechten and Seldes. But when it comes to recognizing the intrinsic irony of the situation he speaks without deference to any authority but his own: "The amusing and yet profoundly significant paradox of the whole situation is the fact that it is the Negroes, who not only can best express the spirit of American life, but who have created the very forms of expression" (133).

For Johnson as for many others of the black intelligentsia, jazz was not especially welcome among those forms of expression. A source of casual entertainment to be sure, jazz hardly seemed a candidate for uplifting the race. William Grant Still, composer of *Afro-American Symphony*, resented the expectation that he incarnate the black experience to the exclusion of anything else. Having studied with the French expatriate innovator Edgar Varèse as well as producing arrangements of sweet jazz for Paul Whiteman, Still was equally at ease with modernism and jazz and did not want to be typecast. Even Duke Ellington, who was identified with jazz his entire career, resisted the term from the outset. "I am not playing jazz. I am trying to play the natural feelings of a people," he insisted in a 1930 interview.[28] Adopting Whitmanian rhetoric in his first published article in 1931, Ellington clarified his aspiration "that an authentic record of my race *written by a member of it* shall be placed on record."[29] The repetition of *record* may slyly attest to the medium in which he worked, but Ellington clearly had the written record in mind as well: "what is being done by Countee Cullen and others in literature is overdue in our music"(50). When, the following year, R. D. Darrell published the most sustained attention yet paid to a jazz figure, the benchmark of his praise was by way of modernism: "Ellington to me is one of Proust's great artists."[30]

"What contributions has jazz made to modernistic music?" asked Alain Locke in one of many discussion questions in *The Negro and His Music*, published by The Associates in Negro Folk Education in 1936.[31] Of the same generation as Pound and Eliot, Locke was nearly forty when his anthology *The New Negro* focused the Harlem Renaissance; and although he had respect for spirituals, his attitude to music was decidedly highbrow and Eurocentric. For him, the best that could be said of jazz was that it "ushered in the first wave of the new modernistic harmony" (81). Consequently, "European musicians, on the look-out for a new modernistic style in music, seized eagerly upon [early jazz]" (85). As with white boosters, Locke was interested mainly in what jazz could offer serious music composition. But, unlike them, he was well informed about African-American music in general. So when it came to the nagging issue of the Jazz Age, Locke could offer a unique perspective: "The Negro, strictly speaking, never had a jazz age; he was born that way" (87). As for the music itself, Locke took a sociological view: "instead of blaming it on jazz, the vogue of jazz should be regarded as the symptom of a profound cultural unrest and change, first a reaction from Puritan repressions and then an escape from the tensions and monotonies of a machine-ridden, extroverted form of civilization" (88). Locke's diagnostic stance involves little concern with the commercialization of African-American folkways by white entrepreneurs. Instead, he prudently remarks that without white participation there would be no "jazz age" (presumably there would be instead "the Negro condition," uninflected by reference to music), and the Jazz Age means modernism: "In some important way," he suggests, "jazz has become diluted and tinctured with modernism. Otherwise, as purely a Negro dialect of emotion, it could not have become the dominant recreational vogue of our time, even to date, the most prolonged fad on record" (90).

In its earliest appearance, in fact, jazz (or any African-derived music) was often clarified with reference to modernism or modernity. "The laws that govern jazz rule in the rhythms of great original prose, verse that sings itself, and opera of ultra modernity. Imagine Walter Pater, Swinburne, and Borodin swaying to the same pulses that rule the moonlit music on the banks of

African rivers."[32] For the 1918 Carnegie Hall premiere of John Powell's
Rhapsodie négre, a program note dedicated the work to Joseph Conrad in
appreciation of *Heart of Darkness*. In 1919, Louis Untermeyer's *The New
Era in American Poetry* proclaimed the virtues of a rediscovered vernacular
("our poets are coming back to the oldest and most stirring tongue," he
wrote, rediscovering "the beauty, the dignity, I might almost say the divine
core, of the casual and commonplace"[33]). "We can hear its counterpart
already in the performance of any Jazz band," a reviewer contemptuously
remarked. *The New York Times* chimed in: "Jazz is to real music exactly
what most of the 'new poetry,' so-called, is to real poetry," and both were
the work "not of innovators, but of incompetents."[34] In an infamous 1921
article, "Plus de Jazz," Clive Bell took "jazz" to be the stylistic affectation
of modernism in all the arts (confusing readers in the process, as he used
the verbs "jazzing" and "ragging" interchangeably). With his "black and
grinning muse," Bell wrote, "Mr. Eliot is about the best of our living poets,
and, like Stravinsky, he is as much a product of the Jazz movement as so
good an artist can be of any."[35] Bell was hardly alone in thinking of jazz and
modernism as labels for any deliberate distortion of the conventional. In its
contemporaneity with the disfigurations of *The Waste Land* and *Manhattan
Transfer*, early jazz seemed to incarnate skyscraper primitivism, affirming
machine-age progress driven by atavistic sources of revitalizing energy. As
Macdonald Moore judiciously explains, jazz was one more key to "the secret
of modernism": "like a guide to the perplexed, 'jazz' lent perceptual coher-
ence to phenomena as discrete as European musical avant-gardism, bureau-
cratic and scientific rationalization, even contemporary faddism."[36] To talk
about jazz or modernism was to talk about novelty (and whatever is novel
is always presumed to have a brief shelf life), even if novelty proved symptomatic of substantive change.

A vivid case of the discomfort imposed by jazz as agent of change may
be found in the case of Vachel Lindsay, acclaimed the "jazz poet" of the
Jazz Age. His 1926 "A Curse for the Saxophone" culminates in a vision of
Lincoln's assassin in the afterlife:

> "John Wilkes Booth, you are welcome to Hell,"
> And they played it on the saxophone, and played it well.
> And he picked up a saxophone, grunting and rasping,
> The red-hot horn in his hot hands clasping,
> And he played a typical radio jazz,
> He started an earthquake, he knew what for,
> And at last he started the late World War.
> Our nerves all razzed, and our thoughts all jazzed,
> Booth and his saxophone started the war![37]

The flamboyant anachronism, coupled with the fantasy of jazz setting America on the warpath, is not quite poetic whimsy like his 1918 poem depicting the Kaiser being vanquished by "the Jazz-bird."[38] By the time *Going-to-the-Stars* was published in 1926, Lindsay had suffered what to him was a deplorable fate: previously known as America's wandering troubador he had unwittingly become its "jazz poet." His affinity for black rhythms, most famously on display in "Congo," along with his oratorical delivery, had long been evident. It was not the racial affiliation but the jazz label that irked him. The poem "The Daniel Jazz"[39] had been his downfall, having been chosen without Lindsay's approval by his English publisher as the title of a collection. Arriving in London in October 1920, he found himself expected to play the role of jazz poet – an agony compounded by his increasing distaste for public recitals – and found himself "cartooned as turning handsprings, and described as whistling and snapping my fingers while I recited."[40] Two years later he was still festering, writing to Harriet Monroe: "I have very much resented being called a 'Jazz' poet, especially by the British Papers, because it was used to mean something synonymous with hysteria, shrieking and fidgets. I abhor the kind of Ball-Room dancing that goes with Jazz, and I abhor the blasphemy that Jazz has made of the beautiful slow whispered Negro Spirituals." Lindsay says he would prefer being called "'The College Yell' poet," whereas jazz "has the leer of the bad-lands in it . . . It is full of the dust of the dirty dance. The Saxophone, its chief instrument is the most diseased instrument in all modern music. It absolutely smells of the hospital" (255). Lindsay was incensed by ulterior expectations he felt being imposed on him by the jazz epithet. In some sense, he never got over it. In 1930 he sullenly accepted $250 to compose a poem on "The Jazz Age," its repeated refrain "Good-bye, Jazz Age. I'm going Home" ominously foreshadowing his suicide the next year.[41]

It is important to note that Lindsay did not at all disavow association with black oratorical rhythms, from which he drew extensively and appreciatively in much of his work. The most striking evidence for Lindsay's assumption that "jazz" had no real connection with African-Americans is brought to light in his encounter with Langston Hughes in a hotel where Hughes was working as a waiter. Hughes slipped copies of several poems to Lindsay at a public dinner ("The Weary Blues," "Jazzonia," and "Negro Dancers," the opening poems of *The Weary Blues*), who read them to the audience during his own recital. The accompanying publicity (which included Carl Van Vechten's prompt report in *Vanity Fair*) was decisive for Hughes's career. If anyone deserved the epithet "jazz poet" it was Hughes, but this episode makes it clear how inexorably the jazz label would adhere to whites, in literature as in music, for in the culture at large black people were rarely accorded the respect of being discussed as individuals. For Lindsay, of course, the label was disrespectful because it implied he was not a bard but an entertainer.

The stigma of entertainment stuck with jazz until bebop, at which point Louis Armstrong began to be viewed with suspicion for being so entertaining. What are the implications, then, behind a 1927 advertisement placard proclaiming Armstrong not only "King of the Trumpet" but also "Master of Modernism"? Did some ad man recognize that Satchmo's versatile scatting was of a piece with Dada sound poems? Was it a furtive acknowledgment that "To call Armstrong, Waller, et al., 'modernists' is to appreciate their procedures as alchemists of the vernacular who have 'jazzed' the ordinary and given it new life"?[42] In any event, when the bebop revolution shook up the jazz world and figures like Charlie Parker and Thelonious Monk were called modernists, some precedent was clearly being followed. Bop challenged jazz orthodoxy in the 1940s with the same reckless intensity as *Ulysses* and *The Waste Land* had imposed on literature in 1922. Bebop "was one of the great modernisms,"[43] says Eric Lott, who emphasizes its cavalier treatment of elements from pop culture, its tendency to make a virtue of defiant isolation, its assertion of aesthetic autonomy as political value, and its exploratory rigor mistaken by outsiders as ugliness. Bebop merited the "modernist" label insofar as it shared many of the formal traits associated with literary and artistic modernism several decades earlier. Self-assured in its resistance to accessibility, bop had all the hallmarks of determined formal experimentation which, coupled with a creative exuberance very different from the crowd pleasing high spirits of earlier jazz, made the music seem the embodiment of the esoteric. Although bop quickly became fashionable, in the romance of its first incarnation as after hours workshop, it also served as a crucible for Parker, Monk, Dizzy Gillespie, Bud Powell, and Kenny Clarke, who incarnated a sort of musical Montmartre with their seemingly effortless avant-gardism (the quality of "cool" that proved addictive, in more ways than one, to rapt fans and fellow musicians alike).

It is all the more poignant, then, that the *literary* fulfillment of jazz modernism dates from the heyday of bebop, but by an author for whom the new music was a deplorable repudiation of jazz as a life affirming force. Ralph Ellison was indebted to the blues based southwest territory jazz of his Oklahoma childhood, which most famously culminated in the Count Basie sound, as well as the literary high modernism to which he was exposed as a student at Tuskegee. For Ellison, *The Waste Land* and "West End Blues" spoke the same language; and "all of these references of Eliot's, all of this snatching of phrases from the German, French, Sanskrit, and so on, were attuned to that type of American cultural expressiveness which one got in jazz."[44] Much the same could be said about *Invisible Man*, a novel deeply infused with jazz cadences while paying intricate thematic homage to modernism. In countless anecdotes and testimonials, Ellison sought to demonstrate how blues-based jazz enabled him to recognize tools for survival in modernist writing and vice versa. "I use folklore in my work not because I am a Negro, but because writers like Eliot and Joyce made me conscious of the literary value of my folk inheritance" (111–112). Like his friend Albert Murray, who never tired of applying to jazz Kenneth Burke's principle of discourse as the dancing of attitudes, Ellison's work was a series of elaborate variations on the basic theme (endemic to both high modernism and the African-American experience) of survival and the attainment of poise in the face of adversity.

Ellison and other "alchemists of the vernacular" offer a practical image of jazz (*as/and*) modernism as a deliberate response to modernity as lived experience. Modernity is functionally different from nostalgic distinctions between now and then, in part because its constitutive features are so vast that they imposed themselves over centuries: Bit by bit, the incremental shocks of modernity have been registered as measurable incitements to complaint as well as enthusiasm; and, each time, the specificity of the provocation (Armory Show or "Experiment in Modern Music") seemed sufficient in itself for the response it provoked. But at some datable threshold (not necessarily Virginia Woolf's "December, 1910"), the cumulative acceleration of historical factors (Protestantism, America, Enlightenment, Democracy, Capitalism, and Industrialism) coalesced into an imperious portent of something weakly named by terms like "modernity" or "modern times." For the first time, a world historical threshold had a *soundtrack*.

Jazz and modernism alike were "post-war": a combination of "cynicism and hedonism that came out of it like a cloud of gas they can't issue masks for."[45] But jazz was also historically timed so as to accompany two decisive technological phenomena: records and radio. It is this conjunction of new media with artistic novelty that made jazz the pre-eminent bearer of cultural modernity in the 1920s. In its initial impact, jazz performed three concurrent roles: as soundtrack for a new social energy largely associated with dancing; as signifier of cultural potential, with connotations ranging from regression to regeneration; and as agent provocateur of modernity, the social consequences of which were viewed as positive, but which exacted certain cultural growing pains in the process. Jazz was hardly yet the incontestable enrichment of American culture it has become, and it had little chance of being recognized as a distinct African-American musical practice. African-Americans were only vaguely associated with jazz, even "jazz was not jazz in the twenties; it was everything else," which meant "the tinkly distillations of toothpaste troubadors"[46] instead of what is now accredited with being jazz. Owing to the discrepancy between early commentary and subsequent developments in the music itself, historians have been inclined to scoff at all the misdirected remarks about jazz as incitement to primitivism, degeneracy, obstacle to cultural progress or refinement, and so forth (a 1921 *Ladies Home Journal* bearing the punchy title "Does Jazz Put the Sin in Syncopation?" being a favorite target). That such remarks miss the point where the music is concerned *is*, however, exactly the point about modernity, which was a continuous provocation to *missing the point*. Homeric epic? – how about a day in Dublin; Grail quest? – listen to the gramophone sob in the haunt of the Fisher King. Stravinsky, too, missed the point, calling Schoenberg's *Pierrot Lunaire* "the solar plexus as well as the mind of early-twentieth-century music."[47]: the real solar plexus hailed from New Orleans, of course, not Vienna.

Everything had a manifesto in the heyday of the avant-garde, but there was no manifesto for jazz – unless, as I think, it was "Portraits and Repetition" by Gertrude Stein. "As I say what one repeats is the scene in which one is acting, the days in which one is living, the coming and going which one is doing, anything one is remembering is a repetition, but existing as a human being, that is being listening and hearing is never repetition. It is not repetition if it is that which you are actually doing because naturally each time the emphasis is different just as the cinema has each time a slightly different thing to make it all be moving."[48] When Stein specifies the value of "keeping two times going at once" and enthuses over the bifocal act of "talk[ing] and listen[ing] all at once, I wondered is there any way of making what I know come out as I know it, come out not as remembering. I found this very exciting," she adds (180, 181). And so did multitudes, except they called it jazz.

NOTES

1. F. Scott Fitzgerald, *The Crack Up*, ed. Edmund Wilson (New York: New Directions, 1956), 16.
2. *New Orleans Times-Picayune*, June 20, 1918, quoted in Francis Newton, *The Jazz Scene* (New York: Monthly Review Press, 1960), 61.
3. Anne Shaw Faulkner, "Does Jazz Put the Sin in Syncopation," *Ladies Home Journal* (August 1921), quoted in Robert Walser, ed., *Keeping Time: Readings in Jazz History* (New York: Oxford University Press, 1999), 35.
4. Clay Smith, "Where is Jazz Leading America?," *The Etude* (August-September 1924), quoted in Walser, *Keeping Time*, 54.
5. R. W. S. Mendl, *The Appeal of Jazz* (London: Philip Allan, 1927), 88.
6. J. Hartley Manners, *The National Anthem*, in Macdonald Smith Moore, *Yankee Blues: Musical Culture and American Identity* (Bloomington: Indiana University Press, 1985), 86.

7. Le Corbusier, quoted in John A. Kouwenhoven, "What's 'American' About America," in *The Jazz Cadence of American Culture*, ed. Robert O'Meally (New York: Columbia University Press, 1998), 127.

8. H. L. Mencken, *Prejudices, Fifth Series* (New York: Knopf, 1926), 293.

9. Waldo Frank, *In the American Jungle [1925–1936]* (New York: Farrar & Rinehart, 1937), 118–119.

10. James Oppenheim, Editorial, *Seven Arts* 1: 2 (December 1916), 156.

11. Hiram Moderwell, "A Modest Proposal," *Seven Arts* 2: 2 (July 1917), 370.

12. Stuart Davis, *Stuart Davis*, ed. Diane Kelder (New York: Praeger, 1971), 23–24.

13. Martin Green, *New York 1913: The Armory Show and the Paterson Strike Pageant* (New York: Scribner's, 1988), 181.

14. Ishmael Reed, *Mumbo Jumbo* (New York: Macmillan, 1972), 20.

15. Hoagy Carmichael, *Sometimes I Wonder* (New York: Farrar, Straus & Giroux, 1965), 42–43.

16. Mezz Mezzrow and Bernard Wolfe, *Really the Blues* (New York: Anchor, 1972), 94.

17. Phillip Ramey, booklet notes, *The Copland Collection: Early Orchestral Works 1922–1935* (Sony, 1991, CD #SM2K 47232), 6.

18. Virgil Thomson, "The Cult of Jazz," *Vanity Fair* 24: 4 (June 1925), 54.

19. Virgil Thomson, "Enter American Music: Why we Must Play More than a Saxophone in the Concert of Nations," *Vanity Fair* 25: 2 (October 1925), 124.

20. Virgil Thomson, *Virgil Thomson* (New York: Knopf, 1966), 70.

21. George Jean Nathan, "The Theater," *American Mercury* 4: 15 (March 1925), 372.

22. [Untitled caption], *Vanity Fair* 24: 2 (April 1925), 43.

23. John Dos Passos, "Is the Realistic Theater Obsolete?" *Vanity Fair* 24: 3 (May 1925), 114.

24. Daniel Gregory Mason, "Stravinsky as Symptom," *American Mercury* 4: 16 (April 1925), 465–466.

25. George Antheil, *Bad Boy of Music* (Garden City, NY: Doubleday, Doran & Co., 1945), 139.

26. Paul Rosenfeld, "Musical Chronicle," *The Dial* 80 (May 1926), 440.

27. Charles S. Johnson, "Jazz," *Opportunity* 3: 29 (May 1925), 132.

28. Florence Zunser, "'Opera Must Die,' Says Galli-Curci! Long Live the Blues!" in *The Duke Ellington Reader*, ed. Mark Tucker (New York: Oxford University Press, 1993), 45.

29. Duke Ellington, "The Duke Steps Out" in *Duke Ellington Reader*, ed. Tucker, 49.

30. R. D. Darrell, "Black Beauty" in *Duke Ellington Reader*, ed. Tucker, 64.

31. Alain Locke, *The Negro and His Music* (Washington, DC: The Associates in Negro Folk Education, 1936), 103.

32. Walter Kingsley, "Whence Comes Jass?" in *Keeping Time*, ed. Walser, 7.

33. Louis Untermeyer, *The New Era in American Poetry* (New York: Henry Holt, 1919), 11.

34. Morroe Berger, "Jazz: Resistance to the Diffusion of a Culture-Pattern," *Journal of Negro History* 32: 3 (July 1947), 467–468.

35. Clive Bell, "Plus de Jazz," *The New Republic* 28 (September 21, 1921), 94.

36. Moore, *Yankee Blues*, 119.

37. Vachel Lindsay, *Going-to-the-Stars* (New York: Appleton, 1926), 51–52.
38. Vachel Lindsay, *The Poetry of Vachel Lindsay*, vol. I, ed. Dennis Camp (Peoria, IL: Spoon River Poetry Press, 1984), 394.
39. "The Daniel Jazz" perpetuated Lindsay's reputation in another medium in 1925, in the form of a solo cantata by Louis Gruenberg, who set several other poems by Lindsay to music as well. Gruenberg (like Kurt Weill, a student of Busoni) conducted the American premiere of Schoenberg's *Pierrot Lunaire* in 1923, going on to achieve some notoriety in the 1920s for his own compositions, including *The Creation* (based on James Weldon Johnson's poem), *Jazzberries* and *Jazz-Masks* for piano, *Jazz Suite* for orchestra, and *The Emperor Jones*, an operatic version of O'Neill's play, premiering at The Met in 1933. Gruenberg also spent time in Germany, where he was instrumental in exposing educators and musicians to principles of jazz performance (albeit from a classical perspective).
40. Vachel Lindsay, *The Letters of Vachel Lindsay*, ed. Marc Chénetier (New York: Burt Franklin & Co., 1979), 283.
41. Lindsay, *Poetry of Vachel Lindsay*, vol. III, 770–771.
42. Alfred Appel, Jr., *Jazz Modernism: From Ellington and Armstrong to Matisse and Joyce* (New York: Knopf, 2002), 13.
43. Eric Lott, "Double V, Double-Time: Bebop's Politics of Style," in *Jazz Cadence*, ed. O'Meally, 462.
44. Ralph Ellison, *Collected Essays*, ed. John F. Callahan (New York: Modern Library, 1995), 520.
45. Frederick Turner, *1929, A Novel of the Jazz Age* (Washington, DC: Counterpoint, 2003), 33.
46. Barry Ulanov, *A History of Jazz in America* (New York: Viking, 1952), 115.
47. Igor Stravinsky, quoted in Michael Chanan, *From Handel to Hendrix: The Composer in the Public Sphere* (New York: Verso, 1999), 223.
48. Gertrude Stein, *Lectures in America* (New York: Random House, 1935), 179.

7

MICHAEL NORTH

Visual culture

As far back as the seventeenth century, when Descartes realized that much of the essential work of eyesight, beginning with the inversion and synthesis of the retinal images, is done by the mind, then the basis for the study of visual culture was established.[1] In 1953, however, when Leo Steinberg published "The Eye is a Part of the Mind," the title was a polemical assertion intended to rebut the influential position of Clement Greenberg, who insisted that "aesthetic judgements are immediate, intuitive, undeliberate, and involuntary."[2] Since that time, the idea that vision is not an automatic, unvarying process has been a part of important controversies in philosophy, history, aesthetic theory, and literary studies. In their very different ways, scholars such as Richard Rorty, Norman Bryson, and Jonathan Crary have worked to replace a mechanistic, essentially mimetic model of vision with one that is physically, historically, and culturally determined.

The idea that vision is at least affected by culture may have occurred to so many scholars at this time because the culture of their period seemed so predominantly visual. It has been common at various different times over the last century or so to bemoan the fact that society has come to be dominated by images, a lament based on the assumption that images require less thought to process than words. The term *visual culture* has also come to stand, therefore, for a host of practices including photography, film, television, and the Web, which together sometimes seem to have assembled a purely spectatorial society. In fact, these two different usages reveal a good deal about the term *visual culture* and the culture that uses it. With the emphasis on the noun, *visual culture* designates a highly intellectualized scholarly practice based on the idea that vision is itself a physically, historically, and culturally intricate process; with the emphasis on the adjective, the term designates a dumbed-down culture, force fed on spectacle. Possibly the truth is to be found in the tense boundary between the adjective and the noun, where the domination of society by images creates its own self-conscious reflex and the increasing turn of culture to the visual makes that sense seem as intricate and complicated as the language it supposedly replaces.

In any case, visual culture in all its definitions has come to be particularly associated with modern culture. There are two very good reasons for this association, even though the term is in principle applicable to any time period.[3] Though modern experience may not be any more intensely dominated by the visual than human experience in earlier periods of time, there is no question that a fundamentally different kind of visual experience is available to the modern eye. Some such experience is simply an accidental by-product of industrialism, as human beings are allowed, or forced, to see at great speed or from dizzying heights, but the most important category of new experience is produced by entirely new media. Photography, to take the first of these, was not simply a new art form but a new medium, as if humankind had one day simply stumbled across the possibility of sculpture. It was, therefore, a medium without rules, standard practices, or common uses, one to which the traditions of art were essentially irrelevant. New media, as it was commonly said in the early days of film, present the means before the end and thus by their very nature provoke basic questions about the nature and purpose of art.[4]

Visual culture is particularly associated with modern culture for another reason as well. Photography was not just a new way of producing images but also an entirely new way of disseminating them. By 1862, paintings were being reproduced and distributed photographically so that millions could now experience what had once been available only to a relative few (Jay, *Downcast Eyes*, 139). Mechanical and then electronic reproduction made the new media particularly appropriate as mass media, with social effects so pervasive and perdurable that they have come to be essentially synonymous with modern social life. The extension to a huge new public of what was thought of from the beginning as a kind of visual literacy attracted the same mistrust and disdain in certain quarters as the spread of literacy itself. Mechanical reproduction of any kind, Robert Ray has argued, always attracts the same complaint: "the new technology makes things too easy. What previously was possible for only a few (storing large amounts of information, producing a figurative representation of a person or object, making a record) becomes possible for many."[5] Thus arguments about the artistic status of photography, which have become, over the years, arguments about the status of art instead, are inseparable from the social status of the millions who produce and enjoy photographic images. Even today, negative attitudes toward visual culture often begin with the simple and apparently innocuous fact that many more people see a popular film than read a new novel.

The history of modern visual culture is therefore the joint history of new media and new audiences, developing symbiotically, since, as Geoffrey Batchen has persuasively suggested, even as astounding an invention as the photograph must have been meant to appease some social appetite that the existing media could not satisfy.[6] Written versions of this history usually begin with transformations in urban street life, especially night-time illumination and outdoor advertisement, which have come to be associated especially with mid-nineteenth-century Paris. Sometime in the 1860s, it is often argued, Paris itself became a spectacle: "Paris was *parade*, phantasmagoria, dream, dumbshow, mirage, masquerade."[7] The display on the boulevards, an amalgam of shop-signs, window displays, posted advertisements, street-side eating and selling, is reproduced inside the *grand magasins*, the great department stores that began to emerge with the Bon Marché in the mid-1860s. The convergence of shopping and visual entertainment is hardly an accident, since the department stores drew self-consciously on techniques of visual display established first in pre-photographic media such as the panorama, which had been attracting urban audiences since the 1780s. In fact, the existence of such displays, which are now commonly included in pre-histories of the film industry, are strong evidence for Batchen's contention that when photography appears in the 1830s it does so in response to a visual desire peculiar to its particular time.

Though photography was a fairly difficult art to practice at the very beginning, it was almost immediately recognized as a mass medium. The daguerreotype, which actually produced unique images, since it did not derive from a negative, was nonetheless turned over to the French public, on the theory that such an invention could belong to no one.[8] The first real photographic craze, inspired by the *carte de visite* in the 1850s, provided the peculiarly modern thrill of duplicating and transmitting oneself as an image, which is structurally impossible outside a mass society. Once photolithography was developed, photographs gradually became the predominant form of printed illustration: the first half-tone photograph appeared in print in 1880, and by 1904 daily newspapers such as London's *Daily Mirror* were using photographs exclusively.[9] At about the same time, still photography was being adapted to display motion as well. In fact, as Tom Gunning reports, it was the popularization of photography, which required film that was much faster and easier to use, that paved the way for the movies. The instantaneous photograph, made possible by the technical advances of Louis Lumière, allowed unskilled photographers to capture spontaneous occurrences in everyday life, but it also made possible the rapid registration of dozens of snapshots a second, enough to make a credible representation of life in motion.[10] Movies did not acquire sound until the late 1920s, and they were not shot effectively in color for another decade, but even in the late nineteenth century, when the camera had come to be an indispensable witness to both private and public life, the basis of modern media society was established.

Almost none of this happened first in the United States. Only in the 1880s, when Thomas Edison laid out the first central power grid in lower Manhattan, bringing the first incandescent light to an urban neighborhood, did American developments begin to rival those in Europe. Edison, of course, is generally credited with developing the motion picture camera, but his understanding of the social possibilities of the new invention was so awry that the lighter, more portable *cinématograph* of the Lumières, which doubled as a projector as well, really established the social institution of cinema as we know it. At a certain point, however, partly because of the global prestige of Edison, modern visual culture came to be identified with American culture, even in France. In fact, Louis Aragon maintained that the French had invented American culture, somewhere around 1914, and if American culture can be taken to mean a fictional mélange of "skyscrapers and cowboys, railroad accidents and cocktail shakers," he is absolutely right.[11] By World War I, a certain kind of urban modernism had come to be considered so quintessentially American that many Europeans debated their own future in terms of capitulation or resistance to the "American age."[12] When European artists such as Marcel Duchamp, reversing the trend of two centuries, began arriving in New York, they brought with them the somewhat surprising news that "the art of Europe is finished – dead – and that America is the country of the art of the future."[13] That there were even a few American artists and writers who agreed is due very largely to the influence of the European avant-garde, which helped to establish America's mass culture as a global style by breaking down elite resistance to it.

American aesthetic acceptance of our own visual culture thus follows a path at least inflected by European influence. As an invention, the camera had inspired a certain intellectual interest, even in New England, where Oliver Wendell Holmes provided enthusiastic and influential essays to the *Atlantic Monthly* in the 1860s (Trachtenberg, *Classic Essays*, 71–82). Holmes was particularly interested in the stereoscope, which meant that he also accepted photography as a development in popular entertainment, which cannot be said for Hawthorne, who gives photography an important place in *The House of the Seven Gables*, or James, who commissioned Alvin Langdon Coburn to produce a series of indistinct plates for the New York Edition of his novels. An interest in photography, in other words, could rather easily coincide with a profound resistance to the mass entertainment it provided, especially so as photography began to figure as a metaphor in debates about aesthetic realism toward the end of the nineteenth century.[14] The Major and Mrs. Monarch are useless as models to the artist protagonist of James's story "The Real Thing" in part because they have posed so frequently for photographs; they have become popular, hackneyed images of themselves and thus have become ineligible for art. As some novelists, notably Crane and Dreiser, began to court the photographic metaphor, others, like James, held out all the more strongly, particularly against the spectatorial attitude implied even by the title of *The American Scene*. James's resistance to America's culture of display is part of a general intellectual mistrust of American visual culture, which can be exemplified by the condescending title of *The People at Play*, a 1909 book by Rollin Lynde Hartt originally published as articles in the *Atlantic Monthly*.[15] An interest that had been relatively innocuous in Holmes was far more difficult to sustain fifty years later, when visual entertainment had become associated with a new mass audience very largely made up of recent immigrants.

Even the Armory Show, that 1913 landmark of the American avant-garde, excluded photography from its galleries. At the same time, however, Alfred Stieglitz had established at *Camera Work* and in his gallery *291* the most important American gateway for European avant-garde aesthetics, which also happened to be, not coincidentally, the center of a sustained polemic on behalf of photography. As Coburn put it, writing in *Camera Work* in 1911, "Photography is the most modern of the arts,"[16] and Stieglitz, because he was a photographer, became, for a time, the epitome of the American modern artist. This did not mean, however, that Stieglitz allowed very much of American spectatorial culture into either his magazine or his studio. In fact, his equivocal attitude toward modern culture generally is revealed quite clearly in his photographs, with their pervasive urban imagery always distanced by mist, haze, clouds, or darkness. Though Stieglitz knew how to handle a movie camera, and though *Camera Work* published one of the first intellectual considerations of the movies, a basic desire to gain artistic acceptance for photography kept Stieglitz away from any of the amateurish or popular uses of it. The more direct approach to American visual culture was accomplished in the offshoots and side projects, such as the magazine *291*, produced by Stieglitz's European allies Picabia and Duchamp.

Stieglitz's ambivalence was fairly typical of the American avant-garde in the early part of the twentieth century. Even a generally liberal and populist magazine like *Seven Arts*, which began its brief life in 1917 with a diatribe against "the weight of mechanical inventions – phonograph, pianola, cinematograph," never managed to express more than a dutiful interest in the mass media of its time (Gorman, 61–63; Lounsbury, 48–49). *The Little Review*, which did so much to introduce modern literature in the United

States, was openly hostile to film and apparently to the audience that followed it (Gorman, *Left Intellectuals*, 68; Lounsbury, 48–49). Of course, it was not difficult to argue, in this as in any other time, that most popular entertainment was as formulaic and in its own way as oppressive as academic art, and yet when *Seven Arts* began publication film had been a thriving medium for nearly thirty years, and there was a considerable difference between the masterpieces of the time, like *Intolerance*, and run-of-the-mill genre pictures. For that matter, it is easier to find intellectual appreciation of the early serials than it is to find a considered analysis of Griffith. *The Soil*, which appeared at about the same time as *Seven Arts*, embraced the serials precisely because they were crude and energetic, for many of the same reasons, that is to say, that they had appealed to the European avant-garde, with which *The Soil*, precisely because of its overt American boosterism, was closely associated (Corn, *Great American Thing*, 81–86; Gorman, Left Intellectuals, 69–70).

When Vachel Lindsay published the first version of *The Art of the Moving Picture* in 1915, therefore, he was quite self-consciously preaching to the unconverted. Lindsay's book was not aimed at the general public, which had already accepted the movies, but the art museums, departments of English, and "the critical and literary world generally." Lindsay was dismayed that the American intellectual world had failed to appreciate the impact of film, which he felt was "as great a step as was the beginning of picture-writing in the stone age" (Lindsay, *Art of the Moving Picture*, 116). Not only did he take specific issue with *The Little Review* for its rather lofty dismissal of the movies, but he also maintained that there was a strong correlation between the poetry of the "new sect, the Imagists" and the new language of images established by film (Lindsay, *Art of the Moving Picture*, 158). Lindsay rhapsodically imagined "Imagist photoplays" that might bring discipline and restraint to the movies while offering poets a language of signs that actualized their rhythmic possibilities in real physical motion (Lindsay, *Art of the Moving Picture*, 158–159). As an act of open boosterism, Lindsay's book effectively illustrates the equivocal relationship of American visual culture to the American avant-garde on the eve of the twenties. Though there was a lively and vociferous argument to the effect that the changes coming over American art and literature at this time were part of a general social change evident also in the new media, this argument was made against the better judgment of the leading critics and magazines, which were still hoping to gain conventional acceptance for new art, not to ally it with popular forms that were devoid of prestige.

This is why the example of the European avant-garde was so crucial, and why the magazines that began to champion the new media in the 1920s were either published in Europe or were strongly influenced by European models.

Harold Loeb and Matthew Josephson, who were responsible for *Broom*, both noticed a little sardonically in 1922, that American expatriate writers in Paris, who hoped "to hear the new literary revival acknowledged, will be told that American advertising, moving pictures, and architecture lead the world."[17] The irony of this situation did not prevent *Broom* from publishing a great deal of European comment on American visual culture, from its very first issue, which opened with Fernand Léger's Chaplin caricatures and Blaise Cendrars's "Profound Today," to the film analysis of Jean Epstein and Philippe Soupault in later issues, soon to be mimicked by the appreciative film articles of Robert Alden Sanborn and Slater Brown.[18] Josephson's own essays, particularly "The Great American Billposter," which *Broom* published in November of 1922, are probably the most concerted literary arguments on behalf of American visual culture to appear at this time, and they are distinct from Lindsay's campaign in linking the European avant-garde, particularly dada, to the popular arts of the United States.

That linkage was more publicly established at *The Dial*, which had a much wider circulation than *Broom* or *The Soil* and thus helped to establish popular visual culture as an intellectual fashion of the modern period. Among the editors and contributors, both Edmund Wilson and Gilbert Seldes were noted devotees of vaudeville and silent film, and several of the regular contributors of the early twenties, most notably e. e. cummings, published work based on or influenced by such popular entertainments.[19] Their taste, in this respect, differs from Lindsay's in its marked cosmopolitanism, for even Seldes's appreciation of slapstick is filtered through a sensibility charmed by the Cirque Medrano. Significantly, the first book-length appreciation of American popular culture, Seldes's *The Seven Lively Arts* (1924), was pulled into shape while Seldes was traveling in Europe, so that his essays on the comic strips and the Keystone Kops were revised while he was hobnobbing with Picasso, Joyce, and Stravinsky (Kammen, *Lively Arts*, 94–95). The seven lively arts that Seldes championed in his book were not all visual – one of the most significant chapters is the one on jazz – but the way in which he links together seemingly disparate forms of entertainment, from Krazy Kat to Jolson, makes Seldes the first really self-conscious exponent of American visual culture as a whole. In fact, it is possible to trace the subsequent history of the new media in the United States almost solely by following Seldes's career, for he went on from *The Dial* to become a popular journalistic spokesman for the movies, one whose work over the years appeared in such different venues as the *Saturday Review of Literature*, the *Village Voice*, and *TV Guide*. He subsequently became the first director of programming for CBS, virtually before there was such as thing as television, and then founding dean of the Annenberg School of Communications at the University of Pennsylvania, where he became almost the only significant spokesman for popular media in the academy (Kammen, *Lively Arts*, 354–355). Though Seldes was apparently not a very effective dean, he did help to establish as an accepted academic discipline what had been in Lindsay's day a lonely, even an insurgent, interest.

Contemporary theoretical accounts of modern visual culture are still very strongly influenced by European models, and most academic assessments of the general influence and significance of visual culture in the modern period are based on European examples. Martin Jay, working primarily from French sources, has argued that there are several different "scopic regimes," different visual subcultures, coexisting in the modern period, though it might be more useful to think of these as different attitudes toward a modern visual culture that is too complex for any single account.[20] What Jay calls the "dominant scopic regime" is a linear descendant of Renaissance perspectivalism, with its desire to systematize and rationalize the sense of sight. In this account, modernity is an unbroken industrial/scientific project that turns the senses into instruments just as surely as it turns individual arms and legs into mechanical tools. When Heidegger calls modernity "the age of the world picture," he means to criticize the act of picturing because it distances and subordinates the thing seen, and though he does not always think of picturing in purely literal terms, he does specifically criticize radio, movies, and television for progressively replacing real nearness to things with a spurious, illusory closeness.[21] In such arguments, the most influential of which has been mounted by Foucault, the link is so close between *voir* and *pouvoir* as to make the very act of seeing one of domination.[22] Foucault has helped to establish an analysis of modern society as one of constant surveillance, in which the collective gaze comes to inhabit the empty center of the panopticon, where it can monitor itself. Thus even an ordinary look on the street can express, in the guise of individual desire, the institutional power relations of a society, and the instruments that record and multiply these looks multiply and extend that power in the name of entertainment. Historians working in this tradition have noted the early use of photography in the surveillance of criminals and the institutionalization of psychoses, while film theorists have studied the ways in which editing and camera placement create an imputed spectator whose position must be occupied and whose very prejudices must be adopted in order to enjoy the film.[23]

If such theories seem to describe an entirely different culture from that which seems so lively in *The Seven Lively Arts*, it is not because such dark suspicions were not shared in Seldes's day. From the very first, establishment opinion mistrusted the new visual arts as potential tools of indoctrination, or, alternatively, gladly embraced them as a new means of extending social control (Gorman, *Left Intellectuals*, 40–41). Though the culture industry may have had to wait for Horkheimer and Adorno to give it a name, the critical point behind the name, that modernity had managed to industrialize even the most purely aesthetic use of the senses, was commonly made even very early in the twentieth century, most obviously and influentially perhaps in the cultural criticism of Walter Lippmann.[24] At the same time, of course, critics of modern culture were also obsessed with what might seem an equal and precisely opposite fear, not that modern sensory experience was too tightly controlled but rather that it was chaotic and indiscriminate. In this account, modern visual culture is so powerfully disorienting that it produces in its subjects what Jean-Louis Comolli has influentially labeled a "frenzy of the visible" (Jay, *Downcast Eyes*, 149–150).

In Jay's formulation, this disordered and decentered visual culture is an alternate "scopic regime" that can be traced back not to the Enlightenment but rather to the Baroque, which also featured a "dazzling, disorienting, ecstatic surplus of images," but it is actually rather hard to think of this disorder as a "regime" at all or to imagine it as arising in any other period than the modern (Jay, "Scopic Regimes," 16). In fact, most early attempts to define this sort of visual experience remark on its unprecedented quality, beginning with Baudelaire, for whom the "ephemeral, the fugitive, the contingent" in urban visual experience was the very essence of the modern, and culminating perhaps in the influential 1903 essay by Georg Simmel, "The Metropolis and Mental Life," which emphasized the "rapid crowding of changing images, the sharp discontinuity in the grasp of a single glance, and the unexpectedness of onrushing impression."[25] In the United States as well, it was common very early in the twentieth century to remark on the quickened pace and unconventional organization of modern visual experience. Lindsay, for example, compared watching a movie to driving in a Ford car, which then became for him the paradigmatic visual experience of the modern era: "To the inevitable speeding-up process of the motion picture quite recently has been added the speeding-up of all other things in America."[26]

Like many other observers of the time, Lindsay also felt that this increase in speed and variety had effected certain phenomenological changes in the sensory organization of human beings: "The whole nervous psychology of the entire American race has thereby been completely revolutionized" (Lindsay, *Progress*, 235). Others, including Simmel, felt the same way, and this conviction, passed down to contemporary theorists by way of Walter Benjamin, has become so widely influential in studies of modern visual culture that these supposed changes in the human sensorium have come to represent modernity itself.[27] The strength of what has come to be called "the modernity thesis" lies in the connection it effects between material history, social change, and aesthetic practices, all linked by the changes technology effects in the senses, but the difficulty also seems to come in making this connection particular. In its most simplistic version, in which the greater speed and variety of modern life in general calls up an equal speed and variety in visual entertainment, this connection has been convincingly criticized by David Bordwell, who wonders just how the human sensorium has been changed and why such changes would prompt similar changes in art, instead of making it slower and more placid, as an anodyne.[28] Some of Bordwell's questions may be answered by the research of Jonathan Crary, which considers the ways in which attention, as a social practice, is derived from modern research on vision as a biological process.[29] Crary's research also has the advantage of linking attentiveness, a necessary modern work habit, with distraction, its apparent opposite in the world of entertainment, thus offering a plausible reconciliation between two influential ways of understanding modern visual culture, which otherwise seem in utter contradiction.

This tension in the theoretical accounts of modern visual culture, which sometimes seem to be describing two completely different experiential systems, is repeated, not unexpectedly, as they are extended to explain aesthetic modernism. The rationalization and ascetic perfection of the visual is an obvious motive in a good deal of modern art: it is, in fact, the feature that seems so overtly "modern" in the work of artists such as Mondrian.[30] Similar motives are apparent all across the arts, from "straight" photography to the architecture of Le Corbusier, but the utter purification of vision is possible only for painting, which can escape all representational and utilitarian necessities. Such, at any rate, was the opinion of Clement Greenberg, for whom the registration of "purely optical experience" was the leading motive of all modern painting (Greenberg, *Collected Essays*, 4: 89). Greenberg's idea of the "purely optical," which excludes illusionary depth, narrative, and overt representation, has come to stand in contemporary controversy for modernism as such, though it accurately describes only a rather small subset of all modern paintings and cannot be extended to literature at all. But Greenberg would hardly have been so influential if his theories did not accurately represent at least one very strong motive among the many behind aesthetic modernism, a motive that is apparent even in the new media that Greenberg generally disdained. The arrival of these new arts, bringing more and more accurate representations of actual life, also gave rise to an almost Promethean desire for a total representation, an art form that would reproduce reality without impediment. The "myth of total cinema," as André Bazin called it,[31] is a myth of eyesight set free from all earthly restraint, and though the exhilaration it offers seems potentially revolutionary, this version of the eye so purified that it can go anywhere and see anything is uncannily like the version that Foucault situates at the center of the panopticon.

At the same time, of course, modernism in all the arts is almost fanatically devoted to reproducing particular perspectives: limited points-of-view in literature; apparently naive glimpses of raw light in painting; snapshots in photography. Though the new media may have presented some with the dream of perfectly limitless sight, they impressed far more with the inevitable distortions inherent in any of looking. In this vein, modernism as a movement attempts to capture and reproduce "the frenzy of the visible" in multiple, conflicting perspectives, the canonical example of which is Duchamp's *Nude Descending a Staircase*, a piled up sequence of images derived from Etienne-Jules Marey's experiments with early film devices.[32] Ezra Pound toyed with the same effect, enlisting Coburn's help in inventing the Vortograph, which superimposed multiple perspectives on a single photographic plate.[33] In film a rapid, abrupt series of apparently arbitrary cuts became so synonymous with urban modernity that it became *de rigueur* in literature as well, most notably perhaps in the work of John Dos Passos.

Though there is always something ecstatic in this frenzied and confused visuality, there is also something deeply skeptical, as multiple perspectives visibly demonstrate the partiality of any single point of view and the impossibility of any inclusive synthesis. Objectivity, in other words, is visibly refuted in many modernist works, and with it goes the reliability of representation. If the camera can lie, as it must if it simultaneously shows two quite different views of the same thing, then how much less reliable is language, which has always been considered even more distant than pictures from the thing itself? The new media, offering new means of representation, prompt in many early modernists a quizzical interest in the very nature of signs, and it is quite common to find the most radical interrogations in the works of artists like Picasso, who was a devotee of both the serials and the comics, or Joyce, who was interested enough in the movies to try to open a cinema.[34] In fact, this convergence of popular visual media with a radical representational irony is the very source of the avant-garde to which contemporary scholars such as Rosalind Krauss have given the pride of place once reserved for Greenberg's abstract expressionists. Where Greenberg had put a modernism devoted to the progressive refinement of the purely optical, Krauss has installed an avant-garde whose sense of sight is embodied, material, and quite literally grounded.[35]

Though it is common to separate and juxtapose these two strains in modernism, almost as if they were opposite camps, they are in fact quite thoroughly implicated in one another, in part because the effects of modern visual culture have been so various. It is quite possible to argue of almost any significant development in the visual culture of the last 200 years that it serves the authoritarian rationalization of the senses and that it disorders and destabilizes sensory regimes long taken for granted. In their early days, even railway trains were thought to offer a dazzling visual spectacle, and the relationship between film and railway travel was established quite early on, as stationary train cars were fitted out as theatres with panoramic displays.[36] But the appeal of this newly mobilized eyesight, hurtled past all sorts of vistas not ordinarily exposed to view, must have been tempered a good deal by the new forms of organization that the railways imposed on the countryside, which had to adopt standardized time so that the trains could run on schedule.[37] Film itself, Tom Gunning has argued, appealed to new audiences because of the "radical heterogeneity" of what it had to offer, while simultaneously imposing new forms of narrative continuity on a mass audience that had not heretofore been tamed into homogeneity.[38] Perhaps for this reason the most influential theorist of modern visual culture is still Walter Benjamin, whose most famous essay, "The Work of Art in the Age of Mechanical Reproduction" includes one of the most positive analyses of "the shock effect of the film" and also an epilogue on the aestheticization of mass politics then leading to Fascism. In the space of a few pages, then, modern visual culture is shown to put the ordinary observer in a newly critical and progressive relation to the work of art and at the same time to lull this observer into inconsequence with empty promises of aesthetic bliss. Of course, Benjamin is talking about such different examples as Chaplin's films and Nazi spectacles, but the point to be made here is that it is difficult to account honestly for modern art and culture without somehow including both.

Taken as seriously as this, the study of modern visual culture might add a great deal to our understanding of modern literature as well. Of course, it has been recognized for many years that certain modern writers have strong affinities with the visual arts, and there is a good deal of empirical research into particular relationships. At least half a dozen very useful books have been written, for example, on William Carlos Williams and the visual arts, but the visual culture scholarship stemming from the historical and theoretical works of Crary, Jay, and Krauss has had remarkably little effect on studies of modern literature, despite the fact that it seems to shed new light on some of the common practices of literary modernism.[39] For example, the new attentiveness studied in such detail by Crary bears an astonishing similarity to the phenomenological virtues preached by the Imagists. Attention, Crary says, became "conceptualized as a physical modality of (relative immobility) within a lifeworld increasingly shaped by the experiences of speed and mobility." Indeed, machines were invented to isolate for measurement the tiny slices of "fixed vision" within the seemingly unbroken welter of modern sensation (Crary, *Suspensions of Perception*, 304).

To any student of modern literature, this definition of attentiveness will sound like an eerily mechanized version of the Imagist desire to render a complex of sensations in an instant of time, and the tachistoscope, which was described in the 1880s as "an instrument for the presentation of visual stimuli, such as a picture, a word, a group of symbols, the duration of each stimulus being extremely short," will sound like a machine for cranking out Imagist poems (Crary, *Suspensions of Perception*, 302). Yet the tachistoscope was not a device for entertainment, closely related though it was to the cinematograph; it was instead part of a widespread laboratory project on attention span and reaction time the ultimate purpose of which was to increase the efficiency of the modern workplace. Attention, in other words, is perception in manufactured form, and the ability to produce it, on demand and in the appropriate quantities, is a modern talent that is highly valued because it is so necessary to subjection (Crary, *Suspensions of Perception*, 309). If Imagism, the cinematograph, and the tachistoscope are parts of some larger perceptual process, then it may be a very sinister one, in which the apparent aesthetic release from time and space constraints offered by films and poems is simply one element in a larger program for the regimentation of the senses.

Though this may seem a rather strained connection, it is one that was stated quite explicitly by Rebecca West, introducing Imagism in *The New Freewoman* in 1913: "Just as Taylor and Gilbreth want to introduce scientific management into industry so the *imagistes* want to discover the most puissant way of whirling the scattered star dust of words into a new star of passion."[40] This could explain why Imagist poems seem to some readers a little cold, why the sharpness and clarity that is so refreshing on one level can seem rigid and even Puritanical on another. But Crary's purpose is not simply to overturn the aesthetic object so as to find political repression wriggling on the underside; though the repressive potentialities of modern attentiveness are real enough, they do not entirely cancel out their opposite. Thus Crary also notes that early researchers were somewhat unsettled by the tendency of fixed attention to waver more the longer it remain fixed, so that the visual field begins "vibrating and oscillating" (Crary, *Suspensions of Perception*, 300). He suggests that it is, in fact, the mobile gaze that allows us to put perceptions together into usable wholes, so that when the gaze is held too long on a single point that point begins to multiply, and one begins to see "its unknown texture, its strangeness, the unfathomable relations of one part of it to another, the uncertainty of how these local elements interact as a dynamic field" (Crary, *Suspensions of Perception*, 298). In other words, one discovers in simple, ordinary perceptions the "optical unconscious" that Benjamin believed had been revealed first when the snapshot split one moment out of the continuum of time and held it up for inspection (Benjamin, *Selected Writings*, 3: 117 and 4: 266). Thus the shock or break so typical of modern perception is not really the antithesis but rather an inescapable part of the rationalization and regimentation of modern vision, as the attentiveness demanded by the assembly line is fundamental also to the enjoyment of film, which it resembles in so many ways. The most innovative, most truly modern, of the artists of this period, for Crary, are those such as Cézanne to whom this relationship appears in all its complexity, so that his "quest for presence disclosed to him its impossibility and opened up for him a view of the mixed and 'broken' character of a fully absorbed perception" (Crary, *Suspensions of Perception*, 328).

This is a description that might usefully be extended to any number of modern writers, including Williams himself. A poem like "The Right of Way," originally published as Poem XI in *Spring and All*, includes at least three layers of attentiveness: the poet's; his own as protagonist; and that of his subjects:

> I saw
> an elderly man who
> smiled and looked away
>
> to the north past a house –
> a woman in blue
>
> who was laughing and
> leaning forward to look up
>
> into the man's half
> averted face . . .[41]

The interest of this simple experience comes from the tension between the fixed attentiveness of the subjects and the mobile gaze of the observer, cruising by in his car. In fact, though, it soon appears that the apparent contrast, in which the subjects seem a little myopic and single-minded as compared to the quick perceptions of the observer, is a false one, since the immobility of the subjects is in fact created by the mobility of the observer, who has not time to watch the full unfolding of any of these little dramatic acts, isolated as snapshots by his speed. As Lindsay suggested about the time that Williams wrote this poem, riding in a car is a lot like watching a movie, except in this case, the ostensible speed of the film is revealed to depend on a whole set of immobilities, single frames flung together in a flash. Ordinarily, the breaks between the frames only appear when the film is made to stop, but in this case, Williams achieves the same effect by speeding up; going very fast, so that each episode shrinks to the size of a frame, turns out to be much the same as going very slow, so that the poem reaches peak velocity just as it stops:

> for I went spinning on the
>
> four wheels of my car
> along the wet road until
>
> I saw a girl with one leg
> over the rail of a balcony

Here, poem and experience come apart along a single seam. The pace of the observer's progress has increased to such a point that it actually breaks his vision into bits that are too small to make sense: he knows the girl really has two legs, but his attention span is so finely tuned at this point that he sees one leg first, so that for a split second she becomes an amputee. The rail of the balcony, which produces this effect by hiding the other leg, works much like the break between film frames, which we are not supposed to notice, or the break between lines in a poem, which Williams forces us not to ignore. In fact, it seems fairly obvious that Williams is hoping to produce with the materials of his poem a creative disorientation originally produced by a purely modern visual experience, that of riding in a car, and reproduced structurally, not just thematically, by modern visual culture in the very form of the movies.

As simple as it is, a poem like this preserves far more subtly the experiential complexity of the modern period than history or theory can. Perhaps for this reason, the most significant recent works on modern visual culture, including Crary's *Suspensions of Perception* and T. J. Clark's *Farewell to an Idea*, have depended heavily on long, searching analyses of particular works, not just as illustrations but also as interrogations of the author's theoretical assumptions. Indeed, such detailed empirical work has always been a part of visual culture studies, even in the difficult theoretical writing of critics such as Krauss, who pays respectfully close attention to all sorts of work, including that of Stieglitz.[42] That the modern period is so full of aesthetic works in all forms that elicit this kind of attention is one of the strongest arguments in favor of the idea that, no matter how uniform or regimented it may be, modern visual culture has made the eye ever more self-consciously a part of the mind.

NOTES

1. Martin Jay, *Downcast Eyes: The Denigration of Vision in Twentieth-Century French Thought* (Berkeley: University of California Press, 1993), 76.
2. Leo Steinberg, *Other Criteria: Confrontations with Twentieth-Century Art* (New York: Oxford University Press, 1972), 293; Clement Greenberg, *The Collected Essays and Criticism*, 4 vols., ed. John O'Brian (University of Chicago Press, 1993), IV: 265.
3. In fact, the earliest use of the term in the discipline of art history came in studies of earlier periods by Michael Baxandall and Svetlana Alpers. See the contributions of Alpers and Thomas Da Costa Kaufman to the "Questionnaire on Visual Studies," *October* 77 (1996), 26, 45–46.
4. See, for example, Ernest Betts, *Heraclitus or The Future of the Films* (London: Kegan Paul, Trench, Trubner, 1928), 13, and Eric Elliott, *Anatomy of Motion Picture Art* (Territet: Pool, 1928), 142.
5. Robert B. Ray, *How a Film Theory Got Lost and Other Mysteries in Cultural Studies* (Bloomington: Indiana University Press, 2001), 70.
6. Geoffrey Batchen, *Burning with Desire: The Conception of Photography* (Cambridge, MA: MIT Press, 1997).
7. T. J. Clark, *The Painting of Modern Life: Paris in the Art of Manet and his Followers* (Princeton University Press, 1984), 66.
8. See the celebrated report of Dominique François Arago to the French Chamber of Deputies, reprinted in *Classic Essays on Photography*, ed. Alan Trachtenberg (New Haven: Leete's Island Books, 1980), 15–25.
9. Gisele Freund, *Photography and Society* (New York: Godine, 1980), 103–104.
10. Tom Gunning, "New Thresholds of Vision: Instantaneous Photography and the Early Cinema of Lumière," in *Impossible Presence: Surface and Screen in the Photogenic Era*, ed. Terry Smith (University of Chicago Press, 2001), 89–91.
11. Quoted in Wanda Corn, *The Great American Thing: Modern Art and National Identity, 1915–1935* (Berkeley: University of California Press, 1999), 52.
12. Miriam Bratu Hansen, "America, Paris, the Alps: Kracauer (and Benjamin) on Cinema and Modernity," in *Cinema and the Invention of Modern Life*, ed. Leo Charney and Vannesa R. Schwartz (Berkeley: University of California Press, 1995), 371.
13. "The Nude-Descending-a-Staircase Man Surveys Us," *New York Tribune*, September 12, 1915. Quoted in Corn, *Great American Thing*, 42, 55.
14. Miles Orvell, *The Real Thing: Imitation and Authenticity in American Culture, 1880–1940* (Chapel Hill: University of North Carolina Press, 1989), 125–127.
15. For a discussion that uses this book as an example of intellectual distance from American popular culture, see Paul R. Gorman, *Left Intellectuals and Popular Culture in Twentieth-Century America* (Chapel Hill: University of North Carolina Press, 1996), 17. See also Myron Lounsbury, *The Origins of American Film Criticism 1909–1939* (New York: Arno Press, 1973), 48–49.
16. Alvin Langdon Coburn, "The Relation of Time to Art," *Camera Work* 36 (1911), 72.
17. Vachel Lindsay, *The Art of the Moving Picture* (1915; rpt. New York: Modern Library, 2000), 30.

18. H. A. L., "Foreign Exchange," *Broom* 2 (May 1922), 178. See also Matthew Josephson, "Made in America," *Broom* 2 (June 1922), 270 and H. A. L., "The Mysticism of Money," *Broom* 3 (September 1922), 127–128.
19. See, in particular, the issue for September 1923, which included Soupault's "The U.S.A. Cinema" (65–69), Sanborn's "Motion Picture Dynamics" (78–82), and Brown's "Note on Sculptural Kinetics" (124–125).
20. Gorman, *Left Intellectuals*, p. 73; Michael Kammen, *The Lively Arts: Gilbert Seldes and the Transformation of Cultural Criticism in the United States* (New York: Oxford University Press, 1996), 100.
21. Jay first catalogued these in "Scopic Regimes of Modernity," in *Vision and Visuality*, ed. Hal Foster (Seattle: Bay Press, 1988), 3–23. As he notes there, the term *scopic regime* is taken from Christian Metz.
22. Martin Heidegger, *Poetry, Language, Thought*, tr. Albert Hofstadter (New York: Harper, 1971), 165–166. See also David Michael Levin, "Decline and Fall: Ocularcentrism in Heidegger's Reading of the History of Metaphysics," in *Modernity and the Hegemony of Vision*, ed. David Michael Levin (Berkeley: University of California Press, 1993), 205, and Jay, *Downcast Eyes*, 269–275.
23. Jay, *Downcast Eyes*, 383, 392–393; Thomas R. Flynn, "Foucault and the Eclipse of Vision," in Levin, "Decline and Fall," 279.
24. Tom Gunning, "Tracing the Individual Body: Photography, Detectives, and Early Cinema," in Charney, pp. 15–45.
25. See, in particular, *Public Opinion* (New York: Harcourt Brace, 1922) and *The Phantom Public* (New York: Harcourt Brace, 1925).
26. Quoted in Ben Singer, *Melodrama and Modernity: Early Sensational Cinema and its Contexts* (New York: Columbia University Press, 2001), 61.
27. Vachel Lindsay, *The Progress and Poetry of the Movies: A Second Book of Film Criticism*, ed. Myron Lounsbury (Lanham, MD: Scarecrow Press, 1995), 235.
28. The essential thesis here is Benjamin's idea that "Just as the entire mode of existence of human collectives changes over long historical periods, so too does their mode of perception." "The Work of Art in the Age of its Technological Reproducibility," in *Selected Writings*, 4 vols., ed. Howard Eiland and Michael W. Jennings (Cambridge, MA: Harvard University Press, 2003), IV: 255.
29. David Bordwell, *On the History of Film Style* (Cambridge, MA: Harvard University Press, 1997), 141–146. See also the detailed response in Singer, *Melodrama and Modernity*, 101–130.
30. Jonathan Crary, *Suspensions of Perception: Attention, Spectacle, and Modern Culture* (Cambridge, MA: MIT Press, 1999).
31. Thierry de Duve, *Kant After Duchamp* (Cambridge, MA: MIT Press, 1996), 155–156.
32. Bart Testa, *Back and Forth: Early Cinema and the Avant-Garde* (Art Gallery of Ontario, 1992), 60.
33. Marta Braun, *Picturing Time: The Work of Etienne-Jules Marey (1830–1904)* (University of Chicago Press, 1992), 287–291; François Dagognet, *Etienne-Jules Marey: A Passion for the Trace*, tr. Robert Galeta with Jeanine Herman (New York: Zone Books, 1992), 159–160.
34. Richard Humphreys, "Demon Pantechnicon Driver: Pound in the London Vortex, 1908–1920," and John Alexander, "Parenthetical Paris, 1920–1925:

Pound, Picabia, Brancusi and Léger," in *Pound's Artists: Ezra Pound and the Visual Arts in London, Paris and Italy* (London: Tate Gallery, 1985).

35. For the most complete discussion of Picasso's interest in film, see Natasha Staller, *A Sum of Destructions: Picasso's Cultures and the Creation of Cubism* (New Haven: Yale University Press, 2001). For a recent discussion of Joyce and film, see Thomas Burkdall, *Joycean Frames: Film and the Fiction of James Joyce* (New York: Routledge, 2001).

36. Rosalind E. Krauss, *The Optical Unconscious* (Cambridge, MA: MIT Press, 1994); Rosalind E. Krauss and Yve-Alain Bois, *Formless: A User's Guide* (New York: Zone Books, 1997). See also de Duve, *Kant After Duchamp*, 171.

37. For a recent discussion of this relationship, see Lynne Kirby, *Parallel Tracks: The Railroad and Silent Cinema* (Durham: Duke University Press, 1997).

38. Stephen Kern, *The Culture of Time and Space, 1880–1918* (Cambridge, MA: Harvard University Press, 1983).

39. Tom Gunning, "The Cinema of Attractions: Early Film, its Spectator and the Avant-Garde," in *Early Cinema: Space, Frame, Narrative*, ed. Thomas Elsaesser with Adam Barker (London: British Film Institute, 1990), 61.

40. For a recent exception, see Karen Jacobs, *The Eye's Mind: Literary Modernism and Visual Culture* (Ithaca: Cornell University Press, 2001), 14–15, 22.

41. Rebecca West, "Imagism," *The New Freewoman*, August 15, 1913, 86.

42. *The Collected Poems of William Carlos Williams*, 2 vols., ed. A. Walton Litz and Christopher MacGowan (New York: New Directions, 1986), 1: 206.

43. Rosalind Krauss, "Stieglitz/*Equivalents*," *October* 11 (Winter 1979).

8

MARJORIE PERLOFF

The avant-garde phase of American modernism

On June 15, 1915, a sweltering day in Manhattan, Marcel Duchamp, then twenty-eight, arrived in New York on the SS Rochambeau. "I am not going to New York, I am leaving Paris," he announced to his American artist-patron Walter Pach.[1] Like a number of other European avant-gardists, Duchamp was escaping the Great War – a war in which both his artist brothers, Jacques Villon and Raymond Duchamp-Villon, were already serving and in which the latter was to be killed in 1918. Duchamp himself was exempt from military service because of a heart murmur, but the very idea of war struck him as insane: "I must say," he later told an interviewer, "I admire the attitude of combating invasion with folded arms."[2]

But it was not only the war that brought Duchamp to America. Increasingly, he had come to dislike the Bohemian "artistic life" of Paris, where scores of artists worked in small suburban studios vying to emulate the great Cubist painters. America, as he told an interviewer in September 1915, was different:

> The capitals of the Old World have labored for hundreds of years to find that which constitutes good taste and one may say that they have found the zenith thereof. But why do people not understand what a bore this is? . . . If only America would realize that the art of Europe is finished – dead – and that America is the country of the art of the future . . . Look at the skyscrapers! Has Europe anything to show more beautiful than these?
>
> New York is a work of art, a complete work of art . . . And I believe that the idea of demolishing old buildings, old souvenirs, is fine . . . The dead should not be permitted to be so much stronger than the living. We must learn to forget the past, to live our own lives in our own time.
>
> (Tomkins, *Duchamp*, 152)

Here is the avant-garde position programmatically stated. The term *avant-garde*, we sometimes forget, was originally a military metaphor: it referred to the front flank of the army, the forerunners in battle who paved the way for the rest.[3] The *avant-garde*, moreover, is by definition oppositional: in Peter Bürger's now famous words, "It radically questions the very principle of art in bourgeois society according to which the individual is considered the creator of the work of art."[4]

By this token, a skyscraper or bridge or, as was to be the case with the mysterious *Fountain*, submitted as an entry to the Society of Independent Artists Exhibition of 1917, a plumbing fixture could be just as much a work of art as a painting by Cézanne. But this was hardly the going view of the New York art world, even at its most sophisticated, at the time of Duchamp's arrival on the scene. It is important to note that it was not the Americans – the Skyscraper Primitives as Dickran Tashjian has called the artists and poets of New York Dada[5] – that invented the "readymades," machine drawings, or "nonsense" poems that we now designate as "avant-garde," for the latter were almost exclusively European imports. Indeed, "New York Dada," the preferred designation for the American modernist avant-garde, is a misnomer on both counts: New York Dada was neither indigenous to New York nor was it Dada, given that Zurich's Cabaret Voltaire, where the Dada movement was invented, came into being only in 1916, two years after Duchamp's first "Dada" readymades were completed. When Dada moved to Paris in the early twenties, Duchamp distanced himself from the movement as much as possible. Invited by Tristan Tzara to contribute to the 1921 Dada Salon, Duchamp responded with a three-word telegram, "PODE BAL-DUCHAMP," with its pun on "peau de balle" or "balls to you."[6] And the same year he wrote to his young protégée, Ettie Stettheimer, "From a distance these things, these Movements take on a charm that they do not have close up – I assure you."[7]

Not only, then, was the so-called American avant-garde a European invention and intervention, but it would not have taken the particular form it did, had Duchamp not settled in New York and quickly become the center of the Walter Arensberg salon, where he met "everyone" from Wallace Stevens and William Carlos Williams to Man Ray and his future patroness Katherine Dreier. The war also brought Francis Picabia, whose "sexy" machine-drawings, published in such journals as *291*, were to have wide repercussions, the British-born poet Mina Loy, and the German Baroness Elsa von Freitag-Loringhoven. At the same time, such native avant-gardists as Gertrude Stein, perhaps the most radical of them all, and Ezra Pound, the founder of Imagism in 1912, and two years later of Vorticism, had become expatriates before the war, even as Man Ray settled in Paris in the postwar years. Those who stayed home – the great photographer Alfred Stieglitz, the painters Charles Demuth and Charles Sheeler, and, for that matter, Williams and Stevens – were not avant-gardists in the strict sense of the word; they did not want to overthrow tradition or to give up painting or lyric poetry.

It can, of course, be argued, that the influx of foreigners who change the very consciousness of the nation is precisely what is "American" about America, and that the fact that Duchamp's interventions took place *in* New York, where he was to spend a good part of his adult life, makes his artworks, even those with French titles and punning French captions, American works. Certainly, they are now part of the very fabric of American, rather than French, consciousness. But it was not until World War II, when a second influx of European avant-gardists arrived in the US, this time primarily surrealists like André Breton and Max Ernst, and Bauhaus artists like Joseph Albers, Walter Gropius, and Lazlo Moholy-Nagy, that an indigenous American avant-garde was born. John Cage, born in Los Angeles, Merce Cunningham in Centralia, Washington, and Jasper Johns in Augusta, Georgia – these were nothing if not homegrown products, as were Frank O'Hara, born in Baltimore, brought up in Grafton, Massachusetts, and John Ashbery, raised on a farm outside Rochester, New York. For the Cage–Cunningham–Johns circle, Duchamp, who was living in lower Manhattan for most of the postwar years, was God. But by this time, the avant-garde had its own momentum, and from then on successive avant-garde movements in the US – Fluxus, conceptual art, language poetry, performance art – were characterized by their artistic independence from the European tradition.

The Duchamp factor

Let me backtrack. The "International Exhibition of Modern Art," organized by Walter Pach, Arthur Davies, and Walt Kuhn, and financially backed by patrons Gertrude Vanderbilt Whitney and Mabel Dodge, opened at the 69th Regiment Armory at 305 Lexington Avenue and 25th Street in New York on February 17, 1913. The Armory Show, as it soon came to be called, exhibited more than a thousand items and quickly became the talk of the town. Ironically, most of the paintings and sculptures shown were not at all outrageous: there were Van Goghs, Cézannes, Odilon Redon, André Derain, Brancusi's *Mademoiselle Pogany*, and so on.

The *succès de scandale* of the show, Duchamp's *Nude Descending a Staircase* (figure 8.1) was, ironically enough, not all that "new" either. The sources of the painting are the motion studies of Etienne-Jules Marey, whose chronophotographs of the 1880s, produced by making multiple exposures of a moving figure on a single photographic plate, had already displayed figures in motion. And, as Calvin Tomkins notes, Eadweard Muybridge's related motion studies, made by using "a battery of cameras mounted side by side to catch fencers, galloping horses and other moving figures in a series of separate views, which he then combined to show the movement's

Figure 8.1 Marcel Duchamp, *Nude Descending a Staircase*, no. 2, oil on canvas.

flow . . . included one sequence of twenty-four images of a nude woman descending a flight of stairs, trailing behind her a white chiffon scarf" (see Tomkins, *Duchamp*, 78). Italian Futurist painters like Giacomo Balla had already adapted these motion studies; Duchamp's *Nude*, for that matter, may well owe something to Balla's charming *Dynamism of a Dog on a Leash* (1912). But if the conception of the *Nude* is Futurist, its technique is largely Cubist. Duchamp's nude is less a woman, or even a human being, than an elaborate machine made up of a series of overlapping geometric planes in brown, gray, and green – the typically muted Cubist colors. There is nothing the least bit erotic about this "woman."

Why, then, all the fuss, beginning with the rejection of the painting by the 1912 Paris Salon des Indépendants? Why the newspaper lampoons, referring to the painting as the "explosion in a shingle factory" or "The Rude Descending a Staircase (Rush Hour at the Subway")? The scandal, it seems, was primarily attributable to the painting's title. Nudes, in Duchamp's day, were lovely creatures, reclining on a chaise-longue (Manet) or bathing in a stream (Renoir); the idea of a nude woman coming down a staircase, even when, as in this case, she was not recognizably a nude woman at all (indeed, there was speculation that "she" was a "he" – see Tomkins, *Duchamp*, 117), was too much for the public of 1912. Ironically, it was the matter-of-fact title that forced the viewer to visualize the scene and to see those curved and rectangular abstracted gray-brown forms as female private parts.

Nude Descending a Staircase was purchased by a San Francisco antiques dealer named Frederick Torrey for $240. Duchamp was glad it sold but he was already questioning the very ontology of painting. Increasingly, he was dissatisfied with the notion of an art for the *eye*, an art that depended on what he came to call "the retinal shudder." Before the nineteenth century, he tells Pierre Cabanne, "painting had other functions: it could be religious, philosophical, moral"; it was only after Courbet that painting was taken to be "completely retinal" (Cabanne, *Dialogues*, 43).

A 1913 journal entry found in *The White Box (A'Linfinitif)* poses the question, "Can one make works which are not works of 'art'"?[8] In answer, Duchamp began to produce – or rather find – what he called, on the analogy of readymade clothing, *readymades*. One of the earliest of these was an ordinary cast-iron bottle-drying rack which he bought at a hardware store in Paris in 1914. Thrifty French families reused their wine bottles in those days, taking the empties to the local wine shop for a refill. Again, it is the title *L'Egouttoir* that transforms ordinary object into artwork. The verb *égoutter* means "able to drain drops" but also plays on the word *goût* ("taste"), thus underscoring Duchamp's insistence that art has nothing to do with "taste," that indeed it must be based on complete "visual indifference" (see

Cabanne, *Dialogues*, 58). But this remark is itself tongue-in-cheek, for the fact is that, as viewers soon noticed, the bottle rack plays on phallic form: those upright rods seem to be waiting to be inserted into their respective "bottles."

In New York, having acquired other such "readymades" as a large snow shovel, inscribed with the title *In Advance of the Broken Arm*, Duchamp wrote his sister, Suzanne: "If you have been up to my place, you will have seen in the studio, a bicycle wheel and a bottle rack. I bought this as a ready-made sculpture . . . Take this bottle rack for yourself. I'm making it a 'readymade,' remotely." And he explains to Suzanne how to inscribe it at the bottom (see Duchamp, *Correspondence*, 44). Unfortunately, Suzanne had thrown both bicycle wheel and bottle rack into the trash. But in the end this did not matter, for the "originality" of the readymades was not in their material existence but in the artist's conception. Accordingly, they could be – and were – readily reproduced. Indeed, Duchamp was to embark on an elaborate project of self-reproduction, placing facsimiles of his readymades inside boxes and *boîtes en valise*, which were to become, in return, sought after artworks.

As such, the readymade paved the way for the conceptual art of the later twentieth century; indeed, that art is inconceivable without Duchamp's example. Then, too, the defamiliarization of ordinary commercial objects – snow shovels, bottle racks, combs, clothes hangers – was the first step in the rapprochement between "high" and "low" art so characteristic of the twentieth century, especially in the US. But this is not to say that the Duchampian readymade functions primarily as a critique of capitalist commodity culture, for as Linda Henderson has so convincingly shown, such "readymades" as the "treated" spool of twine between two metal plates called *With Hidden Noise*, far from being "meaningless," were closely based on the scientific and mathematical discoveries of Duchamp's day, from non-Euclidean geometry to electromagnetism, all of these given a kind of pataphysical spin.[9] *The Bride Stripped Bare By Her Bachelors, Even*, known as *The Large Glass*, begun in New York during the war, and was, so Duchamp insisted, not a "picture" at all but a "delay in glass," rather as one would say "a spittoon in silver" (Duchamp, *Correspondence*, 26), the delay being, among other things, the *temporal* dimension of the conceptual work, the time that elapses between perception and conceptual response.

Photo-secession, abstraction, and mecanomorphs

Duchamp's avant-gardism is thus in a class by itself; it sets the stage for most of the movements of the latter twentieth century and is genuinely radical in opposing the very institution of art in capitalist, bourgeois society. Other New York avant-gardists were less inclined to break with the tradition in such a dramatic way. Take the case of the great photographer Alfred Stieglitz, whose own pictures, together with his journal *Camera Work* (1903–17)[10] and his Photo-Secession Gallery, known, because of its address at 291 Fifth Avenue, as *291*, is central to the American avant-garde.

In its first decade, *Camera Work* was the site of the photographic movement known as Pictorialism. Such photographers as Gertrude Kasebier, Heinrich Kuehn, and Paul R. Haviland produced suggestive, misty landscapes or ethereal portraits of beautiful and mysterious women. In all of these, the image, bathed in *atmosphere*, in soft and delicate shadows, was valued for what Stieglitz called its "individual expression." He himself began as a Pictorialist, but although he continued to publish Pictorialists throughout his career, his own predilection was for the gritty materiality of urban culture, with its skyscrapers, electric lights, machines, and transportation. At the same time, Stieglitz was highly conscious of formal values. The inspiration for his now classic 1907 photograph *The Steerage* (figure 8.2), he once remarked, was that he saw the scene in question as "shapes related to one another – a picture of shapes."[11]

The photograph, reproduced in *Camera Work* 36 (1911) and again in no. 7 (1916) of *291*, uses such compositional elements as a white drawbridge, whose prominent diagonal visually connects the very different upper and lower decks of the ship in a structure of repeated circles, triangles, and rectangles. Again, the narrow stairway on the right, joining the two decks forms a triangle with the mast that cuts into the sky on the top, even as the funnel on the left connects mast and bridge. And the bridge itself has important formal properties: the ovals of the chain railings being juxtaposed to the vertical poles that support them. The geometric composition thus controls the realistic images of the crowd, the ordinary poor people on deck above and below. The lower deck is made up mostly of women and children, dressed in light colors; in the upper, by contrast, men in suits and hats form a dark mass, silhouetted at the top against the white sky. The women below wear flowing garments and have erected a makeshift clothes-line (on the left); the men on the upper deck are mostly standing still, gazing down or into the distance. But a detail like the white hat of the man near the rail at center-right, leads the eye to the lower level and connects to the white shawls and scarfs of the women below.

The Steerage may thus be seen as a classic modernist work, in which representational reference is controlled within a unified formal composition. Stieglitz never wholly abandoned realism for Cubism or Dada. At the same time, as an editor and art dealer, he was wholly receptive to these movements:

Figure 8.2 Alfred Stieglitz, *The Steerage*, 1907, Photogravure, 12 5/8 × 10 1/8″.

in 1912, for example, *Camera Work* put out a special number featuring four-teen reproductions of paintings by Matisse and Picasso. More remarkable: this issue printed Gertrude Stein's astonishing abstract portraits of the two artists. "Picasso" begins:

> One whom some were certainly following was one who was completely charm-ing. One whom some were certainly following was one who was charming. One whom some were following was one who was completely charming. One whom some were following was one who was certainly completely charming.
>
> (Stein, *Camera Work*)

Can we recognize Picasso from this "portrait"? And how do we square the portrait of Matisse with Sadakichi Hartman's essay in the same issue called "Once More Matisse," written after seeing the most recent exhibition of the painter's works at 291? Hartman suggests that Matisse was "not an innovator of form," but praises his extraordinary color, passion, and "ethical dignity," which allows this painter "to accomplish a great task." Stein would have had no truck with terms like "ethical dignity" or "passion," but perhaps she is saying something similar to Hartman when she repeats, in various permutations, the motif that Matisse "was wrong in doing what he had been doing," even though "he certainly was a great one." Still, her mode is entirely other: the repetition in "Matisse" of the words "certain," "doing," and "great," like the repetitions of "charming," "following," "completely," and "working" in the Picasso portrait create a dense, quasi-abstract verbal and rhythmic field, a set of syntactic tensions quite unlike anything that readers of 1912 would have recognized as "poetic." Indeed, most readers thought Stein was simply writing nonsense. But Stieglitz defended her in the Special Issue (1912), arguing as follows:

> . . . the fact is that these articles themselves and not either subjects with which they deal or the illustrations that accompany them, are the true *raison d'etre* of this special issue . . . in these articles by Miss Stein, the Post-Impressionist spirit is found expressing itself in literary form that we thus lay them before the readers of CAMERA WORK in a specially prepared and supplemental number.

And the editor adds somewhat defensively:

> These articles bear, to current interpretative criticism, a relation exactly analogous to that born by the work of the men of whom they treat to the painting and sculpture of older schools.
>   So close, indeed, is this analogy that they will doubtless be regarded by many as no less absurd, unintelligible, radical or revolutionary than the so-called vagaries of the painters whom they seek to interpret.[12]

Here Stieglitz shows himself to be far ahead of his moment, for even today, readers, quite willing to accept non-representational elements in painting, object to their counterpart in literature. "By 1912," writes Janet Malcolm in her 2003 *New Yorker* profile, "[Stein] had started producing work in a language of her own, one that uses English words but in no other way resembles English as it is known."[13] And Malcolm cites what she takes to be an incomprehensible sentence from "Mabel Dodge at the Villa Curonia," a Stein portrait also first published in *Camera Work*, this time in the June 1913 issue.

Despite his appreciation of Stein's language compositions, Stieglitz remained ambivalent about the avant-garde. On the one hand, he continued to publish such "pictorial" Neo-Impressionist photographs as Karl F. Struss's "Ducks, Lake Como 1912," with its shimmery water and heavy, dark leaf-covered branch, and Paul B. Haviland's "Passing Steamer 1912," which looks like one of those delicate turn-of-the century beach scenes by the painter Eugene Boudin (see nos. 38, 39). On the other hand, he joined Haviland and the typographic artist Marius de Zayas in a new venture, the publication of the elegant journal *291*. This large folio publication went through twelve numbers: the first boasted a gorgeous de Zayas cover of an abstracted, geometric figure in black and red and featured, among other typographical experiments, Apollinaire's famous calligramme "Voyage." The "new" typography, as derived from Futurist *parole in libertà* and Dada manifestos, was central to the magazine. But the most significant contribution to *291* was probably Picabia's: no. 2 has his witty erotic "object-portrait" *Voilà Elle*, no. 4, his *Fille née sans mère* ("Girl Born without a Mother"), a set of machine forms without function, made of disconnected springs, rods, and tangled wire, and, in the double issue no. 5–6, two of Picabia's most successful works: the image of a spark plug called *Portrait d'une jeune fille américaine dans l'état de nudité* (figure 8.3), and that of a distorted open camera called *Ici c'est ici Stieglitz* figure 8.4).

These mechanomorphic drawings, as Picabia called them recall, at first glance, the mail-order catalogues and newspaper advertisements of the period. In a 1915 interview, Picabia declared that "This visit to America . . . has brought about a complete revolution in my methods of work . . . it flashed on me that the genius of the modern world is in machinery and that through machinery art ought to find a most vivid expression."[14] But the portraits are hardly straightforward celebrations of the New Technology; on the contrary, like Duchamp's readymades, Picabia's are playful machines, whose subject is eros. The *Portrait d'une jeune fille américaine*, for example, plays on the then well-known archetype of the young American girl, at once liberated and yet virginal – the flirt. Picabia's spark plug is just such a flirt: it has not yet, so to speak, "kindled the flame" of an available engine. Hence its brand name "For-Ever" (in Valentine parlance) is ironic: perhaps this defeminized spark-plug is "forever" chaste. And further, as Tashjian notes, "Drawn in stark black and white, with severely precise lines, the spark plug has a phallic quality that perhaps suggests the latent masculinity of the 'emancipated' American female" (Tashjian, *Skyscraper Primitives*, 38). Word and image thus fuse to create an equivocal erotic machine, quite new to American portraiture.

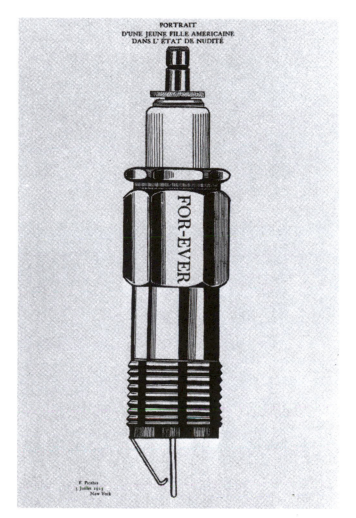

Figure 8.3 Francis Picabia, *Portrait d'une jeune fille américaine*, 291, no. 5–6
(July–August 1915).

Ici c'est ici Stieglitz / Foi et Amour ("Here. It's Stieglitz here / Faith and Love") is even more intricate in its ironies: Picabia, who had his differences with Stieglitz presents the great photographer as an open camera, whose broken bellows cannot make connection with the camera lens, above which the word "IDEAL" is planted. The limp phallic tower, in other words, cannot penetrate the "ideal" hole beyond its reach. Behind the camera box, Picabia improbably places automobile parts in red outline: a gearshift (in neutral) and a brake in locked position, the implication being that this camera/car

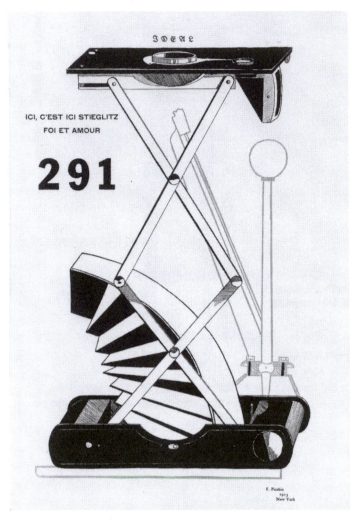

Figure 8.4 Francis Picabia, *Ici c'est ici Stieglitz: Foi et Amour*, cover illustration, *291*, no. 5–6 (July–August 1915).

is a broken machine, its erotic potential frustrated by a useless idealism. So much for the "faith and love" of the caption. Here ("Ici"), Picabia seems to say, is Stieglitz in all his absurdity.

Such portraiture is, of course, largely caricature – and in this sense, a time-honored art. But Picabia's witty identification of persons as machines and his conjunction of the verbal and the visual gave drawing and illustration a new life. Such little magazines as *291*, moreover, provided design standards hitherto entirely unknown in the US. Innovative typography, color, and especially the space of the page: these constituted a decisive change from Victorian book design. A similar avant-garde invention, again influenced by Duchamp but this time involving the new photography, was the "rayography" and related artwork of Man Ray.

Born Emmanuel Radnitsky to Russian-Jewish parents in Philadelphia and growing up in Brooklyn, Man Ray gave the essentially European avant-garde, a decidedly nativist and political inflection. As a young man, he enrolled at the Ferrer Center, a progressive anarchist community in New York, where he studied with the radical painters Robert Henri and George Bellows and published antiwar illustrations for the August 1914 issues of Emma Goldman's journal *Mother Earth*. Allan Antliff reproduces two of these cover illustrations in his recent *Anarchist Modernism*: the first depicts the dual-headed beast of "Capitalism" and "Government," ripping apart "Humanity" with its jaws. The second shows a Christ, crucified on the pole of the American flag, its Stars and Stripes the background for images of war resisters, about to be carried off to jail.[15]

These didactic images are a far cry from Duchamp's apolitical ready-mades and boxes as well as from Picabia's playful sexual innuendos. But Man Ray did not stay with this anarchist mode for long: his early paintings are proto-Cubist, in line with Cézanne, Picasso, and Braque. In 1915, Duchamp visited the Ridgefield, New Jersey artists' colony where Man Ray was then living, and the two artists were soon working on joint projects, Man Ray frequently photographing Duchamp as *Rrose Sélavy*, and transforming the dust-covered, cracked, and unfinished *Large Glass* into *Dust Raising* of 1920, in which the dirty crevices of a confined space are refigured as some kind of moonscape, beautiful in its ridges and hillocks – a kind of proto-earth art piece.

Man Ray's famous "objects," made mostly before he settled in Paris in 1921 and turned to the rayograph, or cameraless photograph, are fascinating analogues to Duchamp's readymades. Take the 1918 silver print of an egg-beater called *Man* (figure 8.5). Whereas Duchamp's readymade art depends on initial choice rather than transformation – a dog comb remains a dog comb – and refigures these objects mainly by means of captions, legends, and framing devices, Man Ray alters the object itself by means of light and shadow of the photograph. Thus the lower part of the eggbeater is duplicated in shadow, suggesting two "legs" or trousers while the assembly of gears above it looks like a torso, and the handle on top, like an oval head. Francis Naumann has posited that "the tapering cylindrical handle attached to the large central gear and carefully positioned between the two floating 'appendages' has obvious phallic implications, a detail that provides the object with its novel male identity."[16]

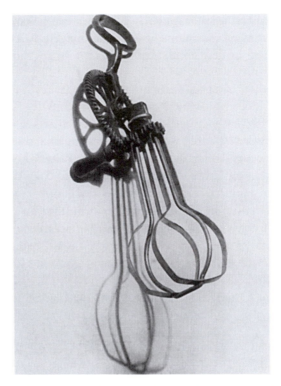

Figure 8.5 Man Ray, *Homme* (Man), 1915. Gelatin silver print, 19 15/16 × 15 1/8″.

But it is not only a matter of equating machine to man. Rosalind Krauss notes that the interest of *Man* and its companion piece *Woman* (an image of photographer's lamps and drying paraphernalia) is "the relation between a readymade and its shadow": "The 'point' is a kind of exfoliation of the physical object into the virtual space of its flattened, wall-bound reflection, where, redoubled by means of cast shadow, it functions to reinterpret the mass-produced object."[17] As such, "the readymade's discursive form is that of the commodity-in-circulation," its exchange value "redoubled by its location in the pages of a magazine and thus ready for dissemination in the world of high culture" (Krauss "Object Caught," 250). The passage from "low" to "high," so important for postmodern art practices, is thus assured.

All the same, *Man* and *Woman* did not provoke the heated controversy generated by Duchamp's most famous readymade, *Fountain by R. Mutt* of 1917. *Man* is, after all, an art photograph that brings out the lovely shape of an ordinary kitchen gadget. The anonymous *Fountain*, on the other hand, was rejected by the Society of Independents, on whose board Duchamp himself served, such members as Katherine Dreier arguing that this urinal was unfit for display in an art gallery. In response, Duchamp arranged for *The Blindman*, the little magazine he edited with Denis Roché in 1917,[18] to produce an elegant protest. First, Duchamp approached Stieglitz and asked him to photograph *Fountain* for the frontispiece. Stieglitz, happy to help the cause against bigotry, did more than just photograph the urinal. He presented it against the backdrop of Mardsen Hartley's 1913 canvas *The Warriors*, which is dominated by a simple, symmetrical form, not unlike the shape of *Fountain*, used as a frame for a seated Buddha in a related painting of 1913. The urinal replaces the Buddha and hence, as Beatrice Wood recalls, it was now dubbed "Madonna of the Bathroom" (Camfield, *Marcel Duchamp*, 33).

Backdrop and lighting transformed the urinal, turned upside down so as to transform male function into female form, into an elegant artwork (figure 8.6). Who, then, was its creator: Duchamp or Stieglitz? And which is the "real" *Fountain*, Stieglitz's photograph or the object itself, now replicated and found in various museums and in Duchamp's boxes? On the page below the Stieglitz image, we find an anonymous article (actually written by Duchamp) called "The Richard Mutt Case," that reads as follows:

> They say any artist paying six dollars may exhibit.
>
> Mr. Richard Mutt sent in a fountain. Without discussion this article disappeared and never was exhibited.
>
> What were the grounds for refusing Mr. Mutt's fountain –
>
> 1. Some contended it was immoral, vulgar.
> 2. Others, it was plagiarism, a plain piece of plumbing.
>
> Now Mr. Mott's fountain is not immoral, that is absurd, no more than a bathtub is immoral. It is a fixture that you see every day in plumbers' show windows.
>
> Whether Mr. Mutt with his own hands made the fountain or not has no importance. He CHOSE it. He took an ordinary article of life, placed it so that its useful significance disappeared under the new title and point of view – created a new thought for that object.
>
> As for plumbing, that is absurd. The only works of art America has given are her plumbing and her bridges.   (Camfield, *Marcel Duchamp*, 37–38)

This seems to me one of the pivotal manifestos of American avant-gardism. The notion that art can be made from everyday objects and materials and that the artist is not so much a talented draftsman or painter but simply the person *who chose it*, has been central to our arts from Smithson's "Monuments of Passaic, New Jersey" to Cindy Sherman's costume pieces to such "found art" works as Kenneth Goldsmith's recent *Day*, which is a transcription of one day's issue of the *New York Times*, transcribed from left to right and top to bottom on the consecutive pages of a book, thus revealing the absurdity and

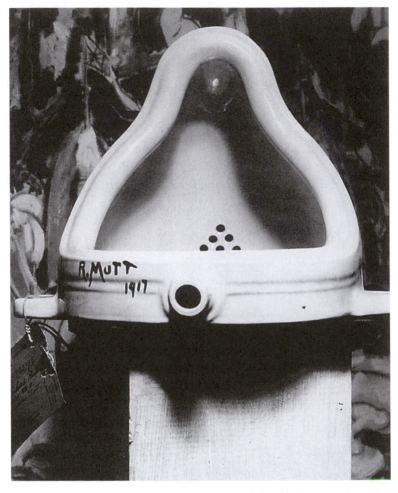

Figure 8.6 Marcel Duchamp, *Fountain*, 1917. Photograph by Alfred Stieglitz from *The Blind Man*, no. 2 (New York, May 1917), 4.

wonder of our daily discourse. The urinal is given further resonance by and its attribution to R. Mutt, bringing to mind the J. L. Mott Iron Works, where Duchamp purchased it, the cartoon *Mutt and Jeff*, and the references to dogs (mutts), mothers (German *Mutti*), and even *Armut* (poverty). The erotic and playful meanings of *Fountain*, whose female shape actually resembles the great fountains of Roman villas, are multiple.

"He CHOSE it." In the same year (1917), the notorious Baroness Elsa von Freytag-Loringhoven (née Elsa Plötz in Swinemunde, Germany, a sometime show girl, artist's model, veteran of endless affairs and short-lived marriages, made, with the help of the artist Morton Schamberg, a "sculpture" called *God*, consisting of a cast-iron inverted plumbing trap on a carpenter's miter-box. It was designed, so the Baroness claimed, to take up Duchamp's challenge that plumbing was America's great art mode and also to expose America's shallowness and prudery, its refusal to accept the body's own "machinery." Duchamp thus emerges as the God of plumbing, but also the God who had set a trap for the female artist (Elsa), who had pursued him assiduously with no luck. The Baroness had already made an earlier portrait of Duchamp, described by Rudolf Kuenzli as "a metallic gear and clock spring intermixed with feathers and twigs in a wine glass, and a cog-wheel and feather on top of what looks like a section of a fishing pole with lure."[19] And she wrote poetry, some of it published in *The Little Review*, that contained lines like the following:

> Thou now livest motionless in a mirror!
> Everything is a mirage in thee – thine world is glass – glassy!
> Glassy are thine ears – thine hands – thine feet and thine face.
> SO long must I love it until I myself will become glass and
> Everything around me glassy
>
> (Kuenzli, "Baroness Elsa," 449)

These lines appeared in the June 1918 issue under the title "Love – Chemical Relationship," and subtitled "Un Enfant Français: Marcel (A futurist) / Ein deutsches Kind: Else (a Future Futurist)." Duchamp, the poem posits, had turned himself into his own art object – a piece of motionless glass, devoid of all feeling and passion. Indeed, the Baroness's favorite topic was rage and contempt for those American artists – Williams turned out to be her chief target – too impotent and prudish to respond to her sexual overtures.

Feminist critics have recently made much of the Baroness: Irene Gammel's 500-plus-page biography, sumptuously produced by the MIT Press, presents the Baroness as a touchstone for the New York avant-garde, superior to her male counterparts in daring and originality. If greatness is measured by sheer outrageousness, then Elsa Plötz was undoubtedly great: her escapades on the New York streets are now legendary. But if we focus on the work rather than the life, I find the Baroness's productions, even her so called proto-performance art, both derivative and negligible. Indeed, Gammel's reference to *God* and *Fountain* as "companion pieces" strikes me as merely frivolous, as does her assessment of the Baroness's invective against Williams's *Kora in Hell* (1920) as "powerful cultural critique, in which syntactic breaks and hyperbolic rhetoric enact her point that art equals a state of ecstatic intoxication of which Williams was not capable."[20]

The lyric's other

Syntactic breaks and hyperbolic rhetoric are not in themselves a sign of genius. The much more important female avant-garde figure, in this regard, was Mina Loy. Pound's comment in *The Little Review* (1918) that Loy and Marianne Moore "have written a distinctly national product"[21] is at first puzzling since Loy was not American at all; she was born in England as Mina Gertrude Löwy to a Hungarian-Jewish father and an English mother. Loy settled on the Continent when she was nineteen, was part of the Futurist movement in Italy in 1914–1915 (she had affairs with both F. T. Marinetti and the poet Giovanni Papini), and did not come to New York until 1916 when she was thirty-four, departing again in 1918, when she eloped to Mexico with the "Dada boxer" Arthur Cravan. Nevertheless Pound was right to think of Loy as an American for it was the American avant-garde periodicals – *Camera Work, Trend, Rogue, Blind Man,* and *Dial* – that published her poetry. Indeed, *Others* brought out the entire sequence *Songs to Johannes* in its April 1917 issue.

What makes Loy's "logopoeia" (Pound's epithet, meaning "the dance of the intellect among words")[22] so distinctive is that her poetic language is not only aggressively disjunctive, fragmented, and anti-lyric but that it absorbs foreign locutions (e.g. "Once in a mezzanino," "padded porte-enfant"), coinages ("cymophaneous sweat"), and jarring conjunctions of abstract and concrete as in "bed-ridden monopoly of a moment." In *Anglo-Mongrels and the Rose* (1923), borrowings from French, Italian, Hebrew, and Yiddish, words and phrases crowded into unpunctuated and syntactically odd line units, constitute a "mongrelist" verse that has surely had a central influence on the "mongrelisme" of such contemporary poets as Kamau Brathwaite, Theresa Hak Kung Cha, and Joan Retallack.

In 1917, the shock value of *Songs to Joannes* was considerable. "Had a man written these poems," remarked Alfred Kreymborg, they might have been tolerated. "But a woman wrote them, a woman who dressed like a lady and painted charming lamp-shades."[23] Ladies were not supposed to talk about private parts, satirize their lovers' sexual foibles, or narrate, however obliquely, the undergoing of an abortion that had evidently marked the end of the poet's affair with "Joannes." Loy's lyric, moreover, makes few concessions to musical rhythm, graceful imagery, or coherent description. More narrative than lyric, the sequence's main emotions seem to be disgust, contempt, and a sense of profound loss. "We might have lived together / In the lights of the Arno," we read in XVI, "or gone apple stealing under the sea / Or played / Hide and seek in love and cob-webs / and a lullaby on a tin pan" (Loy, *Lost Lunar*, 39). But such a happy union was not to be. Here is XVII:

> I don't care
> Where the legs of the legs of the furniture are walking to
> Or what is hidden in the shadows they stride
> Or what would look at me
> If the shutters were not shut
> Red a warm colour on the battle-field
> Heavy on my knees as a counterpane
> Count counter
> I counted the fringe of the towel
> Till two tassels clinging together
> Let the square room fall away
> From a round vacuum
> Dilating with my breath.   (Loy, *Lost Lunar*, 59–60)

In the poet's delirious state, the "legs of the furniture" are interchangeable with her own legs, held apart (perhaps in stirrups?) to facilitate the abortion. She no longer cares what she looks like or what the world beyond her "closed shutters" might think. Her only reality is the pain felt as the blood spurts from her womb, weighing her down like a red counterpane even as she is told to count and breathe so that the dead fetus will be ejected. The image of the towel fringe, with its "two tassels clinging together" is especially effective: it underscores the *wetness* of the scene with its sweat and blood – the soaked towel – even as it suggests that, unlike the two tassels, the poet has no one to cling to, the "square room fall[ing] away / From a round vacuum" which is her uterus, "Dilating with [my] breath."

Loy's poem, like the others in the sequence, is by no means realistic: she doesn't *describe* the actual abortion. The atmosphere is surreal in its focus on the "legs of the legs of the furniture," the ominous shadows, and the unknown face "look[ing] at me / If the shutters were not shut." The equation of menstrual blood with the blood of the battlefield refers here, not only to the battle of the sexes, but also to the battlefield of World War I, where the Futurists Boccioni and Sant'Elia had already been killed. No earlier or even subsequent poet, I think, has given us such a horrific image of the fruits of "love." As for love itself, it is strangely absent from these love songs, even as "Nature" is dismissed as "that irate pornographist" (Loy, *Lost Lunar*, 63).

Tomorrow / the stiff curl of wildcarrot leaf

In 1921, Walter and Lou Arensberg moved to California, thus signaling an end to the avant-garde phase of modernism, which their salon had both created and nourished. Picabia had left for Switzerland in 1917, never to return to America except for brief visits. Mina Loy was gone and the Baroness Elsa had returned to Germany. In August 1918, Duchamp sailed for Buenos Aires: the US was now at war with Germany, and he was anxious, once again, to avoid war at all costs. Katherine Dreier followed him there in 1919. And by 1920, the scene of Dada manifestation had become Paris, where Tristan Tzara was now the *chef d'école*.

Of those who remained behind and carried on the avant-garde experiment, the most prominent was probably William Carlos Williams. But after *Kora in Hell* of 1920, which the poet's fellow artists and his critics regarded as something of a failed experiment, Williams incorporated Cubist and Dada technique in an American idiom that was, in fact, quite unlike the ready-mades of Duchamp or mechanomorphic drawings of Picabia. *Spring and All* (1923), his great sequence of short lyrics, embedded in a disjunctive, didactic, theoretical prose, represents a fusion of Futurist/Dada typography with Romantic lyric subjectivity. Consider one of the sequence's less well-known lyrics, no. IV:

> The Easter stars are shining
> above lights that are flashing –
> coronal of the black –
>
> > > Nobody
>
> to say it –
> > > Nobody to say: pinholes
>
> Thither I would carry her
>
> among the lights –
>
> Burst it asunder
> break through to the fifty words
> necessary –
>
> > > a crown for her head with
> castles upon it, skyscrapers
> filled with nut-chocolates –
>
> > > dovetame winds –
> stars of tinsel
> from the great end of a cornucopia
> of glass[24]

Williams's note to this poem, as recorded by John Thirwall, is "For the 13-year-old girl next door in Rutherford. Fresh, and rough and tough" (see Williams, *Collected Poems*, 502). The poem is one of Williams's characteristic sexual fantasies, the expression of unfulfilled desire for an unavailable – indeed unaware – young girl: "Thither I would carry her / among the lights." The Romantic note is reinforced by the nature setting: "The Easter stars are shining" and the night is one of "dovetame winds." Such recourse to nature and the seasons is, of course, quite alien to the urban avant-garde, the closest analogue being the early photography of Stieglitz, in which trees and flowers play a similar role to that in Williams's poetry.

But "Flight to the City," as Williams titled no. 4 in subsequent printings of individual *Spring and All* poems (see Williams, *Collected Poems*, 500), also has elements that testify to Williams's apprenticeship to New York Dada. Visual form for one thing: the poem begins with a normal free-verse tercet but with the word "Nobody," isolated in line four in the center of the page, "Flight to the City" uses typography and quirky line break (e.g., "a crown for her head with / castles upon it"), to create a tense verbal field that defies the linear norm of American poetry of the early twenties. Again, the love scene is deflated by a series of non-sequiturs and missing antecedents. What is the "it" that "Nobody" will say? The next line answers the question with the word "pinholes," but the reference is confusing because the image of the stars as mere "pinholes" in the "coronal" of black night hardly seems shocking or inappropriate. The "it" in line nine is even more enigmatic: what is the *it* the poet wants to "burst asunder"? The nameless girl's body? Her hymen? The bourgeois suburban world in which he must function? And what would those "fifty words" be that he wants to "break through to"? a declaration of love, an argument persuading the girl to surrender? We are never told but, of course, the general drift is quite clear.

Indeed, the "crown" the poet longs to place on the girl's head is not the Romantic prop we expect for it is decorated with "castles" and "skyscrapers / filled with nut-chocolates." The stars, moreover, turn out to be "tinsel," and emanate from "the great end of a cornucopia / of glass." The Easter scene, it seems, was never a "natural" one at all, but an urban invention in which glass, as in Duchamp's *Large Glass*, is the dominant material. In this context, the word "cornucopia" is especially interesting. It suggests, on the one hand, the sheer abundance of glass in the skyscrapers that surround the poet. But the cornucopia was the horn of the goat that suckled Zeus and thus refers, in this landscape of tinsel stars, to the young girl's private parts as well. One is reminded of Man Ray's charmingly erotic eggbeater. But whereas Man Ray and Duchamp eroticize the objects themselves, Williams always inserts himself into the picture art as *delay*, as Duchamp would have it, is not Williams's métier. For him, as for his painter friends Demuth and Sheeler, the object, however "objectively" rendered, is endowed with a direct emotive charge – a charge absent from those "silent" readymades *Fountain* and *Bottle Rack*, whose eroticism is, so to speak, "colder," more conceptual.

The avant-garde incursion of the teens had left a lasting legacy, but the immediate future for American poetry and the visual arts was thus elsewhere. American poetry would return to its own roots, to a "realism" that would be consonant with the social upheavals of the 1920s and 1930s. No more "skyscrapers / filled with nut-chocolates," no more Dada hilarity and *double-entendre*. As the title poem of *Spring and All* puts it (Williams, *Collected Poems*, 183):

> Now the grass, tomorrow
> the stiff curl of wildcarrot leaf
>
> One by one objects are defined –
> It quickens: clarity, outline of leaf

Definition, clarity, outline: a new ethos was in the air.

NOTES

1. Marcel Duchamp, *Affect. Marcel: The Selected Correspondence of Marcel Duchamp*, ed. Francis M. Naumann and Hector Obalk, tr. Jill Taylor (London: Thames & Hudson, 2000), 35–36.
2. Calvin Tomkins, *Duchamp, A Biography* (New York: Henry Holt, 1996), 253.
3. See Matei Calinescu, *Five Faces of Modernity, Modernism, Avant-Garde, Decadence, Kitsch, Postmodernism* (Durham: Duke University Press, 1987), 98–99.
4. Peter Bürger, *Theory of the Avant-Garde*, ed. Wlad Godzich, tr. Michael Shaw (Minneapolis: University of Minnesota Press, 1984), 51.
5. See Dickran Tashjian, *Skyscraper Primitives: Dada and the American Avant-Garde 1910–1925* (Middletown, CT: Wesleyan University Press, 1975).
6. Pierre Cabanne, *Dialogues with Marcel Duchamp*, tr. Ron Padgett (New York: Viking, 1971), 65.
7. Rudolf Kuenzli, *Marcel Duchamp: Artist of the Century*, ed. Rudolf and Francis M. Naumann (Cambridge, MA: MIT Press, 1989), 220.
8. Marcel Duchamp, *A l'Infinitif*, in *The Essential Writings of Marcel Duchamp*, ed. Michel Sanouillet and Elmer Peterson (New York: Oxford, 1973), 74.
9. Linda Dalrymple Henderson, *Duchamp in Context: Science and Technology in The Large Glass and Related Works* (Princeton University Press, 1998), passim.
10. For a facsimile edition of the entire journal, see Alfred Stieglitz, *Camera Work, The Complete Illustrations 1903–1917*, ed. Pam Roberts (Cologne: Taschen, 1997).
11. Henry Sayre, *The Visual Text of William Carlos Williams* (Urbana: University of Illinois Press, 1983), 46.
12. Alfred Stieglitz, *Camera Work, The Complete Illustrations 1903–1917*, ed. Pam Roberts (Cologne: Taschen, 1997), 1912 issue, unpaginated.
13. Janet Malcolm, "The Mystery of Gertrude Stein," *The New Yorker*, 2 June 2003: 58–81, 60.

14. Pontus Hulten, *The Machine as Seen at the End of the Mechanical Age* (New York: Museum of Modern Art, 1968), 83.

15. Allan Antliff, *Anarchist Modernism: Art, Politics, and the First American Avant-Garde* (University of Chicago Press, 2001), 84–85.

16. Francis Naumann, "Man Ray, 1908–1921: From an Art in Two Dimensions to the Higher Dimension of Ideas," in *Perpetual Motif: The Art of Man Ray*, ed. Merry Foresta (New York: Abbeville Press, 1989), 51–87; see 77.

17. Rosalind Krauss, "The Object Caught by the Heel," in *Making Mischief: Dada Invades New York*, Francis M. Naumann, with Beth Venn (New York: Whitney Museum of American Art, 1996), 249–51; see 249.

18. See William A. Camfield, *Marcel Duchamp, Fountain* (Houston: The Menil Collection, 1989), 24–40.

19. Rudolf E. Kuenzli, "Baroness Elsa von Freytag-Loringhoven and New York Dada," in *Women in Dada: Essays on Sex, Gender, and Identity*, ed. Naomi Sawelson-Gorse (Cambridge, MA: MIT Press, 1998), 442–75, see 448.

20. Irene Gammel, *Baroness Elsa: Gender, Dada, and Everyday Modernity* (Cambridge, MA: MIT Press, 2002), 227, 270.

21. Ezra Pound, "A List of Books," *The Little Review* (March 1918); rpt. in Ezra Pound, *Selected Prose 1909–1965*, ed. William Cookson (New York: New Directions, 1973), 424–425.

22. Ezra Pound, *Literary Essays of Ezra Pound*, ed. T. S. Eliot (London: Faber and Faber, 1954), 25.

23. See Notes, Mina Loy, *The Lost Lunar Baedeker*, selected and edited by Roger L. Conover (New York: Farrar Straus Giroux, 1996), 189.

24. William Carlos Williams, *The Collected Poems of William Carlos Williams*, vol. 1, 1909–1939, ed. A. Walton Litz and Christopher MacGowan (New York: New Directions, 1986), 186–87.

3
SOCIETY

9

JANET LYON

Gender and sexuality

In the past twenty years, the voluminous work done by scholars of feminism, gender, and sexuality has helped to restructure the field of modernist scholarship. Women writers who had been excluded from canonical consideration have become the subjects of extensive literary study; gay and lesbian networks that had been cursorily overlooked or underread have been revalued as matrices of modernist aesthetic experimentation; recent theoretical elaborations of sexual identity and gender formation have been put to use in new and sometimes startlingly revisionary interpretations of modernist texts. The sources of these new paths of inquiry have been many. Some were groundbreaking works of historical scholarship, like John D'Emilio and Estelle Freedman's 1988 account of American sexuality, *Intimate Matters*, or Nancy Cott's 1987 study, *The Grounding of Modern Feminism*. Feminist reconsiderations of canon formation, popular culture, and the sociological force of women's burgeoning entry into public life owe debts to foundational works like Shari Benstock's *Women of the Left Bank* (1986), Sandra Gilbert and Susan Gubar's three-volume study, *No Man's Land* (1988–1994), and Ann Ardis's *New Women, New Novels* (1990).[1] Perhaps one of the most far-reaching essays from this period of scholarship, in terms of the wide debates it immediately produced, was Andreas Huyssen's "Mass Culture as Woman: Modernism's Other" (1986), which triangulated the relations among mass culture, modernism, and gender with its provocative claim that turn of the century mass culture was "consistently and obsessively" gendered as feminine by a male-dominated high culture.[2]

All of these studies are now more than a decade old; their original force has been diffused and supplemented by explorations of modernism that elaborate the roles of gender and sexuality through studies of national identity and citizenship, racial identity and race politics, queer identity and aesthetics, marketing and magazine culture, performance, visual culture, capitalism and market economies, and historical accounts of twentieth-century political modernity. It will be my aim in this chapter to incorporate some of these recent shifts in the academic field of modernism into a general overview of gender and sexuality in American modernism. The first section sketches out the climate in which an influential "modern" feminism emerged alongside an explosion of what was sometimes called "sex-talk," fueled by the popularization of Freudian theory and concomitant discourses of Comstockian censorship and personal liberation. The second section provides a differential reading of gender and sexuality and their representations in a handful of American modernist texts. In the third section I examine some of the "difficult" aesthetic techniques and practices brought to bear on the exploration of gender and sexuality by modernists, in order to examine "difficulty's" relation to non-normative sexuality within heterosexual culture. The fourth section returns to a more sociological perspective on American modernism, focusing especially on race, sociability, and transient communities of difference.

Feminism's political climate

In 1914, the English poet and painter Mina Loy, writing from Italy to her American friend, the Greenwich Village salonnière Mabel Dodge, enclosed with her letter a Futurist-style manifesto which began with the declaration that "the feminist movement as at present instituted is *Inadequate*."[3] Loy had been living in Florence among American itinerants and Italian Futurists, and watching from the sidelines as the Anglo-American suffrage campaigns reached their zenith in the militant street actions of 1913 and 1914. Like many modernist-identified artists, her relation to organized feminism was one of ambivalence, born largely of an avant-garde suspicion of reformism and a related commitment to radical individualism. The women's movement had grown out of nineteenth-century campaigns for economic and political rights, most of the arguments for which were arrayed across the problem of sexual difference. On the one side was the position insisting on the equality of men and women in the eyes of the law and within the fundamental principles of the republic; according to this set of arguments, the "disabilities" accruing to the female sex were man-made and therefore remediable through egalitarian legal and social reforms. On the other side was the position insisting on women's biological or cultural or transcendental differences from men; from this perspective, women could never be adequately represented by men and must therefore represent themselves, not only in government but in the institutional and cultural formations through which the nation continually renewed itself. For the adherents of both of these positions, a republic which did not include a differential representation of its plurality of female citizens invited a kind of national anemia which threatened its very lifeblood.

By the turn into the twentieth century, the question of women's rights had partially crystallized into a popular movement organized around the demand for the vote, which was amplified through contemporary Progressive era rhetorics of social justice. Predictably, the organs of the cultural Left endorsed this dramatic campaign for the vote, including and especially *The Masses*, the Greenwich Village monthly (1911–1917). Most of its myriad feminist writers and artists agreed on the necessity of the franchise for women, though for varying reasons. Some like Dorothy Day were socialists aiming to expand the popular mandate on all fronts; others like Margaret Sanger articulated the vote to the promotion of birth control and other forms of sexual self-determination; Elizabeth Gurney Flynn, an outspoken labor advocate, pursued the vote on behalf of working-class women; still others linked suffrage with personal autonomy and free expression.

But there were many who viewed the dominant suffrage apparatus with indifference or suspicion. African-American women suffragists were repeatedly betrayed by white organizers like Alice Paul and Carrie Chapman Catt, who viewed racial justice as a distraction (at best) rather than a principle. Most women involved in the African-American suffrage movement were multiply affiliated with or sympathetic to nascent civil rights activities, and could not abide the single-issue stratagems that characterized a good deal of white suffragism. They were perforce a part of the African-American identity politics coalescing around issues that could not be disarticulated from the importance of black women's votes: the proliferation of Jim Crow laws in the South and their increasing appearance in the North, the unchecked lynchings throughout the country, and the explosion of racial violence and race riots in the teens.

In these same years, the anarcho-feminist Emma Goldman famously dismissed the vote as a tool of the state which would bring neither economic justice nor personal independence to women. Goldman's assertion that "true liberation begins neither at the polls nor in courts," but rather "in woman's soul"[4] was of a piece with her libertarian dismissal of institutional reform generally, but as I have noted it was a belief shared by many members of the cultural avant-garde in both Europe and the US, among them Loy, whose influential experimental poems appeared regularly in New York little magazines beginning in 1914. What was generally preferred in place of a reformist, "equalizing" campaign to win qualified recognition from the state was a more philosophically amorphous feminism that could accommodate simultaneously the desiderata of sexual autonomy, personal freedom, and social critique, even as it acknowledged the inequities generated by sexual difference. Loy's "Feminist Manifesto" chides women to "cease to place your confidence in economic legislation, vice-crusades & uniform education – you are glossing over **Reality**. Professional & commercial careers are opening up for you – **Is that all you want?**" (153). Like Goldman, Loy traces women's cultural disadvantages to asymmetrical relations between men and women, and both writers see "equality" as a superficial patch for these disadvantages. Indeed, from the perspective of the avant-garde axis of feminism, sexual difference could not simply be negated by efforts of the state; and even if sexual difference was in fact a product of institutional apparatuses – wrought by legal codifications, moral prescriptions, and medical prognostications, for instance – the uneven social organization of that sexual difference could never be addressed by a handful of legal alterations. More desirable instead, for Loy at least, was an exploratory (and, ideally, diagnostic) elaboration of sexual difference by women themselves, through the media available to them, including art and literature, but also conversation, performance, correspondence, and fashion. Thus for example Loy's poem "Parturition" (*Trend*, 1914), which shocked New York readers with its exceedingly experimental account of childbirth, stages that childbirth simultaneously as a path to unparalleled Bergsonian enlightenment and as a cultural event that secures the mother's unexalted role as a mere reproductive animal. Her "genius" will go unrecognized; the mother is doomed to the frustrating double-consciousness that characterizes the cultural position of the Other.

Loy's feminist critique, however philosophical its focus may have been, was not indifferent to the economic foundations of women's oppression; on the contrary, that theme forms a leitmotif in several of her early poems. "Virgins Plus Curtains Minus Dots" (*Rogue*, 1915), for example, paratactically renders the fate of poor girls without doweries ("dots") whose unmarriagability reifies them as failed commodities. The virgins' subjectivities are created wholecloth by their own surplus: they can do nothing but mark time, imagine marriage, and peer out into the street of sexual commerce, where men "may look everywhere," with eyes that "look into things." The virgins, by contrast, can only "look out" from a room where "Somebody who was never / a virgin / Has bolted the door / Put curtains at our windows" (21–22). These are the village girls of the "Latin Borghese," in the poem's epigraph, imprisoned by Catholic culture and the bride price; but their envy of "Men's eyes" bears the principal weight of the poem's critique. These girls know enough to know that they cannot know, which is to say that the agnotology so central to uneven gender relations is here rendered by Loy as fatally flawed. Even surplus village girls, even girls who "flutter . . . flutter" (22) at the thought of a man, can recognize their own reification; they can see, in fleeting moments, that life and even subjectivity might be otherwise.

Loy's most famous and most scandalous poem of this period, "Love Songs" (*Others*, 1915),[5] repeats "Virgins"'s artificially cloistered isolation by way of a poetic persona who "must live in [her] lantern / Trimming subliminal flicker / Virginal to the bellows / Of Experience" (53). But "Love Songs" also baldly challenges the gendered hierarchy of sexuality that would leave to women the passive role of coital helpmeet: its speaker is mystified by and, in turn, demystifies her sexual partner as a curious "skin-sack," "Something the shape of a man / To the casual vulgarity of the merely observant / More of a clock-work mechanism / Running down against time / To which I am not paced" (53–54). This lyric example of what was more broadly known as "sex-talk" is stunning both for the focus it places on a woman's sexual disappointment and for the balance it strikes between clinical frankness and poetic indirection, which was Loy's unique metier. Her lexical exploration of sex in this and other poems found an audience in nascent American cosmopolitan communities that were forming around dialogic explorations of the physical and psychological dimensions of sexuality.

The discourse of sex ran through stories in popular and sentimental fiction depicting the intricacies of love or marriage; it formed the bedrock for defenses of a new phase of free love and the concomitant promotion of birth control by Goldman and Sanger; it anchored a praxis of auto-analysis through which self-styled cultural radicals challenged bourgeois conventions of "character" and sought instead to discover or fashion a "self." All of these endeavors were buoyed by a high tide of popular Freudianism, which crested in the decade after Freud's famous 1909 Clark University lectures. Freud's principles of drives, of defense mechanisms, and especially of the unconscious were transformed by lay enthusiasts into plot devices for a cycle of new narratives about an unexplored interiority; this was eagerly mapped and re-mapped in novels, plays, cultural analyses, and above all personal accounts of Puritanical repression and cathartic self-disclosure. Loy's friend Mabel Dodge's salon was a significant site for the early exfoliation of Freud's ideas in the US. Dodge invited A. A. Brill, Freud's American translator and the head of the New York Psychoanalytic Society, to a "Psychoanalytic Evening" in 1913. In spite of Brill's professional opposition to lay analysis, his dramatic salon visit produced a wave of converts, most of whom blithely substituted Freud's theoretical pessimism with pragmatic optimism, thus allowing for the transformation of psychoanalytic principles into widespread and flexible therapeutic applications. Principal among these was the therapeutic practice, popular with Village radicals, of locating and exposing sexual repression through anamnesis and dream interpretation, converting it through various methods of diligent attention into sexual candor, and distilling from that a more "authentic" form of self-expression (thereby producing a healthier and more orderly society into the bargain). Freud's insight that "the impulses of sexual life are among those which, even normally, are the least controlled by the higher activities of the mind"[6] became an invitation to the Village intelligentsia to turn the higher mind against itself in ever more astute ways.

This practice of sexual self-knowledge helped to bolster new feminist arguments against sexual double standards while at the same time grounding liberatory programs ranging from free motherhood to the joys of masturbation to female intellectual achievement to homosexual openness. However, it did little to address, let alone ameliorate, the hard facts of economic gender discrimination, or the broader sense, among many modernist women, that the promises of modernity were neither universal nor binding, but, rather, partial and arbitrary. For some American modernists like Isadora Duncan and H. D., this perception of the incompleteness of modernity led back to an exploration of the "origins" of western civilization and a subsequent feminist re-imagining of what went wrong in the transmission of culture. H. D.'s palimpsestic poems from this period – poems that register narrative behind myth, epic tension beneath image – re-animate dynamic women of antiquity who were subsequently papered over in patriarchal history. "Eurydice" (*Egoist*, 1917), for example, renders Orpheus mute while granting his silent lover Eurydice the place of monologist: she angrily accuses him of "ruthlessness" and "arrogance" for turning back to see if she has followed him out of hell; his insecure faithlessness loses for her "the earth / and the flowers of the earth," leaving "everything . . . crossed with black, / black upon black."[7] It is his gaze, she suspects, that effects her undoing: he turns back to capture his face's reflection from hers; she very nearly becomes an image of Irigaray's speculum, reproducing the One in her role as other. But she recovers herself, and like Milton's Satan she performatively fashions for herself light from darkness and a heaven from hell, claiming it as her own: "I tell you this: such loss is no loss / . . . my hell is no worse than yours / . . . I have the fervour of myself for a presence / and my own spirit for light" (*Collected Poems*, 54–55). Thus does H. D. install agency and presence into an historical void; thus also does she negotiate the difficulty of being "modern" when there is so little to work with: women may light themselves up and may make a heaven from hell, but they must do it themselves, through art or polemic, in community or in utter isolation.

Gender identity and sexuality

The study of gender as a sign of power relations (in authors' lives, within texts, in the cultural fabric of the modern) has formed a substantial vector within modernist studies of the past several decades. But recent histories of gender and sexuality have pointed in a somewhat different direction by providing detailed accounts of the complicated and shifting relations among sexual difference, the identity and performance of gender, and the various practices and desires issuing from sexuality. Those theories of gender that were powerfully elaborated in feminist theories of the 1980s and 1990s understood gender to be a critical analytic category for making sense of the disadvantages that accrue to women through uneven distributions of power. Such discussions focused on the ideological link between, on the one hand, the highly variable set of cultural attributes called "femininity" and the equally unstable social category called "woman," on the other. Generally speaking, according to this theoretical approach, "sexual difference" denotes the space of meanings between males and females, while "gender" addresses the inflection of those meanings. Both concepts are relational, insofar as both are part of a heterosexual paradigm within which the nexus of female/femininity/woman necessarily derives critical significance in relation to male/masculinity/man. By contrast, theories of sexuality tended to insist on a non-relational perspective from which to describe and analyze sexual practices and desires. According to this approach, the epistemological category of homosexuality, especially, suffered multiple deformations from – indeed, was determined by – its inscription into a heterosexual paradigm. Thus the corrective move to disarticulate the study of sexuality from the study of gender was one of the founding events of queer theory.

Some recent work in modernist studies, however, has mediated the gap between the analytical categories of gender and sexuality. For, as scholars have argued, it is impossible not to notice the emphasis that some modernists themselves placed on the creatively flexible relations between negotiated gender identity, on the one hand, and the practices and objects of sexuality, on the other. George Chauncey, for one, has shown that in gay New York subcultures before World War II, the "fairy" was a central (and highly public) figure distinguished primarily by a cultivated feminine gender persona rather than by same-sex desire.[8] The fairy's adoption of the dominant culture's gender ideology – however witty or wry that adoption may have been – stands as evidence for Chauncey of the interplay between the prescriptive force of gender ideology and the less determinate zone of sexuality. Indeed, in Chauncey's (and, more recently, Jennifer Terry's) accounts of nineteenth-century sexologists' descriptions of "inversion," the "invert" (sometimes called the "third sex") cannot be understood except through gender categories: inversion signaled a disavowal – conscious or otherwise – of one's assigned gender.[9] "Homosexual," by contrast, signaled no such disavowal, and was distinguished primarily through sexual practices related to same-sex desire, or, more generally, through sexual object-choice. Whereas in the case of the invert, a characterological portrait could be extrapolated through cultural traits associated with femininity (or, in the case of the butch, masculinity), no such definitive portrait was forthcoming from the homosexual, whose object-choice was not necessarily connected to persona or performance. Freud's influential 1905 study of "sexual aberrations" highlighted the unpredictability of object-choice: noting that "all human beings are capable of making a homosexual object-choice and have, in fact, made one in their unconscious,"[10] he effectively blurred the sociological figure of the homosexual – though not the myriad regulatory discourses surrounding homosexuality.

Thus, within the historical frame of modernist studies, homosexuality and inversion may well lead down separate paths of inquiry, but they are paths closely connected by cultural anxiety, political identification, and aesthetic experimentation. Willa Cather's 1905 story "Paul's Case" illustrates these imbrications. Paul is a doomed adolescent-turning-invert, and Cather frames his death-tale with the indices of a medical "case." An aesthete who loves theatre and abhors the grimy banality of his bourgeois family life in Pittsburgh, Paul assembles with great care a persona that crosses out of his assigned gender of boorish, middle-class masculinity: he wears red carnations, exasperates his teachers with his mannered detachment, and falls at the feet of a visiting diva. Driven by fervid dreams of an urban life of upscale beauty, he steals money from his father's company, takes a train to New York, spends an ecstatic week at the Waldorf, and then, knowing that he will be pursued and returned to his intolerable old life, commits suicide with great delicacy on a snow-covered train track. On one level, of course, Cather's is a sympathetic account of gender dysphoria and the hell of heteronormativity; "Paul's Case" is the ur-story of the urban hejira of queer youth. At the same time, however (and because of his ur-role), "Paul" is no more than the name assigned to an individual case study: his move toward inversion, though never directly named, is evidenced in his eyes' "hysterical brilliance," in his "hysterically defiant manner," his physical weakness, his "white, blue-veined face,"[11] all symptoms of gender under fatal pressure. Paul's sustained solitude heightens the inevitability of his fate: had he arrived in Greenwich Village rather than in midtown, he might have found a fairy community, collaborators in queer self-invention; but Cather's invert lives and dies alone in the telos of pathology.

It should be noted that Paul's case is not a case of same-sex desire – his is as much a story about class fantasy as it is about deviant gender, and sexuality plays no part in the story. Nevertheless, homoeroticism is the implicit threat forestalled by his suicide: for where gender goes, so must sexuality, in the anxious cultural imaginary of this and other modern stories. Ernest Hemingway's much later "The Sea Change" (1930) elaborates the anxieties of a reversed version of this algorithm. In an empty Paris bar, a "handsome young couple" is engaged in one of Hemingway's typically paratactic, nearly referentless dialogues; they are splitting up because the "girl" – tanned, with short blonde hair, in a tweed suit – has begun an affair with another woman. The man, Phil, protests as much against her object-choice as against the breakup itself: "Couldn't you have gotten into some other jam?" he asks; "It seems not," she answers.[12] He reluctantly admits that he understands her leaving, and "That's the trouble. I understand" (398). When he tries to taunt her with a botched quote from Pope about vice,[13] she protests against his use of the words "vice" and "perversion," preferring not to "put any name to it," and reminding him that "We're made up of all sorts of things. You've known that. You've used it well enough." His own apparent "perversions" are now on the table, and he feels himself changed utterly as he suddenly, avidly tells her to go. "And when you come back tell me all about it," he says in a voice he does "not recognize" (399–400). After she leaves, he addresses the barman: "'I'm a different man, James . . . You see in me quite a different man." James notices only that he is a "brown young man," tanned from the summer, but Phil continues: "Vice," he says "is a very strange thing." As the story closes Phil gazes in the mirror at the different-looking man and repeats to James for a third time that he is "a different man." The barman sees nothing, saying only "You look very well, sir." But Phil's admission of his own "vice" – and his anticipation of future "perversions" – has effected in him a phenomenological transformation, a "sea change" that he hears in his own voice and reads on his own face, as if to suggest that when sexual practices and the desires that drive them are named and put into discourse, they produce legible signs, or, perhaps, symptoms. Such a suggestion is not out of line with Foucault's observation that sexual "types" proliferate through the extension of sexual discourses, but in this story Phil's transformation is connected not only to sexuality but also to gender, and especially to gender's perceptible coding. He had been studying the girl's face in the crucial moment of telling her to go, imagining, perhaps, in "the way her hair grew on her forehead" (400) a link between features and perversions; or, to put it another way, seeking signs of sexuality in the effects of the gendered body. Thus the "handsome" girl's short hair and brown skin are part of the "sea change" as well: now they signify an interpretive shift from femininity to masculinity, in line with her new object-choice, just as Phil's voice and reflection and performative declaration that he is a "different" man signal a shift in both sexuality and gender, if we understand gender to be the performance of identification. In the unedited manuscript version of *The Garden of Eden*, Hemingway's unfinished posthumous novel, a Phil-like character quietly becomes a sexual bottom in his marital bed; but in "Sea Change" the sexual modulation is more active: Phil embraces the "vice" of Pope's quatrain as a familiar, as he awaits the return of the girl who will tell him "all about" her homoerotic adventure.

The fungibility of sexuality and gender alluded to in "The Sea Change" – the fact that "we're made up of all sorts of things" that may manifest themselves in "different" sexual desires or gendered effects – returns us to the modernist problem of gender, namely, that a focus on the increasingly labile bodily performance of gender in these years further undermined its already (and always) unstable role as an index of cultural value. Gender critics have long noted the variety of ways that modernism adapted as a central aesthetic tenet the disavowal of femininity, with femininity standing in for a whole incoherent host of artistic disorders, including sentimentality, mystification, dissolution, optimism, and naturalized passivity, all of them deemed impediments to the task of forging an art that wrestles with the synthesizing forces of modernity. This sometimes monolithic critique of gender's evaluative role in culture has been qualified repeatedly by critics engaged in careful local readings, but it is nevertheless the case that evidence of a disavowal of femininity may be seen everywhere in American formulations of a national aesthetic prospectus. Writers from John Dos Passos to Ezra Pound, Mina Loy, Ernest Hemingway, and (painter) Marsden Hartley pursued what Ann Douglas has called a doctrine of "terrible honesty" in their quest for a modern American literary ethos. Dos Passos, for example, protested in 1916 that the prevailing "tone" of "higher"American writing "is undoubtedly that of a well brought up and intelligent woman . . . bound tightly in the fetters of 'niceness.'"[14] Hartley completed the thought with his 1919 "injunction to some 'girl' poets": poetry is not "an ivory trinket. It calls for an arm. We need not be afraid of muscularity or even of 'brutality.'"[15]

Ironically, for both writers – as for a wide array of American artists (including Duncan, Gertrude Stein, and Hart Crane) – the cure for American temerity could be found in the paradigmatic masculinity of Walt Whitman, who "abandoned the vague genteelness" of American writing (Dos Passos, "Against American Literature," 335) and, with "simple frankness," removed its "loin-cloth because it always hints at secrecy and cheap morality" (Hartley, "Business of Poetry," 355). Clearly, Whitman's masculinity coincided with a form of homosexuality that was untainted by the "femininity" of inversion; his sexuality, while openly homoerotic, was simultaneously vigorously homosocial, bodying forth a national imaginary of fellowship and futurity that suited the architects (both homosexual and heterosexual) of American modernism. And while the example of Whitman's homosexual masculinity stands in marked contrast to Hemingway's anxious explorations of sexuality, both are emblems in a wider epistemological shift occasioned in part by the mutability of the relations between gender and sexuality, and the attendant erosion of gender as an epistemological ground for judging culture and its artifacts.

This erosion is foregrounded in Djuna Barnes's extraordinary novel *Nightwood*, an experimental text which, through its sheer excess of imagined relationships, thoroughly disaggregates any constitutive relations among gender, sex, and cultural valuation. The lexical markers for sexuality – "invert," "homosexual," "heterosexual" – are rendered not only ineffectual but inert by the novel's insistent dislocation of any normative ideals against which to assess desiring subjectivity. The novel's queer *raisonneur*, Dr. Matthew O'Connor, is a transvestite who "never asked better than to boil some good man's potatoes and toss up a child for him every nine months by the calendar";[16] the *somnabule* of the night's wood, Robin Vote, sleepwalks through a brief marriage, the birth of a child, auratic relations with animals, and countless lesbian encounters; Nora Flood, a woman with a house and a job, is torn to shreds by her impossible desire for stable love with Robin; Felix Volkbien, a deracinated Jew, longs for an aristocratic lineage but receives a form of aristocratic futurity instead, through a son (Robin's) whose disability is said to be the effect of sanguinal degeneracy. Familial constructions exceed "family" in all directions, just as night exceeds day, dreaming exceeds waking, and the insistent trauma of desire exceeds all narrative possibilities for desire's resolution. In short, the novel overwhelms normative categories of knowledge and experience, including, and especially, gender and sexuality. As Barnes's friend Emily Coleman put it in her repeated book pitches to T. S. Eliot, *Nightwood* "go[es] beyond sex, to that world where there is no marriage or giving in marriage – *where no modern writer ever goes.*"[17]

Textual difficulty

Nightwood appears to stand as a strong example of the modernist "difficulty" that Eliot prescribed for the "poets of our civilization" who must become "more comprehensive, more allusive, more indirect, in order to force, to dislocate if necessary, language into his meaning."[18] Barnes's novel resists virtually all narrative conventions, including expository dialogue, character development, and chronological plotting. It consists instead of eight semi-detached chapters that proceed by way of a nearly rhizomatic proliferation of oblique metaphors whose tenors and vehicles are quickly layered over by secondary and tertiary figures. Robin's flesh, for example, is "the texture of plant life, and beneath it one sensed a frame, broad, porous and sleep-worn, as if sleep were a decay fishing her beneath the visible surface" (34). Fishing is a central trope in the novel: here, in a secondary image, it figures the unseen erosion of a skeleton (a "sea change," as it were); elsewhere it is used to depict the relations between, on the one hand, the massive, uncharted seas of night, of sleep, of the unconscious, and, on the other hand, the singular images that are "fished out" of these seas and naively taken to be representations of empirical truth. "The face is what anglers catch in the daylight, but the sea is the night" (93) Matthew tells Nora, by which he means, roughly, that for every face of "true love," there are countless others forming and unforming in the flux beyond the borders of rational thought.

Nearly all of Barnes's metaphors are anti-metaphorical, if the purpose of metaphor is to clarify one concept through its juxtaposition to another. Whatever "clarification" occurs in *Nightwood*'s metaphors occurs not through reference or juxtaposition but through kinetic accretion: the novel's figurations point insistently toward the folly of looking for "truth" in the logical light of day. This movement involves a series of conceptual inversions that structure the novel, most of which are elaborated by the "invert" O'Connor. In a central meditation on the causal primacy of dreaming over waking life, O'Connor maintains that waking life – featuring the seemingly autonomous and autotelic "self" of the day – is, in fact, a vastly reduced precipitation of the dreaming night. Whatever "facts" the self depends upon in the day are vanquished by the chaotic enormity of night: "dreams have only the pigmentation of fact" (a sort of reverse-day residue [86]), for theirs is the originating realm of multiplicity and possibility, where identity dissolves into boundlessly recombinant elements. The sleeper "lies down with his Nelly and drops off into the arms of his Gretchen" (86), O'Connor tells the distraught Nora; Robin is lawless like all sleepers: "when she sleeps, is she not moving her leg aside for an unknown garrison? Or in a moment, that takes but a second, murdering us with an axe? Eating our ear in a pie?" (87). Thus the lawless matrix of the unconscious both dwarfs and mocks its fussy, myopic daytime creations. Nora's quest for an answer to her heartache is repeatedly turned back by O'Connor, who reminds her that there can be no answers, least of all in conventional narratives or elucidating metaphors.

Barnes's relentlessly queer deformation of identity is perhaps a far cry from the "terrible honesty" ascribed to a good deal of American modernism. And while her practice of excessive indirection could be read as an example of an Eliotic writer's attempts to force "language into his meaning," such an explanation leaves unasked the crucial question of whether "his meaning" can ever be intelligible within the strictures of heteronormative culture, or whether difficulty itself might not be an artifact of that which cannot mean. This is perhaps another way of suggesting that some forms of poetic difficulty may be a necessary function of the homosexual "closet," insofar as difficulty's opacity may at once indicate the presence of and the cordoning

off of a textual space of non-heterosexuality. Eve Sedgwick famously elaborated this thesis in her groundbreaking *Epistemology of the Closet*, and
Judith Butler's complementary theorizations of sex as a regulatory norm for
the body's cultural intelligibility further support the argument that queer
texts produce opacity as a strategy of resistence or a mark of refusal.[19]
Indeed Butler reads Cather's story "On the Gull's Road" (1908) from this
approximate perspective: the pointedly unnamed gender of a narrator who
has fallen in love with a beautiful dying woman indicates for Butler an active
textual avoidance of gender, whose prohibitions "[preempt] the possibility of
homosexual attachment" and graft into its place a grievous and unspeakable
loss of futurity.[20]

But it is possible to see other queer uses for a poetics of difficulty besides
those of strategic resistance. When Hart Crane's poem "At Melville's Tomb"
(1926) prompted Harriet Monroe at *Poetry* magazine to request an explica-
tion of the poem's difficult metaphors, Crane patiently invoked, among other
things, a potential ("however small") audience for whom certain "experiences" supply "the necessary connotations to complete [the] connection"
within the poem's images.[21] This seemingly coded response understandably
has been read as a closeted reference to a knowing audience bound by homosexual experience; but Tim Dean has argued to the contrary that, in fact,
Crane deplored the logic of the closet. In Dean's reading, Crane's textual difficulty stems from his poetic commitment to the "privacy of inviolate experience – that which remains private even when known and communicated."[22]
Thus Crane's indirection is neither a decoy nor a set of cues, but rather arises
from the representational aim itself. In lines like "The calyx of death's bounty
giving back / A scattered chapter, livid hieroglyph,"[23] mixed metaphors
and elliptical syntax constitute the media through which the intensity of
sui generic experiences – of modernity and endurance, as well as sex and
desire – leaves its indelible if inscrutable textual record.

In contrast to Crane's poetics of intensive experience, Gertrude Stein's infamous experimental difficulty has often been discussed by way of its extensivity and its refusal of the closed codes of experience. An example of this
extensivity may be found in her early assemblage of prose poems, *Tender
Buttons* (1914), which is grouped into three sections, "Objects," Food," and
"Rooms"; each section offers a series of word portraits that proceed by way
of a continuous recalibration of grammar and a thorough reconceptualiza-
tion of representation. Eschewing as much as possible the deadening closure
of nouns – which, in naming a thing always in the same way, render it inert –
Stein aims in these portraits to expand the phenomenal world through the
generative kinesis of language itself. The "objects" of the poems, as they
appear in their noun forms in the individual titles, are for the most part the

apparently inactive denizens of the quotidian realm – "A long dress," "A red hat," "A plate," "A box," "Cold climate," and so on; but they are activated by the poems, set into motion through a grammar that names them through relations, associations, departures, proximities, extensions, passion, in the service of radiant possibility.

Take, for example, the second of two short "Food" entries titled "Milk": "Climb up in sight climb in the whole utter needles and a guess a whole guess is hanging. Hanging hanging."[24] The title "Milk" lights up an interpretive network, linking the pun of "utter" / udder with the "hanging" udder, and perhaps with the tit-like "needles" through which milk is delivered; the debriding power of Stein's habitual punning – marking covert connections among words – soon extends to "whole" / hole, which in turn marks out "climb in the whole utter" as a variant of "climb in the hole udder." Since Stein frequently figured sexual pleasure with her partner Alice Toklas as "a cow," the chain of homophones in "Milk" may then be seized upon as route to interpretive stability: the poem is "about" sex with Alice. But of course it is "about" no such thing. Although intimacy with Alice forms a crucial component in a good deal of Stein's poetry, the poems of *Tender Buttons* work insistently beyond referentiality: they are not "about" anything, or rather, they are about the everythingness that is language's ontological domain, but which has been constricted through language's ideological conscription into instrumental use. Domestic objects (including unlikely "objects" like "A time to eat" and "In between") are tenderly granted a new *quidditas* in *Tender Buttons*, not through attempts to render an object's singularity or uniqueness, but rather through a display of endlessly mobile relationality. In prepositional phrases, via the verbs prized by Stein because they "can be so mistaken,"[25] through conjunctions and repetition, relations exceed the predation of "meaning." As Stein explains in her marvelous "Lectures in America" (1934–1935), the work of *Tender Buttons* involves finding "a way of naming things that would not invent names, but mean names without naming them," rendering not the figure of the thing but its kinetic ground, its multiple, fungible situations, so that "the thing being alive [is] always new."[26]

As I have indicated, Stein's lesbian sexuality forms one crucial and nearly continuous "situation" through which her experimental writing unfolds, and while there are elements of coding that frequently accompany this situation (the "cow" of orgasm, the "Caesar" of a particular sexual role), such codes can hardly be confused with a practice of closeting, or with an appeal to an implied audience's "experience" of gendered or sexualized otherness. On the contrary, Stein is suspicious of the very concept of "audience," insisting that "when there are two [subjectivities] present instead of one . . . creation breaks down" into merely referential communication; "identity . . . takes[s] the place of entity," which is to say that art fails to become a "masterpiece."[27] But to note this is not to imply an indifference on Stein's part to the radical possibilities of her work for those genders and/or sexualities rendered superfluous or problematic within the domain of (ideological) language. The very title of her monumental prose poem "Patriarchal Poetry" (1927) explicitly names the dilemma of language: it is patriarchal, that is, it "means," it patrols boundaries, it "makes no mistake in estimating the value to be placed upon the best."[28] Stein's poetics effectively undo patriarchal poetry from within, in part by breaking up the apparatuses through which meaning is determined and distributed: the logic of telos and the syntax of order. Those critics who confuse these effects with the aims of her contemporary Dadaists miss altogether the force of Stein's powerful insight into the workings of heteronormative partriarchy.

In 1911 or so – a few years before the first Dada manifesto – Stein wrote "Orta or One Dancing," a prose poem alluding to the American modernist dancer Isadora Duncan. Duncan's sensational European performances were creating a large audience for feminist experimentation: she not only danced, but also spoke and wrote exultantly of "the dancer of the future" who will "dance the freedom of woman."[29] Like Stein and so many other American women modernists (including H. D. and Barnes), Duncan left the United States to pursue her work, doubting the aesthetic capacities of an American public that was as perplexed by her diaphanous attire and bare feet as by her revolutionary approach to formal technique and performance, the latter of which presented an insuperable challenge to patriarchal traditions of dance in the west. Her targets within the culture of dance included the dance-master, who manipulated the specularized bodies of women; the dance school which commodified movement itself; the flashy role of the soloist, which demeaned or subsumed what Duncan held to be the authentic site of dance, the chorus. Duncan's innovations in performance were similarly far-reaching: she danced alone (in the role of the chorus, as she said) in front of a single gauze curtain to short classical compositions; she used a reduced vocabulary of movement that included just a few walking steps, light glides, and skips. But her most important work was the technical development of a limitless syntax of movement. Like Stein, Duncan focused on relationality, which, for Duncan, meant a concentration on the continuous modifications of the body by space and of space by the body: there were no poses or stops in Duncan's movement (even during moments of standing still); body parts did not exist independently, but neither was their relation one of dependence. The labels of "organic" and "natural" that have been attached to her dance (even by Duncan herself) tend to obscure the core of its "difficulty," which is its constitutive resistance to the stasis of meaning, and its pursuit instead of "unending sequences" (57) through a syntax of repetition, conjunction, endless modification. Stein's prose poem recognizes and recapitulates this in its own unending sequences: "In dancing she was dancing. She was dancing and dancing and in being that one the one dancing and dancing she was dancing and dancing. In dancing, dancing being existing, she was dancing, and in being one dancing dancing was being existing."[30]

Modern communities

Both Stein and Duncan were part of a widespread, overlapping salon community: Duncan danced frequently in US and European salons, while Stein and Toklas's long-standing Saturday evenings in the rue de Fleurus magnetized a whole stratum of international modernists. For these women, as for many other salonnières and guests of their generation, the salon represented an unusual intersection of public discourses and intimate interiority. The modernist salon was a site of, among other things, the development of modernist aesthetics and practices. Mabel Dodge's regular evenings on lower Fifth Avenue, Alfred Stieglitz's reverent 291 meetings, Stein's and Natalie Barney's Paris gatherings, A'Lelia Walker's Dark Tower at-homes in Harlem and Villa Lewaro weekend retreats on the Hudson River: all of these and many other transient, semi-private assemblages incorporated various experiences of experimental art. Paintings and photography were exhibited, dancing performed, poems read, jazz played, interior design displayed, political, philosophical, and aesthetic ideas exchanged. If, as some have argued, modernism emerged from the foundational lacuna of modernity – that is, from the gap between modern self-conscious subjectivity and the world that it reduces to epistemological images – then one might say that the development of modernism was inconceivable without these embodied circulations of art. And if the US was the vortex of modernity in these years (or if "No one who has not lived in New York has lived in the Modern World," as Loy put it[31]), then it was the American salon that displayed most nakedly the conflicts of a disenchanting modernity and their attempted solutions through art and its proxy, sociability.

Sociability as a distinctively modern concept emerged in these years, mainly in the work of German sociologists; their thesis that sociability offered a detached refuge from modern alienation was tested in the role of the modernist hostess, who typically aimed to create a space in which modern conversation (however disjunctive or polemical) could flourish as an art unto itself. The final, deadly scene in Nella Larsen's *Passing* (1929) shocks all the more because it has begun with what Georg Simmel and others would characterize as perfect party conversation, people "throwing nonsensical shining things into the pool of talk, which the others . . . picked up and flung back with fresh adornment."[32] For Stein, conversation was high art: she declared that "the essence of being a genius is to be able to talk and listen to listen while talking and talk while listening."[33] Other salonnières, like Dodge, Walker, and Toklas, were nearly non-conversant stage-setters who kept the conversation going through attentions to space-making, well-plotted guest lists, food, intoxicants, ambience, and sometimes topics for discussion.

What distinguished these American modern salons from many earlier salons were their self-conscious attempts at cultural mixing, as if to demonstrate the principle that true sociability – detached, rhythmic, impersonal – transcended social difference. But of course, "mixing" in the US was an especially fraught enterprise, since the problem of race relations – proliferating in every discursive direction in these years – haunted the very concept of modern community. Dodge's salon performed class mixing in careful proportions, producing into the bargain a "transgressive" frisson from the rubbing elbows of labor organizers, bourgeoises, and intellectuals. Dodge's salon also mixed genders and sexualities up to a point. But the performance of mixing (and, by extension, the performance of redressing the social striations symptomatic of modernity) was limited: hers was an all-white, largely non-hyphenated salon whose only African-American guests, brought on the first evening by the cultural tourist Carl Van Vechten, were "entertainers" whom Dodge rejected with horror when they "leered and rolled their suggestive eyes,"[34] in Dodge's painfully racist account.

The literary record of white salons tends to hyperbolize their levels of mixing – tends, that is, to stage American modernism's "thousand languages"[35] as a product of actual interracial, inter-ethnic intimacy, however fleeting or impersonal. Wallace Thurman's *Infants of the Spring* (1932) participates in this impulse as well, though from the perspective of African-American artistic gatherings. The novel's cynical portrayal of a Harlem Renaissance salon focuses on the stultifying effects of its racial uplift agenda: an Alain Locke figure assembles a guest list of "young hopefuls"[36] and then kills off the conversation in advance by perorating about white decadence and the need for African-American artists to return to their "racial roots" (152). This lurching salon is pointedly contrasted in the novel to a much more proliferative formation of sociability, that is, an interracial, cross-class, inter-sexual Donation Party, thrown by the protagonist Raymond's housemates when their pantry runs dry. The party, which has been widely publicized, builds through the night, piling up "black people, white people, and all the in-between shades" (113); gin is consumed in huge quantities, donated groceries spill underfoot, "Greenwich Village uranians" (118) admire a beautiful black youth in one room while women embrace in another, "shouts of joy" (119) blare through the house, and the party climaxes in a darkened mass of black and white dancers clinging "passionately together as if trying to effect a permanent merger. Liquor, jazz music, and close physical contact had achieved what decades of propaganda had advocated with little success."

"Here," thinks Raymond wryly, "is social equality"; this is "the Negro renaissance, and this is about all the whole damn thing is going to amount to" (120) – "this" meaning interracial sexual contact in a sculptural mass of impersonal intimacy. "This" is where the color line dissolves, however fleetingly. "Social equality" may as well be synonymous with sexual intimacy for Raymond, who fiercely opposes identity politics, but who also recognizes that, like "social equality," this kind of collective intimacy is an unreal performance dictated by hegemonic power relations. The whites at the party are there because they have the option of touring and slumming; for them, as for Van Vechten, "Harlem" is an extrusion of (white) modern sexuality leavened by the thrill of racial interdiction. This is not to say that Raymond views the party's mass contact as "inauthentic" – it is, for him, a pleasing moment of aesthetic consummation – but rather that he understands race and sex to be discourses of control converging around black bodies: "sexual difference," from this important perspective, means not simply the space between males and females, but the space between sexualized races.[37] And while this space might offer a site of art-making for African-Americans as well as for whites – especially for performers like Josephine Baker[38], who worked it in Europe with broad improvisational freedom – it was nevertheless a space determined in the main by white appropriations of how race could "mean." Baker was a hostess in her own Paris cabarets, where she taught jazz dancing, passed hors d'oeuvres, modeled haute couture, and kept the cosmopolitan conversation going; but she also made a huge fortune, which is to say that in commodifying interracial sociability, she shrewdly appropriated white appropriation.

When Hemingway stages race as a symptom or co-factor of shifting sexuality in the Paris story "The Sea Change" – when he textually insists on an isomorphism between white-skin-going-dark (Phil and the girl's "tanning") and sexuality-going-queer – we must recognize the sharp disjuncture between his unreflective primitivism and the vibrant African-American agency by which he is surrounded in the Montmartran modernist community (and not only in the figure of Baker, for whom Hemingway confessed a sexual attraction). His thematic elision of skin color and sexuality is part of a larger American tendency – seen as well in Hartley's and Crane's treatments of Native Americans[39] and in Larsen's treatment of passing – to produce a sexed aesthetic discourse that relies on emphatic racial or ethnic alterity for its abstraction of sexual alterity. At once regulatory and creative, as Foucault would say, this drive in modernist aesthetics may be coterminous with the proliferative "sex-talk" that marked American modernism's historical conditions of possibility. It may be, that is to say, part of American modernism's discursive elaboration of the "pleasure and power"[40] of sexuality. But it may also be symptomatic of American modernism's filial relations with modernity itself, which it alternately vocalizes and critiques. This is a modernity that casts race and gender and sexuality as categorical problems, and then takes its own categories for truths; modernism, a house of many mansions, is of necessity home both to the hiatuses of modernity and to the elaborate modern project of generating a greater truth.

NOTES

1. John D'Emilio and Estelle Freedman, *Intimate Matters: A History of Sexuality in America* [1988], second edition (University of Chicago Press, 1997); Nancy F. Cott, *The Grounding of Modern Feminism* (New Haven: Yale University Press, 1987); Shari Benstock, *Women of the Left Bank* (Austin: University of Texas Press, 1986); Sandra Gilbert and Susan Gubar, *No Man's Land*, vol. I, *The War of the Words* (New Haven: Yale University Press, 1988), *No Man's Land*, vol. II, *Sexchanges* (New Haven: Yale University Press, 1989), and *No Man's Land*, vol. III, *Letters From the Front* (New Haven: Yale University Press, 1994); Ann Ardis, *New Women, New Novels: Feminism and Early Modernism* (New Brunswick, NJ: Rutgers University Press, 1990).

2. Andreas Huyssen, "Mass Culture as Woman: Modernism's Other," *After the Great Divide: Modernism, Mass Culture, Postmodernism* (Bloomington: Indiana University Press, 1986), 47.

3. Mina Loy, *The Lost Lunar Baedeker: Poems*, ed. Roger L. Conover (New York: Farrar, Straus & Giroux, 1996), 153.

4. Emma Goldman, *Red Emma Speaks: Selected Writings and Speeches*, ed. Alix Kates Shulman (New York: Random House, 1972), 142.

5. "Love Songs" was the first published section of the much longer "Songs to Joannes," the latter of which appeared in 1917. "Love Songs" was included in the inaugural issue of *Others: A Magazine of the New Verse*, edited by Arthur Kreymborg, who later described the poem's tumultuous reception by readers insulted by its textual experimentalism and outraged by Loy's "utter nonchalance in revealing the secrets of sex" (Loy, *Lost Lunar*, 189).

6. Sigmund Freud, *Three Essays on the Theory of Sexuality* [1905], tr. James Strachey (New York: Basic Books, 1975), 15.

7. H. D., *Collected Poems, 1912–1944*, ed. Louis L. Martz (New York: New Directions, 1983), 52–53.

8. See George Chauncey, *Gay New York: Gender, Urban Culture, and the Making of the Gay Male World, 1890–1940* (New York: Basic Books, 1994).

9. See Jennifer Terry, *An American Obsession: Science, Medicine, and Homosexuality in Modern Society* (University of Chicago Press, 1999).

10. Freud, *Three Essays*, 11. Freud added the footnote containing this passage in 1915.

11. Willa Cather, "Paul's Case," *Willa Cather's Collected Short Fiction: 1892–1912*, revised edition, ed. Virginia Faulkner (Lincoln: University of Nebraska Press, 1970), 243, 245.
12. Ernest Hemingway, "The Sea Change," *The Short Stories of Ernest Hemingway* (New York: Scribner's, 1953), 397.
13. Phil can produce only a few telegraphic phrases from Pope's *Essay on Man* (1734), the original quatrain of which is: "Vice is a monster of so frightful mien, / As to be hated, needs to be seen; / Yet seen too oft, familiar with her face / We first endure, then pity, then embrace." Cf. Phil's fragmented rendering: "'Vice is a monster of such fearful mien,' the young man said bitterly, 'that to be something or other needs but to be seen. Then we something, something, then embrace'" (399).
14. John Dos Passos, "Against American Literature," reprinted in *Modernism: An Anthology of Sources and Documents*, ed. Vassiliki Kolocontroni, Jane Goldman, and Olga Taxidou (University of Chicago Press, 1998), 336.
15. Marsden Hartley, "The Business of Poetry," reprinted in *Manifesto: A Century of Isms*, ed. Mary Ann Caws (Lincoln: University of Nebraska Press, 2001), 354.
16. Djuna Barnes, *Nightwood* [1937] (New York: New Directions, 1961), 91.
17. Cheryl Plumb, "Introduction," *Nightwood: The Original Version and Related Drafts* (Normal, IL: Dalkey Archive Press, 1995), xxi.
18. T. S. Eliot, "The Metaphysical Poets" [1921], *Selected Prose of T. S. Eliot*, ed. Frank Kermode (London: Faber and Faber, 1975), 65.
19. Eve Kosofsky Sedgwick, *Epistemology of the Closet* (Berkeley: University of California Press, 1990); and see especially the introduction to Judith Butler's *Bodies that Matter: On the Discursive Limits of Sex* (New York: Routledge, 1993).
20. Judith Butler, "Withholding the Name: Translating Gender in Cather's 'On the Gull's Road,'" *Modernist Sexualities*, ed. Hugh Stevens and Caroline Howlett (Manchester University Press, 2000), 60.
21. Hart Crane, "The Dynamics of Metaphor," *The Modern Tradition: Backgrounds of Modern Literature*, ed. Richard Ellmann and Charles Feidelson, Jr. (New York: Oxford University Press, 1965), 160.
22. Tim Dean, "Hart Crane's Poetics of Privacy," *American Literary History*, 8.1 (1996), 91.
23. Hart Crane, "Melville's Tomb," *Collected Poems*, ed. Waldo Frank (New York: Liveright, 1946), 100.
24. Gertrude Stein, *Writings 1903–1932*, ed. Catharine R. Stimpson and Harriet Chessman (New York: Library of America, 1998), 336.
25. Gertrude Stein, "Poetry and Grammar," *Writings 1932–1946*, ed. Catharine R. Stimpson and Harriet Chessman (New York: Library of America, 1998), 314.
26. *Ibid.*, 330.
27. Stein, "What Are Master-pieces and Why Are There So Few of Them?" *Writings 1932–1946*, 356–357.
28. Stein, *Writings 1903–1932*, 571, 585.
29. Isadora Duncan, "The Dance of the Future" [1903], *The Art of the Dance*, ed. Sheldon Cheney (New York: Theatre Arts, Inc., 1928), 62–63.
30. Stein, *Writings 1903–1932*, 300.

31. Loy, interview in *New York Evening Sun*, February 17, 1917, quoted in Steven Watson, *Strange Bedfellows: The First American Avant-Garde* (New York: Abbeville, 1991), 241.

32. Nella Larsen, *Passing* [1929], ed. Deborah McDowell (New Brunswick, NJ: Rutgers University Press, 1986), 237.

33. "What Are Master-pieces?" 355.

34. Mabel Luhan Dodge, *Movers and Shakers* (Albuquerque: University of New Mexico Press, 1985), 79–80.

35. Loy, *Lost Lunar*, 158.

36. Wallace Thurman, *Infants of the Spring* (London: Black Classics/X Press, 1998), 148.

37. Ida B. Wells offers an extraordinarily incisive account of the political orchestration of racialized sexual difference, "Southern Horror: The Lynch Law in All its Phases" [1892], reprinted in *Man Cannot Speak for Her*, vol. II, ed. Karlyn Kohrs Campbell (New York: Praeger, 1989).

38. Baker's wondrous dancing was, like Duncan's, driven by the syntactical pursuit of "endless sequences," but Duncan indirectly discredited Baker's work in an essay written at the pinnacle of Baker's fame: "It seems monstrous to me for anyone to believe that the Jazz rhythm expresses America" she wrote in the Whitmanesque "I See America Dancing" (1927). For Duncan, Whitman's America cannot be found in the "ape-like convulsions of the Charleston" or the "sensual convulsion of the South African negro" (Duncan, *The Art of the Dance*, 48–49).

39. See Robert K. Martin, "Myths of Native Masculinity: Hart Crane and the Poem of the Nation," *American Modernism Across the Arts*, ed. Jay Bochner and Justin D. Edwards (New York: Peter Lang, 1999), 203–217.

40. Michel Foucault, *The History of Sexuality*, vol. I: "An Introduction," tr. Robert Hurley (New York: Vintage, 1980), 45.

10

JOHN N. DUVALL

Regionalism in American modernism

Any attempt to link regionalism to American modernism may seem, at first blush, a perverse enterprise. After all, definitions of modernism tend to cast it as nearly the antithesis of regionalism. If regionalist fiction between the 1890s and 1910s typically focused on matters of domesticity in rural localities, modernism was an international movement, encompassing the fine arts as well as literature. In so many of its manifestations, from Cubism in painting to atonality in music and stream-of-conscious narration in fiction, modernism bespeaks a self-conscious difficulty intended to shock the middle class out of its complacency and to create the possibility of fresh perception. The radical formal experiments of modernism often are accompanied by an equally radical politics, from Ezra Pound's open embracing of fascism to the many American authors who were drawn to Communism in the 1930s. Not surprisingly then, modernism is typically associated with urban centers, places where the arts flourish; Vienna, Paris, London, and New York more immediately come to mind when thinking of cutting edge aesthetic and political thought than, say, Red Cloud, Nebraska; Richmond, Virginia; or even Oxford, Mississippi.

The years this volume covers (1890–1939) also create problems for seeking the ground of regionalism and modernism. In an American context, modernism is typically thought to "happen" between World Wars I and II, as writers respond to T. S. Eliot's diagnosis of the spiritual wasteland of modernity, a world in which all the institutions (the Church, the State, the University) that previously had sustained value seemed for many intellectuals to have failed. Writers such as Ernest Hemingway, Djuna Barnes, F. Scott Fitzgerald, and William Faulkner all specifically engaged *The Waste Land* so that, even when critical of Eliot, they nevertheless signaled their membership in the club of international modernism. No one would call Eliot (born in St. Louis, Missouri) a Midwestern writer. Nor, for that matter, would Midwestern literature typically claim Hemingway or Fitzgerald, despite their being from, respectively, Oak Park, Illinois, and St. Paul, Minnesota.

If, however, we take literary modernism as all imaginative writing that responds to the intense forces of modernization that occur from the 1890s to the eve of World War II, then we might speak of a broader range of writers, often those whose regionalism is associated with realism and naturalism, who contribute to an understanding of modernism. From the mid-nineteenth century onward, Charles Darwin's theory of evolution, Karl Marx's critique of capital, and Fredric Nietzsche's transvaluation of values all laid the ground for modernism prior to 1914. The double consciousness that W. E. B. Du Bois wrote about in *The Souls of Black Folk* (1903), although specifically addressing the gap between the promise of America and the lived experience of African-Americans, also resonates with the experience of other marginalized people. Quite simply, minority and women writers did not need a world war in order to feel alienated.

Regionalism presents its own definitional problems. For much of its history, the term was synonymous with the phrase, "writers of local color," a designation frequently used to devalue women writers by signaling that they were of only regional, not national, importance. Even when credited more seriously, regionalism was generally seen as an outgrowth of realism and naturalism, playing out in rural settings the same thematics of realist ethics or naturalist determinism that urban writers had already staked out. In short, to label something as regional has been, until quite recently, a minoritizing gesture, one relegating the regional text to a supplemental status in the canon of a national literature.

The last decade, though, has seen a renewed interest in regionalism, often from feminist critics who use the term as a tool to reclaim certain women authors. Among the most significant recent attempts to reconfigure regionalism are Judith Fetterley and Marjorie Pryse's Norton anthology, *American Women Regionalists* (as well as their critical justification for it, *Writing out of Place: Regionalism, Women, and American Literary Culture*), Kate McCullough's *Regions of Identity: The Construction of America in Women's Fiction, 1885–1914*, and *Breaking Boundaries: New Perspectives on Women's Regional Writing*.[1] These interventions focus on re-presenting the fiction primarily of women but in some cases of writers of color. This recovery work, however, may not immediately seem pertinent to a consideration of regionalism and modernism, since one will not find the word "modernism" in the indexes of any of these books. Nevertheless, the reintroduction of forgotten texts by twentieth-century American authors necessarily affects our sense of the modern.

While unquestionably useful in recovering out-of-print texts, the feminist remapping of regionalism has certain limitations, not the least of which is its exclusive focus on fiction. Other problems arise from the politicizing of regionalism to make it a weapon in the canon wars. Because Fetterley and Pryse have taken such a prominent role in revaluing and canonizing regionalism, I would like to consider their work in greater detail. Fetterley and Pryse wish to liberate regionalist fiction from its subservient relation to realism, and in a bold stroke they radically devalue the importance of region in regionalism on the grounds that regions are "far more local and specific than" such designations as the South, the Midwest, the Northeast, and the West (*Writing*, 11). For example, if one uses "Southern literature" to group authors from north Mississippi, Appalachia, and Louisiana, there may be little that the authors' local cultures have in common.

Their critique of typical regional designations leads Fetterley and Pryse to their most important claim, which is that one should regard regionalism "less as a term of geographical determinism and more as a discourse or a mode of analysis, a vantage point within the network of power relations that provides a location for critique and resistance" (*Writing*, 11). Thus, Fetterley and Pryse effectively identify regionalism as a form of minor literature in which "everything is political."[2] In other words, like Deleuze and Guattari's minor literature, Fetterley and Pryse's regionalism maps an alternative space of ethics that critiques the received wisdom of literary history. Proposing a regionalism without regions, Fetterley and Pryse construct a feminist fictional form that takes its identity from feminist concerns. "Regionalism," they write, "marks that point where region becomes mobilized as a tool for critique of hierarchies based on gender as well as race, class, age, and economic resources" to which they will later add national identity (*Writing*, 14). As far as they are concerned, realism is a disciplinary category in the service of the dominant patriarchal ideology, asserting that it is largely deaf to issues of identity and their politics. In short, they argue, if a text does not critique hierarchies, it cannot be regionalist. This orientation leads Fetterley and Pryse to exclude Hamlin Garland (1860–1940) from regionalism, because although his stories in *Main-Traveled Roads* (1891) and *Prairie Folks* (1893) may detail the harshness of rural life in the Midwest, he "is unable to critique the ideological operations of gender." Similarly, Mark Twain's *Huckleberry Finn* (1885) also falls short of regionalism because, whatever it may or may not say about race, it "does not problematize gender" (*Writing*, 16).

At the same time, by insisting that we include urban writers in this new and localized way of understanding region, Fetterley and Pryse create a different kind of problem for any thinking about regionalism. If, for example, one claims Sui Sin Far's stories about the gender problems that arise in half-assimilated immigrants in Seattle and San Francisco's Chinatown and Grace Elizabeth King's depictions of gender matters in urban New Orleans, then why not name Edith Wharton as a fellow urban regionalist? In such major novels as *The House of Mirth* (1907), *The Custom of the Country* (1913), and *The Age of Innocence* (1920), Wharton unquestionably mobilizes her localized region, the upper echelons of society in New York City and the Hudson River Valley, to critique hierarchies of gender and class. Instead of trying to position Wharton in relation to her most proper region, Fetterley and Pryse consider only *Ethan Frome* (1911). Wharton was critical of the regionalism of Mary Wilkins and Sarah Orne Jewett, which leads Fetterley and Pryse to develop a perspective that sees *Ethan Frome* as a parody of the conventions of women's regionalist fiction and to question Wharton's motives for this parody. Whether one accepts Fetterley and Pryse's portrayal of Wharton as a writer who, by focusing on a male character's story, fails "to create sympathy for women and to present alternative feminist values" (*Writing*, 61) and who aligns herself with a patriarchal male literary tradition, it is precisely in Wharton's exploding the formal conventions of rural regionalist fiction that one might locate an intersection of regionalism and modernism. What remains useful in negotiating the conceptions of regionalism and modernism is Fetterley and Pryse's sense that regionalism is a form of critique rather than a type of geographical determinism. This recognition allows regionalist readings to cross geographical boundaries so as to underscore resonances between writers typically contextualized within their particular region. Thus, in "Toward modernism" I look at two pairs of regional women writers who came to their literary voices prior to World War I yet whose thematics remain germane in the interwar period of American modernism. Next, in "Regional poetry" I consider four male poets whose personal and poetic identities are grounded in region. Finally, in "Southern sectionalism and the rise of Southern modernism" I turn to that region with the clearest and most self-conscious relation to modernism where both New Criticism and the institutional study of Southern literature grew out of an engagement with modernist poetics. But again crossing institutional markers of region, this section looks at how African-American writers who migrated to Harlem from the South create a different purchase on Southern modernism.

Toward modernism

Pairing two transregional women writers suggests ways that both urban and rural regionalists contribute to an understanding of American modernism. The first pair delineates the mores of the city – Kate Chopin and Sui Sin Far – while the second looks at rural community – Willa Cather and Ellen Glasgow; Chopin and Sui Sin Far map gender and racial difference, while

Cather and Chopin focus their gender critique through the lens of agricultural modernization.

Born in St. Louis into Irish-American O'Flaherty family, Kate Chopin (1850–1904) married New Orleans businessman Oscar Chopin in 1870. After his death in 1882, Chopin returned to St. Louis with her six children and began to turn her experiences in Louisiana into fiction. Although her literary career is limited to two novels and two collections of short stories, her work questions the authenticity of personal identity in ways that would become central to modernist writing.

Although best known for *The Awakening* (1899), which focuses on life in New Orleans, Chopin also addressed rural Louisiana life in her early stories. One of the most relevant to modernism is "Désirée's Baby," originally published in *Vogue* in 1893. This story not only addresses miscegenation but also actively transfigures the genre of the tragic mulatta – established in the 1850s – in ways that anticipate the work of both the Harlem Renaissance and the Southern Renascence. The tragic mulatta, in brief, is a beautiful, light-skinned, well-mannered young woman whose "black blood" is uncovered resulting either in her return to the victimization of slavery or (in later versions) in her white lover's rejection of her. Chopin inverts this narrative arc by a deft switch. Désirée is happily married to a slave owner, the darkly handsome Armand, but their happiness is shattered when her baby's skin appears to turn too dark. For Armand this can only mean that his wife is not white. When her mother does not confirm her whiteness, she drowns herself and the baby. While burning Désirée's things, Armand discovers a letter from his mother to his father. In the final line of the story, which quotes her letter, she expresses gratitude that Armand is light enough that he will never need to know that his mother is part black. Reversing the reader's assumption that "Désirée's Baby" is yet another narrative of the tragic mulatta, Chopin deftly reveals that the abusive slave master Armand is himself already a Negro by the laws and customs of the South. Thus, in the story's subversive rendering, Désirée's racial identity is both unknowable and not even the point. Unlike his father, who overlooked his own wife's racial identity, Armand cannot, and consequently he produces a racial tragedy that ensures his self-loathing.

As an outsider herself to French Creole society, Chopin surely encodes in Edna Pontellier some of the cultural misunderstandings she herself experienced in moving to New Orleans. We might understand Edna's story as her failure to assimilate to the values of New Orleans Creole culture because Edna is transplanted from Kentucky by marriage. She observes the apparent freedom of married Creole women (their cigarettes, their drinking, and their flirtatious behavior with unmarried men), but fails to see how this apparent freedom actually operates in a set of unspoken social rules that in fact masks men's property rights in women. Whether we take Edna's suicide as the deterministic result of her disruption of the gender codes of Creole society or as her ethical critique of that same patriarchal society, Edna's awakening, as critics have recognized, is a sexual one. Well before Freud's dissemination in America, Chopin locates sexuality as a cornerstone of Edna's identity, a move that points us toward later modernist explorations of the sexual woman from Ernest Hemingway's Brett Ashley to Djuna Barnes's Robin Vote.

For Sui Sin Far, the matter of difference extends beyond misunderstandings arising from ethnicity to the more visible difference of race. Sui Sin Far is the pen name of Edith Maude Eaton (1865–1914), a Eurasian woman born of a British merchant father and a Chinese mother. A native of Macclesfield, England, Eaton, at age seven, moved with her family to New York and later to Montreal. Eaton's formal education ended when she was ten because of the family's poverty. Although she began her journalistic career in Canada, it was not until she moved to Seattle, Washington, in 1898 that she found the locale that would become the subject matter of her mature fiction. One of the first Asian-North American writers, Sui Sin Far could be regarded as the literary foremother of contemporary Asan-American writers. This role is problematic, however, because her one collection of short stories, *Mrs. Spring Fragrance* (1912), was soon out of print and only reissued in a different form in 1995.[3]

Like Chopin's, Sui Sin Far's fiction uses her setting to underscore cultural differences, but her Asian heritage in a sinophobic America reveals that the dilemma of Du Boisian double consciousness was not exclusively an African-American problem. The matter of authentic identity – certainly a modernist thematic – repeatedly emerges in her stories, often drawing on her own racially mixed position. This notion of authenticity plays out formally in her very attempts to render Asian-American speech and thought. As Amy Ling points out, Sui Sin Far did not herself know Chinese. By making her English appear as though it were translated, she attempts to represent in her Asian characters both an English that is a second language and the impression that these characters think and speak in Chinese.[4] Her stories take up the matter of miscegenation, assimilation, and the possibility of passing as white, issues that are addressed in the works of a number of modernist writers. For example, "Its Wavering Image," tells the story of a young Eurasian woman, Pan, who falls in love with a white newspaper reporter. He urges her to reject her Chinese upbringing and to pass as white, a proposition that clearly tempts her. However, when he publishes a feature article on Chinatown based on insider information taken from his intimacy with Pan, the young woman feels betrayed. In their final meeting, she rejects both the reporter and his claim that she is white.

Unlike Chopin, who often works in the tragic mode, Sui Sin Far treats even the most serious subjects with a humorous touch. Certainly the title story of her 1912 volume, Mrs. *Spring Fragrance*, humorously examines the degree to which Mr. and Mrs. Spring Fragrance consciously and unconsciously assimilate to an American culture in which shifting gender roles afford women more freedom than Chinese culture. Much of the humor results from Mr. Spring Fragrance's unfounded fears about his wife's fidelity. In its self-reflexivity, another story, "The Inferior Woman," is an especially playful modernist narrative. Mrs. Spring Fragrance decides that, if American women can write about Chinese women, she will write a journalistic book about American women on the subject of the "inferior woman." Her research consists of eavesdropping on a conversation between a white mother and daughter. Pointedly, Mrs. Spring Fragrance's writing has an effect on a white reader, another white mother who objects to her son's love interest, a woman who has risen from the working class. Mrs. Spring Fragrance's narrative makes the white woman recognize her sexism and classism, leading her to accept the "inferior woman."

Similarly, two other women writers whose relation to modernism becomes clearer if we draw them out of their typical regional designations are the near contemporaries Willa Cather (1873–1947) and Ellen Glasgow (1873–1945). Both authors were born in Virginia, but Cather's family moved to Red Cloud, Nebraska, when she was nine. After graduating from the University of Nebraska, Cather worked for several years as the managing editor of *McClure's*. Cather fictionalizes her small community as Hanover in O *Pioneers!* (1913) and as Black Hawk in *My Antonia* (1918), her second and fourth novels respectively. Although typically thought of as a writer of the Nebraska prairie, by 1926, with the publication of *Death Comes for the Archbishop*, Cather explores the Southwest of the nineteenth century. Ellen Glasgow, generally seen as a precursor of the Southern Renascence, was born in Richmond, Virginia. A rebellious child, she rejected her father's Presbyterian religion and very early turned to reading and writing as a form of protest. Like Cather, Glasgow never married. As would be the case with Faulkner a generation later, Glasgow found herself as a writer when she discovered her local subject matter, her native region of Virginia, in her third novel, *The Voice of the People* (1900), material that would sustain her for the rest of her career.

Cather's fiction draws on the strategies of realism, though there can be decided modernist tendencies. For example, because of his lack of self-knowledge, Jim Burden in *My Ántonia* is as classically unreliable as Fitzgerald's Nick Caraway; and though Cather expressed distaste for Freudianism, her representations of sexual dreams (such as Jim Burden's and Alexandra

Bergson's in *O Pioneers!*) means that she was aware of modern psychology. Glasgow's reading of Charles Darwin undoubtedly creates a more naturalist world in which men and women are ground down by the constraints of heredity, sexual passion, and the crushing labor of environment. Nevertheless there is a psychological complexity in her later fiction that resonates with modernism. Reading Cather's *O Pioneers!* against Glasgow's *Barren Ground* (1922) illuminates the modernist elements present in both works. To begin with, both plots reveal striking likenesses. Alexandra and Dorinda Oakley similarly inherit their family farms from well-meaning but ineffectual fathers. Pointedly, the daughters receive title to the farms rather than the sons, who are less well-meaning but equally ineffectual. Through heroic (though largely unrepresented) struggles with the land, both Alexandra and Dorinda turn their farms into showplaces. They prosper financially and are able to increase their acreage. Neither marries. Alexandra (never interested in heterosexuality) and Dorinda (who renounces heterosexual passion after being jilted by Jason Graylock) are not afraid to dress in overalls and both end up in asexual, companionate relations with men who do not conform to traditional cultural scripts of masculinity.

O Pioneers! and *Barren Ground* both serve as pro-modernization responses to technology and the applied sciences and see the new as a positive means to an end. Cather and Glasgow link utopian possibility with innovation in farming. Alexandra and Dorinda both embrace new agricultural techniques (against the wisdom of patriarchal male agrarian communities) to refigure gendered identity. By championing new production concepts (such as crop rotation and the introduction of alfalfa), both these female protagonists simultaneously produce new technologies of gender. Having renounced motherhood, they are both in an older and pejorative sense "barren" inasmuch as they are childless. Nevertheless, the fruits of the earth that they bring forth are the displaced expression of a modern fertility. Dorinda's turn to modern dairy production underscores her sexual choice. By seizing the means of modern production, she helps to nourish thousands and connects the rural to the urban.

Regional poetry

Despite the overwhelming amount of scholarship that treats regionalism as though it were exclusively a form of fictional production, regionalist poetry often thematizes alienation and an awareness of the forces of modernization, and much of this work occurs prior to America's entry into World War I. If women fiction writers have in certain cases been marginalized by the regional designation, it is surprising how many early-twentieth-century male poets risked identifying themselves so thoroughly with regional subject matter. Carl Sandburg (1878–1963) carries Whitman's celebratory poetics of the common man and woman into the twentieth century and, perhaps even more than Glasgow and Cather, delineates the positive potential of modernization. His "Chicago" (1914) deploys the Whitmanesque catalogue to celebrate the spirit of the laborer, who represents the vitality of urban life. At times, though, Sandburg, in a poem such as "Fog" (1916) – six lines that figure the fog as coming in "on little cat feet" – seems to move beyond Whitman and to anticipate the Imagist poetics of William Carlos Williams's famous "Red Wheelbarrow" (1923). The cat imagery in "Fog," in fact, resonates with that of Eliot's "Love Song of J. Alfred Prufrock" (1915) in which the fog "rubs its back upon the window-panes."

More typically, though, regionalist poets depict rural life and have a much less sanguine view of the forces of modernization than does Sandburg. In particular Sandburg's fellow Midwesterner, Edgar Lee Masters, and the New England poets Edwin Arlington Robinson and Robert Frost each explores different aspects of alienated consciousness. Like Sandburg, Edgar Lee Masters (1869–1950) is associated with the Chicago Renaissance, an arts movement intended to highlight the city's significance. The literary heart of this movement is represented by two little magazines, *Poetry: A Magazine of Verse*, founded in 1912, and *The Little Review*, which began operation in 1914. Despite their Chicago connection, Masters seems much more a poet of the twentieth century than Sandburg. Based on his memories of growing up in rural western Illinois, his *Spoon River Anthology* (1915) depicts the voices of the dead who lie in the town's cemetery. These voices reveal the distance between the public and the private, between what is manifest to the world and what is latent in their souls. Doc Hill may seem an altruistic man of medicine to the community, but we learn that his love for the people is a substitute for a loveless marriage and an unsatisfying family life. Fully seven years before *The Waste Land*, Masters delineates a world highly resonant with the one that the more intellectual Eliot would create. In *Spoon River Anthology*, as in *The Waste Land*, the relations between women and men mean little more than a series of sexual acts, one of "the unseen forces/That govern the processes of life" as Masters puts it in "Serepta Mason."

Having found his Illinois subject matter, Masters continued to mythologize the Midwestern prairie in such volumes as *Songs and Satires* (1916), *The Great Valley* (1916), *Toward the Gulf* (1918), *Starved Rock* (1919), *The Open Sea* (1921), *Return to Spoon River* (1924), *Poems of People* (1936) and *More People* (1939), *Illinois Poems* (1941), and *Along the Illinois* (1942).

Although none of the later received the acclaim or popularity of *Spoon River*, it would be difficult to deny the impact of Masters's regionalism on American modernism. The collection of voices that comprise *Spoon River Anthology* points toward the more overtly modernist experiments with character and voice that one later finds in Sherwood Anderson's collection of short stories *Winesburg, Ohio* (1919), Faulkner's novel *As I Lay Dying* (1930), and Thornton Wilder's play *Our Town* (1938). Yet Masters stands as another problematic figure in the feminist reconstructive work on regionalism. A white, male poet, Masters certainly does not need to be recovered, even if his reputation has diminished in the last fifty years. Perhaps his portrayal of character in "Margaret Fuller Slack" might earn Masters a moment of notice in Fetterley and Pryse's regionalism-as-gender-critique because the poem represents the voice of a female character aware of the social limitations placed on women. But probably not, since, Masters's poem, like Slack's accidental death from lock-jaw, is "ironical"; her intellectual aspirations are merely a pose.

Like Masters, Edwin Arlington Robinson (1869–1935) turned his childhood experiences into the subject matter of his poetry. Robinson transforms his home of Gardner, Maine, into the Tilbury Town of a number of his poems. More traditional in his prosody than Masters, Robinson typically produced rhyming quatrains and eight-line stanzas, as well as a number of sonnets. Although Robinson was quite productive until his death, most of his best poetry was written by 1921, when his *Collected Poems* appeared. "Luke Havergal" and "Richard Corey," for example, appeared in his first volume of poetry, *The Torrent and the Night Before* (1896). The cost of publishing this volume, as well as his second, *The Children of the Night* (1897), was paid for by friends, a situation that points to the poverty Robinson lived in until the 1920s when his critical reputation was finally secured. (His *Collected Poems* won a Pulitzer Prize, the first of three he would receive during the 1920s.)

Critical of the mores of small town life, Robinson created characters, much as Masters did, that often are themselves gently satirized. Robinson does not spare himself in certain of his portraits. In "Miniver Cheevy," the title character is a genial failure whose love of Arthurian stories and alcohol surely provides a wry self-portrait of the alcoholic Robinson who published three long poems based on Arthurian legend; alcoholism recurs in "Mr. Flood's Party," as Eben Flood drinks alone and talks to himself. But Robinson's portraits do more than speak to individual failure. Like so many modernist texts, Robinson's poems at times address the forces of modernization. For example "The Mill" (whether we take the suicides of the miller and his wife as literal or as the product of the wife's overactive imagination) represents the alienation certain workers feel in light of new technologies that render older forms of communal commerce obsolete.

Perhaps the poet who most cannily used region as a form of poetic and personal self-fashioning was Robert Frost (1874–1963). Born in San Francisco where he spent the first eleven years of his life, Frost came to embody for the American public the quintessential New England poet-farmer. Unlike Robinson, Frost was immediately embraced by the critical establishment after the publication of his first volume of poetry, *A Boy's Will* (1913). This was followed a year later by *North of Boston*. Although Frost would win four Pulitzer prizes in the 1920s and 1930s, these first two volumes contain a disproportionate number of the poems for which he is best remembered. Both establish themes and techniques that would sustain Frost throughout his career. In poems such as "The Death of the Hired Man" and "Home Burial," one sees Frost's use of dramatic dialogue to experiment with the possibilities of colloquial diction. But Frost was also adept at traditional forms, as the sonnet "Mowing" reveals. Typical of so many of these early poems is the way that the poet-farmer-philosopher begins with physical description of some rural activity only to end in metaphysical speculation, as in "Mending Wall," "After Apple Picking," "The Wood-Pile," and "The Road Not Taken." For this reason, it is easy to see why Frost can be taken as a descendant of the Transcendentalists; however, Frost's movement from the world to metaphysics does not reproduce Emerson's optimism but is more in line with Melville's skepticism. Nowhere is this better exemplified than in Frost's Italian sonnet, "Design," which appeared in *A Further Range* (1936), though it is a revision of an earlier poem, "In White" (1922). The octave of the sonnet details something the speaker discovers on a walk – a white spider sitting on an albino version of a wild flower eating a white moth. The sestet, however, does not answer or resolve anything, but only asks a series of questions about this ironic Trinity. Frost's questions, in fact, lead to a speculation about the possible nature of a designer, in lines that recall nothing so much as an extremely condensed version of Ishmael's speculations about the uncanny horror of misplaced whiteness in "The Whiteness of the Whale" chapter of *Moby-Dick*. The sonnet, which begins with a regional poet acutely aware of nature, concludes with a couplet clearly revealing a poet fully aware of the modernist questioning of larger purpose: "What but design of darkness to appall? – / If design govern in a thing so small."

As this section has shown, male regional poets found national recognition despite their engagement with specific locale, a situation that is more pronounced in the most self-conscious of all the regions during American modernism – the South.

Southern sectionalism and the rise of Southern modernism

The previous section might have included the Fugitive poets, who around 1915 began meeting informally in Nashville, Tennessee, if it were not for the prominent role that several of these poets and their students later played in developing both New Criticism and Southern Literature as an academic subject. By the early 1920s the group included such notables as John Crowe Ransom, Robert Penn Warren, Donald Davidson, John Gould Fletcher, and Allen Tate. What had begun as a gathering of teachers and students to discuss poetry and share their verse lead to a stronger sense of shared purpose that formalized itself in the creation of a literary magazine.

The Fugitive first appeared in April of that watershed year of international modernism, 1922, in which both James Joyce's *Ulysses* and Eliot's *The Waste Land* were published and in which Eliot's *Criterion* began. The magazine's formation may be understood in part as a response to H. L. Mencken's harsh dismissal of post-Civil War Southern culture in "The Sahara of the Bozart" (1917). In it, Mencken flatly states "you will not find a single southern poet above the rank of a neighborhood rhymester" and, with the exception of James Branch Cabell, "you will not find a single southern prose writer who can actually write."[5] Not surprisingly, then, Ransom announces his group's difference in the foreword to the first issue, proclaiming that "a literary phase known rather euphemistically as Southern Literature has expired" and that "THE FUGITIVE flees from nothing faster than the high-caste Brahmins of the Old South."[6] Although the Fugitives embraced the past as subject matter, in terms of poetics, they self-consciously attempted to be modern. A key moment in Fugitive poetics was Allen Tate's championing *The Waste Land* against the objections of Davidson and Ransom (who had reviewed the poem negatively). Eliot's influence can be seen in Tate's most famous poem, "Ode to the Confederate Dead" (1928), which reads like nothing so much as a Southern "waste land," with many images echoing Eliot's poem.

The Fugitive ceased publication in December 1925 and the members of the group dispersed. These literary rebels, however, reunited to develop a decidedly sectionalist, anti-modernization political agenda known as Southern Agrarianism. All of the poets named above contribute to a collection of essays, *I'll Take My Stand: The South and the Agrarian Tradition* (1930). The opening statement of principles sharply critiques modernity, particularly the encroachment of Northern industrial society and an attendant materialism, while praising Southern culture as the last repository of European tradition. The Agrarians condemn the alienation that results from consumer society, a move that resonates with contemporary Marxist critiques of capital, yet the Agrarians were staunchly anti-Communist. Accusing the Marxists of idealism and utopianism, the Agrarians themselves posited a golden age in the Southern past that they sought to preserve. Their solution to the problems of modernization was to return to an organic community in which most people earned their living through agriculture. The Agrarian's idealized community in which leisure allows for the flourishing of the arts was predicated on the exploited labor of African-Americans, who were already migrating to other areas of the US.

Although the Agrarian reactionary and segregationist political agenda clearly could not stop the development of the New South, this group of men continued their culture wars as tenured conservatives at prominent universities where their scholarship continued in more coded forms the vision of the South that they championed. Cleanth Brooks, for example, was a student of Tate's and Warren's at Vanderbilt in the mid-1920s, and contributed to the second Agrarian forum, *Who Owns America?* (1936). Brooks and Warren's many pedagogical collaborations were instrumental to the dissemination of New Criticism, but Brooks also helped shape both Faulkner studies and the discipline of Southern literature. Brooks's help is warmly acknowledged by Louis D. Rubin, Jr., and Robert D. Jacobs, the editors of *Southern Renascence: The Literature of the Modern South* (1953), a collection that is the first instance of canon making in Southern modernism.[7] The poets examined are Ransom, Tate, John Peale Bishop, Davidson, and Merrill Moore; the essays on fiction focus on Faulkner, Warren, Glasgow, James Branch Cabell, Stark Young, Katherine Anne Porter, Thomas Wolfe, Eudora Welty, Erskine Caldwell, and Caroline Gordon. Where Agrarian politics is most evident is in the absence of African-American writers from Southern modernism. A second collection of essays edited by Rubin and Jacobs, *South: Modern Southern Literature in its Cultural Setting* (1961), again has no essays on Southern African-Americans, though the editors struggle for several pages in the volume's introduction over the questions "What of the Southern writer who is a Negro? What does the question of the Negro's role in the South mean to him?"[8] Rubin and Jacobs dismiss Countée Cullen and James Weldon Johnson as merely topical and Richard Wright as a propagandist but find Ralph Ellison's treatment of his college experience in *Invisible Man* to be a worthy augur that African-Americans might play a role in the future of Southern letters. It would not be until a generation later and the publication of the comprehensive *History of Southern Literature* (1985), for which Rubin served as general editor, that African-American literature would begin to become visible in Southern literary studies.

Rubin might have had to rethink his assessment much earlier had he taken into consideration other African-Americans writers born in the South. But since these African-Americans often left the South, it is crucial to link the

Southern Renascence with the Harlem Renaissance.[9] Juxtaposing these two movements creates a more nuanced critical understanding of what might be meant by "Southern literature" and its relation to modernism.[10] For example, Eudora Welty's collection of stories *A Curtain of Green and Other Stories* (1941) details the manners of small town life in mid-Mississippi and remains a compelling example of Southern modernism. Welty's experiments with narrative voice and orality in the family chaos of "Why I Live at the P. O." is exceeded perhaps only by the way her beautician, Leota, in "Petrified Man" uses her storytelling powers to invent Mrs. Pike as a surrogate in a covert class antagonism with her customer Mrs. Fletcher. However, reading Welty's fiction against that of Zora Neale Hurston (1891–1960) and her depiction of the all-black community of Eatonsville, Florida, may provide a better purchase on what is modernist about both these writers.

Overcoming childhood poverty, Hurston graduated from Howard University and went on to Barnard where she studied with the leading anthropologist of the day, Franz Boas, which accounts for the ethnographic impulse behind much of her writing. "The Eatonville Anthology" (1926), a collection of fourteen sketches of people from this community that reveal their human foibles, is a first attempt at material that she would mine in her later writing, such as her ethnographic *Mules and Men* (1935) and her now canonical novel, *Their Eyes Were Watching God* (1938). These early sketches also point to why Hurston was frequently ostracized by other members of the Harlem Renaissance; by depicting sexual black women, black men who drink, gamble, and steal, and who have folk superstitions, Hurston was faulted for not following the approved Renaissance line of racial uplift.

If we base our judgment exclusively on the volume of scholarship produced annually, William Faulkner (1897–1963) remains the leading figure of Southern modernism, but the Faulkner one reads today is very different than the one read forty years ago. Far from the champion of the cohesive (white) Southern community that Southern critics in the Agrarian tradition construed, we read a Faulkner today whose fiction maps and critiques the complex coordinates of race, gender, and class in his fictional northern Mississippi Yoknapatawpha County. Well acquainted with European modernism (from *fin-de-siècle* decadents to Eliot and James Joyce), Faulkner blends formal experimentation and commitment to place that makes him an exemplar both of international modernism and regionalism. Capable of tour de force uses of stream-of-consciousness narration and radical perspectivism in *The Sound and the Fury* (1929) to tell the story of the decline of a once aristocratic family and in the tragi-comic funeral journey of *As I Lay Dying* (1930), Faulkner at his best explores the social contradictions growing out of race in the South. What Faulkner is acutely aware of is that, in a white community that wishes both to make absolute the distinctions between the races and to demonize black male sexuality, the races have already been mixed, almost exclusively by white men's abuse of black women. In *Light in August* (1932), Joe Christmas is the supremely alienated, ironic Christ figure; his racial identity unknowable, Joe is killed and castrated less for any crime than for his uncertain status in a world that would absolutize all differences of identity: racial (white/African-American), religious (saved/damned), political (Southern/Northern), sexual (hetero-homo); Christmas, however, disrupts these binaries by figuring the possibility of a repressed and mediating third term. *Absalom, Abaslom!* (1936) examines the poor white become wealthy planter, Thomas Sutpen, who denies his black son, Charles Bon; and *Go Down, Moses* (1942) tells the story of Isaac McCaslin's repudiation of his patrimony after learning of his grandfather's incestuous miscegenation with his slaves. What destroys whites in all of these narratives is their failure to acknowledge their literal and symbolic kinship with African-Americans.

While fifty years ago, novelists such as Thomas Wolfe (1900–1938) and Erskine Caldwell (1903–1987) were considered Faulkner's peers, the reputations of both have fallen sharply. Wolfe's thinly disguised autobiographical tale of Eugene Gant, his college education, and his alienation from his rural North Carolina hometown in *Look Homeward, Angel* (1929) may have made Wolfe the star of the Southern literary scene at the time, but his subsequent fiction repeatedly illustrates his failure to grow as a novelist. The posthumously published *You Can't Go Home Again* (1940) is more of collaboration than the work of Wolfe alone, edited as it was into existence by Edward Aswell at Harper's. Caldwell, best known for his sensational depictions of morally degenerate poor whites in *Tobacco Road* (1932) and *God's Little Acre* (1933), is another figure whose initial fame has now diminished.

An alternative path to a critical contextualizing of Faulkner's racialized South runs through the works of James Weldon Johnson (1871–1938), Jean Toomer (1894–1967), and Richard Wright (1908–1960). Born in Jackson, Florida, Johnson was the product of the black middle class. Educated at Atlanta University, he went on to study literature at Columbia. Written while Johnson was serving as US consul in Nicaragua, *The Autobiography of an Ex-Coloured Man* first appeared in 1912, but was republished with an introduction by the white patron of black art, Carl Van Vechten, at the height of the Harlem Renaissance in 1927. Because of his light skin, Johnson's protagonist is able to pass back and forth across the color line and reiterates the lesson of *Plessey v. Ferguson* (1896), namely, that white skin and a white legal identity were not one and the same. Travelling north and south in America and on tour with a wealthy patron in Europe, the ex-colored man, who at times is down on his luck and at other times is flush with cash, has seen all society from many angles and clearly articulates the rules of the society as he sees them – from the colorism and class difference within black communities to the prohibitions governing a "black" man's desire for a white woman. Moreover, the homoeroticism in the white patron's relation with the ex-colored man provides a useful point of entry for thinking about the homoerotic in Faulkner's depiction of Joe Christmas's relations with other men.

Jean Toomer, a light-skinned African-American, born of a planter father and the daughter of prominent African-American politician during Reconstruction in Louisiana, almost seems to live the life of Johnson's ex-colored man, moving as he does across the color line almost at will. Born in privilege in Washington, DC, the college-educated Toomer decides to explore his racial identity by taking a teaching position in Sparta, Georgia. The result of his sojourn to the segregated South is his formally experimental *Cane* (1923), which mixes narrative sketches, poetry, and drama. The work was enthusiastically reviewed but fell out of print before the end of the decade.

Faulkner often identified himself as a failed poet and his fiction is often noted for its lyric quality. The prose of Toomer's narrative sketches also has a pronounced lyricism. The second of these, "Becky," reverses the typical portrayal of miscegenation as the result of white men and black women and begins and ends with the same words: "Becky was the white woman who had two Negro sons. She's dead; they've gone away. The pines whisper to Jesus. The Bible flaps its leave with an aimless rustle on her mound."[11] With little revision, these words could be set as poetry and the repetition has the effect of a refrain reflecting the communally known story. What is striking about some of the poems that Toomer reprints in *Cane* is their uncanny kinship with Fugitive poetics. The sonnet "November Cotton Flower" and the quatrain structure of "Georgia Dusk" both combine classical form with a celebration of disappearing agrarian culture. What prevents Toomer from being an Afro-Agrarian, though, is the critique of Southern racism that appears in a poem such as "Portrait of Georgia," in which a woman's hair is "braided chestnut, coiled like a lyncher's rope" (29).

Richard Wright, the son of an illiterate sharecropper father who abandoned his family, often portrays what is largely missing from Faulkner's fiction, the direct representation of the African-American angle of vision. Although he leaves the South for Chicago in 1927, Wright produces stories in *Uncle Tom's Children* (1938) that represent elements of the South unavailable in Faulkner. In particular, Wright's "The Man Who Was Almost a Man" (1939), details the dawning political awareness of the son of a black sharecropper as he fails in his bid to be recognized by his community as a man; it was, of course, a goal destined to fail in a world where a white could hail any African-American male as "boy." Wright's story surely should be read against Faulkner's "Barn Burning," which tells of Sarty Snopes, the son of a white sharecropper, and his equally difficult attempt to negotiate Southern manhood in a charged atmosphere of class difference. Sarty's sense of justice causes him to identify with the landed gentry over his barn-burning father. On a novelistic canvas, Bigger Thomas, who becomes the embodiment of black criminality to the white community in *Native Son* (1940), serves as an intertextual commentary on Faulkner's Joe Christmas. As Philip Weinstein has noted, if Faulkner uses the racially invisible Christmas to focus "on his white culture's fear of racial contamination," Wright reverses the situation in Bigger, whose invisibility to white culture is his "all too visible black mask," in order to examine "the deformity his culture has undergone at the hands of a virulent white racism."[12]

Previously mentioned in relation to Eudora Welty, Zora Neale Hurston also provides another way to recontextualize Faulkner's place in Southern modernism. Hurston's retelling of the Moses story and its resonances for African-Americans in *Moses, Man of the Mountain* (1939) may be read against Faulkner's *Go Down, Moses*. Through her use of dialect, Hurston casts the Hebrews as rural African-Americans who come to believe that the princess's son, Moses, is actually a Jew. As Hurston makes clear from her introduction, the novel is an attempt to understand Moses in a pan-African context by mixing the biblical story with Haitian voodoo; from this syncretic perspective, Moses is himself a deity, perhaps the most important one to African-Americans.[13] Barbara Johnson has explored the issue of why both Hurston and Freud in *Moses and Monotheism* (1937) insist that Moses was an Egyptian,[14] an insistence that speaks also to Faulkner's *Go Down, Moses*, inviting one to add his novel to the intertextual matrix. Because he repudiates his patrimony, Isaac McCaslin undergoes a kind of figurative race change that renders him in old age as Uncle Ike; without property and a proper white identity as a "mister," Uncle Ike has become symbolically black. It is precisely in such an intertextual space of Freud, Hurston, and Faulkner that one sees how regionalism and modernism meet in an American context. Taking on one of the master narratives of western culture (Moses, the lawgiver), Hurston and Faulkner remap territory central to Freud, himself the author of one of modernism's master narratives (oedipal desire), in order to represent and critique racialized thinking. In doing so, they reveal themselves as practitioners of international modernism while remaining regionalist in precisely the minoritarian, politicized fashion that Fetterley and Pryse advocate.

Coda

The relation between regionalism and modernism in the future will likely become more rather than less pronounced, especially if American texts from the late-nineteenth and the first quarter of the twentieth century continue to be recovered under the rubric of regionalism. This work of recovery has helped expand the canon of American literature, first in the form of alternative canons (such as *American Women Regionalists*) and later in the reshaping of anthologies of American literature. In its most recent avatar, the sixth edition of the *Norton Anthology of American Literature* has expanded from two volumes to five (though, in fact, adding fewer than 250 additional pages of content). New material cannot simply be added, and at a certain point authors who have been in the anthology necessarily must be removed. While few will care that the current *NAAL* decanonizes Frank Norris, the relegation of William Dean Howells to the trash heap of history is not without a certain irony. While serving as editor of the *Atlantic Monthly* and subsequently, Howells, against the trend of his male colleagues, championed a number of regionalist women authors who might not even exist as textual traces to be recovered had he not helped them publish their fiction in the first place. Howells would probably care less about the current ranking of his fiction than the staying power of his poetics and surely would applaud the work of modernism's regionalists, from Cather and Glasgow to Faulkner and Hurston, for engaging and implicating the reader in ethically complex fictions.

Twenty years from now the difficulty I noted at the outset about reconciling regionalism and modernism may seem quaint as increasingly diverse regional writers are incorporated into the modern section of anthologies. The result doubtless will be that what we mean by the regional will be more fully a part of the modern, and our modernity will be unknowable apart from the various regions of identity represented by American literature.

NOTES

1. *American Women Regionalists, 1850–1910: A Norton Anthology*, ed. Judith Fetterley and Marjorie Pryse; Judith Fetterley and Marjorie Pryse, *Writing out of Place: Regionalism, Women, and American Literary Culture* (Urbana: University of Illinois Press, 2003); Kate McCullough, *Regions of Identity: The Construction of America in Women's Fiction, 1885–1914* (Stanford University Press, 1999); Kate McCullough, *Breaking Boundaries: New Perspectives on Women's Regional Writing*, ed. Sherrie A. Inness and Diana Royer (Iowa City: University of Iowa Press, 1997).
2. Deleuze and Guattari, *Kafka: Toward a Minor Literature*, tr. Dana Polan (Minneapolis: University of Minnesota Press, 1987), 17.

3. Sui Sin Far, Mrs. *Spring Fragrance and Other Writings*, ed. Amy Ling and Annette White-Parks (Urbana: University of Illinois Press, 1995).

4. "Introduction" to Part 1, Mrs. *Spring Fragrance* 12–13.

5. Mencken, "The Sahara of the Bozart," *The Literature of the American South*, ed. William L. Andrews, *et al.* (New York: W. W. Norton, 1998), 371.

6. John Crowe Ransom, "Foreword," *The Fugitive* 1 (1922), 2.

7. For a fuller treatment of the role of Southern literature anthologies and collections, see chapter 3 of Richard Gray's *Southern Aberrations* (Baton Rogue: Louisiana State University Press, 2000) and chapter 4 of Michael Kreyling's *Inventing Southern Literature* (Jackson: University Press of Mississippi, 1998).

8. Rubin and Jacobs, "Introduction: Southern Writing and the Changing South," *South: Modern Southern Literature in its Cultural Setting*, ed. Louis D. Rubin, Jr. and Robert D. Jacobs (Garden City, NY: Doubleday, 1961), 18.

9. Thadious Davis begins this task in her essay, "Southern Standard-Bearers in the New Negro Renaissance" in *The History of Southern Literature*, ed. Louise D. Rubin, Jr., *et al.* (Baton Rouge: Louisiana State University Press, 1985), 291–313.

10. Such a linkage is made much easier by the publication of *The Literature of the American South: A Norton Anthology*, ed. William L. Andrews, *et al.* (New York: W. W. Norton, 1998), which is the most comprehensive collection of texts by black and white Southerners to date.

11. Toomer, *Cane*, Norton Critical Edition, ed. Darwin T. Turner (New York: Norton, 1988), 7, 9.

12. Weinstein, "Postmodern Intimations: Musing on Invisibility: William Faulkner, Richard Wright, and Ralph Ellison," in *Faulkner and Postmodernism*, ed. John N. Duvall and Ann J. Abadie (Jackson: University of Mississippi Press, 2002), 26.

13. Hurston, "Introduction," *Moses, Man of the Mountain* (Philadelphia: J. P. Lippincott, 1939), 7–8.

14. Johnson, "Moses and Intertextuality: Sigmund Freud, Zora Neale Hurston, and the Bible" in *Poetics of the Americas*, ed. Bainard Cowan and Jefferson Humphries (Baton Rouge: Louisiana State University Press, 1997), 15–30.

11

PAULA RABINOWITZ

Social representations within American modernism

Measuring density

Unreal city . . .
A crowd flowed over London Bridge, so many . . .
Vienna London
Unreal

T. S. Eliot,
The Waste Land

"It's curious," she said. "After the war New York . . . Nobody can keep away from it."   John Dos Passos, *Nineteen Nineteen*

A man is indeed a city, and for the poet there are no ideas but in things.
William Carlos Williams, *Paterson*

We have the bright-lights, the bridges, the Yankee Stadium . . .
Joy Davidman, *Twentieth-Century Americanism*

The modern city, as astute critic and vast walker of European cities Walter Benjamin noted, seems at once to epitomize and refute Marx's famous description of Capitalism: All that is solid melts into air.[1] A location understood at its roots to be solidly constructed of bricks and mortar, of concrete and steel, it is full of the ephemera of paper handbills flying down a windy alley, discarded trash left on a street corner, myriad faces glimpsed momentarily in the flow of the crowd: "The apparition of these faces in the crowd; / Petals on a wet, black bough."[2] The city as site of modern life is a cliché by now. In America, modernism was always an afterthought. So, in *Nineteen Nineteen*, when ace pilot, Lieutenant Charley Anderson, returns from the war to New York, he looks up Paul and Eveline Johnson in their Greenwich Village apartment because they are the only people he knows in the city after meeting on a ship crossing over, flirting, and drinking together in the mad joy of armistice. "'My brother wanted me to go into a Ford agency with him out in the Twin Cities, but how can you keep them down on the farm after they've seen Paree?' 'But New York's the capital now,'"³ replies his hostess.

But why is this so?

Modern life is characterized by movement, by mass movement; by multiplication and multiplicity. What a city affords its inhabitants and visitors, its players and its bystanders, is a view of others, of the rich texture of social experience. The field of sociology, first among the new professions to institutionalize (the American Social Science Association was formed in 1865) was spawning a whole army of professionals – social workers, economists, historians, folklorists, political scientists, criminologists – who were studying and more significantly attempting "to set apart, regulate, and contain" the face of the American city.⁴ This new force – millions of immigrants and migrants inhabiting the same territory – unsettled the class and ethnic geography of America. While the city was segregated – Jacob Riis provided a detailed mapping of the class, racial, and ethnic boundaries enclosing where the other half lived – throngs moved throughout it, under its streets and above them on trains, subways, trolleys, and along their sidewalks on foot. Maids and deliverymen left one sector for another, sales girls and shoppers spread from residential neighborhoods to commercial areas.

This density and mobility of capital, of people, gave rise to new forms of viewing human culture. For Gustave Le Bon, writing in 1896 of the militant French working class, the Crowd presented a spectre of violence and anarchy.⁵ (Recently uncovered files indicate that Pablo Picasso was denied French citizenship during the 1930s because his first Paris roommate (1909) was a known anarchist.⁶) This newly (dis)organized mass offered inspiration for generations of artists – beginning with Charles Baudelaire of course. By the 1930s, New York painter Reginald Marsh was extolling the "crowds – crowds of people in all directions, in all positions, without clothing, moving" he found at Coney Island Beach, which became the subject of many of his etchings and paintings.⁷ While Marsh's sprawling enmeshed figures owe much to Michelangelo's *Last Judgment* in the Sistine Chapel, it also presented an antidote to the angular verticality of the cityscape. Bodies overflow; entwined, they become solid objects. The density of bodies found in public places – streets, subways, beaches, boardwalks, sweatshops – mimics the incursion of stuff into the private homes of the middle class. The city itself becomes a giant display case for the various figure(in)es collected there.

This dense mass interrupts the orderly structures of bridges, skyscrapers, sidewalks, the steel and concrete that gives the city its heavily geometric carapace. It swarms, a mass, the fear is that the collectivity of bodies is all encompassing and endlessly the same; yet the features of each body might be discernibly differentiated, though not necessarily through the usual means. Clothing, for instance, may not be an accurate marker of social distinction – consumerism and the attendant mass media of magazines and movies made fashion, and fashion sense, widely available. John Dos Passos's three-volume saga of modern times, *U. S. A.*, details how this density transformed every aspect of American life. His trilogy, written during the 1930s, retrospectively surveys the exuberant yet deadly histories – interior and exterior – of people and events contributing to this. The very heft of the work – its density – weaves several plotlines, many characters, multiple voices, varying styles that combine journalism, stream-of-consciousness memoir, dime novels, and newsreel collages of urban detritus: headlines, song lyrics, advertising slogans, "But mostly U. S. A. is the speech of the people" (*U. S. A.*, vii).

He begins his trilogy on the streets – the emptying streets of a crowded city, its varied citizens hurrying along, unremarkable in their dailiness, achieving a sort of poetic highlight in the accumulating catalogue:

> The young man walks by himself searching through the crowd with greedy eyes, greedy ears taut to hear, by himself, alone.
>
> The streets are empty. People have packed into subways, climbed into street-cars and buses; in the stations they've scampered for suburban trains; they've filtered into lodgings and tenements, gone up in elevators into apartment-houses. In a showwindow two sallow windowdressers in their shirtsleeves are bringing out a dummy girl in a red evening dress, at a corner welders in masks lean into sheets of blue flame repairing a cartrack, a few drunk bums shamble along, a sad streetwalker fidgets under an arclight. (v)

Dos Passos's evocation of Vag's reverie owes much to cinematic conventions of setting the city scene. The solidity of the city, its density, is matched by its fluidity – by the constant movement of bodies and machinery along its arteries. The crowd is a formation, at once dense and mobile; mobility becomes the aesthetic counterpart to the density of the urban throng. Its form is also modern – the cinema – in which the literally moving images track the physical movement of objects through space. By the 1930s, the image of the American city within cinema was a firmly established cliché: Muriel Rukeyser, for instance, invokes it in her poem "Movie," "Here is a city, she writes, "here the village grows / Here are the rich men standing rows on rows, / But the crowd seeps behind the cowboy the lover the king / Past the constructed sets America rises / . . . in a wave of a mass."[8]

The cinema at once called forth the masses – crowds lined up to see representations of crowds in the spectacles offered by D. W. Griffith's (among many other directors) one and two-reelers – and depicted them. For *Orphans of the Storm*, Griffith employed the entire population of Mamaroneck, New York, where he shot the film, as the cast of thousands.[9]

The framed image of anonymous masses owes much to one of the earliest modern novels of New York: William Dean Howells's *A Hazard of New Fortune*. His 1890 depiction of middle-class urban househunting, as the Marches search in vain for the ideal flat to move their two children, two servants and themselves into from Boston, established the cinematic trope of visualizing the crowd by focusing momentarily on distinctive faces passing by. Riding uptown on the Third Avenue L, the Marches note "the theatre . . . what drama" of the isolated yet massed scenes they are passing – "the fleeing intimacy you formed with people in second and third floor interiors." Framed by their windowsills, this panoramic vista of the crowd anticipates the archetypal establishing shot of urban cinema. Instead of the picture moving, the elevated train shuttles along, passing: "a family party of workfolk at a late tea, some of the men in their shirt-sleeves; a woman sewing by a lamp; a mother laying her child in its cradle; a man with his head fallen on his hands upon a table; a girl and her lover leaning over the window-sill together."[10] This sensation of fleeting intimacy with others, of the spectacle private life offered, unwittingly, for public display, but done so on the run, also established the element of documentary representation of the social – through fiction, poetry, film, and photography – that is one significant element of American modernism.[11]

D. W. Griffith's *Musketeers of Pig Alley* (1912) features Lillian Gish radiantly transcending the streets of New York. Her key-lit face is never in danger of being engulfed by the busy mob crowding the Lower East Side streets. It teems with immigrants, described in vivid terms by Jacob Riis: "picturesque, if not very tidy, element" (The Italians); "the scrupulous neatness" and "crafty submissiveness" of "the Chinaman" – it makes sense his business includes laundries; the "intensely bald and materialistic" Jews with their "native combativeness" crowding the tenements of the East Side, stuffing dozens into rooms filled with sweatshop sewing machines; the "imperturbable cheerfulness" of the Negro; the "vagabond Street Arabs" and on and on. Riis found all these types readily recognizable in the few square blocks he documented between the 1870s and 1890s for the New York *Tribune* in a series of articles and photographs of tenement life.[12] The Other Half represented the masses of new immigrants flooding the city between the Gilded Age and the Roaring Twenties when the Immigration Act of 1924 curtailed most foreign immigration. Black migration into New York continued as the KKK increased its violence after World War I sparked the Great Migration of African-Americans. Riis's characterizations of the social types swarming through downtown alleys and bends – Anarchist Bohemians, feisty Irish, orderly Germans, living cheek-by-jowl with the less fortunate (and darker) newcomers noted above – were meant to spark sympathy and outrage. They were a primary impetus for the New York Tenement Commission's research into housing conditions. But they relied on stereotypes, even as they sought to debunk them, to convey a sense of the massive influx of aliens onto the streets of New York. These racial types were immediately recognizable from "their unmistakable physiognomy." Facial markers denoted racial differences.

On a more intimate level, Gertrude Stein's *Three Lives* (1909) had also isolated fragmentary bits of lives often overlooked – immigrant servant girls or their daughters, like the Good Anna of "solid lower middle-class south german stock," and the German cousin, Gentle Lena, or wandering girls, like "a graceful, pale yellow, intelligent, attractive negress," Melanctha.[13] These dreamy young women living in a second-rate working-class city, Bridgeport, Connecticut, avoided crowds. For the most part, their activities were domesticated, their ambitions limited, their pleasures rare. Stein's intimate portrait of the mundane lives of working women, however, also invoked cinema: montage and close-up. Her cubist biographies cut up and reassembled stock figures, much as the quick-cut montages of urban scenery glimpsed from the sidewalks or the L had within cityscapes. *Three Lives*, like Edgar Lee Masters's *Spoon River Anthology* and novels and short stories from Sherwood Anderson and Sinclair Lewis (in the Midwest) and William Faulkner (in the South) through Ann Petry's *Country Place* (also set in a small-sized city on the Connecticut shore), limned the outlines of America's claustrophobic heartland as a dark and sinister zone of social disarray. Where social chaos was openly visible on the teeming city streets, rural America, with its drowsy small towns and its mid-sized cities built around a single industry (Howells's newspaper syndicator, Fulkerson, details the rise of Moffitt, Indiana, as a natural gas center enriching the Pennsylvania Dutch farmer, Dryfoos [who promptly hightails it for New York society where he bankrolls March's magazine]), masked class and ethnic and racial tensions within mostly impenetrable homes and isolated landscapes. It was not the sidewalks that seethed but the lone merchant or farm wife trapped by four walls. Still, despite rejecting Howells's realist style, Stein maintains a camera eye; if the Marches observe a panorama of New York as tracking shot, Stein's *Three Lives* are held in close-up. Trapped and immobile, they are dense with the accrual of repetitious detail.

How did the modern – the technological changes in transportation and communication and the social upheavals wrought by capitalism, revolution, and war – translate into American modernism? Modernism in America links a demotic urge to represent the plebeian, the everyday, the regular Joe, through experiments with diverse forms – realist, naturalist, cubist, lyric – in various media – prose, poetry, photography, film. Often, these two aspects – the social and the experimental – appear opposed as if they inhabited different eras, different locations. To some extent, this is so. Experimentation seems to be tied to expatriates shedding an insular and philistine nation for the sophistication of Europe, while the indigenous American culture exudes either a folksy regionalism or is tainted by industrial mass production. But then, how does one explain Stein's insistent use of the American vernacular? Or Fitzgerald's building his anti-ode to American self-fashioning around the automobile trips back and forth between Manhattan and East Egg? Or even Eliot's return to the pubs of East End as respite from the walking dead flowing toward King William Street?

The American modernist afterthought, freed from the need to be original, could be redundant; it could be vernacular; it could be pulpy, embracing Whitman's ecstatic catalogues and Dickinson's wacky prosody as it accommodated *Main Street*, Fordism, Hollywood, and the New Deal.[14] It could constantly focus and refocus its lens on the variety of contending social and economic forces in a nation as rich and large as the United States. One might note, from opposite poles, that between 1911 and 1917, the most important radical magazine was called simply, *The Masses*, and the most significant, albeit racist, film of the silent era was titled, *Birth of a Nation*; nothing was less than grand scale. After the devastation of Europe during World War I, the US ascended unquestionably to economic power and political hegemony. The triumphalism, however, was always tempered among writers and artists by the knowledge that violence – slavery, extermination, imperial wars, land annexation – was buried just below the surface of the nation pledged to make the world safe for democracy.

Dos Passos's anatomy of the nation presents an anthology from the grave of late-nineteenth-century American types becoming early twentieth-century American failures. His web of fictional and historical characters traces paths from hopeful restlessness and imagination to death, disease, madness, suicide, bloated alcoholic disaffection, or wizened barren loneliness. The terrible impact of World War I and American imperialism in Asia and Latin America rips the heart out of the naive enthusiasms of these sons of farmers, workers, and small-time businessmen. Dos Passos's characters are the last generation of Northern European immigrants – Swedes, Germans, Irishmen, and Scots – whose forbears made up the white Republic. The spectacle of capitalism – with its public relations, celebrity, advertising, and commodities – and war – with its weapons of mass death and mutilation, and overheated production – dislodged the sleepy remains of postbellum

Jim Crow isolationism. Viewed from the midst of the 1930s – with the Depression and Fascism the ultimate products of all this entrepreneurial energy by young men and women seeking to escape the dullness of America's heartland – the years of Progressivism and the Jazz Age appeared as a heady distraction. The form of *U. S. A.* forged a methodology that revealed the volume and velocity – the density and mobility – of America's pulp modernity.

In the 1890s, when the population of New York City was nearly two million, the middle-class Marches observe the newly visible working class from the L; by the 1930s, when the city's population had more than tripled, middle-class writers and artists were joining them on the streets, entering their homes. Thus Vag begins *U. S. A.* walking the streets. Charlie Chaplin's Tramp in *Modern Times* (1936), wandering the empty streets after losing his assembly-line job, finds himself engulfed by a mass of striking workers, then hauled off to jail as its leader because he has picked up a red flag fallen from an overloaded truck passing by. Joy Davidman's epic poem, "Twentieth-Century Americanism" (the campaign slogan used by the Communist Party's 1936 presidential candidate, Earl Browder), moves into the rooms the Marches had merely watched: "We have the radio . . . // Beside the bedroom window long trains ride, / the harsh lights come and go outside."[15] So, too, does Muriel Rukeyser's "Boy With His Hair Cut Short." "[O]n this twentieth-century evening. / The L passes." What begins as an observation of the scene: "He sits at the table . . . exposed, / watching the drugstore sign," quickly moves into his private exchange with his sister and "her cheap shears," as she prepares him for another futile Monday morning of job hunting.[16] Rukeyser's speaker has more than a fleeting intimacy with the boy; he is not simply on display but possesses a rich subjectivity, alive to the familiar sights and sounds of his surroundings.

Erasing the space between social others – the middle class from the poor and working class, Jews from Gentiles, blacks and whites from each other – became an aesthetic as well as a political imperative by the 1930s. During the last years of the Depression, for instance, photographer Walker Evans would ride the subways of New York, his camera hidden inside his jacket and shoot the unwitting passengers nodding off after a long night out, exhausted from a day at work, or worse another day without it. But, in 1936, when he and writer James Agee were sent on assignment by *Fortune* magazine (Evans was on loan from Roy Stryker's Farm Security Administration) to Hale County, Alabama, to report on the lives of tenant farmers, he had allowed his subjects to pose themselves. He and Agee were living with the families who would eventually people their "postmodern realist" work of "cubist sociology," as T. V. Reed calls *Let Us Now Praise Famous Men.* This connection, this identification, and its troubling swill of voyeurism and

Figure 11.1 Walker Evans, 1936, movie poster, vicinity of Moundsville, Alabama.

Figure 11.2 Walker Evans, 1936, Fireplace and wall detail in bedroom of
Floyd Burroughs' cabin.

sentimentality involved in cross-class representation became a crucial facet of the book's form and content.[17] Documentary, no matter how experimental its narrative resort to interiority, deconstruction, and self-disclosure, could never fully escape the invasive quality it had had since Jacob Riis rushed into the tenement homes of astonished workers, exploding mercury flashes like gunshot, and capturing poverty's victims unawares. Privacy itself had become public; photography assured that there could be no haven from the crowds of the city – even rural shacks hidden in the Alabama cotton fields were decorated with torn out advertisements from mass-marketed magazines.

The density of *Let Us Now Praise Famous Men* – its many-layered text including photographs and prose, newspaper clippings and chore lists, acute observation and wild fantasy – owed much to the cut-up and repieced narrative form of *U. S. A.* (no matter how much Agee despised proletarian fiction). But it was primarily an unconscious heir to the signal work of modern(ist) American social representation: W. E. B. Du Bois's 1903 *Souls of Black Folk*. Du Bois invented a new form of sociology that could account for African-Americans (but clearly any invisible group – poor and rural) as a culture – black folk – possessing a deep interiority and symbolic system – souls; one that listened attentively to the rhythms of speech, "the soundings," as Houston Baker calls it, of daily life, church gatherings, work, and leisure in their "sorrow songs." Putting himself at the center of political, sociological, and economic data – data that could not accurately account for his life experiences, however – Du Bois reversed the migratory path North to freedom to return South as a teacher in rural black schools. His dinners, his rides in Jim Crow cars, his casual exchanges with students and their families, his memories and finally his anguished acceptance of his son's death – a death that will save the boy from the humiliations his father had suffered when the "Veil of Race" descended on him at a white girl's birthday party, producing thereafter "ever a twoness" – contribute to its complex form. Du Bois takes on icons – challenging Booker T. Washington's accommodation to Jim Crow, celebrating unsung heroes like Alexander Crummell – to expound his theories of education and desire that linked African-American literacy to the voice. Alive to the sounds of black folk, and to his own reveries stirred by the transportation of one's own memory, of a night train wailing through a Southern landscape, of the books one has read, *Souls* challenged modern America to cross its color line. Declaring race the "problem of the twentieth century," it revamped its expression, folding various genres and media – music, autobiography, fiction, scholarship among them – into a new force for social change. Like so many modernists concerned with representing the complex social fabric of America, he was author and activist – at once pursuing scholarship, writing fiction, founding the NAACP, editing *The Crisis*, teaching, lecturing, agitating.

Reading mobility

So the 20th Century – so
whizzed the Limited – roared by and left
Hart Crane, "The Bridge"

Answer motion with motion . . .
go answering answering FLY
Muriel Rukeyser, "Theory of Flight"

In early November 1936, a fifteen-year-old girl, daughter of Russian-Jewish immigrants, found a copy of the newly published first issue of *Life* magazine. Its cover story, by noted photographer Margaret Bourke-White, one of the highest paid women professionals in Depression America, featured a dramatic image of the Fort Peck Dam, a beautiful modernist structure of gleaming white poured concrete gently arching across the wide Missouri River, the first of the massive Western hydroelectric projects initiated by FDR. Bourke-White's story tracked the rise of one of the eighteen company boom towns, "New Deal, Montana," grown up to accommodate the workers and their families, but also the service economy required for the survival of any community – bars, laundries, hotels, brothels. Perhaps Esther Bubley read this article in the local Superior, Wisconsin, or Duluth, Minnesota, Public Library; perhaps she perused it at a drugstore newsstand while wandering the hillside community of Duluth's "Little Jerusalem," the Eastern European Jewish ghetto in the hills above Lake Superior, like the one her mother Ida ran.[18] In any case, she attributes its inspiration to her desire to emulate Bourke-White's profession.[19]

Bubley's photographs of 1940s women on the loose in bars, hotels, bus stations, and street corners situate these mobile modern women within a disturbing, because typical, American landscape. They circulate within a system of security linking industry and government – a war economy fully realizing the capacities of capital to regroup after the devastation of worldwide depression.[20] Bubley's work comes after the usual date demarking the end of modernism. However, her work suggests new paradigms for understanding social representation and modernism, bringing new personalities to the surface, revising its outlines. Bubley was inspired to pursue her thoroughly modern(ist) art form, photography, through her circuitry within a system of mass circulation – itself a thoroughly modern process requiring technologies to meld image and print seamlessly and cheaply devised by European modernist artists such as Futurists, Dadaists, and Surrealists and first used to broad effect in German worker's magazines of the late 1920s and early 1930s. Henry Luce's *Life* magazine brought these modernist sensibilities to a massive American middle class, "Middletown-in-transition," by featuring a cover of that most modernist icon, a massive poured concrete dam,[21] thus marrying aesthetic, industrial, and governmental icons and marketing them through a mass-mediated form meant to sell the very idea of modern circulation. People and magazines circulated in this circular process, wherein American modernity – in the form of mass culture, industrial capitalism and the liberal corporate state – were celebrated, produced, and consumed through a mass-mediated, middle-brow modernism. Bubley's images extended into the 1940s a process of "making a New Deal," as Lizabeth Cohen calls it, begun during the 1920s and radically extended during the 1930s in the US by mass culture, consumerism and the New Deal.

The mobile female, a working woman, is a paradoxical figure. At once thoroughly modern, she is also a throwback. The woman on the move could be nothing more than the streetwalker, practitioner of the "oldest profession," or she might be a farm girl sent to the mills of Lancashire or Lowell, or she might be a newly emancipated woman seeking thrills or escape from stifling family life. This working woman, shopgirl, office worker, shopper was the subject of the Fourteenth Street School of American Scene painters – Raphael Soyer, Isabel Bishop, Reginald Marsh, Kenneth Hayes Miller – whose studios surrounded Union Square. They found in the massing groups of working-class women crowding the "people's Fifth Avenue" shops on Fourteenth Street inspiration for an American vernacular genre painting that speculated on and imaged the democratization of consumerism and the New Woman within the working class.[22] These artists, the offspring of the Ashcan School of American urban painters, saw in the masses swarming through the Fourteenth Street subway station or cramming themselves against shop windows, or crowding to hear soapbox orators during lunch hour in Union Square, an enormous new energy.

Women were literally bursting the seams of their city. Swelling breasts and curving hips and bellies overpower the gaunt working men whom they elbow aside for a seat or to get a better view. These working girls seem to relish their ability to walk seven abreast and control the pedestrian traffic. They represent a new image of work for women – an exuberant sense of power not seen in the abject images of sweatshop cash girls Jacob Riis had found only a few years earlier, only a few blocks south. Much as painter Georgia O'Keeffe reworked the desiccated bones T. S. Eliot found amid the wasteland by playfully adding a floral corsage to a cow skull – as if the dried bones were a bleached version of Billie Holiday's sleek black hair framed by white camellias – these bold women recast the image of the girl on the street from pitiful debased creature to forceful desiring and desirable actor.

Bubley's bar girls and the Fourteenth Street working girls would seem a far cry from the shy, gingham-dressed young women Du Bois or Agee and Evans found in the rural South. These mobile women were a distinctively urban phenomenon; yet the daughters of sharecroppers and tenant farmers also circulated, albeit vicariously, in consumer culture. Josie, Du Bois's one-time student tucked away in a Tennessee hollow, yearns for "Progress" over the hill in Alexandria and Nashville; Du Bois reaches her home after a long walk across the countryside from the Jim Crow train that brought him South. Jean Toomer's 1923 multi-genre narrative, *Cane*, also is indebted to the form and content of *Souls*, mixing poetry, drama, sketch, novella, into a picture of class and color that moves between Northern cities and rural Georgia. Toomer's cut-up and knitted-together fragments focus on the seemingly immobile women found living nearby the railroad tracks in smalltown Georgia or walking the streets of Chicago's Southside or Washington's Southeast. They are the women with whom a traveling man – white or black – might meet and enjoy a night of lovemaking. Those in Georgia seem stuck in a dreamy past that locks them into familiar roles of mother, whore, virgin. But even they dare to desire and sometimes do escape. The insistent train whistle calls everyone north to "Seventh Street . . . a bastard of Prohibition and the War. A crude-bonded, soft-skinned wedge of nigger life breathing its loafer air, jazz songs and love, thrusting unconscious rhythms, black reddish blood into the white and whitewashed wood of Washington." *Cane*'s social typology distinguishes among more than rural and urban womanhood; its eye is on the subtleties of color differences within the "mass-heart of black people," where "Within this black hive to-night/ There swarm a million bees." Dorris, a dancer at the Howard Theatre, considers an affair with its director: "I'd get a pair of silk stockings out of it. Red silk. I got purple."[23] Finding a style that suggested the languor of Southern summers and the jagged intensity of big-city Saturday nights, Toomer imagined a form that could convey social fragmentation.

Both Toomer and Du Bois travel a circuit South then North then back again, leaving the city to look for the future in the past. But as Du Bois finds when he returns ten years after teaching Josie in the tiny schoolhouse, the trajectory of modernism – out of the domestic embrace into the violence of the streets – can be fatal. Dos Passos and Agee reiterated this dirge. Yet the women who crowded the streets relished their dangers anyway. These dangers were part of the extreme mix of the crowd, the mass. Its racial divisions appeared visible on the surface of skin colors Toomer lingers over and were etched onto the streets of the ghettos segregating the city; but they were hardly stable. A well-dressed man or woman might come from anywhere and slide into most places. As immigrants became white, detectable ethnic differences became increasingly clouded; part of the anxiety and exhilaration of the crowd was in this fluidity. As such, America swallowed up modernism, which, in turn, worked to produce it and make legible its inherent modernity.

One might never be sure who a person passing by on the street actually was: perhaps those elegant white women sipping iced tea, as Irene Redfield and Clare Bellew do in Nella Larsen's *Passing*, were actually "colored"; perhaps that woman you eyed was a man; maybe that man checking you out was a woman. After the 1901 revelation that Murray Hall, politician and New York poker-playing, beer-swilling gadfly of Tammany Hall, was actually a woman, who "fooled many shrewd men," according to the *New York Times*, hardly a year went by without some urban tabloid exposé of a prominent woman passing. Pictures of Murray Hall or Mary Walker or Cora Anderson, or any number of passing women, show them attired in the debonaire clothing of the period – top hats and cloaks, and later, bowlers and three-pieced suits.[24] Anzia Yezierska's Sonya Vrunsky, "Salome of the Tenements," like Dorris and Clare, is drawn to men with the goods; she too wants to pass from one class to another. Restless and available, urban men, unmoored from the constraints of domesticity, appeal to these ambitious women who desire them. America became a nation passing.[25] The erotic conventions of cross-class, cross-sex and cross-ethnic relations reveal the dangerous yet promising lure of urban spaces for desire, democracy, and criminality. They unsettle the myth of the American dream.

Yezierska's Salome, like Dreiser's Sister Carrie, refashioned herself by carefully observing the men and women she passed on the streets to get a series of men to do her bidding. In her quest for riches, impoverished Russian-Jewish reporter, Sonya Vrunsky, succeeds in charming first one, then another hard-nosed ghetto businessman into giving her clothes, a new paint job for her tenement room, and money to redecorate it. Yezierska's novel updates Shaw's *Pygmalion*: with the right outfit a girl can go anywhere, transform herself, and leave her past behind.

Indeed, "a temptress . . . this siren," Sonya leaves behind a trail of men, each with a past that connects her to him, as she quests for money, refinement, beauty, and a better life.[26] Her desire appears tempered by her sense of class injustice and her efforts to work on behalf of the poor. "Flight is intolerable contradiction," in Muriel Rukeyser's words.[27] In this, she resembles the gangsters who would populate Warner Brothers films a decade later. Like Paul Muni's Tony Camonte, aka Scarface, or Edward G. Robinson's Little

Caesar, Rico, or James Cagney's Tommy Powers – The Public Enemy – Sonya rises out of the ghetto through both extraordinary will power and careful planning. Her ultimate return to its vital source via marriage to Jacques Hollins, Fifth Avenue designer for New York's WASP elite whom Sonya knew back when he was Jaky Solomon, is an act of self-fashioning and sheer will as well; it occurs because of the slights and discrimination thrown in their paths. These "city boys," as Robert Sklar calls them, gangsters – immigrant men set loose on American soil – are the siblings of Sonya and her fatal sisters. They organize themselves into mutant forms of capitalism to control their neighborhoods and cities.

In *King Kong*, New York (and the newly erected Empire State Building) is terrorized by the captive animal from abroad. Kong's lustful desire for Fay Wray recalled antebellum (and recently revived Ku Klux Klan, note the repetitive Ks) hysteria of miscegenation between African men and white women. Giant gorillas signified racial anxiety; urban gangsters embodied ethnic contamination as their outfits – monstrous replicas of legit business (albeit dressed with too big lapels, too white spats) – spread across the city streets. The unleashed man who dresses (and ultimately, of course, undresses) the woman, the sensitive brute (even King Kong is careful with Fay Wray, caressing her and sniffing her like the lover he truly is) is essential for the construction of the New American (working) woman, a modern woman, often one who is rising from her poverty, her immigrant status, to achieve a new spectacular publicity. She is on display: Fay Wray hangs over the entire New York City skyline; Sonya rules the Lower East Side. She can control these complex and contradictory spaces because she is properly attired. Like the traffic lights and neon signs, she stands out on the street corner.

Critics Elizabeth Wilson and Giuliana Bruno have discussed the differences between Benjamin's male *flaneur*, who possesses the modern city by interrupting its hustle and bustle to become an object of contemplation as he observes the passing sight of the city's streets and arcades, and his non-corresponding female streetwalker.[28] For Benjamin, the arcade, the structure designed to facilitate shopping by encouraging pedestrian window-shopping, made of glass and steel, at once fragile and breakable, and sturdy and permanent, is the precursor of the modern glass and steel skyscraper whose exterior walls of glass serve as both decoration and structure. Exteriority and the interior rapidly exchange places: glass architecture "appears in the context of utopia" because its transparent surface appearance provides its strength.[29] In the arcade, records Benjamin, the "young and beautiful woman under glass was called 'the Absolute'" (33). Women remained immobile – as merchandise, as shopgirls, as manikins – and men strolled regarding them. Women appear frozen, under glass, interruptions of the male flow within the arcade – a space of commerce, of commodities; but soon they, too, move through them as shoppers. They take refuge from the street under this protective glass. It sheathes them, like couture. Paris fashion remakes both Jaky/Jacques and Sonya into denizens of Fifth Avenue, alienated from its wealth and upper-crust WASP mores, but residents nonetheless. He owns a shop; she moves into a townhouse. Clothing enables this shift in ethnicity and class, encourages this passing, the social mobility the city makes it possible by hiding origins.[30]

Meridel Le Sueur's 1939 pulpy novel *The Girl* traces the developing class consciousness of the anonymous waitress through connections to her co-worker and roommate, Clara, her boss, Belle, and the community organizer, Amelia. The unnamed girl's sexual infatuation with a young gangster, his death, and her pregnancy are all steps in her female *Bildungsroman*; but it is walking the streets with Clara and turning a trick with the gang boss, Ganz, that cements her knowledge about the political economy of sex under capitalism. Le Sueur turned to a pulp fiction genre – the gangster tale – to critique this sexual economy. The gun moll, usually depicted in gangster films as a trophy, an appendage to the rising "city boy" gangster, decenters the narrative of capital accumulation. Mother and criminal, the originally naive Girl transforms, like Elizabeth Gurley Flynn, into a "Rebel Girl."

Classical Marxism analyses the prostitute as an abject figure to be eliminated by bringing her into productive social work (through a social worker); her recurrent invocation – the woman on the street – crystallizes the contradictions of modernity for the female working-class body, which is at once a (re)productive and consumptive (all puns intended) body. Walter Benjamin intuited the prostitute's power to undo masculine visions of fraternity; she figures as the only female presence in his monumental *Arcades Project*. Woman may work, even shop, in the Arcades, but in all cases those are merely guises; they are always for sale. Perhaps Benjamin's archetype for urban modernity, the *flaneur*, is nothing more than a wannabe whore. Le Sueur envisions woman on the street as a new form of collectivity, a maternal mass, that, like Virginia Woolf's modernist woman writer, sets up a printing press amid its communal squat in a St. Paul warehouse to organize daughters and mothers.

Esther Bubley worked within a state bureaucracy designed first to document and so ameliorate the ravaged lives of ordinary Americans caught by the Depression then to record their changing situations during the war. Her photographs of the young women inhabiting Washington, DC, rooming houses detailed the ways in which a new kind of home life developed for single women. These women, many of them young Jewish girls freed from the restrictions of their immigrant parents' homes, living together in

Figure 11.3 Esther Bubley, 1943, Washington, DC. Girls window-shopping.

Figure 11.4 Esther Bubley, Washington, DC. A radio is company for this girl in her boarding house room.

Figure 11.5 Esther Bubley 1943, Washington, DC. Girl sitting alone in the Sea Grill, a bar and restaurant, waiting for a pickup. "I come in here pretty often, sometimes alone, mostly with another girl, we drink beer, and talk, and of course we keep our eyes open – you'd be surprised at how often nice, lonesome soldiers ask Sue, the waitress, to introduce them to us."

restricted dormitories, sit together or alone, often framed within doorways or windows like manikins in department store windows or *femme fatales* in Hollywood movies, poised to act. They lean on a dresser, engrossed in a radio show; they lounge on a bed flipping through a magazine; they clot a stairway waiting to use a pay phone. Each solitary yet connected to the modern nation through her work as a government employee or a switchboard operator at Western Union and through her leisurely consumption and use of the tools of mass communication – mass media and telephones. The women form an odd community of rootless cosmopolitans (as Stalin called Jews). Bubley found an endless parade of lonely women aggressively waiting for the few servicemen also on the prowl. One photograph, "Girl sitting alone in the Sea Grill, a bar and restaurant waiting for a pickup," provides all the iconic totems of the urban woman on the make. She sits, like Toulouse-Lautrec's absinthe drinkers, at a table, a half-finished beer before her, cigarette in hand, clutch purse beside her; bereft but determined, she waits for action. Framed by the large picture window covered by half-opened Venetian blinds, she is caught, under surveillance by a passing figure, his Fedora hat barely visible in the black night: "I come in here pretty often, sometimes alone, mostly with another girl, we drink beer, and talk, and of course we keep our eyes open you'd be surprised at how often nice, lonesome, soldiers ask Sue, the waitress to introduce them to us," she explains.[31]

Bubley's images portray a new kind of transience, one that makes possible working women's unmoored mobility. Unlike Dorothea Lange's suffering but heroic images of "An American Exodus" in such Depression-era iconic images as "Migrant Mother," Bubley's well-fed, wholesome women hardly seem worthy of recognition. They are on the move, but not because of extreme privation or because of extreme abjection; neither mother nor whore, they are picking up the slack, passing time. They are working girls, passing through, washing their nylons every night before retiring after another day on the job or in transit to one. This focus on the mundane is precisely what makes Bubley's 1940s photographs so unsettling. At the moment Bubley catches them, they are emblems of the dullness attendant upon the working life. They are neither defiant nor defeated; instead they appear haunted. Their movement endlessly deferred, arrested, they are ghostly presences; they display perhaps the hidden faces of the Migrant Mother's daughters now sporting shoulder pads as they head off for war work. They participate in a national mobilization, a nationalist modernism, progressive, mass-mediated, industrialized, and federally-funded, designed to spread information, including the knowledge of modernism itself through modern technologies to cement a modern nation.

Now

"Northern America which is all new, the old gets lost before it becomes new because the new is always becoming new."
Gertrude Stein, "And Now," *Vanity Fair*, 1934.

"The modern has really become unmodern."
Theodor Adorno, *Minima Moralia*.

Poet Kenneth Fearing, whose 1935 portrait painter Alice Neel placed at a desk sitting just below the Third Avenue L, crowds of New Yorkers strolling across his papers and books, ransacked popular culture – its magazines, movies, ad copy, billboards, neon signs – for emblems of this pastiche nation, this agitated crowd that was modern America. Ever attuned to "Now," his poems etch the daily routines of lovers who must go to work, of workers who might glimpse love: "Now that we know life: / Breakfast in the morning; office and theater and sleep; no memory; / Only desire and profit are real."[32] A grim dirge. Yet his quirky speakers – oddballs drinking too much, staying up too late, sleeping through the alarm clock – find a way to coexist in the present. Their immobility, their flatness, offers a perverse vision of the crowd.

His are social types whose banality subverts typology. Stripped down pulpy versions of *The Waste Land*, Fearing's poems find a way to enjoy the crowd flowing over the bridge by embracing its voice, its vernacular, its inertia, its pulp.

A vernacular, pulp modernism – corporate, industrial, mass-mediated schlock – exceeds the bounds of the aesthetics and practices usually associated with high modernism. Tracing modernist representations of the social means thinking about who gets to be modernist and how the modern and modernism get contaminated and thus realigned by popular culture and by politics. An American working-class, ethnic, racial, and women's modernism reworks the iconography of prostitution within mass-mediated forms, for instance. In dialectic tension, density and mobility animate the never-ending present. During the 1920s, 1930s, and 1940s, the enormous machinery of mass culture – Hollywood, paperback publishing, mass-marketed magazines, advertising, grocery chains, and department stores, and so forth – spread pulp modernist sensibilities across the landscape of America into small towns and working- and middle-class homes from Decatur, Georgia, to Decatur, Illinois, from Portland, Maine, to Portland, Oregon.

The language of pulp speaks of pent-up desire or keyed-up anger; its simple suggestive prose burst the cheap bindings of the Avon, Fawcett, Dell, Ace, Medallion, Gold Medal, Bantam, Cardinal, Penguin, Lion, and Signet paperbacks. Virtually anything could be pulped: Nobel Prize winner William Faulkner's *Wild Palms* became "a haunting story of lovers confronted by the relentless pressures of a morality which no one can defy without disaster." French classics, like Honore de Balzac's *Droll Stories*, reveal "wit and wickedness in the sixteenth century." And, of course, soft-core paperback "originals" brought readers to *The Lusting Drive* by Ovid Demaris. Even the new sciences of evolution, psychoanalysis, anthropology, and physics could be pulped; Freud, Margaret Mead, Darwin and George Gamov were transformed into sensational packages. Pulp, lower grade than newsprint, is a paper stock destined to disappear. Made from the leftovers of paper production, pulp paperbacks were meant for the trashcan. Kin to the penny dreadfuls and dime novels of the nineteenth century, pulp fiction became popular in the 1920s and 1930s mass-marketed magazines devoted to crime, passion, and science: *True Love, Amazing Stories, Black Mask*. By the mid-1920s, pulp had entered slang as a term for nonsense and excess – over-the-top sentimentality and sleaze. The first successful pulp paperback line in the United States was published in 1939 by Pocket Books. War rationing made them patriotic. The paperback revolution opened a landscape of pulp novels that ranged from bohemian enclaves and artists' colonies in Greenwich Village to gothic mansions in Greenwich, Connecticut. It included the steamy bayous of Louisiana, the divorce ranches of Reno, Nevada, Los Angeles bungalows, and Viennese cafes.

These cheap twenty-five-cent books, found in bus and train stations, soda fountains and candy stores, drug stores and newspaper kiosks, called out to a mobile population of men and women commuting on trolleys and subways to work. Their lurid colorful covers telegraphed stories of sex and violence that traversed class and racial boundaries. Small enough to be tucked into a breast pocket or handbag and read at a lunch counter or on the streetcar, the more risqué and daring books could be hidden and read late into the night, firing the imaginations of young women like *The Girls in 3-B*. They are portable tokens of the public experience of the movie theatre to be savored alone.

These are novels of escape, escapist literature, where rebellious daughters attend art school or sing in nightclubs running from their conventional middle-class homes only to discover their dreary stay-at-home mothers harbor deep secrets and hidden desires for escape, also. They are incantations of a private world of fantasy lived behind *The Blank Wall*. Pulp fiction offered writers a means to imagine the exotic in everyday life. Dangerous men, even men with Princeton or Harvard degrees and combat medals, menace placid suburbs. College dormitories might be brothels. An apartment complex houses a murderer; housewives hide dead bodies. Simple household objects, like a hammer, transform into deadly weapons. But pulp also domesticates the unusual, transforming the foreign into a conventional middle-class narrative. On the back cover of the Pocket Book edition of Eve Curie's biography of her mother, Marie Curie becomes more than a brilliant scientist – she is also "the young Polish girl, poor, beautiful . . . whom Pierre Curie found . . . strangely sweet." And there's more: stories about white trash, jungle explorers, schoolteachers, artists, chanteuses, secretaries, divorcees, movie extras – any woman anywhere could become a *femme fatale*; it is a thoroughly demotic literary universe.

Charles Baudelaire had discerned just how this modern literary strategy might work. Writing in 1857 about Gustave Flaubert's scandalous pulp novel, *Madame Bovary*, he observes "our new novelist was faced with a society wholly worn-out – worse than worn-out – brutalized and greedy, wholly repelled by fiction, adoring only material possession," in short, the Eighteenth Brumaire of Louis Bonaparte was a world none too different from the one mid-twentieth-century American writers found. Flaubert's ingenious solution: "the most trivial adventure . . . the most vacuous . . . the most insufferable characters . . . the most threadbare and hackneyed theme" – that is, write a story of adultery amid small fry provincial fools.[33] Flaubert's novel, considered the first modern work of fiction, inscribes a vision of seemingly insignificant social types as *the* means to dissolve the formulaic. Steeped in cliché, nothing profound happens and thus everything of meaning takes place. In the Unreal City, "where fishmen lounge at noon" speaking "demotic French,"[34] vernacular modernism, the low modernism of the street, follows that guy Fearing overheard on the subway confessing murder into the diner for a late-night sandwich and a cup of coffee, lingers to watch that lone woman standing under the corner streetlamp check her lipstick, wiping a stray smudge off her front tooth Bubley had caught eyeing a sailor, then turns and dreams it all again. Now.

NOTES

1. See Marshall Berman, *All that is Solid Melts into Air: The Experience of Modernity* (New York: Simon and Schuster, 1982).
2. Ezra Pound, "In the Station of the Metro," [1916] in *The Norton Anthology of Modern Poetry*, ed. Richard Ellmann and Robert O'Clair (New York: W. W. Norton, 1973), 338.
3. John Dos Passos, *Nineteen Nineteen* in *U. S. A.* (New York: Modern Library, 1937), 65.
4. Burton J. Bledstein, *The Culture of Professionalism: The Middle Class and the Development of Higher Education in America* (New York: Norton: 1976), 93, traces the emergence of a professional class in the United States to new self-ideas within the middle class about the role of knowledge and instrumentality in establishing an expert class.
5. Gustave Le Bon, *The Crowd: A Study of the Popular Mind* [1896] (London: E. Benn, 1952). Elias Canetti identifies four traits of the crowd: growth, equality, density, direction. Within Canetti's typology, the crowd, or more accurately the mass, is boundless, in a state of absolute equality, discharges a feeling of density and is in constant movement. *Crowds and Power*, tr. Carol Stewart (New York: Farrar Strauss Giroux, 1984), 29.
6. BBC, "The World," July 17, 2003.
7. Reginald Marsh, *Coney Island Beach* (1935) in *Modern Metropolis*, ed. Leslie Nolan (New York: New Press, 1993), n.p. Reginald Marsh, "Let's Get Back to Painting," *Magazine of Art* 37 (December 1944), 296. Quoted in Ellen Wiley Todd, *"New Woman" Revisited: Painting and Gender Politics on Fourteenth Street* (Berkeley: University of California Press, 1993), 337.
8. Muriel Rukeyser, "Movie," in *Theory of Flight* (New Haven: Yale University Press, 1935), 87.
9. As early as 1915, in *The Art of the Moving Picture*, film critic Vachel Lindsay theorized about how the new medium both depicted and created the crowd. The most well-known argument to this effect appears in Walter Benjamin, "The Work of Art in the Age of Mechanical Reproduction," in *Illuminations*, ed. Hannah Arendt, tr. Harry Zohn (New York: Schocken Books, 1968), 217–252.
10. William Dean Howells, *A Hazard of New Fortunes* [1890] (New York: Bantam Books, 1960), 61.

11. See Wolfgang Schivelbusch, *The Railway Journey: Industrialization and the Perception of Time and Space in the 19th Century* (Berkeley: University of California Press, 1986) for a theory of the interconnections among cinema, machinery and the railroad. Thanks to Melanie Brown who analyzed the spectacle imbedded in this scene.

12. Jacob A. Riis, *How the Other Half Lives: Studies Among the Tenements of New York* [1890] (New York: Dover, 1971), 43, *passim*. The same year, Howells has his editor, March, travel to the Lower East Side and notice "the people of Germanic, of Slavonic, of Pelasgic, of Mongolian stock . . . [t]he small eyes, the high cheeks, the broad noses, the puff lips, the bare cue-filleted skulls, of Russians, Poles, Czechs, Chinese; the furtive glitter of Italians; the blonde dullness of Germans; the cold quiet of Scandinavians" (*Hazard*, 155). His language dovetails with Riis's, for instance: "the Chinese dwellers in Mott Street . . . stood . . . along the dirty pavement . . . aloof in immaculate cleanliness from the filth around them . . ." (*Hazard*, 157).

13. Gertrude Stein, *Three Lives* [1909] (New York: Vintage, 1936), 24, 239, 86.

14. Recent work by Michael Szalay, Saverio Giovacchini, Lizabeth Cohen, among many others, continues the focus on Popular Front Modernism articulated by Michael Denning. It has outlined the contours of an expressly popular and populist modernism after the fact which is as indebted to mass consumption, mass organizing, and mass media, thus embraces modernity, as it is to traditional views of modernist rejections of modern life and mass society (best articulated by Andreas Huysmann as a modernist refusal of femininity).

15. Joy Davidman, "Twentieth-Century Americanism," in *Letter to a Comrade* (New Haven: Yale University Press, 1938), 25–28, 26.

16. Muriel Rukeyser, "Boy With His Hair Cut Short," in *U. S. 1* (New York: Covici, Friede, 1938), 89.

17. T. V. Reed calls *Let Us Now Praise Famous Men* the first, most fully realized version of "postmodern realism," in "Aesthetics and the Overprivileged: The Politics and Ethics of Representation in *Let Us Now Praise Famous Men*," *Fifteen Jugglers, Five Believers: Literary Politics and the Politics of American Social Movements* (Berkeley: University of California Press, 1992), 22.

18. For a description of Duluth's poor Jewish immigrant community during the early years of the twentieth century, including its connections to Sholom Aleichem's Ukraine and its experiences of anti-Semitism, see, Gayla Ellis *et al.*, eds., *Irene: Selected Writings of Irene Paull* (Minneapolis: Midwest Villages & Voices, 1996).

19. For more on Bubley's work, see Paula Rabinowitz, *Black & White & Noir: America's Pulp Modernism* (New York: Columbia University Press, 2002), ch. 1; Beverly Brannan and Carl Flesichhauer, *Documenting America: 1935–1943* (Berkeley: University of California Press, 1989).

20. See Michael Szalay, *New Deal Modernism: American Literature and the Invention of the Welfare State* (Durham: Duke University Press, 2000).

21. See Daniel Rosenberg, "No One is Buried in Hoover Dam," in *Modernism, Inc.: Body, Memory, Capital*, ed. Jani Scandura and Michael Thurston (New York University Press, 2001), 84–106.

22. See Todd, *"New Woman" Revisited*, for an exhaustive study of the style and context for these images of women crowding the sidewalks as workers and shoppers.

23. Jean Toomer, *Cane* (New York: Liveright, 1923), 39, 50, 52.

24. For the story of Murray Hall and many other passing women in modern American history, see, Jonathan Katz, ed., *Gay American History: Lesbians and Gay Men in the U. S. A.* (New York: Thomas Crowell Company, 1976), 230–279, *Times* headline, p. 232; George Chauncey, *Gay New York: Gender, Urban Culture and the Makings of the Gay Male World, 1890–1940* (New York: Basic Books, 1994) outlines a comprehensive geography of the spatial sexuality of turn-of-the-century New York.

25. For a detailed history of Jewish men's passing (as another other) by adopting black face (or in this case a tanned one), see Michael Rogin, *Blackface, White Noise: Jewish Immigrants in the Hollywood Melting Pot* (Berkeley: University of California Press, 1996). Alan Wald investigates why Jewish Communists relied so extensively on "racial cross dressing." For another version – Black man passing as Jewish – see, Philip Roth, *The Human Stain* (Boston: Houghton Mifflin: 2000).

26. Anzia Yezierska, *Salome of the Tenements* [1923] (Urbana: University of Illinois Press, 1995), 60, 63.

27. Rukeyser, "Theory of Flight," in *Theory of Flight*, 67.

28. See Elizabeth Wilson, *The Sphinx in the City: Urban Life, the Control of Disorder, and Women* (Los Angeles: University of California Press, 1991).

29. Walter Benjamin, *The Arcades Project*, tr. Howard Eiland and Kevin McLaughlin (Cambridge, MA.: Belknap Press of Harvard University Press, 1999), 4.

30. For an analysis of the "politics of envy" as it is played out by one ambitious mill girl who moved to the city, London, during the 1930s and refashioned herself through good shoes and a well-cut suit, see Carolyn Steedman, *Landscape for a Good Woman: A Story of Two Lives* (New Brunswick, NJ: Rutgers University Press, 1986).

31. Esther Bubley, U. S. OWI Negative # 21005-E.

32. Kenneth Fearing, "Now," in *Collected Poems* (New York: Random House, 1940), 19. "Now" was originally published in *Menorah Journal* as "No War." See Robert M. Ryeley, ed., *Kenneth Fearing, Complete Poems* (Orono, ME: The National Poetry Foundation, 1994), 284.

33. Charles Baudelaire, "*Madame Bovary* by Gustave Flaubert," *Selected Writings on Art and Artists*, tr. and ed. P. E. Charvet (Harmondsworth: Penguin, 1972), 248–249.

34. T. S. Eliot, "The Waste Land," *The Waste Land and Other Poems* (New York: Harcourt, Brace and World, Inc. 1934), 39, 37.

12

DOUGLAS MAO

Modern American literary criticism

If by "modern American literary criticism" we mean the evaluative and theoretical discourse most closely related to the high modernist literature of the United States, we would need, in this kind of survey, to focus mainly on statements by that literature's makers. Undoubtedly, the most illuminating criticism of modernism is to be found in polemics such as Pound's Imagist manifesto, Hughes's delineation of the racial mountain, and Stein's lectures in America, as well as the poetry, prose writing, and plays that – just as a longstanding commonplace holds – execute the most potent criticism of all in their formal ruptures, their surprising modes of being, their nervy materializations of the unexpected. The writers in question tried hard to outdistance assimilation by criticism as such, and for the most part they succeeded: although their experimentalism was noted at once, it was only around mid-century that modernism as we now think of it began to be written about as a coherent formation. And this recognition, as we will see, was inseparable from a sense that what had rendered modernism visible was nothing other than its recent death.

We might, however, construe "modern American literary criticism" in a different way: as the discourse produced in this period by writers who regarded themselves principally or significantly as critics.[1] This discourse had much to say about the literature of its own moment, but it was at least as concerned with the Elizabethans as with the moderns, at least as apt to dwell on Dryden or Poe as to take up Frost or Cather. Moreover, this discourse failed to take most of the makers of literary modernism especially seriously *as critics*, however vigorous or groundbreaking their polemics. Why, then, should a reader interested primarily in American modernism bother with this body of writing?

One answer is simply that putting it together with the texts of modernism proper gives a more rounded picture of the literary life of the period. Few would now disagree that it is impoverishing to read the high modernists in isolation from less evidently experimental writers or contemporary mass cultural forms, and the same could be said of ignoring early twentieth-century criticism. But another answer is that our own ways of reading were shaped decisively by this criticism, which grappled – sometimes haltingly, sometimes brilliantly – with questions about the nature of the literary object, the value of literary study, the continuity of human experience, the differences between poetic and scientific language, the future of an immigrant nation, and the meanings of art in a society dominated by commerce. In his introduction to a 1958 critical anthology, Irving Howe remarked that criticism had become "the vehicle through which a cultivated elite not only exercised its powers of perception but reflected upon its sense of the human condition in the middle of the twentieth century . . . one of the last humane disciplines in which it was still possible to take a 'total view.'"[2] Whether or not critics had a right to assume this role can be debated, but there is no question of the accuracy of Howe's description. The story of modern American literary criticism is indeed the story of what seemed a last refuge of the total view – of an attempt to survey modern life in terms of broad ends as well as local means, and of a fear that society was conspiring to render that attempt, and even the literature from which it might draw sustenance, impossible.

There are many ways of beginning to tell this story. One would be to note the precipitating effects of changes in higher education in the United States during the last decades of the nineteenth century. At this time, many American colleges transformed themselves into universities on the European model, advanced educators importing from Germany the view that faculty should be professional specialists in research fields. Within the area of modern languages and literature, this lent a special luster to the meticulous investigations of philologists, which both resembled the natural sciences' mode of contribution to knowledge and rebuffed the claim of classicists that only the study of Greek and Latin could promote the mental discipline colleges were meant to instill. By the turn of the century, as Gerald Graff observes, the university had become the home of a "new academic professional" whose "loyalties went to his 'field' rather than to the classroom dedication that had made the older type of college teacher seem a mere schoolmaster."[3] Yet in addition to philologists and literary historians who similarly molded themselves to the research paradigm, faculties of modern language departments retained generalists who sought for themselves and their students a wider acquaintance with world literatures. Much of the most significant criticism of the first years of the century emerged from a generalist opposition to philological and historical narrowing – an opposition virtually definitional inasmuch as the essence of "criticism" had long been held to consist in precisely the acts of evaluation that more scientific approaches eschewed.

No generalist insisted on the importance of evaluation more forcefully than Irving Babbitt, professor of French and comparative literature at Harvard from 1892 to 1933. In his 1908 *Literature and the American College*, Babbitt advocated, against philological specialization, the adoption of a version of Renaissance humanism emphasizing breadth of reading, critical judgment, moral cultivation, and the exploration of "relationships of language and literature to the human spirit."[4] In *The New Laokoon* of 1910, Babbitt praised the late Renaissance's "love of clear and logical distinctions" and insisted that "the function of criticism at the present hour" must be to restore the intellect to art, to

> make as many and as clear distinctions as possible and then project them like vivid sunbeams into the romantic twilight . . . to bring once more into honor the broad, masculine, and vigorous distinction. We might then have a type of writing that is not intended primarily for women and men in their unmasculine moods, – for the tired scientist and the fagged philologist and the weary man of business.[5]

This passage is worth quoting at length because it indicates how the New Humanism, as it came to be called, constituted itself in opposition to a constellation of enemies who would not have recognized each other as allies. One enemy was the bourgeois philistine who could value nothing apart from acquisition; another was the producer of popular writing for women (a literature that for Babbitt confirmed a sort of absolute linkage between the feminine and the trivial); a third was the proponent of literary or philosophical romanticism, which in Babbitt's view terminated in the deplorable fuzziness of impressionistic criticism; yet a final one was the drily delimiting philologist. What linked these four was their rootedness in a "naturalistic" philosophy that Babbitt traced back to Jean Jacques Rousseau, and which he saw as advocating the wildest license for behavior while deterministically denying that individuals could shape their own moral destinies. Babbitt's antipathies echo through early polemics by Pound and Eliot and continued to influence the latter (who was briefly Babbitt's student) for decades; as we shall see, the matter on which Eliot finally diverged from Babbitt was humanism itself.

Babbitt was not the only exponent of the humanist position. Frequently grouped with him in period debates was his friend Paul Elmer More, who agreed that the cultivation of discrimination and self-control was central to humanistic education, stressed the importance of literature as cultural memory, and found much to admire in the literature of the Puritans. Stuart P. Sherman, who had studied with Babbitt, also lamented declining standards and lambasted naturalistic philosophy for reducing humans to mere animals of appetite, but by the time of his 1922 collection, *Americans*, had come to criticize what he saw as an anti-democratic strain leading More and company to a regrettable disengagement from contemporary American life. The most prominent humanist forays into the American field, however, were made by Norman Foerster, a professor at North Carolina and Iowa. In books like *American Criticism: A Study in Literary Theory from Poe to the Present* (1928) and *The American Scholar* (1929), Foerster outlined specific principles guiding a renovated humanism and chided United States critics for their belief that a viable national literature could be produced only out of a severing from the European past. "[W]hile it would be interesting for us to be American," Foerster declared contrarily, "it is far more important for us to be human."[6]

Humanism was not, however, the only mode of generalist contestation in the early years of the century. John Erskine, a teacher of Randolph Bourne and Lionel Trilling and the initiator of the Columbia great books course, admired Sherman and joined the New Humanists in decrying anti-intellectualism (his 1915 essay collection is called *The Moral Obligation to Be Intelligent*) but also embraced the more impressionistic criticism that the New Humanists abhorred. In *The Kinds of Poetry* (1920), Erskine insisted in Paterian tones that the teacher of poetry should be concerned less with "meter or verse forms" or "the subject-matter of poems" than with "multiplying ... those fortunate moments when the soul is dilated and the universe enlarged."[7] Another Columbia professor, Joel Spingarn, promoted the aesthetic theory of Benedetto Croce and recommended that criticism abandon its obsession with rules, genres, moral judgments, and literary history in favor of the single question, "What has the poet tried to express and how has he expressed it?"[8] In an essay of 1913–1914, Spingarn attacked Babbitt specifically for failing to talk about literature, for lacking an aesthetic theory (though it is not clear that Spingarn himself had a particularly developed one), and for caring not "what art or criticism is" but only that "young men and women should have discipline, training, tradition, ideals" (198).

One can witness Babbitt and Spingarn going head to head, and incidentally get a fair sense of the critical terrain of the 1910s and early 1920s, by turning to the now scarcely remembered 1924 volume *Criticism in America* (one of many critical anthologies published in this period). Opening with one of the Spingarn polemics just quoted, the collection also featured two seminal essays by T. S. Eliot; a rebuke of Spingarn by Babbitt; a broadside in which Sherman railed against the younger generation for rejecting Puritanism, democracy, and morality in favor of psychology, sex, and Spingarn; a 1921 reconsideration in which a more muted Spingarn, responding to a temporary rout of professors by "dilettanti," "amateurs," and "journalists," mourned a want of "philosophic insight and precision" in critical writing[9]; and a stinging attack by Ernest Boyd on what he called "Ku Klux Kriticism" – an effort, which Boyd somewhat unfairly identified with Sherman, to elim-inate from consideration in American letters "those names which have not the familiar Anglo-Saxon ring."[10]

Also represented in *Criticism in America* were Van Wyck Brooks and H. L. Mencken, two critics who shared Boyd's anti-Puritanism and journal-istic distance from the academy but are far more widely remembered today. In his essay on "The Critics and Young America," Brooks presented con-cisely many of the ideas unfolded at greater length in key books such as *The Wine of the Puritans* (1909) and *America's Coming-of-Age* (1915) – above all that American literature had been prevented from maturing by the domi-nance of the acquisitive impulse and the Puritanism with which that impulse had long and curiously been entangled. Mencken, who through his columns for *Smart Set* and later the *American Mercury* became the most fearsome book reviewer of the twentieth century, denounced Puritanism, middlebrow culture, anti-intellectualism, and the timorous literature of cheerfulness yet more witheringly. In his own contribution to *Criticism in America* – enti-tled "Criticism of Criticism of Criticism" – this hardest-to-please of readers found fault with psychological critics, rule-obsessed critics, aesthetic critics, and above all the moralizers who would have literature serve an improv-ing function. According to Mencken, only Spingarn's question about what the poet is trying to do and how he has done it grounded itself in the idea that "there should be free speech in art, and no protective tariffs," and even Spingarn erred in suggesting that beauty could appear "*in vacuo*," divorced from social, political, and moral implications.[11]

The principal fault line in American criticism from the 1910s through the late 1920s, then, lay between critics principally concerned with the continuity of literary tradition, the honing of the evaluative faculty, and the cultivation of moral self-discipline, on the one hand, and a group privileging artistic experience in a more fluid, spontaneous, and self-fulfilling mode, on the other. Both sides resisted what they saw as a narrowing of sensibility in philological and historical specialists, and both agreed that the great conflict of the age lay between art's vitality and the deadness of the commercial temper. But whereas the first tended to be wary of social change – not only industrial expansion but also an array of progressive ideas – the second associated Puritan self-discipline itself with the acquisitive urge, and embraced developments that promised to loosen the Puritan hold.

In this second group, Spingarn, Boyd, Brooks, and Mencken were joined by a number of influential critics who did not appear in *Criticism in America*, including Max Eastman, Waldo Frank, and Randolph Bourne. Eastman's particular emphasis was on the opposition between poetic language and practical language – or even, as he formulated it in his 1913 *Enjoyment of Poetry*, between poetic people, interested in "receiving experiences," and practical people, "chiefly occupied with attaining ends." For Eastman, poetry was "not only a realization of things, but . . . also a thing itself" that demands of its audience a "power of lingering with energy."[12] Six years later came the publication of *Our America*, in which Frank, surveying the history of various regions since colonial times, at once acknowledged the contributions of Puritanism and stressed the need to move beyond it. A common devotion to "conserv[ing] energy," "sharpen[ing] wits," and "quicken[ing] all the machinery of action," Frank argued, had allowed the Puritan to meet the Pioneer "on a base of psychological and temperamental unity" wonderfully adapted to dominating a "virgin and hostile continent." But it also left Americans no time to cultivate "inner peace" or "that sensation of harmony which is the sense of beauty."[13] Bourne, who died in 1918 at the age of thirty-two, assumed the role of speaker for a younger, more egalitarian generation in critiquing the New Humanists' form of elitism ("The calm of Mr. More's style cannot keep the claws of class-exploitation from showing through"[14]), condemning Puritan xenophobia, and cheering the decline of what George Santayana had in 1911 named the "genteel tradition" in American letters and thinking. In his crucial 1916 essay, "Trans-National America," Bourne insisted, against calls for the cultural assimilation of immigrants, that there must be "a higher ideal than the 'melting-pot,'" that distinctive regional and ethnic qualities must not be "washed out into a tasteless, colorless fluid of uniformity," but rather encouraged in a United States whose lot was "to be a federation of cultures" (249, 254, 256).

Not surprisingly, these more progressive critics were more receptive to new modes of writing than the classically oriented humanists. Erskine argued that contemporary experimenters had revitalized a poetry gone moribund, consciously or unconsciously learning from the masters of modern realist fiction the importance of close fidelity to experience. Frank saw glimmerings of hope in the fiction of Theodore Dreiser and Sherwood Anderson and discerned "the flower of a great American poetic renaissance" in the work of Edgar Lee Masters, Robert Frost, and Amy Lowell; "The first true 'man of letters' of Our America," wrote Frank, in appreciation of Lowell's campaign on behalf of Imagism as well as her own verse, "turns out to be a woman" (164–165). Bourne, similarly, saw a laudably revolutionary attack on the genteel tradition in Lowell's *Tendencies in Modern American Poetry* and praised Dreiser for getting down "the pattern of life, sincere, wistful, and unredeemed" (481–482, 461). And although Mencken's taste in poetry was conservative, he championed fiercely fiction writers such as Anderson, Willa

Cather, and above all Dreiser, whom he saw as locked in a struggle against American prudery.

Absent from most white critics' considerations of the future of the arts in America in the first quarter of the century was the role that might be played by black writers: Boyd's "Ku Klux Kriticism," for example, is concerned with the writing of European immigrants, and the subject goes similarly unmentioned in Bourne's brief for cultural federalism. Yet many black intellectuals shared the belief that the materialist tendency of American life presented an obstacle to cultural efflorescence, and this agreement was one basis for important connections between black and white critics emerging at this time – as, for example, between Spingarn, who served as chair of the NAACP, and W. E. B. Du Bois, who served as editor of the NAACP-sponsored magazine *The Crisis* from 1910 to 1934. For Du Bois, black Americans' very marginalization lent them a special distance on the acquisitive urge: "pushed aside as we have been in America," he wrote in his 1926 statement on "Criteria of Negro Art," "there has come to us . . . a vision of what the world could be if it were really a beautiful world."[15] Like many of his fellow black writers and critics, moreover, Du Bois saw the distinctively bitter experience of American black life as providing matter for a powerful new body of writing. "[N]ever in the world has a richer mass of material been accumulated by a people than that which the Negroes possess today," he declared in a 1913 piece, while in "Criteria" he described struggles in Africa and the South as the "true and stirring stuff" of tragedy and romance (866, 996–997). Other leading black critics such as James Weldon Johnson placed African-American innovation at the center of America's contribution to the arts: "there is nothing of artistic value belonging to America," wrote Johnson, "which has not been originated by the Negro . . . everything else is borrowed from the old world."[16] Still others evoked the importance of Africa for modern Western artists, black and white, as when in his landmark 1925 anthology, *The New Negro*, Alain Locke observed that African art has brought "the lesson of discipline, of style, of technical control pushed to the limits of technical mastery."[17]

It was also clear to black critics in this period that a forceful emergence of African-American art would have consequences reaching far beyond art itself. Locke insisted that work of the sort collected in *The New Negro* pushed beyond the limitations of the "Negro problem" because – as the contemporary examples of India, China, Egypt, Ireland, Russia, Bohemia, Palestine, and Mexico also revealed – "self-expression" was closely involved with "self-determination."[18] Johnson declared in 1918 that the "world does not know that a race is great until that race produces great literature" (272), and Du Bois remarked near the end of "Criteria" that "until the art of the black folk compels recognition they will not be rated as human" (1002). When Du Bois wrote elsewhere in the same essay that "all Art is propaganda and ever must be," he was by no means embracing a vision of art as ideological manipulation; the rest of the piece reiterates his devotion to aesthetic experience. But he was asserting, as he immediately explains, that the social legitimacy conferred by new developments must be embraced: "whatever art I have for writing has been used always for propaganda for gaining the right of black folk to love and enjoy" (1000).

If there was a broad consensus that the vitality of black artistic production would owe something to the distinctiveness of black experience, there was far less agreement on what should *count* as black experience in literary representation. Particularly contentious in this regard was the question of how large the "low-down" side of life should loom in African-American drama, fiction, and poetry. Du Bois and other literati at *The Crisis*, notably William Stanley Braithwaite and Jessie Fauset, have been associated with the view that over-representation of violence, sexual looseness, and degradation in African-American life obscured the existence of a significant black middle class whose ways offered something for both white and black readers to admire, while Locke and others like Charles Johnson, editor of *Opportunity* magazine from 1923 to 1928, have been linked with a belief that the greatest benefit to the community would accrue where black artists were able to express themselves with maximum freedom. Although the positions of these critics were much more complicated than such a dichotomy acknowledges, the debate as such was vividly enacted in reviews of particular works. And the question was further complicated by the fact that more sordid representations could be identified not with expressive freedom but rather with a commercial constraint allegedly imposed by white readers' taste for the sensational or morbidly documentary. Some of the more poignant articulations of this point were made by (an increasingly marginalized) Zora Neale Hurston in the years after the fading of the Harlem Renaissance, as, for example, in a 1950 article for the *Negro Digest* in which she remarked her amazement at "the Anglo-Saxon's lack of curiosity about the internal lives and emotions of the Negroes" and asserted that publishers continue to "shy away from romantic stories about Negroes and Jews because they feel that they know the public indifference to such works, unless the story or play involves racial tension. It can then be offered as a study in Sociology . . ."[19]

For the Marxian critics who emerged as a force in the 1920s and 1930s, meanwhile, the task was not to maintain the separation between sociology and literature but to draw the two closer together. Mike Gold, the novelist and fiercely revolutionary editor of *New Masses*, noted his respect for artists who resisted having their content defined by others, but insisted nonetheless that the future of literature lay in the experience of the proletariat: the intellectuals "have created, out of their solitary pain, confusions, doubts and complexities," but the "masses are still primitive and clean, and artists must turn to them for strength again."[20] Criticism, meanwhile, had to turn its attention to the social grounding of art. "Marxians, for at least fifty years, have been grubbing and burrowing among the economic roots of the shining rose bush of art," wrote Gold in 1926's "America Needs a Critic," and a properly Marxian criticism would provide "a sense of the social changes which precede each new school of art and which determine the individual psychology of the artist, however 'free' he thinks he is" (133). An even stronger emphasis on social determination marked the work of V. F. Calverton, founder of *The Modern Quarterly*. In his 1925 collection, *The Newer Spirit: A Sociological Criticism of Literature*, Calverton declared flatly that "all of the theories and concepts, the dicta and shibboleths, of creative and critical effort are but the outgrowths of the social system in which they have their being, and which in turn is the product of the material conditions of the time."[21] Proceeding to unfold a history of these determinations from the feudal period forward, Calverton asserted that "the impossible" had given way to the "improbable, thence to the probable and finally to the inevitable" in the literature of recent centuries, thanks to science's demonstration of how "the reactions of mind and body" follow the "inescapable law of cause and effect" (43, 45). Thus if academic historical scholarship found its rationale in a certain neutrality that set it apart from the evaluative discourse of criticism, the Marxian critics deployed history to the quite different end of exposing and ultimately altering the otherwise mystified conditions of modern production. Needless to say, the Marxians' emphasis on social causation and hostility to individualism also set them at a distance from the New Humanists' abhorrence of "naturalistic philosophy"; *The Newer Spirit*, as it happens, carried an introduction in which Boyd once again lambasted the "Ku Kluxers of criticism."[22]

Yet the combination of revolutionary agenda and historical determinism presented a difficulty for the Marxian critics, as for other Marxist theoreticians. If the ascent of the proletariat was historically inevitable, what could be the need for any particular intervention by any particular activist (or artist) at any particular time? Calverton confronted this problem in his 1932 volume, *The Liberation of American Literature*. Stressing that the "literary artist is not . . . a hopeless victim of his environment but is a creative part of it, able to assist in [its] transformation," he unfolded a narrative of breakthrough in which twentieth-century writers at last overcame what had been the two major impediments to a strong American literature: a "colonial complex" of inferiority toward Europe and the interference of the "petty bourgeois censor."[23] Though unsympathetic to modernist self-absorption, Calverton – a fervent promoter of *The New Negro* and himself the editor of a 1929 *Anthology of American Negro Literature* – credited African-American writers with a high degree of freedom from the colonial complex, and noted approvingly the growth of interest in "indigenous materials" evidenced by Mary Austin's collecting of "Amerindian" songs, John Lomax's quest for cowboy ballads, and the wide dissemination of "Negro spirituals . . . blues . . . folk-lore . . . and . . . jazz" (Calverton, *Liberation*, 433, 438). A year later, Granville Hicks, who would become literary editor of the *New Masses*, published a study with similar bearings in *The Great Tradition: An Interpretation of American Literature Since the Civil War*. More elegant and less dogmatic than Calverton, Hicks was also somewhat more sympathetic to modernist innovation: where Calverton likened the Imagists to "petty bourgeois individualists in the economic and political sphere" on the basis of their determination "that nothing should be permitted to stand in the way of the expression of individuality in the poetic sphere" (*Liberation*, 414), Hicks praised the "vitality of literature in the modern period" of 1912 to 1925 and declared it "not wholly an exaggeration" to "speak of the rebirth of American culture" at this time. Yet Hicks also faulted this "middle generation" for its pessimism, and joined with Calverton in finding more hopeful signs in the fiction of Dreiser, Anderson, and especially Gold and John Dos Passos.[24]

In this period, a number of critics sympathetic to the Marxians' broad aims but averse to their deterministic and propagandistic inclinations attempted to negotiate between the call of social justice and the desideratum of freedom in art. In his 1934 collection *Art and the Life of Action*, for example, Eastman rejected as symptoms of "a troubled condition" *both* the doctrine of art for art's sake and the subordination of art to partisan politics. Deploying a historical narrative of his own against the high proletarian line, Eastman wrote that "to dismiss 'pure art' as a decadent indulgence of the bourgeoisie is mere cant and nonsense," because the anti-purposive tendency of modern art is "an intrinsic item in the general march of human culture, not to be wished away by any theory."[25] In studies such as *The Philosophy of Literary Form* (1941), meanwhile, the endlessly inventive critic Kenneth Burke elaborated a theory of art as "linguistic, or symbolic, or literary action."[26] Burke's method of avoiding what he called "the *excess* of environmentalist schools" was to conceive of "[c]ritical and imaginative works" as "*strategic* answers, *stylized* answers" to "questions posed by the situation in which they arose" (xvii, 1). Much interested in the structure of literary works – one of his widely consequential contributions lay in showing how writers

unconsciously produce meaning through "associational clusters" of images –
Burke nonetheless stressed that "a poem's structure is to be described most
accurately by thinking always of the poem's function" (20, 89).

Yet another fascinating negotiation between engagement and autonomy
is to be found in the work of Edmund Wilson. In *Axel's Castle: A Study in
the Imaginative Literature of 1870–1930*, published in 1931, Wilson argued
that "what literary criticism ought to be" is "a history of man's ideas and
imaginings in the setting of the conditions which have shaped them"[27] – thus
recommending attention to the socioeconomic "base" without implying that
it fully determines the cultural "superstructure." But the intricacies of this
relation were not merely a methodological concern for *Axel's Castle*; they
were also its central theme. In Wilson's telling, the literary history of the six
decades preceding – as exemplified by Yeats, Eliot, Joyce, Stein, Proust, and
Valéry – was "to a great extent that of the development of Symbolism and of
its fusion or conflict with Naturalism" (25), where Symbolism was defined by
a belief that "it is the poet's task to find, to invent, the special language which
will alone be capable of expressing his personality and feelings" (21). The
Brooks-Frank-Bourne notion of a distinctively American conflict between
poetry and practicality thus emerges in Wilson as the great conflict of modern
European literature. Yet it was less easy for Wilson, in 1930, to imagine a
liberated literature as inherently resistant to acquisitive culture: sympathetic
though his presentation of the Symbolist side often was, he finally condemned
as a dead end its way of withdrawing from "an experience shared with
society to an experience savored in solitude" (266). Notably, Wilson's other
most celebrated book, 1940's *To the Finland Station*, traces from Vico and
Michelet through Renan, Taine, Saint-Simon, Marx, Lenin, and others the
fate of the idea that, in Vico's words, *"the social world is certainly the work
of men."*[28]

Another study by Wilson, *The Wound and the Bow* (1941), contributed to
the uneven but collectively significant flow of psychoanalytic criticism in the
first half of the century. Lacking the kind of organizational base that Marxian
theory had in the Communist Party and the proletarian magazines, Freudian
(and Jungian) concepts were deployed by a more diffuse array of writers
and more subject to dilution in criticism. Wilson's book, for example, visits
Dickens, James, Kipling, Proust, and others in working through the rather
broad idea that in producing art writers could address their own emotional
traumas in addition to obtaining worldly esteem. Some analyses adhered
closely to Freudian doctrine: in his celebrated "Psychoanalytical Study of
Hamlet" (first published in 1910, revised and enlarged in 1923, and then
expanded to book length in 1949), the psychoanalyst Ernest Jones proposed that the power of the play derives from the latent content of Hamlet's

repressed erotic feelings for his mother, and advanced a general defense of the application of psychoanalytic models to fictional characters. In books such as *Poetry and Dreams* (1913) and *The Poetic Mind* (1922), the critic and scholar F. C. Prescott elaborated on matters such as the dreamwork's relation to poetic language and the literary text's realization of unconscious wishes. Other studies adapted psychoanalytic terms much more loosely, however: in *The Ordeal of Mark Twain* (1920), Van Wyck Brooks argued that all of Twain's work grew out of a division of personality (artist versus conformist) traceable to his early family life, while in *Edgar Allan Poe: A Study in Genius* (1926), Joseph Wood Krutch attributed Poe's few strengths and many limitations to his "abnormal condition of the nerves."[29] Clearly, the new psychology was attractive to those seeking to undo the repressive power of Puritan thinking; this effort found perhaps its purest articulation in Ludwig Lewisohn's 1932 *Story of American Literature*, which detailed the artistic costs of repression from the colonial era forward.

The period of the late twenties through early forties also saw the publication of several more influential revisions of American literary history. In his astonishing, monumental, and unfinished *Main Currents in American Thought* (1927–1930), V. L. Parrington set out to trace the origins of "certain germinal ideas that have come to be reckoned traditionally American," to explore "forces that are anterior to literary schools and movements, creating the body of ideas from which literary culture eventually springs."[30] Parrington was especially interested in documenting "the transplanting to America of old-world liberalisms" (iv), but he also gave a detailed account of the way in which regional conditions shaped American political thinking, thus demonstrating that non-Marxists (he was a liberal) could also be vitally concerned with the economic and social determinants of literature. Like Parrington, Constance Rourke was absorbed with recovering lost strands of American cultural history, but where much of Parrington's interest lay with European sources, Rourke's lay with indigenous ones. In *American Humor* (1931) and *The Roots of American Culture* (1942), Rourke brought to light forgotten "pools or pockets of the arts" in places such as late eighteenth-century Salem and Annapolis; assembled a capacious survey of early American music; revealed a tradition of theatricals in the United States extending back to pre-colonial times; demonstrated that the recent "absorption in Negro art and character" was "a partial culmination of a long stream of expression in which the white American and the Negro have often joined"; and, perhaps most significant, collected and analyzed a multiplicity of tall tales, ballads, and other folk forms whose further investigation she saw as "open[ing] possibilities for criticism and scholarship of a most radical, refreshing kind."[30]

Like Parrington's, Rourke's work participated in a vast effort to document the lost or disappearing folk forms of the United States and to unsettle the dominance of New York and New England by drawing attention to the diversity of regional arts. Among many other contributors to this project were Mary Austin, who in *The American Rhythm* (1923) tried to show how poems by Sandburg, Amy Lowell, and others had the same underlying rhythms as American Indian songs, and Mabel Major, Rebecca W. Smith, and T. M. Pearce, who in *Southwest Heritage* (1938) offered a literary history of the region including (though not emphasizing) Indian and Spanish poems and stories. Working in a quite different direction was F. O. Matthiessen's *American Renaissance: Art and Expression in the Age of Emerson and Whitman* (1941), which in its way of concentrating on its titular authors, plus Thoreau, Hawthorne, and Melville, secured these five writers' position at the core of the nineteenth-century American canon for decades. Introducing the "method and scope" of *American Renaissance*, Matthiessen noted his admiration of Parrington, but stressed that his very different approach arose from a conviction that literature not only "reflects an age" but "also illuminates it" and that the "common reader" reads books "whether of the present or past, because they have an immediate life of their own."[31] Even so, *American Renaissance* included enormous quantities of historical and biographical material, which were brought to bear on themes such as the friction between individual and society and the "split between art and the other functions of the community" (xiv–xv). Matthiessen thus placed extensive historical knowledge not principally in the service of historiography per se or in that of the master narratives of Marxism, but rather in that of the electric encounter between enduring text and contemporary reader.

In so doing, he marked his proximity to the school that dominated criticism from the late 1930s through the late 1950s: that of T. S. Eliot and the New Critics whom Eliot inspired. (Matthiessen himself had published a book-length study of Eliot in 1935, and his affinity with the prevailing New Critical temper was certainly part of the reason *American Renaissance* enjoyed so much success.) Critics of the day often attributed Eliot's eminence to his ability to vie with academic scholars in historical knowledge while yet producing a firmly critical – that is, evaluative – criticism, and certainly his most important writing brought the past to bear on the present in striking ways. His most famous statement was 1919's "Tradition and the Individual Talent," in which he argued that a proper engagement with literary tradition lies not in "blind or timid adherence" to old styles but in a "historical sense" that prevents the modern writer from merely repeating what has already been done. "[W]hat happens when a new work of art is created," he wrote in a celebrated passage, "is something that happens simultaneously to all the works of art which preceded it. The existing monuments form an ideal order among themselves, which is modified by the introduction of the new (the really new) work of art among them."[32]

This negotiation between experiment and tradition might in itself have been enough to render "Tradition" noteworthy, but Eliot went on to make a second significant move. Comparing the mind of the artist to a catalyst, he asserted that artistic progress "is a continual self-sacrifice, a continual extinction of personality," that "the poet has, not a 'personality' to express, but a particular medium . . . in which impressions and experiences combine in peculiar and unexpected ways" (40, 42). The aesthetic of impersonality, already a guiding principle for some early twentieth-century artists, was still more widely adopted thanks to Eliot, and variations on the theme appeared in much of his later writing. In the "The Perfect Critic," which led off his 1920 selection of his critical prose, *The Sacred Wood* (and, incidentally, appeared with "Tradition" in the aforementioned *Criticism in America*), Eliot insisted – against impressionistic criticism – that the true "end of the enjoyment of poetry" is not momentary delight in a single line here or there, but "a pure contemplation from which all the accidents of personal emotion are removed" (57). In another well-known analysis, 1919's "*Hamlet*," Eliot argued that Shakespeare's play is marred by its failure to find an "objective correlative" for its hero's emotion – that is, "a set of objects, a situation, a chain of events which shall be the formula of that *particular* emotion; such that when the external facts . . . are given, the emotion is immediately evoked . . . Hamlet (the man) is dominated by an emotion which is inexpressible, because it is in *excess* of the facts as they appear" (48). Possible objections to this formulation are many (not least among them that approaches to the inexpressible are a crucial feature of Eliot's own poetry), but the idea of the objective correlative took root and remains in the critical vocabulary to this day.

For all his resistance to uncontrolled emotionalism, Eliot assumed – as did many other critics of the day, led by the British theorist I. A. Richards – that emotions were the matter and currency of works of art. In "Tradition," for instance, Eliot stated that the "business of the poet is not to find new emotions, but to use the ordinary ones and, in working them up into poetry, to express feelings which are not in actual emotions at all" (43). His thesis in the widely read "Metaphysical Poets" essay of 1921, meanwhile, was that the English poets of the seventeenth century felt "their thought as immediately as the odour of a rose," but that a "dissociation of sensibility," a severing of thought from feeling, set in thereafter (64). Eliot's advocacy of the metaphysicals led to the most dramatic canon revision of early twentieth-century English-language criticism: long neglected, Donne, Herbert, Marvell, and company came into prominence, while all the poets between them and the moderns – especially the Romantics – suffered some devaluation.

Eliot's difficulties with the emotional character of art were part of a larger conflict (evocative of his teacher Babbitt's anxieties) between his admiration for the cultivated, sensitive personality and his mistrust of what he saw as the egocentric, anti-communal excesses of Romanticism. Like the Marxian critics, Eliot required some theory of mediation between individual and society. But where the Marxians concentrated on relations of process and cause – above all, the determination of the individual by antecedent social forces – Eliot thought in terms of patterns, systems, and orders in which individual elements could be fit. Eliot's belief that "men cannot get on without giving allegiance to something outside themselves" (70) led him to join the Church of England in 1927, and after this his criticism was increasingly driven by a belief that cultural continuity could be sustained only through the order provided by a state-sponsored church. It was from this position that Eliot came to attack humanism, which he derided as "sporadic" and "parasitical" upon the more authentic continuity of institutional Christianity (278–279).

Eliot's devotion to art of high complexity pervades the work of those writers who came to be associated with the New Criticism: principally John Crowe Ransom, Cleanth Brooks, Allen Tate, Robert Penn Warren, R. P. Blackmur, Kenneth Burke, Yvor Winters, René Wellek, Austin Warren, and W. K. Wimsatt in the United States, and William Empson (with, sometimes, Richards and F. R. and Q. D. Leavis) in England. Among these, it was Tate who reiterated Eliot's pronouncements most faithfully: his 1936 collection, *Reactionary Essays on Poetry and Ideas*, included observations that Emily Dickinson "like Donne, . . . *perceives abstraction* and *thinks sensation*," that though valid poetry "probes the deficiencies of a tradition" it "must have a tradition to probe," and that "the background of an objective religion, a universal scheme of reference, is necessary" if humanism's "eclecticism" of values is to be avoided.[33] Ransom's 1938 collection, *The World's Body*, also showed a clear debt to Eliot in its claims that a "good poem . . . intends as a work of art to lose the identity of the author," that "expression" is not "the essential quality of poetry," that interesting poetry is "the act of a fallen mind, since ours too are fallen," and that the hallmark of modern "literary taste" lay in the recovery of "the admirable John Donne."[34]

But the New Critics did more than merely reiterate Eliotic doctrine. In *The World's Body*, Ransom was already framing a somewhat different poetics, and three years later he published an extensive critique of Eliot (as well as Richards and Winters) in *The New Criticism*. According to Ransom in 1941, criticism would do well to "drop the vocabulary of emotions" dear to Richards and Eliot, and instead "talk about the respective cognitive objects, or the cognitive situations, which identify them."[35] In Ransom's formulation, poems become the distinctive things they are thanks to a certain resistance of the medium: the poet sets out with some point to make, but as writing proceeds, formal constraints (stanza, meter, rhyme) turn the poem into something other than a simple statement of the intended argument. Interwoven with the structure of argument in the finished poem, in other words, is always a texture of irrelevancies, of "incessant particularity" in which "each fresh particular is capable of enlisting emotions and attitudes" (25).

This theory would seem to have immediate consequences for the assessment of modern experimentation, since if texture cannot develop without constraints, authentically free verse must verge on the non-poetic. And indeed, although Ransom pressed the cause of contemporary poets against academic fixation on works of the past, the new poetry he favored was marked by the regular form, elaborate conceits, and coolly intellectual cast of the metaphysicals. In 1939, Ransom's New Critical confrere Cleanth Brooks had helped solidify this aesthetic with *Modern Poetry and the Tradition*, another defense of the new verse that gave priority to difficult poets manipulating more or less traditional structures. Echoing Eliot, Brooks insisted that modern innovation is itself traditional, in the sense that worthwhile poets have always altered readers' sense of what poetry can be, and stressed a resemblance between the metaphysicals and the best of the moderns. Both, in his telling, show that figuration is integral to the poem's being, not a dissociable ornament; that wit is compatible with high seriousness; and that poetry draws its life from the "qualifying irony" and "conflict of opposites" that poets following the metaphysicals tried to eschew.[36] Such ideas had an enormous impact on poetic production in the middle decades of the century: Ransom and Tate were often numbered among poetry's leading lights, Auden (who had returned to traditional forms in the mid-1930s) was embraced, and poets who would later break out in other directions, such as Robert Lowell and Adrienne Rich, honed their skills in lyrics of intricate patterning and relative emotional detachment.

Ransom's poetics also marked a reworking, in a more intimately technical register, of the familiar opposition between poetry and industry. Evoking closely Eastman's adaptation of Kantian aesthetics, Ransom had argued in *The World's Body* that the role of art is to restrain "natural man," with his "predatory and acquisitive interest in the object" – to remove him to a position from which he could not "hurt the object, nor disrespect it by taking his practical attitude towards it." Whereas science tries to "wring physical satisfaction" out of the object, in art one is not impelled "to lay hands on the object immediately" or "to ticket it for tomorrow's outrage," but rather desires to "know it for its own sake, and conceive it as having its own existence" (38, 45). It was this understanding of art's office that undergirded the structure-texture theory of *The New Criticism*, with its claim that poetic language "conducts a cognitive discourse in terms of details which are no more neutral or void of interest than is its main line of argument," whereas in "science . . . the terms are entirely functional to the main discourse" (25).

For Ransom and the other Southerners who would become New Critics, the anti-commercial animus was at first inseparable from a regional one. In the notorious 1930 collection *I'll Take My Stand*, twelve Southern "Agrarians," (including Ransom, Tate, and Warren) argued that encroaching Northern norms of competition and acquisition were threatening whatever remained of the leisured, cultivated way of the old South – for them the last redoubt of American civilization. As they themselves made clear, however, what was meant by the way of the old South was principally the lifestyle of the white male plantation owner; and it is thus not surprising to find in the volume appalling defenses of post-Civil-War racism as an expedient against the potential savagery of freed slaves, nods of approval to the Tuskegee compromise for its recognition of the limited capacities of the Negro, and a staggering underplaying of the moral issues surrounding slavery. ("Slavery was a feature monstrous enough in theory," writes Ransom at one point, "but, more often than not, humane in practice; and it is impossible to believe that its abolition alone could have effected any great revolution in society."[37]) To be sure, *I'll Take My Stand* preceded the New Criticism by several years, and Ransom and others would eventually distance themselves from the Agrarian position. But a glance at the volume does reveal how the most democratic aspiration in the New Critical agenda – that of bringing the good of aesthetic contemplation to the widest possible audience in an anti-contemplative age – was at first entwined with a myopic nostalgia for an aristocratic past.

The most deliberate vehicle of the New Critics' democratizing agenda was 1938's *Understanding Poetry*, an anthology-textbook co-edited by Cleanth Brooks and Robert Penn Warren that, after some initial opposition, became a standard in college instruction. (*Understanding Fiction*, edited by Brooks and Warren, and *Understanding Drama*, edited by Brooks and Robert B. Heilman, followed in 1943 and 1945.) In keeping with the New Critical emphasis on the complexity of the poetic artifact, *Understanding Poetry* encouraged students to proceed from "Narrative Poems" to poems with "Implied Narrative," and from there to poems illustrative of "Objective Description," "Metrics," "Tone and Attitude," "Imagery," and "Theme"; they would thus come to see (ideally) how much was going on in what could appear a simple or casual arrangement of words. (In the first edition, 240 poems, most followed by questions for students to consider, were grouped under these seven headings.) In their introductory remarks, the editors warned students against merely impressionistic comment and the temptation to privilege "logical and narrative content," "biographical and historical materials," and "[i]nspirational and didactic interpretation" at the expense of the poem itself[38]; they also stressed the differences between poetic language and scientific language, reiterated that all parts of the poem contribute to the total effect, and suggested that any poem may usefully be conceived as a dramatic speech by an implied character.

In this, the textbook dovetailed with essays that Brooks would eventually collect in 1947's *Well Wrought Urn* – a volume as important for scholars as *Understanding Poetry* was for students. In the collection's preface, Brooks once again argued that while historical study has its place, there is also a value to recognizing the "miracle of communication" by which poems seem able to speak to readers of later eras; in its appendices he decried professors who resist criticism's "burden of making normative judgments" and reiterated that the study of poetry must not become the study of morals, history, or sociology.[39] In between, Brooks placed eleven essays that became influential in part because they offered concrete ways of understanding the distinctiveness of literary discourse. In "The Language of Paradox," for example, he insisted that although not all poets consciously aim at paradox, all are "forced into paradoxes" by the nature of poems, in which "terms are continually modifying each other, and thus violating their dictionary meanings" (9–10); in "The Heresy of Paraphrase," he argued that a poem can never be completely paraphrased because its total meaning is indissociable from its particular organization of words. The essays were equally significant, however, for their exemplification of New Critical reading practices – Brooks illustrating his claim about paradox (for instance) with an analysis of how in Donne's "Canonization" profane love is holy and the poem's "lovers in rejecting life actually win to the most intense life" (15).

What accounts for the preeminence enjoyed by the New Critics in the middle of the twentieth century, and the resilience of many of their procedures thereafter? One reason often advanced is the sheer suitability of their artifact-centered approach to the university classroom; another is that their downplaying of political elements jibed with cold war mistrust not merely of left-wing writing but of all suggestions that specific historical determinants shaped works otherwise exhibitable as outgrowths of pure human freedom. Both of these propositions have substantial merit, but there were additional reasons for the New Criticism's early success and subsequent longevity. For one thing, it may be argued that if New Critical methods continue to be deployed by scholars and teachers concerned with the ideological work texts perform, this is so because the capacity those methods sought to develop is precisely the one most needed for demystification: the ability to discern the tension, contradiction, or paradox of "both . . . and . . ." in situations that public rhetoric strives to reduce to "either . . . or . . ."

Surely the most basic reason for the New Criticism's ascent, however, was that it managed to show how the analysis of literature qua literature could actually be interesting, and in this provided criticism with the substantive justification of its own existence that it had long been seeking. In the early part of the twentieth century, as we have seen, critics seemed forced to choose between two equally problematic alternatives. On the one hand, they could insist, as Spingarn did, that the only proper subject for criticism was literature itself; but this often seemed – on the evidence of the thin analysis that resulted – to leave little of moment to say about any particular text. On the other hand, they could consider works of literature in the light of philology, history, sociology, or philosophy; but then the question became why literary study should constitute a special branch of inquiry rather than being subordinated to one of these other fields. The achievement of the New Critics was to take the former line while demonstrating that the study of the textual object "in itself" could be fruitful and exciting. And they did so chiefly by showing, as few critics had shown before, how extraordinarily complex the workings of the verbal artifact could be. The New Critics did not merely reiterate the lesson that poetry is the language of paradox or that the poem is hard to paraphrase; they also – and here the ingenious individual readings of critics like Blackmur and Empson became especially important – disclosed in particular texts resonant paradoxes and ambiguities pertaining to a wide range of problems and experiences.

What happened in the years after the dominance of the New Criticism falls outside the bounds of this story, but a few subsequent developments have at least to be indicated. The first major challenge to the New Critics came from the so-called "Chicago" school, led by R. S. Crane and embodied in *Critics and Criticism: Ancient and Modern*, which Crane edited, and *The Languages of Criticism and the Structure of Poetry*, which Crane wrote. The Chicago contributors – who also included Elder Olson, W. R. Keast, Richard McKeon, Norman Maclean, and Bernard Weinberg – argued that criticism should embrace a plurality of approaches, but at the same time that an approach derived from Aristotelian poetics had a certain logical priority over all others. For Crane and company, the foundational problems for criticism were what the verbal artifact was attempting to achieve and how it did so; in their view, the New Critics were right to train attention on the text as a functional structure, but failed to live up to their own insights when they obsessed about the differences between poetic and scientific language (as if both were not made of words), lumped the many genres (and hence purposes) of literature together, and overingeniously analyzed parts of a work instead of considering the effect achieved by the whole. The eminent good sense of the Chicago School offered salutary readjustments to the somewhat less rigorously theorized New Criticism, but as subsequent critics have noted, it engendered relatively few engaging readings. One might say that the balance of scholarly and critical tendencies in the New Criticism (emblematized by the trajectory of most of the New Critics themselves, from non-academic to academic positions) lost something in the Chicago tilt toward weighty and sober scholarship.

Ensuing years witnessed the rise of "archetypal" or "myth" criticism, which had already informed studies like Maud Bodkin's *Archetypal Patterns in Poetry* (1934), Joseph Campbell's *Hero with a Thousand Faces* (1949), and Philip Wheelwright's *Burning Fountain* (1954), but which displaced the New Criticism from center stage on the publication of Northrop Frye's *Anatomy of Criticism* in 1957. Archetypal criticism's pivotal move was, in effect, to reformulate the problem of the distinctiveness of literature as that of the distinctiveness of myth: instead of risking the subordination of literary study to an existing discipline, it found a kind of superdisciplinary framework (touching the anthropology of Levi-Strauss, the psychology of Jung, and other fields) in basic myths said to structure all human cultural production. In archetypal criticism, the universalizing impulse that had informed virtually all of the critical thinking of previous decades – not just the classicizing of Babbitt but also the cultural federalism of Bourne, not just Brooks's "miracle of communication" but also the Marxist master narrative of Calverton – reached its apogee. But it also reached a kind of terminus. For the most important movements in United States criticism beginning in the 1960s were energized less by continuities than by disjunctions – by instructive differences between canonical writing and texts from hitherto marginalized groups (women, members of racial minorities, colonial subjects, gay people) and by elements resisting assimilation to the mainstream or main line (recalcitrant desire in a newly vigorous psychoanalytic criticism; cunning ideology in a newly inventive Marxist criticism; the footnote, the pun, the lacuna in deconstruction; the anecdote, the advertisement, the ledger in New Historicism; the messy sprawl of culture in general, including mass culture, in Cultural Studies).

One other group of critics requires mention here, for it was with some of its members that modernism came retrospectively to be formulated as a coherent, meaningful, and powerful movement in the arts. Like the New Critics, the "New York intellectuals" associated with Philip Rahv and William Phillips's *Partisan Review* (beginning in the late 1930s) accorded their highest admiration to works that were intricate and original. But for the most theoretically influential among them (Clement Greenberg, Irving Howe, Lionel and Diana Trilling, Susan Sontag, and others), metaphysical tension and relation to the tradition were less important than the ways in which a work expanded the possibilities of its medium and, in so doing, mounted a challenge to prevailing artistic and social norms. For these critics, whose acknowledged forerunner was Edmund Wilson and who bore a limited likeness to the German philosopher and critic T. W. Adorno, the point was neither that art should be disconnected from society in an absolute sense nor that it should be engaged in any immediately evident way. It was rather that under the peculiar conditions of capitalism, art's political resistance had come to reside in a certain resistance to the political. For Greenberg (primarily a critic of the visual arts), the protest of modernism lay in its way of turning its back on a society out to destroy art; for Trilling, the flattening tendencies of partisan politics were countered by literature's "variousness, possibility, complexity, and difficulty"[40]; for Howe, the crucial modernist stance was one of antagonism to any complacencies its audience might bring.

As was remarked at the beginning of this essay, the great irony attending the consolidation of "modernism" as an object of analysis after midcentury lay in an accompanying sense that modernism had, or might have, ended. An important 1960 essay in which Harry Levin outlined the major characteristics of modernist art was called "What Was Modernism?", while Howe's similarly definitional "Culture of Modernism" (1970, adapted from 1967's "Idea of the Modern") appeared in a collection called *The Decline of the New*. Ever since, writings on "modernism" have been haunted by the question of whether it is most adequately conceived as an ongoing, perhaps endless, project or style; as a movement or cluster of schools that ended in 1930 or 1945 or 1960; or as the whole field of cultural production, "high" and "low," in the first half of the twentieth century. The question has only gained urgency in recent years, with architects, designers, and some writers and visual artists beginning to treat "postmodernism" as an aberration or phase within a larger modernist trajectory.

If "modernism" still names variously a style, a movement, and a period, the reason arguably has much to do with the New York intellectuals' influence on the academy – for so powerful was their case for the importance of experimental writers that it became standard scholarly practice to divide writing in English since the nineteenth century into Romantic, Victorian (or Nineteenth-Century), Modernist, and Postmodernist. Recent expansions of the canon have demonstrated the inadequacy of this nomenclature, with its tendentious intimation that early twentieth-century works seeming not to fit modernist criteria are beneath the interest of literary study, but it is notable that much more effort has been expended in trying to enlarge the scope of "modernism" than in attempting to replace it with a more neutral term.

Why? The answer surely has something to do with sheer inertia, something to do also with a certain edgy glamour that the term "modernism" retains. But it may also point to the quiet persistence, among many kinds of scholars and critics today, of a belief visible in earlier writers as diverse as Babbitt, Spingarn, Bourne, Du Bois, Eastman, Burke, Wilson, Hicks, Ransom, and Trilling. This is the belief that a crucial office of literary art is the very one that the New York intellectuals did so much to affiliate with modernism: the office of resisting the acquisitive, anti-contemplative propulsions of modernity, by engendering a capacity for criticism.

NOTES

1. This limitation may illuminate, though it does not resolve, some of the problems of exclusion raised by the global terms "modern" and "American" in this essay's title (and discussed in the introduction to this collection). Many kinds of discourse produced in the early twentieth-century United States could be considered critical; the focus here is on writing that self-consciously marked itself as criticism and concerned itself with the possibilities of the critical enterprise. That the writers mentioned here turn out to be overwhelmingly male reflects the dearth of institutional positions from which female critics could gain a hearing in these years; that most of the writers mentioned are also white reflects the fact that few non-white writers were widely attended to for their views on the nature of criticism, and that African-American, Caribbean, Asian-American, Hispanic-American, American Indian, and related criticisms appear to have gathered momentum as coherent discourses only after the period covered by this survey (that is, beginning in the 1960s). Although this essay does not dispense attention in exact proportion to individual critics' fame or influence, it does attempt to give a broad sense of what voices would have been heard by those most explicitly concerned with criticism as such in the early twentieth-century United States, and this means, among other things, signaling the erasure of many perspectives that have become integral to criticism since.

     My sincere thanks to Jeremy Braddock for his advice on some questions arising in the preparation of this article.
2. Irving Howe, *Modern Literary Criticism: An Anthology* (Boston: Beacon Press, 1958), 8–9.
3. Gerald Graff, *Professing Literature: An Institutional History* (University of Chicago Press, 1987), 62.
4. Irving Babbitt, *Literature and the American College* (Washington, DC: National Humanities Institute, 1986), 136.
5. Babbitt, *The New Laokoon: An Essay on the Confusion of the Arts* (Boston: Houghton Mifflin, 1910), 29, 244.
6. Norman Foerster, *American Criticism: A Study in Literary Theory from Poe to the Present* (Boston: Houghton Mifflin, 1928), 225.
7. John Erskine, *The Kinds of Poetry* (New York: Duffield, 1920), 47.
8. Joel Spingarn, *Creative Criticism* (New York: Harcourt Brace, 1931), 36. In this instance and in all subsequent ones, further citations from the same text will be given parenthetically in the body of the essay.

9. Spingarn, "Criticism in the United States," in *Criticism in America: Its Function and Status* (New York: Harcourt Brace,1924), 287–288.

10. Ernest Boyd, "Ku Klux Kriticism," in *Criticism in America*, 313.

11. H. L. Mencken, "Criticism of Criticism of Criticism," in *Criticism in America*, 180, 188, 187.

12. Max Eastman, *Enjoyment of Poetry*, revised edn (New York: Scribner's, 1921), 3, 154, 175.

13. Waldo Frank, *Our America* (New York: Boni and Liveright, 1919), 63, 20.

14. Randolph Bourne, *The Radical Will: Selected Writings 1911–1918* (New York: Urizen, 1977), 469.

15. W. E. B. Du Bois, *Writings* (New York: Library of America, 1986), 994.

16. James Weldon Johnson, *Selected Writings*, vol. 1 (New York: Oxford University Press, 1995), 262.

17. Alain Locke, "The Legacy of the Ancestral Arts," in *The New Negro*, ed. Alain Locke (New York: Atheneum, 1968), 256.

18. Locke, foreword to *The New Negro*, ed., xvii.

19. Zora Neale Hurston, *Folklore, Memoirs, and Other Writings* (New York: Library of America, 1995), 950–951.

20. Mike Gold, *Mike Gold: A Literary Anthology* (New York: International Publishers), 66.

21. V. F. Calverton, *The Newer Spirit: A Sociological Criticism of Literature* (New York: Boni and Liveright, 1925), 21.

22. Ernest Boyd, introduction to Calverton, *The Newer Spirit*, xiii.

23. V. F. Calverton, *The Liberation of American Literature* (New York: Scribner's, 1932), 474.

24. Granville Hicks, *The Great Tradition: An Interpretation of American Literature Since the Civil War* (New York: Macmillan, 1935), 210.

25. Max Eastman, *Art and the Life of Action* (New York: Knopf, 1934), 5, 15, 24.

26. Kenneth Burke, *The Philosophy of Literary Form*, 2nd edn (Baton Rouge: Louisiana State University Press, 1957), xvii.

27. Edmund Wilson, *Axel's Castle: A Study in the Imaginative Literature of 1870–1930* (New York: W. W. Norton, 1984), i.

28. Quoted in Wilson, *To the Finland Station* (Garden City, NY: Doubleday, 1940), 3.

29. Joseph Wood Krutch, *Edgar Allan Poe: A Study in Genius* (New York: Russell & Russell, 1954), 234.

30. Vernon L. Parrington, *Main Currents in American Thought* (New York: Harcourt Brace, 1930), vol. 1, iii.

31. Constance Rourke, *The Roots of American Culture* (New York: Harcourt Brace, 1942), 43, 263, 248.

32. F. O. Matthiessen, *American Renaissance: Art and Expression in the Age of Emerson and Whitman* (London: Oxford University Press, 1941), ix–x.

33. T. S. Eliot, *Selected Prose* (New York: Harcourt Brace, 1975), 38.

34. Allen Tate, *Reactionary Essays on Poetry and Ideas* (New York: Scribner's, 1936), 13, 18, 139, 124.

35. John Crowe Ransom, *The World's Body* (New York: Scribner's, 1938), 2, 4, viii, 78.

36. Ransom, *The New Criticism* (Norfolk: New Directions, 1941), 155.

37. Cleanth Brooks, *Modern Poetry and the Tradition* (Chapel Hill: University of North Carolina Press, 1939), 32.
38. Ransom, "Reconstructed but Unregenerate," in *I'll Take My Stand* (New York: Harper and Brothers, 1930), 14.
39. Cleanth Brooks and Robert Penn Warren, eds., *Understanding Poetry* (New York: Henry Holt, 1938), iv.
40. Cleanth Brooks, *The Well Wrought Urn* (San Diego: Harcourt Brace, 1947), xi, 235.
41. Lionel Trilling, *The Liberal Imagination* (New York: Viking, 1950), xv.

FURTHER READING

Nationalism and the modern American canon

Alexander, Charles C. *Here the Country Lies: Nationalism and the Arts in Twentieth-Century America.* Bloomington: Indiana University Press, 1980.

Anderson, Benedict. *Imagined Communities: Reflections on the Origin and Spread of Nationalism.* London and New York: Verso, 1983.

Baker, Houston A. *Modernism and the Harlem Renaissance.* University of Chicago Press, 1987.

Daniels, Stephen. *Fields of Vision: Landscape Imagery and National Identity in England and the United States.* Princeton University Press, 1993.

Golding, Alan. *From Outlaw to Classic: Canons in American Poetry.* Madison: University of Wisconsin Press, 1995.

Kusch, Celena E. "How the West Was One: American Modernism's Song of Itself." *American Literature* 74: 3 (2002), 517–538.

Lauter, Paul. *Canons and Contexts.* New York and Oxford: Oxford University Press, 1991.

Lentricchia, Frank. *After the New Criticism.* University of Chicago Press, 1980.

Michaels, Walter Benn. *Our America: Nativism, Modernism, and Pluralism.* Durham: Duke University Press, 1995.

Miller, Angela. *The Empire of the Eye: Landscape Representation and American Cultural Politics, 1825–1875.* Ithaca and London: Cornell University Press, 1993.

Miller, Karen A. J. *Populist Nationalism: Republican Insurgency and American Foreign Policy Making, 1918–1925.* Westport, CN: Greenwood Press, 1999.

Morris, Timothy. *Becoming Canonical in American Poetry.* Urbana and Chicago: University of Illinois Press, 1995.

Nelson, Cary. *Repression and Recovery: Modern American Poetry and the Politics of Cultural Memory, 1910–1945.* Madison: University of Wisconsin Press, 1989.

North, Michael. *The Dialect of Modernism: Race, Language and Twentieth-Century Literature.* New York and Oxford: Oxford University Press, 1994.

Rainey, Lawrence. *Institutions of Modernism: Literary Elites and Public Culture.* New Haven and London: Yale University Press, 1998.

Schwartz, Lawrence H. *Creating Faulkner's Reputation: The Politics of Modern Literary Criticism.* Knoxville: The University of Tennessee Press, 1988.

Von Hallberg, Robert, ed. *Canons.* University of Chicago Press, 1984.

Modern American fiction

Barnard, Rita. *The Great Depression and the Culture of Abundance: Kenneth Fearing, Nathanael West, and Mass Culture in the 1930s*. New York: Cambridge University Press, 1995.

Cowley, Malcolm. *Exile's Return: A Literary Odyssey of the 1920s*. New York: Penguin, 1994.

Davidson, Arnold E. and Cathy N. Davidson. "Decoding the Hemingway Hero in *The Sun Also Rises*." In *New Essays on* The Sun Also Rises. Ed. Linda Wagner-Martin. New York: Cambridge University Press, 1987. 83–108.

Delany, Paul. "Who Paid for Modernism?" In *The New Economic Criticism: Studies at the Intersection of Literature and Economics*. Ed. Martha Woodmansee and Mark Osteen. New York: Routledge, 1999. 335–351.

Donaldson, Scott. "Hemingway's Morality of Compensation." In *Ernest Hemingway's* The Sun Also Rises. Ed. Harold Bloom. New York: Chelsea House, 1987. 71–90.

Foley, Barbara. "The Treatment of Time in *The Big Money*: An Examination of Ideology and Literary Form." *Modern Fiction Studies* 26 (Autumn 1980), 447–467.

Godden, Richard. *Fictions of Capital: The American Novel from James to Mailer*. New York: Cambridge University Press, 1999.

Irr, Caren. *The Suburb of Dissent: Cultural Politics in the United States and Canada during the 1930s*. Durham: Duke University Press, 1998.

Kazin, Alfred. *On Native Grounds: An Interpretation of Modern American Prose Literature*. New York: Harcourt Brace, 1942.

Kennedy, Gerald, ed. *The Modern American Short Story Sequence: Composite Fiction of Fictive Communities*. New York: Cambridge University Press, 1995.

Kenner, Hugh. *A Homemade World: The American Modernist Writers*. Baltimore: John Hopkins University Press, 1975.

Klein, Marcus. *Foreigners: The Making of American Literature 1900–1940*. University of Chicago Press, 1981.

Levine, Lawrence. *The Unpredictable Past*. New York: Oxford University Press, 1993.

Litz, A. Walton, ed. *Modern American Fiction: Essays in Criticism*. New York: Oxford University Press, 1963. 25–31.

Matthews, John T. "Touching Race in *Go Down, Moses*." In *New Essays on* Go Down, Moses. Ed. Linda Wagner-Martin. New York: Cambridge University Press, 1996. 21–48.

Messent, Peter. *Ernest Hemingway*. New York: St. Martin's, 1986.

Michaels, Walter Benn. *Our America: Nativism, Modernism, and Pluralism*. Durham: Duke University Press, 1995.

Rhodes, Chip. *Structures of the Jazz Age: Mass Culture, Progressive Education and Racial Discourse in American Modernism*. London: Verso, 1998.

Rideout, Walter. *The Radical Novel in the United States; 1900–1954*. Cambridge, MA: Harvard University Press, 1956.

Scruggs, Charles. *Sweet Home: Invisible Cities in the Afro-American Novel*. Baltimore: Johns Hopkins University Press, 1993.

Singal, Daniel Joseph, ed. Special Issue: Modernist Culture in America. *American Quarterly* 39:1 (Spring 1987).

Sollers, Werner. "Ethnic Modernism." In *The Cambridge History of American Literature. Volume 6: Prose Writing 1910–1950*. Ed. Sacvan Bercovitch. New York: Cambridge University Press, 2002.

Solomon, William. *Literature, Amusement, and Technology in the Great Depression*. New York: Cambridge University Press, 2002.

Stouck, David. "Anderson's Expressionist Art." In *New Essays on* Winesburg, Ohio. Ed. John W. Crowley. New York: Cambridge University Press, 1990. 27–52.

Strychacz, Thomas. *Modernism, Mass Culture, and Professionalism*. New York: Cambridge University Press, 1993.

Susman, Warren I. *Culture as History: The Transformation of American Society in the Twentieth Century*. Washington, DC: Smithsonian Institution Press, 2003.

Tratner, Michael. "A Man is His Bonds: *The Great Gatsby* and Deficit Spending." In *The New Economic Criticism: Studies at the Intersection of Literature and Economics*. 365–387.

Yingling, Thomas. "*Winesburg, Ohio* and the End of Collective Experience." In *New Essays on* Winesburg, Ohio. 99–128.

Modern American poetry

Aragon, Louis. In *An Other e. e. cummings*. Ed. Richard Kostelanetz. New York: Liveright, 1998.

Beecher, John. *Collected Poems*. New York: Macmillan, 1974.

Benet, Stephen Vincent. *Burning City*. New York: Farrar & Rinehart, 1936.

Burnshaw, Stanley. *The Iron Land*. New York: Centaur Press, 1936.

Crane, Hart. *Complete Poems of Hart Crane*. Ed. Marc Simon. New York: Liveright, 1966.

Eliot, T. S. *Collected Poems 1909–1962*. Boston: Harcourt Brace, 1963.

Fearing, Kenneth. *Kenneth Fearing: Complete Poems*. Ed. Robert M. Ryley. Orono, ME: National Poetry Foundation, 1994.

Fletcher, John Gould. *Preludes and Symphonies*. Boston: Houghton Mifflin, 1922.

Freeman, Joseph. "Six Poems," *Dynamo* (January 1934).

Frost, Robert. *The Poetry of Robert Frost*. Ed. Edward Connery Lathem. New York: Henry Holt & Company, 1969.

Funaroff, Sol. *Exile from a Future Time*. New York: Dynamo, 1943.

Gessner, Robert. *Upsurge*. New York: Farrar & Rinehart, 1933.

Ginsberg, Allen. *Collected Poems 1947–1980*. New York: HarperCollins, 1984.

Gold, Mike. In *Social Poetry of the 1930s*. Ed. Jack Salzman and Leo Zanderer. Philadelphia, PA: Burt Franklin, 1978.

Gregory, Horace. *Poems 1930–1940*. New York: Harcourt, 1941.

H. D. *Collected Poems 1912–1944*. New York: New Directions, 1982.

Hughes, Langston. *Collected Poems*. New York: Alfred A. Knopf, 1994.

Kalar, Joseph. *Selected Poems*. Urbana: University of Illinois Press, 2004.

Kramer, Aaron. *Wicked Times: Selected Poems*. Ed. Cary Nelson and Donald Gilzinger. Urbana: University of Illinois Press, 2004.

Lechliner, Ruth. *Tomorrow's Phoenix*. New York: Alcestis Press, 1937.

Lowell, Amy. *The Complete Poetical Works of Amy Lowell*. Boston: Houghton Mifflin, 1955.

Loy, Mina. *The Lost Lunar Baedeker*. Ed. Robert Conover. New York: Farrar Straus Giroux, 1996.

MacLeod, Norman. In *Social Poetry of the 1930s*. Ed. Jack Salzman and Leo Zanderer. Philadelphia, PA: Burt Franklin, 1978.

McKay, Claude. *Collected Poems*. Ed. William Maxwell. Urbana: University of Illinois Press, 2004.

Millay, Edna St. Vincent. *Collected Poems*. New York: HarperCollins, 1968.

Moore, Marianne. *The Collected Poems of Marianne Moore*. New York: Simon & Schuster, 1969.

Olsen, Tillie. "I Want You Women up North to Know." In *Anthology Of Modern American Poetry*. Ed. Cary Nelson. New York: Oxford University Press, 2000.

Patchen, Kenneth. *Collected Poems*. New York: New Directions, 1980.

Pound, Ezra. *The Cantos of Ezra Pound*. New York: New Directions, 1985.
Personae. New York: New Directions, 1990.

Rolfe, Edwin. *Collected Poems*. Ed. Cary Nelson and Jefferson Hendricks. Urbana: University of Illinois Press, 1993.

Rukeyser, Muriel. *Collected Poems*. New York: McGraw Hill, 1978.

Schneider, Isidor. *Comrade: Mister*. New York: Equinox Cooperative Press, 1934.

Stein, Gertrude. *Bee Time Vine*. New Haven: Yale University Press, 1953.

Stevens, Wallace. *Collected Poems*. New York: Alfred A. Knopf, 1957.

Swift, Morrison I. *Advent of Empire*. Los Angeles: The Rombroke Press, 1900.

Taggard, Genevieve. *Calling Western Union*. New York: Harper & Brothers, 1936.

Trent, Lucia. *Children of Fire and Shadow*. New York: Packard, 1929.

Williams, William Carlos. *Collected Poems 1909–1962*. New York: New Directions, 1986.

Weiss, Henry George. *Lenin Lives*. Holt, MN: B. C. Hagglund, 1935.

Modern American drama

Bigsby, C. W. E. *A Critical Introduction to Twentieth-Century American Drama*. 2 vols. Cambridge University Press, 1984.

Bogard, Travis. *Contour in Time: The Plays of Eugene O'Neill*. New York: Oxford University Press, 1972.

Clurman, Harold. *The Fervent Years*. New York: Harcourt, Brace, Jovanovich, 1975.

Hatch, James V., ed. *Black Theater, U. S. A.: Forty-Five Plays by Black Americans, 1847–1974*. New York: Free Press, 1974.

Hewitt, Barnard. *Theatre U. S. A. – 1665–1957*. New York: McGraw-Hill, 1959.

Krutch, Joseph Wood. *The American Drama Since 1918: An Introduction*. New York: George Braziller, 1957.

Richardson, Gary A. *American Drama from the Colonial Period through World War I: A Critical History*. New York: Twayne Publishers, 1993.

Sarlos, Robert. *Jig Cook and the Provincetown Players: Theatre in Ferment*. Amherst: University of Massachusetts Press, 1982.

Schlueter, June, ed. *Modern American Drama: The Female Canon*. London and Toronto: Associated University Presses, 1990.

Sievers, W. David. *Freud on Broadway: A History of Psychoanalysis American Drama*. New York: Heritage House, 1955.

Smiley, Sam. *The Drama of Attack: Didactic Plays of the American Depression*. Columbia: University of Missouri Press, 1972.

Wilmeth, Don B. and Tice L Miller, eds. *The Cambridge Guide to American Theatre*. Cambridge University Press, 1993.

American modernism and the New Negro Renaissance

Baker, Houston A., Jr. *Modernism and the Harlem Renaissance*. University of Chicago Press, 1987.

Bell, Bernard W. "Jean Toomer's 'Blue Meridian': The Poet as Prophet of a New Order of Man." *Jean Toomer: A Critical Evaluation*. Ed. Therman B. O'Daniel. Washington, DC: Howard University Press, 1988, pp. 343–352.

"A Key to the Poems of *Cane*." *Jean Toomer: A Critical Evaluation*. Ed. Therman B. O'Daniel. Washington, DC: Howard University Press, 1988, pp. 321–327.

Bentson, Kimberly W. "Sterling Brown's After-Song: 'When de Saints Go Ma'ching Home' and the Performance of the Afro-American Voice." *Callaloo* 5: 14 and 15 (February–May 1982): 33–42.

Boas, Franz. *Anthropology and Modern Life*. New York: Norton, 1928.

Race, Language, and Culture. The University of Chicago Press, 1982.

Brooks, Van Wyck. *Van Wyck Brooks: An Autobiography*. New York: E. P. Dutton and Co., 1965.

Brown, Sterling A. "The New Negro in Literature (1925–1955)." *The New Negro Thirty Years Afterward*. Ed. Rayford L. Logan. Washington, DC: Howard University Press, 1955, pp. 57–72.

"The Odyssey of Big Boy." *The Collected Poems of Sterling A. Brown*. Ed. Michael S. Harper. New York: Harper & Row Publishers, 1980, pp. 20–21.

"Ragtime and the Blues." *Sterling A. Brown: A UMUM Tribute*. Ed. Black History Museum Committee. Philadelphia, PA: Black History Museum UMUM Publishers, 1982, pp. 76–88.

Jean Toomer's Years with Gurdjieff: Portrait of an Artist, 1923–1936. Athens: University of Georgia Press, 1990.

De Jong, James. *Vicious Modernism: Black Harlem and the Literary Imagination*. Cambridge University Press, 1990.

Dekoven, Marianne. "Modernism and Gender." *The Cambridge Companion to Modernism*. Ed. Michael Levenson. Cambridge University Press, 1999, pp. 174–193.

Dett, Nathaniel. *Religious Folk Songs of the Negro*. Hampton, VA: Hampton Institute Press, 1927.

Dewey, John. *Reconstruction in Philosophy*. Ed. Jo Ann Boyston. The Middle Works, 1899–1924. Vol. XII. Carbondale: Southern Illinois University Press, 1976.

Diggins, John P. *The American Left in Twentieth Century*. New York: Harcourt Brace Jovanovich, 1973.

Douglas, Ann. *Terrible Honesty: Mongrel Manhattan in the 1920s*. New York: Noon Day Press, 1995.

Dray, Philip. *At the Hands of Persons Unknown: The Lynching of Black America*. New York: Random House, 2002.

DuBois, W. E. B. *The Souls of Black Folk*. New York: Penguin Books, 1989.

Eastman, Max. "Introduction." *Harlem Shadows: The Poems of Claude McKay*. New York: Harcourt, Brace, and Company, 1922.

The Literary Mind: Its Place in an Age of Science. New York: Charles Scribner's Sons, 1935.

Ellison, Ralph. *The Collected Essays of Ralph Ellison.* Ed. John F. Callahan. New York: Modern Library, 1995.

Shadow and Act. New York: Vintage Books, 1964.

Frank, Waldo. *Our America.* New York: Boni and Liveright, 1919.

Gabbin, Joanne V. *Sterling A. Brown: Building the Black Aesthetic Tradition.* Westport, CT: Greenwood Press, 1985.

Gates, Henry Louis, Jr. Afterword: "Zora Neale Hurston: 'A New Negro Way of Saying.'" *Their Eyes Were Watching God.* New York: Harper & Row Publishers, 1999.

Figures in Black: Words, Signs and the "Racial" Self. New York: Oxford University Press, 1987.

"Their Eyes Were Watching God: Hurston and The Speakerly Text." *Zora Neale Hurston: Critical Perspectives Past and Present.* Ed. Henry Louis Gates, Jr. and K. A. Appiah. New York: Amistad, 1993, pp. 154–203.

The Signifying Monkey: A Theory of Afro-American Literary Criticism. New York: Oxford University Press, 1986.

Hutchinson, George. *The Harlem Renaissance in Black and White.* Cambridge, MA: Harvard University Press, Belknap Press, 1995.

"Langston Hughes and the 'Other' Whitman." *The Continuing Presence of Walt Whitman: The Life and After the Life.* Ed. Robert K. Martin. Iowa City: University of Iowa Press, 1992, pp. 16–27.

"The Whitman Legacy and the Harlem Renaissance." *Walt Whitman: The Centennial Essays.* Ed. Ed Folsom. Iowa City: University of Iowa Press, 1991, pp. 201–216.

James, William. *A Pluralist Universe.* Cambridge, MA: Harvard University Press, 1977.

Johnson, James Weldon. *Black Manhattan.* New York: Da Capo Press, 1991.

Kalaidjian, Walter. *American Culture between the Wars: Revisionary Modernism and Postmodern Critique.* New York: Columbia University Press, 1993.

Kutzinksi, Vera M. "The Distant Closeness of Dancing Doubles: Sterling Brown and William Carlos Williams." *Black American Literature Forum* 22 (Spring 1982), 19–25.

Levine, Lawrence W. *Black Culture and Black Consciousness: Afro-American Folk Thought from Slavery to Freedom.* New York: Oxford University Press, 1977.

Lewis, David Levering. *W. E. B. Du Bois: Biography of a Race, 1868–1919.* New York: Henry Holt and Co., 1993.

When Harlem was in Vogue. New York: Oxford University Press, 1981.

Litwack, Leon F. *Trouble in Mind: Black Southerners in the Age of Jim Crow.* New York: Vintage Books, 1998.

Locke, Alain. *The Negro and His Music: Negro Art Past and Present.* New York: Arno Press, 1969.

"The New Negro." *The New Negro: An Interpretation.* Ed. Alain Locke. New York: Albert and Charles Boni, 1925, pp. 3–16.

"Sterling Brown: The New Negro Folk-Poet." *Negro: An Anthology.* Ed. Nancy Cunard and abridged by Hugh Ford. New York: Frederick Ungar Publishing Co., 1935, pp. 111–115.

Martin, Robert K. "Introduction." *Continuing Presence of Walt Whitman: The Life After the Life*. Iowa City: University of Iowa Press, 1992.

Maxwell, William J. *New Negro, Old Left: African American Writing and Communism between the Wars*. New York: Columbia University Press, 1999.

McFarlane, James, and Malcolm Bradbury, eds. *Modernism, 1890–1930*. New York: Penguin Books, 1976.

Moses, Wilson. "The Lost World of the Negro, 1895–1919: Black Intellectual Life before the 'Renaissance.'" *Black American Literature Forum* 21 (Spring-Summer 1987), 61–64.

Nelson, Cary. *Repression and Recovery: Modern American Poetry and the Politics of Cultural Memory, 1910–1945*. Madison: University of Wisconsin Press, 1988.

Nielson, Aldon Lynn. *Reading Race: White American Poets and the Racial Discourse in the Twentieth Century*. Athens: University of Georgia Press, 1988.

North, Michael. *The Dialect of Modernism: Race, Language, and Twentieth-Century Literature*. New York: Oxford University Press, 1994.

O'Daniel, Therman B., ed. *Jean Toomer: A Critical Evaluation*. Washington, DC: Howard University Press, 1988.

Pickens, William. *The New Negro: His Political, Civil, and Mental Status*. New York: Neale Publishing Co., 1916.

Rampersad, Arnold. *The Life of Langston Hughes., 1902–1941: I, Too, Sing America*. Vol. 1. New York: Oxford University Press, 1986.

Sanders, Mark A., *Afro-Modernist Aesthetics and the Poetry of Sterling A. Brown*. Athens: University of Georgia Press, 1999.

Singal, Daniel Joseph. "Towards a Definition of American Modernism." *American Quarterly* 39 (Spring 1987), 7–26.

Toomer, Jean. *Cane*. New York: Boni and Liveright, 1923.

Untermeyer, Louis. "New Light from an Old Mine." *Opportunity* 10 (August 1932), 250–251.

West, Cornell. *The American Evasion of Philosophy: A Genealogy of Pragmatism*. Madison: University of Wisconsin Press, 1989.

Whitman, Walt. *Democratic Vistas*. New York: Liberal Arts Press, 1949.
  Leaves of Grass. New York: W. W. Norton & Co., 1973.

Jazz and American modernism

Alexander, Charles C. *Here the Country Lies: Nationalism and the Arts in Twentieth-Century America*. Bloomington: Indiana University Press, 1980.

Collier, James Lincoln. *Jazz, the American Theme Song*. New York: Oxford University Press, 1993.

Crunden, Robert M. *Body and Soul: The Making of American Modernism*. New York: Basic Books, 2000.

Evans, Nicholas M. *Writing Jazz: Race, Nationalism, and Modern Culture in the 1920s*. New York: Garland, 2000.

Hutchinson, George. *The Harlem Renaissance in Black and White*. Cambridge, MA: The Belknap Press of Harvard University Press, 1995.

Leonard, Neil. *Jazz and the White Americans: The Acceptance of a New Art Form*. University of Chicago Press, 1962.

Levine, Lawrence W. *The Unpredictable Past: Explorations in American Cultural History*. New York: Oxford University Press, 1993.

Lopes, Paul. *The Rise of a Jazz Art World*. New York: Cambridge University Press, 2002.

Meltzer, David, ed. *Reading Jazz*. San Francisco: Mercury House, 1993.
ed. *Writing Jazz*. San Francisco: Mercury House, 1999.

Moore, Macdonald Smith. *Yankee Blues: Musical Culture and American Identity*. Bloomington: Indiana University Press, 1985.

Ogren, Kathy J. *The Jazz Revolution: Twenties America and the Meaning of Jazz*. New York: Oxford University Press, 1989.

Oja, Carol J. *Making Music Modern: New York in the 1920s*. New York: Oxford University Press, 2000.

O'Meally, Robert G., ed. *The Jazz Cadence of American Culture*. New York: Columbia University Press, 1998.

Peretti, Burton W. *Jazz in American Culture*. Chicago: Ivan Dee, 1997.

Tischler, Barbara L. *An American Music: The Search for an American Musical Identity*. New York: Oxford University Press, 1986.

Walser, Robert, ed. *Keeping Time: Readings in Jazz History*. New York: Oxford University Press, 1999.

Visual culture

Bryson, Norman. *Vision and Painting: The Logic of the Gaze*. New Haven: Yale University Press, 1983.

Clark, T. J. *Farewell to an Idea: Episodes from a History of Modernism*. New Haven: Yale University Press, 1999.

Crary, Jonathan. *Techniques of the Observer: On Vision and Modernity in the Nineteenth Century*. Cambridge, MA: MIT Press, 1990.

Dijkstra, Bram. *The Hieroglyphics of a New Speech: Cubism, Stieglitz and the Early Poetry of William Carlos Williams*. Princeton University Press, 1969.

Hansen, Miriam. *Babel and Babylon: Spectatorship in American Silent Film*. University of Chicago Press, 1991.

Jenks, Chris. *Visual Culture*. London: Routledge, 1995.

Matthew Teitelbaum, ed. *Montage and Modern Life 1919–1942*. Cambridge, MA: MIT Press, 1992.

Rorty, Richard. *Philosophy and the Mirror of Nature*. Princeton University Press, 1979.

Shloss, Carol. *In Visible Light: Photography and the American Writer, 1840–1940*. New York: Oxford University Press, 1987.

Smith, Terry. *Making the Modern: Industry, Art, and Design in America*. University of Chicago Press, 1993.

The avant-garde phase of American modernism

Antliff, Allan. *Anarchist Modernism: Art, Politics, and the First American Avant-Garde*. University of Chicago Press, 2001.

Bürger, Peter. *Theory of the Avant-Garde*. Tr. Michael Shaw. Minneapolis: University of Minnesota Press, 1984.

Cabanne, Pierre. *Dialogues with Marcel Duchamp*. Tr. Ron Padgett. New York: Viking, 1971.

Calinescu, Matei. *Five Faces of Modernity, Modernism, Avant-Garde, Decadence, Kitsch, Postmodernism*. Durham, NC: Duke University Press, 1987.

Duchamp, Marcel. *The Essential Writings of Marcel Duchamp*. Ed. Michel Sanouillet and Elmer Peterson. New York: Oxford, 1973.

Foresta, Merry, ed. *Perpetual Motif: The Art of Man Ray*. New York: Abbeville Press, 1989.

Henderson, Linda Dalrymple. *Duchamp in Context: Science and Technology in the Large Glass and Related Works*. Princeton University Press, 1998.

  The Fourth Dimension and Non-Euclidean Geometry in Modern Art. Princeton University Press, 1983.

Hulten, Pontus. *The Machine as Seen at the End of the Mechanical Age*. New York: Museum of Modern Art, 1968.

Kuenzli, Rudolf and Francis M. Naumann. *Marcel Duchamp: Artist of the Century*. Cambridge, MA: MIT Press, 1989.

Mina Loy. *The Lost Lunar Baedeker*, selected and edited by Roger L. Conover, NY: Farrar Straus Giroux, 1996.

Naumann, Francis M. with Beth Venn. *Making Mischief: Dada Invades New York*. New York: Whitney Museum of American Art, 1996.

Perloff, Marjorie. *Twenty-First Century Modernism*. Oxford: Blackwell, 2002.

Pound, Ezra. *Literary Essays of Ezra Pound*. Ed. T. S. Eliot. London: Faber and Faber, 1954.

Sawelson-Gorse, Naomi, ed. *Women in Dada: Essays on Sex, Gender, and Identity*. Cambridge, MA: MIT Press, 1998.

Sayre, Henry. *The Visual Text of William Carlos Williams*. Urbana: University of Illinois Press, 1983.

Shreiber, Maeera and Keith Tuma, eds. *Mina Loy: Woman and Poet*. Orono: National Poetry Foundation, 1998.

Stieglitz, Alfred. *Camera Work, The Complete Illustrations 1903–1917*. Ed. Pam Roberts. Cologne: Taschen, 1997.

Tashjian, Dickran. *Skyscraper Primitives: Dada and the American Avant-Garde 1910–1925*. Middletown, CT: Wesleyan University Press, 1975.

Tomkins, Calvin. *Duchamp, A Biography*. New York: Henry Holt, 1996.

Williams, William Carlos. *The Collected Poems of William Carlos Williams*. Volume I, 1909–1939. Ed. A. Walton Litz and Christopher MacGowan. New York: New Directions, 1986.

Gender and sexuality

Boone, Joseph Allen. *Libidinal Currents: Sexuality and the Shaping of Modernism*. Chicago University Press, 1998.

Comley, Nancy R., and Robert Scholes. *Hemingway's Genders: Rereading the Hemingway Text*. New Haven: Yale University Press, 1994.

Crunden, Robert M. *American Salons: Encounters with European Modernism, 1885–1917*. New York: Oxford University Press, 1993.

Daly, Ann. *Done into Dance: Isadora Duncan in America*. Bloomington: Indiana Univeristy Press, 1995.

De Lauretis, Teresa. *The Practice of Love: Lesbian Sexuality and Perverse Desire.* Bloomington: Indiana University Press, 1994.

DuPlessis, Rachel Blau. *Genders, Races and Religious Cultures in Modern American Poetry, 1908–1934.* Cambridge University Press, 2001.

Foulkes, Julia L. *Modern Bodies: Dance and American Modernism from Martha Graham to Alvin Ailey.* Chapel Hill: University North Carolina Press, 2002.

Gambrell, Alice. *Women Intellectuals, Modernism, and Difference: Transatlantic Culture, 1919–1945.* Cambridge University Press, 1997.

Halberstam, Judith. *Female Masculinity.* Durham, NC: Duke University Press, 1998.

Haralson, Eric. *Henry James and Queer Modernity.* Cambridge University Press, 2003.

Jameson, Fredric. *A Singular Modernity: Essay on the Ontology of the Present.* New York: Verso, 2002.

Jarraway, David R. *Going the Distance: Dissident Subjectivity in Modernist American Literature.* Baton Rouge: Louisiana State University Press, 2003.

Jones, Margaret C. *Heretics and Hellraisers: Women Contributors to The Masses, 1911–1917.* Austin: University of Texas Press, 1991.

Laqueur, Thomas. *Making Sex: Body and Gender from the Greeks to Freud.* Cambridge, MA: Harvard University Press, 1990.

Scandura, Jani, and Michael Thurston, eds. *Modernism, Inc.: Body, Memory, Capital.* New York University Press, 2001.

Scott, Bonnie Kime, ed. *The Gender Complex of Modernism.* Urbana: University of Illinois Press, forthcoming.

Segal, Lynn. *Why Feminism?: Gender, Psychology, Politics.* New York: Columbia University Press, 1999.

Shreiber, Maeera, and Keith Tuma, eds. *Mina Loy: Woman and Poet.* Orono, ME: National Poetry Foundation, 1998.

Stevens, Hugh, and Caroline Howlett, eds. *Modernist Sexualities.* Manchester University Press, 2000.

Watson, Steven. *Strange Bedfellows: The First American Avant-Garde.* New York: Abbeville, 1991.

Regionalism in American modernism

Cox, James M. "Regionalism: A Diminished Thing." In *Columbia Literary History of the United States.* Ed. Emory Elliot, et al. New York: Columbia University Press, 1988. 761–784.

Fetterley, Judith, and Marjorie Pryse, eds. *American Women Regionalists, 1850–1910: A Norton Anthology.* New York: Norton, 1995.

Fetterley, Judith, and Marjorie Pryse. *Writing out of Place: Regionalism, Women, and American Literary Culture.* Urbana: University of Illinois Press, 2003.

Foote, Stephanie. *Regional Fictions: Culture and Identity in Nineteenth-Century American Literature.* Madison: University of Wisconsin Press, 2001.

I'll Take My Stand: The South and the Agrarian Tradition. New York: Harper and Brothers, 1930.

Inness, Sherrie A., and Diana Royer, eds. *Breaking Boundaries: New Perspectives on Women's Regional Writing.* Iowa City: University of Iowa Press, 1997.

Jones, Anne Goodwyn. *Tomorrow is Another Day: The Woman Writer in the South, 1859–1936*. Baton Rouge: Louisiana State University Press, 1981.

Jordan, David. *Regionalism Reconsidered: New Approaches to the Field*. New York: Garland, 1994.

McCullough, Kate. *Regions of Identity: The Construction of America in Women's Fiction, 1885–1914*. Stanford University Press, 1999.

Rubin, Jr., Louis D. and Robert D. Jacobs. *Southern Renascence: The Literature of the Modern South*. Baltimore: Johns Hopkins University Press, 1953.

Social representations within American modernism

Baker, Houston A., Jr. *Modernism and the Harlem Renaissance*. University of Chicago Press, 1987.

Berman, Marshall. *All That is Solid Melts into Air: The Experience of Modernity*. New York: Simon and Schuster, 1982.

Brannan, Beverly, and Carl Flesichhauer. *Documenting America: 1935–1943*. Berkeley: University of California Press, 1989.

Bruno, Giuliana. *Streetwalking on a Ruined Map: Cultural Theory and the City Films of Elvira Notari*. Princeton University Press, 1993.

Cappetti, Carla. *Writing Chicago: Modernism, Ethnography and the Novel*. New York: Columbia University Press, 1993.

Cohen, Lizabeth. *Making a New Deal: Industrial Workers in Chicago, 1919–1939*. Cambridge University Press, 1990.

Cooper, Mark Garrett. *Love Rules: Silent Hollywood and the Rise of the Managerial Class*. Minneapolis: University of Minnesota Press, 2003.

Cucullu, Lois. *Expert Modernists, Matricide and Modern Culture: Woolf, Forster, Joyce*. London: Palgrave, forthcoming.

Dennning, Michael. *The Cultural Front*. London: Verso, 1996.

Dieckmann, Katherine. "Photography: A Nation of Zombies." *Art in America* 77 (November 1989), 55–57.

Fisher, Andrea. *Let Us Now Praise Famous Women: Women Photographers for the U.S. Government, 1935–1944*. London: Pandora Press, 1987.

Giovacchini, Saverio. *Hollywood Modernism*. Philadelphic, Temple University Press, 2001.

Huyssen, Andreas. *After the Great Divide*. Bloomington: University of Indiana Press, 1986.

Nelson, Cary. *Revolutionary Memory*. New York: Routledge, 2000.

Rabinowitz, Paula. *They Must Be Represented: The Politics of Documentary*. London: Verso, 1994.

   Black & White & Noir: America's Pulp Modernism. New York: Columbia University Press, 2002.

Reed, T. V. *Fifteen Jugglers, Five Believers: Literary Politics and the Politics of American Social Movements*. Berkeley: University of California Press, 1992.

Scandura, Jani, and Michael Thurston, eds. *Modernism, Inc.: Body, Memory, Capital*. New York University Press, 2001.

Szalay, Michae. *New Deal Modernism: American Literature and the Invention of the Welfare State*. Durham, NJ: Duke University Press, 2000.

Todd, Ellen Wiley. *The "New Woman" Revisited: Painting and Gender Politics on Fourteenth Street*. Berkeley: University of California Press, 1993.

Wald, Alan. *Exiles from a Future Time*. Chapel Hill: University of North Carolina Press, 2002.

Wilson, Elizabeth. *The Sphinx in the City: Urban Life, the Control of Disorder, and Women*. Berkeley: University of California Press, 1991.

Modern American literary criticism

Cain, William E. *The Crisis in Criticism: Theory, Literature, and Reform in English Studies*. Baltimore: The Johns Hopkins University Press, 1984.

Eagleton, Terry. *Literary Theory: An Introduction*. Minneapolis: University of Minnesota Press, 1983.

Fekete, John. *The Critical Twilight : Explorations in the Ideology of Anglo-American Literary Theory from Eliot to McLuhan*. London: Routledge, 1977.

Filreis, Alan. *Modernism from Right to Left: Wallace Stevens, the Thirties, and Literary Radicalism*. Cambridge University Press, 1994.

Fraiberg, Louis. *Psychoanalysis and Literary Criticism*. Detroit, MI: Wayne State University Press, 1960.

Goldsmith, Arnold L. *American Literary Criticism: 1905–1965*. Boston: Twayne, 1979.

Graff, Gerald. *Professing Literature: An Institutional History*. University of Chicago Press, 1987.

Graff, Gerald, and Michael Warner, eds. *The Origins of Literary Studies in America: A Documentary Anthology*. New York: Routledge, 1989.

Guillory, John. *Cultural Capital: The Problem of Literary Canon Formation*. University of Chicago Press, 1993.

Hegeman, Susan. *Patterns for America: Modernism and the Concept of Culture*. Princeton University Press, 1999.

Hutchinson, George. *The Harlem Renaissance in Black and White*. Cambridge, MA: Harvard University Press, 1995.

Hyman, Stanley Edgar. *The Armed Vision: A Study in the Methods of Modern Literary Criticism*. New York: Knopf, 1948.

Jancovich, Mark. *The Cultural Politics of the New Criticism*. Cambridge University Press, 1993.

Jay, Gregory S., ed. *Modern American Literary Critics, 1920–1955*. Vol. 63 of the *Dictionary of Literary Biography*. Detroit, MI: Gale, 1988.

Leitch, Vincent B. *American Literary Criticism from the Thirties to the Eighties*. New York: Columbia University Press, 1988.

Lentricchia, Frank. *After the New Criticism*. University of Chicago Press, 1980.

Morrison, Claudia C. *Freud and the Critic*. Chapel Hill: University of North Carolina Press, 1968.

Posnock, Ross. *Color and Culture: Black Writers and the Making of the Modern Intellectual*. Cambridge, MA: Harvard University Press, 1998.

Webster, Grant. *The Republic of Letters: A History of Postwar American Literary Opinion*. Baltimore: The Johns Hopkins University Press, 1979.

Wellek, René. *American Criticism, 1900–1950*. Vol. 6 of *A History of Modern Criticism, 1750–1950*. New Haven: Yale University Press, 1986.

INDEX

CAMBRIDGE COMPANIONS TO LITERATURE

Period and Thematic

The Cambridge Companion to the
Italian Novel
edited by Peter Bondanella and
Andrea Ciccarelli

The Cambridge Companion to the Modern
German Novel
edited by Graham Bartram

The Cambridge Companion to Jewish
American Literature
edited by Hana Wirth-Nesher and
Michael P. Kramer

The Cambridge Companion to the African
American Novel
edited by Maryemma Graham

The Cambridge Companion to Canadian
Literature
edited by Eva-Marie Kröller

The Cambridge Companion to
Contemporary Irish Poetry
edited by Matthew Campbell

The Cambridge Companion to Modernism
edited by Michael Levenson

The Cambridge Companion to American
Modernism
edited by Walter Kalaidjian

The Cambridge Companion to
Postmodernism
edited by Steven Connor

The Cambridge Companion to Postcolonial
Literary Studies
edited by Neil Lazarus

The Cambridge Companion to Australian
Literature
edited by Elizabeth Webby

The Cambridge Companion to American
Women Playwrights
edited by Brenda Murphy

The Cambridge Companion to Modern
British Women Playwrights
edited by Elaine Aston and
Janelle Reinelt

The Cambridge Companion to
Twentieth-Century Irish Drama
edited by Shaun Richards

European authors

The Cambridge Companion to Homer
edited by Robert Fowler

The Cambridge Companion to Virgil
edited by Charles Martindale

The Cambridge Companion to Ovid
edited by Philip Hardie

The Cambridge Companion to Dante
edited by Rachel Jacoff

The Cambridge Companion to Cervantes
edited by Anthony J. Cascardi

The Cambridge Companion to Goethe
edited by Lesley Sharpe

The Cambridge Companion to Dostoevskii
edited by W. J. Leatherbarrow

The Cambridge Companion to Tolstoy
edited by Donna Tussing Orwin

The Cambridge Companion to Chekhov
edited by Vera Gottlieb and Paul Allain

The Cambridge Companion to Ibsen
edited by James McFarlane

The Cambridge Companion to Flaubert
edited by Timothy Unwin

The Cambridge Companion to Proust
edited by Richard Bales

The Cambridge Companion to Thomas
Mann
edited by Ritchie Robertson

The Cambridge Companion to Kafka
edited by Julian Preece

The Cambridge Companion to Brecht
edited by Peter Thomson and
Glendyr Sacks

The Cambridge Companion to Walter
Benjamin
edited by David S. Ferris

The Cambridge Companion to Lacan
edited by Jean-Michel Rabaté

UK writers

The Cambridge Companion to Chaucer,
second edition
edited by Piero Boitani and Jill Mann

The Cambridge Companion to Shakespeare
edited by Margareta de Grazia and
Stanley Wells

US writers

The Cambridge Companion to Herman Melville
edited by Robert S. Levine

The Cambridge Companion to Nathaniel Hawthorne
edited by Richard Millington

The Cambridge Companion to Harriet Beecher Stowe
edited by Cindy Weinstein

The Cambridge Companion to Theodore Dreiser
edited by Leonard Cassuto and Claire Virginia Eby

The Cambridge Companion to Edith Wharton
edited by Millicent Bell

The Cambridge Companion to Henry James
edited by Jonathan Freedman

The Cambridge Companion to Walt Whitman
edited by Ezra Greenspan

The Cambridge Companion to Ralph Waldo Emerson
edited by Joel Porte and Saundra Morris

The Cambridge Companion to Henry David Thoreau
edited by Joel Myerson

The Cambridge Companion to Mark Twain
edited by Forrest G. Robinson

The Cambridge Companion to Edgar Allan Poe
edited by Kevin J. Hayes

The Cambridge Companion to Emily Dickinson
edited by Wendy Martin

The Cambridge Companion to William Faulkner
edited by Philip M. Weinstein

The Cambridge Companion to Ernest Hemingway
edited by Scott Donaldson

The Cambridge Companion to F. Scott Fitzgerald
edited by Ruth Prigozy

The Cambridge Companion to Robert Frost
edited by Robert Faggen

The Cambridge Companion to Eugene O'Neill
edited by Michael Manheim

The Cambridge Companion to Tennessee Williams
edited by Matthew C. Roudané

The Cambridge Companion to Arthur Miller
edited by Christopher Bigsby

The Cambridge Companion to Sam Shepard
edited by Matthew C. Roudané

CAMBRIDGE COMPANIONS TO CULTURE

Culture Companions

The Cambridge Companion to Modern German Culture
edited by Eva Kolinsky and Wilfried van der Will

The Cambridge Companion to Modern Russian Culture
edited by Nicholas Rzhevsky

The Cambridge Companion to Modern Spanish Culture
edited by David T. Gies

The Cambridge Companion to Modern Italian Culture
edited by Zygmunt G. Barański and Rebecca J. West

The Cambridge Companion to Modern French Culture
edited by Nicholas Hewitt

The Cambridge Companion to Modern Latin American Literature
edited by John King